D1765619

University of Edinburgh

30150   027726675

ISBN 978-90-5972-204-0

Eburon Academic Publishers
PO Box 2867
2601 CW Delft
The Netherlands
Fax: (+31) 15 2146888 / Phone: (+31) 15 2131484
www.eburon.nl / info@eburon.nl

Graphic design: Bjørn Hatteng
Cover illustration: Per Kleiva's lithograph *Kort møte* (Short encounter)

Indigenous Peoples:
Self-determination
Knowledge
Indigeneity

Henry Minde (ed.)

In collaboration with:
Svein Jentoft, Harald Gaski and Georges Midré

Eburon Delft
2008

Contents

Part I
Indigenous Movements and their Opponents

Part II
Self-determination, Social Justice and Natural Resources

Part III
Politics of Knowledge

Acknowledgements

This book emerged from a workshop held in Tromsø, Norway in October of 2005 arranged by the research project *The Challenge of Indigenousness: Politics of Rights, Resources and Knowledge* which had its financial support from The Norwegian Science Council. Many of the authors in this volume presented a draft of the present chapters at this workshop. Some of our contributors were also invited to present a paper at the annual conference held by the *Forum for Development Cooperation with Indigenous Peoples*, also in October, 2005. I thank the Forum for allowing us to publish two of the papers from that conference. Three chapters have later been commissioned to be included in this book. I thank all of the authors for their contribution and their patience.

As the main editor I am grateful for the most rewarding editorial cooperation with Harald Gaski, Svein Jentoft and Georges Midré. I am also grateful for the support of Terje Brantenberg and Vigdis Stordahl, the other members of the research project, and for their contributions to the workshop. Special thanks go to Ellen Marie Jensen who did a tremendous job with language editing. Jill Wolfe added aditional language comments to the inroduction.

The support from the Centre for Sámi Studies at the University of Tromsø must also be warmly acknowledged. The Centre's graphic designer, Bjørn Hatteng, has helped us make this book look very appealing. My gratitude is also extended to the artist Per Kleiva for allowing us to use his lithograph *Kort møte* (Short encounter) for the cover, and to Mary Nicholson for permission to include Peter Nicholson's cartoon in chapter 15.

Except for the Introduction, all of the chapters had gone to print before the watershed moment on September 13, 2007 when the United Nations adopted the Declaration on the Rights of Indigenous Peoples.

Tromsø, January 2008

Henry Minde

Introduction

Henry Minde, Harald Gaski, Svein Jentoft and Georges Midré

Globalisation is a category that describes the flow of goods, capital, people, information, images and risks across national borders. Globalisation is also manifested by the emergence of networks and institutions, in many instances championed by multinational corporations, as well as by international organisations such as the UN (see Nash (ed.) 2000; Held (et.al.., eds.) 1999). Many of the contributions in this book demonstrate how these developments have had negative impacts for indigenous peoples. Yet, despite setbacks, recent international developments also have promising features. A page was turned in indigenous peoples' history when on September 13, 2007 the General Assembly of the United Nations with an overwhelming majority voted to adopt the Declaration of the Rights of Indigenous Peoples. Issues of principal importance for the world's indigenous peoples have now been settled. The highest authority of global governance has stated that indigenous peoples have basic human rights and these rights must be respected and adhered to at every level of governance – from global to the local. But the final page in this narrative will not be turned until the principles of the Declaration are acted upon. Thus, much remains to be done before indigenous peoples have obtained the justice that a sizable majority of the United Nations members have acknowledged that they are entitled to when they voted in favour of the Declaration. There is a long way to go from principle to policy to tangible results and there is every reason to assume that this process will be far from linear. The challenge that lies ahead is to make sure that indigenous peoples' rights are confirmed and materialized in those concrete settings where indigenous peoples find themselves.

Although the Declaration refers to issues and concerns that indigenous peoples share, their situations differ greatly from geographic area to area, and also within countries. This must be taken into account during implementation because one formula does not fit every situation. Indigenous peoples' rights as delineated in the Declaration must be transformed into policies that apply to situations where the livelihoods, institutions, history, cultures and identities of indigenous peoples are at stake. Indigenous people must be able to see and feel the difference that these rights and principles make in their daily lives.

This book draws on case studies from a number of countries and discusses how the process of globalization impacts indigenous peoples and the academic and political discourses pertaining to their rights. The contributions to follow clearly demonstrate the challenges involved and the need for a contextualized policy implementation along many dimensions that are common for indigenous peoples, regardless of where they live. These issues and concerns have global relevance but at the end of the day they must have a local manifestation. This introduction will briefly discuss those issues and concerns. The introduction and the chapters are structured along three subject matters that we believe are central to the implementation of the Declaration:

- The continued focus of indigenous peoples' concerns and interests globally and the role of the international indigenous movement
- The issue of self-determination and social justice with regard to territorial control, political participation, and resource management
- The importance of indigenous knowledge, research and education as being inherent to the empowerment of indigenous peoples

Methodological Considerations

Social research has tended to limit Indigenous Studies to events and processes at "intermediate" scales, i.e. the local, regional and national levels, focusing on issues such as the interplay of indigenous leadership and associations, parties, national governments and bureaucracies within nation-states. Less emphasis has been placed on the global diffusion of indigenous claims and trans-national political, legal and cultural discourses and practices. Sami Studies in the Nordic countries are a case in point; research in each country continues to focus on the particular history and circumstances of Sami affairs as they relate to the distinct history and circumstances of each respective country (cf. Stordahl and Kuok-kanen in this volume). Academics who work on indigenous issues thus become experts on matters mostly within their respective countries. Comparative Indigenous Studies that focus on the different national contexts of law, culture, and politics are therefore rare, with some important exceptions (see Haver-mann (ed.) 1999, and Brysk 2000 on land rights; Tauli-Corpuz and Cariño (eds.) 2004, Cant, Goodall and Inns (eds.) 2005 on environment and sustainable development; Smith and Ward (eds.) 2000 on culture and globalisation; and Ivison, Patton and Sanders (eds.) 2000 on politics). Studies of indigenous movements as the trans-national process of the flow of ideas, organisation, and events are almost absent. With this volume we hope to make up in part for this deficiency.

The interplay and contradictions between different levels in thematic and institutionalised fields of activity are relevant for discourse analysis of indigenous movements. In Part I of this book, such analysis will consist of content analysis of essential thematic discourses and fields of activity. Some discourse analysis involves the mapping of power positions, as these can be disclosed

2

through content analysis, decision processes, and policy outcomes. Despite the differences in history, culture, language and legal and political systems, indigenous peoples' relations to majority populations and the nation-state involve the same basic issues which include claims for and the recognition of their legal rights, political autonomy, and management and access to natural resources. Of particular interest is why and how indigenous interests and demands in some countries are translated into effective collective action with regard to the management of natural resources, the development of legal rights and jurisprudence and forms of self-government. As demonstrated in Part I of this book, indigenous peoples' issues are currently contentious, not only in terms of minority policy, but also within academic disciplines, a point which is raised consistently throughout this volume.

The growth of the global economy and the reduced significance of the nation-state as a governing institution relative to international institutions and agencies during the 1990s onwards has created another, and quite different, context for indigenous peoples' interests and policy formation. In this context, collective interests and peoplehood are seen as contradictory to individuality and primordiality. One of the most disputed outcomes of this process is how the rise of indigenous nationhood also opens up a fundamental restructuring of indigenous peoples' relations to the outside world, including their constitutional status within nation-states (Tully 1994; Kymlicka 1995; and Part II of this volume). By virtue of the very same processes, indigenous peoples are also not only becoming involved in and dependent on globalisation processes in various ways, but they are also participating and becoming integrated in public institutions and life within their respective nation-states. Thus, globalisation has the potential to empower indigenous peoples within their own states (see Part III of this volume).

Part I: Indigenous Movements and their Opponents

> *United Nations Declaration on the Rights of Indigenous Peoples*
> Article 1:
> Indigenous peoples have the right to the full enjoyment, as a collective or as individuals, of all human rights and fundamental freedoms as recognized in the Charter of the United Nations, the Universal Declaration of Human Rights and international human rights law.
> Article 3:
> Indigenous peoples have the right to self-determination. By virtue of that right they freely determine their political status and freely pursue their economic, social and cultural development.

> Article 9:
> Indigenous peoples and individuals have the right to belong to an indige-
> nous community or nation, in accordance with the traditions and customs
> of the community or nation concerned. No discrimination of any kind
> may arise from the exercise of such a right.

The political mobilisation of indigenous peoples in nation-states undergoes various but apparently parallel phases, which reflect general conditions and also the increasing international involvement of indigenous leaders. At the beginning of the 20th century, the first organised modern indigenous movements emerged with varying forms and purposes, not only in North America and the Nordic countries (Minde 1996) but also in New Zealand (Walker 1990) and Australia (Meynard 2007). These movements were triggered by the economic and socio-cultural dynamics of industrialisation, increased mobility, and political unrest during that period. However, the overall emphasis on assimilation, class struggle, and nationalism of early modernisation provided few incentives and caused modest resistance from indigenous activists.

The conditions which provided space for a gradual development of indigenous organisations, political claims and a flowering of indigenous forms of self-expressions began with the development of the modern welfare states and the policies of industrial development and ideologies of common benefits. Notably, a precondition for indigenous revitalisation and the cultural and political movement was the emergence of a fairly small political elite from among the indigenous peoples which led to more effective organisation. The grievances of indigenous peoples could now be channeled on to the political arena (see the chapters by Friedman, Minde and Reynolds).

The indigenous movement had its inception at the end of the 1960s and then flourished in the decades to follow. At that time, this movement was a part of the dramatic ethnic revival which was underway in western countries. It paved the way for the cumulative growth of these movements in other continents (Africa and Asia) from the late 1980s onwards (see Saugestad, Chapter 7). Most importantly, these movements managed to forge international and global dimensions during the 1970s, which eventually gained them a lot of political clout (Minde and Nilsen 2003; and Minde, Chapter 2). The conventional wisdom in the early period after the Second World War was to provide individuals with equality under the law as a means to avoid war and conflict, whereas collective rights were associated with the destructive forces of fascism and nationalist ideologies. Thus, the indigenous claims for special collective rights challenged the older model of assimilation and homogenisation of nation-states (Kymlicka 1995; Falk 2000:127 ff). The chapters in the first part of this book explore the cultural and political dimensions of the political mobilisations around indigenous-based rights claims on local, national and global level. A short list of events in the UN as it pertains to indigenous peoples, illustrate the changing political mood on this matter:

- In 1971 the Economic and Social Council in the UN (ECCOSOC) favoured the preparation of a study of indigenous populations under the Human Rights Sub-Commission, the so-called "Martínez-Cobo-Report" (1971-1984).
- NGO conferences were held in the UN buildings in Geneva in 1977 and 1981 about indigenous peoples' issues, respectively "Discrimination against Indigenous Populations in the Americas" and "Indigenous Peoples [!] and the Land"
- The World Conference to Combat Racial Discrimination in Geneva 1978 endorsed the rights of indigenous peoples and included this issue in their plan of action.
- The UN formed a Working Group on Indigenous Population (WGIP) under the Sub-Commission in 1982. At their meeting in 1985, the Group decided to begin the work of standard-setting with the aim to produce a Draft Declaration.
- Meanwhile a new Convention–No. 169 –on indigenous peoples was adopted by The International Labour Organisation (ILO) in 1989.
- The UN Conference on Environment and Development in Rio de Janeiro in 1992 stated in Chapter 26 *inter alia* that indigenous land should be protected from activities that are environmentally unsound or that the people concerned consider to be socially and culturally inappropriate.
- At the WGIP session in 1993, members of the Working Group agreed upon a final text of the Draft Declaration on the Rights of Indigenous Peoples and submitted the text to its parent body, the Sub-Commission. The Sub-Commission of experts adopted the text without changes in its 1994 session and transmitted the text to the Commission of Human Rights (CHR). The CHR consisting of state members established in its session in 1995 a new Working Group with a sole purpose to elaborate a revised Draft. The representatives of indigenous groups were then also given the opportunity to continue to participate in these elaborations. A somewhat revised text proposed by the chairperson of the CHR Working Group was adopted by the successor of the CHR, the Council of Human Rights in its first session in 2006.
- In the meantime, many of the UN's bodies responded to questions and demands raised by the Indigenous International Movement, issues which were discussed in many conferences arranged by the UN. An example of one important new concern has been the protection of the heritage of indigenous peoples in relation to the process in the UN on Biological Diversity.
- The World Conference on Human Rights in Vienna 1993 recommended the UN establish a permanent forum. Such an organisation, called "Permanent Forum for Indigenous Issues," located at the UN in New York had its first

session in 2002. Compared with the WGIP, the Permanent Forum has a much wider mandate. The indigenous peoples themselves propose half of the sixteen experts who formally constitute the Forum. However, the Forum has only advisory status under ECOSOC.

- The further process of adoption of a Declaration on the Rights of Indigenous Peoples by the UN unexpected opposition and delay when the General Assembly 3rd Committee in November 2006 adopted an amendment proposed by Namibia on behalf of the African Group of States to allow time for further consultations.
- However, after a few changes the General Assembly approved the Declaration on the Rights of Indigenous Peoples on September 13, 2007 after 143 states voted in favour, 11 abstained and four–Australia, Canada, New Zealand and the USA voted against.

During the political mobilisation of indigenous peoples in the 1960s and 70s, liberal politicians and social scientists who sympathised with the international indigenous movement actuated a discourse of compensation and moral restitution. This opened up for indigenous interests and representation both within the UN system and in many countries (see chapters in Part I by Minde, Nyyssõnen, Warren, Reynolds, and Saugestad). However, regardless of the progress made by the indigenous over the years globally, indigenous peoples have been confronted with new and different challenges in relation to some national governments and majority populations (see Reynolds' Chapter 5 and Johansen Dahre's Chapter 6 in Part I).

Firstly, we are dealing with movements which were on the forefront of the indigenous struggle and which are now entering a many-sided process of formalisation and institutionalisation in terms of negotiating different kinds of self-determination, (as demonstrated in the Norwegian context by Lina Gaski in Part II) and which during the last years have been in the forefront of the political agenda in Australia (see Robbins 2007; Altman and Hinkson (eds.) 2007; and Reynolds in this part). Secondly, the ethnic conflicts after the collapse of the Soviet Union in Europe and in other parts of the world have contributed to a growing scepticism towards indigenous leaders and their organisations from national governments and the public at large. Thirdly, we have seen an increasingly outspoken critique of indigenous organisations and their goals and perspectives. The critique covers a wide range of arguments and attitudes–from the warnings of national politicians against collective rights and indigenous self-determination as being dangerous political strategies to academics branding indigenous movements as "essentialist" and as outdated nationalism–reinforced by the growing influence of the ideas of equality, individualism and multiculturalism. As explored in Part I, accusations against indigenous movements as being imbedded in apartheid reasoning are often espoused by powerful industrial companies and political parties in countries like Australia, Guatemala and the USA as well as in some African states (see respectively Reynolds, Warren, Johansson Dahre and Saugestad in Part I).

This kind of academic opposition has been spearheaded by the anthropologist Adam Kuper (2003), and it coincides with the sociologist Ulrich Beck's opposition to multiculturalism, which he views as a path to essentialism and rivalry between cultures (Beck 2006). However, in Chapter 1, Jonathan Friedman criticises such perspectives with regard to indigeneity. He argues that with their particular history of political marginalisation the idea that indigenous peoples should represent a threat to a modern cosmopolite is an exaggeration. In Chapter 2, Henry Minde also regards Kuper's critique as missing the mark because the arguments used by the indigenous movement in the UN to support their claims during the declaration process were not inflamed by essentialist portrayals or illustrated in primordial terms. On the contrary, they were filtered and framed through the language of human rights, democratic citizenship and the modern anthropological theory of ethnicity. Therefore, it is due to explore how the modern indigenous discourses have changed since the 1970s. What has been the economic and political context for the opponents? How have indigenous intellectuals and leadership responded to the current critique of their movement? Which dilemmas have to be confronted and how can this process then be reconceived? These are some of the questions that will be highlighted not only in Part I of the book, but also in the parts to follow. It remains to be seen whether the new Declaration or books such as this one can help transform such discourses.

About the chapters in Part I

In Chapter 1 Jonathan Friedman explores the relational nature of the concept of indigeneity. He argues that it is a category that is always defined within the larger context of a state, an empire or political system within which it refers to the marginalized, less developed populations that pre-dated the advent of the former. It discusses the variations in the way in which indigeneity is constructed as a function of the nature of the state forms within which it is constituted. The second section of his chapter deals with the historical disappearance and re-emergence of indigenous groups. He argues that such groups can be constituted and in part created out of shreds and patches of historical experience, and that indigeneity is a position more than a particular kind of population. The history of Hawai'i is used to illustrate the way in which indigenous identity that had once all but disappeared has come back in force since the mid 1970s. The last section of the chapter deals with the complementary opposition to indigeneity that is expressed in the new process of globalisation, one that has had a great deal of influence in a certain anthropology that, following the "invention of tradition" school, which claimed that indigenous movements were false–because instrumental phenomena in which artificial representations of the past were used in present politics–has now taken a further step toward denying the validity of the concept of indigenous as such.

In Chapter 2, Henry Minde investigates why and how the development of the Declaration on the Rights of Indigenous Peoples found its way into the UN system. This question has mostly been overlooked in the academic literature on indigenous issues in international law. The mostly North American literature does not take notice of, or has even misrepresented, contributions made by the indigenous peoples' movement and states from other regions of the world. This preoccupation led to the exclusion of the complex and ambiguous cultural and political processes among the indigenous peoples themselves and also of the larger historical context within the UN. Lately, some social anthropologists have criticised not only the authenticity of the movement, but also questioned the reality of the term "indigenous peoples." In this study, Minde demonstrates how participants within the UN and different indigenous organisations used the demand for a Declaration to frame indigenous-state relations in new ways. The application of certain concepts had their background in colonial history, but they were marked by the counter-hegemonic discourses linked to the process of decolonisation from the 1960s. Secondly, he analyses how the category "indigenous peoples" was understood and defined in the UN, and how this term has been strongly connected to the question of self-determination and land rights. Since the Declaration of Indigenous Rights has not been studied properly in its historical context, Minde argues that in recent academic and political debate, these issues have become more confusing and misleading than they rightfully deserve.

The focus in Jukka Nyyssönen's Chapter 3 is the use of the global rights discourse, which was introduced by the Indigenous peoples' movement, in the Finnish political context. The possibility to "guilt-trip" the national bodies was stunted by the simultaneous institutionalisation of the Sami movement in Finland by the establishment of the Sami Delegation in 1973, the first of the Sami Parliaments in the Nordic countries. Institutionalisation enclosed Sami activity to the national political frame, in its required political culture, and rendered parts of the global indigenous imagery useless. There also occurred an internal division within Sami identity politics, as the institutionalised Sami movement chose to concentrate on judicial reasoning, while the "Independents" used more radical "ecologized" representational strategies. Neither of these strategies was legitimised in the minority politics of Finland. The land rights claims were ignored as encroachments on the formal equality provided by Finnish society and the ecological reputation of the Sami under the new hegemonic discourse of environmentalism quickly deteriorated. The Sami in Finland can only point out restricted successes in "soft" issues, not in those of their own interests, i.e. the land rights.

In Chapter 4, Kay Warren discusses the challenges of representing the dynamics of the multi-faceted Pan-Maya movement in Guatemala through the complex decades of Central America's Cold War, peace process, and reconstruction. The chapter discusses the roots of indigenous activism in rural communities, the interplay of culturalist and class-oriented activism, and power-knowledge issues across the rural-urban divide. It examines the relation between social movements and the state during the drafting of the 1995 Indigenous Accord by civil society groups recruited to consult on the Peace Accords which were formally signed in 1996. The defeat of the indigenous rights referendum in 1999 offers a case study of how different state and business interests set up the referendum to fail, how dirty campaigns and a savvy Maya opposition leadership used the media to critique "special rights" that would fragment the nation-state, and how Pan-Mayanist groups, on both sides of the culturalist-class analysis divide, failed to mobilize voters. The chapter ends with a discussion of the current tensions between the movement for collective rights, liberal views of identity as a private rather than a public policy issue, and the rise of a new generation of leftist movements in Latin America.

In Chapter 5 Henry Reynolds takes as his point of departure the mass bridge marches of May 29, 2000 in Australia's biggest cities. More than a million people endorsed these walks in support of reconciliation between indigenous and settler Australians. The question he poses is: Why did these marches turn out to be the end of a reform era instead of being a new and more active phase of Aboriginal politics? The modern campaign for reforms had its breakthrough in 1967 when a referendum accepted Aboriginal peoples as citizens so they could participate in elections and at the same time paved the way for an increasing role for the national government in Aboriginal affairs. Simultaneously, the reform movement within this field was overtaken by Aboriginals and Torres Strait Islanders themselves. Demands for land rights and treaties were placed on the political agenda, but were opposed by State governments and the mining industry. Instead, the Labour Government in the 1980s and early 1990s established The Aboriginal and Torres-Straits Islander Commission and launched the idea of reconciliation. The aims were to promote a deeper understanding of the Aboriginal history of past dispossession and their continued disadvantage. This campaign culminated in the aforementioned bridge walks. In addition, the verdict in the Mabo case in 1992, when Australia's highest court discarded the doctrine of terra nullius, and the following political negotiations between the federal government and the indigenous movement contributed to the rise of Pauline Hanson's One Nation party and a shift of government in the 1996 election. It was enough to shatter the implicit, but important, consensus on questions of race and migration, questions which came to the forefront in the following elections. Reynolds concludes that behind these developments is a strong reassertion of nationalism, persistent attacks on the idea of multiculturalism, and anxiety about cultural difference.

Ulf Johansson Dahre, in Chapter 6, examines the changes in policies concerning the claims of indigenous people during the last forty years with a special focus on Hawai'i. Since the end of the 1960s, indigenous peoples' movements have been salient factors on international and national political arenas. Indigenous people of Hawai'i and elsewhere have become increasingly politicised in the hope of changing the relationship between them and the states where they live. The policy changes regarding indigenous peoples in western democracies were called "silent revolutions" in the 1990s. However, during the last decade, the general recognition of indigenous claims in western democracies have ignited a strong current of critique and opposition that have led to considerable changes in political and legal attitudes, and to changes in public opinion regarding constitutional and legal concessions for indigenous peoples. In the same way that the dramatic pro-indigenous changes in the 1980s and 90s swept over western democracies, the critique and opposition to indigenous movements are now sweeping over those same states. This opposition towards indigenous claims shows that human rights are not beyond dispute: contrary to the general view of human rights being instruments of conflict resolution, human rights can actually fuel ethnic conflicts.

Sidsel Saugestad's contribution in Chapter 7 takes as a point of departure the development of an international indigenous movement over the past decades, and looks at the way new organisations and trans-national structures have affected and interacted with indigenous peoples in Africa. The chapter points to important differences between the way indigenous organisations developed from local into more encompassing national and transnational structures in other parts of the world during the 1970s and 1980s, while indigenous organisations only emerged in Africa during the 1990s. The fact that African organisations already had established meeting places at the UN in New York and Geneva meant that the process of developing a leadership to participate in these forums was complicated.The chapter examines some of the problems of dispossession and marginalisation that have characterised relationships between indigenous peoples and African states, and concludes that for the African continent, the First UN Decade on the World's Indigenous Peoples probably had more effect than in many other places, as it served to introduce the concept of "indigenous" to the African context.

Part II: Self-determination, Social Justice and Natural Resources

> *United Nations Declaration on the Rights of Indigenous Peoples:*
> Article 26:
> 1. Indigenous peoples have the right to the lands, territories and resources which they have traditionally owned, occupied or otherwise used or acquired.
> 2. Indigenous peoples have the right to own, use, develop and control the lands, territories and resources that they possess by reason of traditional ownership or other traditional occupation or use, as well as those which they have otherwise acquired.
> 3. States shall give legal recognition and protection to these lands, territories and resources. Such recognition shall be conducted with due respect to the customs, traditions and land tenure systems of the indigenous peoples concerned.

Human rights, social justice and self-determination are all key issues in the global indigenous discourse. Notably, they are not separate but overlapping issues; indeed, they are all elements of the same equation. Human rights are basically about social justice; without such rights there is no justice. Social justice is a human right that is partly realised through self-determination. To what extent human rights and social justice for indigenous peoples are secured in particular situations is largely determined by the degree to which they enjoy self-determination. Thus, it makes sense to discuss these concepts as elements of the same whole. Together they also form a key research topic in social research that targets indigenous peoples, for instance with regard to how they are implemented in concrete settings.

These concepts have a long history in global politics and nation-building, and they have figured prominently on the agenda of major institutions such as the UN for a long time. Introduced by President Woodrow Wilson, self-determination became a key issue during the Versailles treaty negotiations in the aftermath of World War I, where a number of new states originated on the world map (MacMillan 2003). The concept caused as much turmoil then as it has caused in the negotiations leading up to the UN Declaration of the Rights of Indigenous peoples. What does self-determination really mean, and what constitutes a people to whom self-determination should be a right? For some peoples, the decisions made in the Versailles were felt as a violation of their basic right to statehood and self-determination, which created traumas that are still haunting us today, for example in the Middle East. Thus, the hopes and aspirations that are linked to these concepts have not vanished and they continue to be contested, for example, when indigenous peoples raise political claims in international forums. But as the following chapters in Part II demonstrate, human rights, social justice, and self-determination not only relate to high ideals and principles that still remain to be implemented globally; they also pertain to tangible matters on the ground, for instance to land and resource rights, income distribution, and political participation. Thus, human rights, social justice, and self-determination are also micro-issues. They are about the development of local communities, access to and control of natural resources, sustainable livelihoods and food security, and social cohesion and cultural identity. These are all matters of great relevance to indigenous peoples who across the globe often find themselves in a situation where they are discriminated against, impoverished, disempowered and excluded from the political processes that affect their lives.

These concepts are further problemitized when the focus switches from the global to the local level. Their operationalisation and implementation into concrete situations are imbued with obstacles and controversies on the ground. The situation for the Sami is a case in point. In the endeavour to create Sami nationhood, the discursive formation found among the Sami political elite often point to historical injustices, that the Sami are victims of Norwegian oppression, and Sami culture is then often presented as an essential, reified entity as demonstrated in the chapter by Lina Gaski. At the same time, it may be difficult to base a theoretical argument pertaining to special rights for indigenous peoples on the grounds that they have suffered injustices (cf. Kymlicka's review (1999) of Anaya's book *Indigenous Peoples in International Law*). Indigenous people are not the only disadvantaged people in the world; many people find themselves in situations where they are oppressed and poor. Is it then fair that some categories of people– such as indigenous peoples–should have special rights? How should such claims be justified? In order to answer such questions one must explore the various meanings of justice and fairness, in particular, the different concepts of justice to which such claims are attached. According to Weigård, the legitimation of special rights for indigenous peoples can be based on notions of desert and entitlement, as well as to notions of fairness to compensate for injustices of the past. Still, even legitimate claims are often contested, because legitimacy is not only an issue of philosophical reasoning but something that is up for interpretation amongst the people involved in a rights struggle. Justice is often a zero-sum game. Thus, the concern in many of the contributions in this section addresses issues of social justice. The actual employment of these concepts determines how indigenous peoples' cultural lives and welfare develops in relation to other categories of citizens. Some governments insist on basing their policies on formal equality rather than equity, that is, where the whole population is considered to have the same rights and opportunities regardless of the position they find themselves in. Nyyssönen's chapter in Part I discusses how this resulted in the rejection of Sami claims for land rights in Northern Finland.

In most countries indigenous peoples are small minorities, as is the case with the Sami in the Nordic countries and Russia. In Guatemala by contrast, the Mayas represent around half of the total population. Their claims for special rights have been rejected on the same grounds as in the example from Finland: considering entitlements or social rights to one category of the citizens is often thought to represent a kind of discrimination of the other citizens. In Guatemala, these kinds of arguments justify policies that in effect marginalise the large indigenous population, keeping a majority of them in poverty.

In welfare states such as those in Scandinavia, we find concepts of justice that are concerned with the outcome of the distributional processes, not only equality regarding access to institutions like education, health care, and the labour market, etc. As discussed by Midré in his chapter, there is a tension between welfare policies based on distributional equality and respect for differences in lifestyles and worldviews. For instance, in its formative years the Norwegian welfare state not only tried to reduce differences in living conditions, but it also seemed to demand a willingness to refrain from expressing differences in ethnic identities as a precondition for obtaining status as full citizens. Different notions of equality may have similar consequences for the relation between the state and the indigenous peoples. If there is no recognition of the right to be different, the indigenous populations tend to be marginalised in relation to the distribution of wealth and other goods, as well as to the right to self-determination.

Self-determination and the right to use, own, and live on ancestral lands and to have access to other natural resources are central to notions of justice, as stressed in the Declaration of the Rights of Indigenous Peoples. However, the relation between property rights, poverty alleviation and fairness is not straightforward. Jentoft's contribution in Part II demonstrates how the basic tenets of effective management of natural resources reside in property rights to land and other natural resources coupled with social justice. Poverty as well as considerations about the legitimacy of rules for harvesting natural resources will affect how people use resources; injustices may lead to mismanagement. Property rights may not be the answer without considering whether or not these rights are fair. When no reference is made to social justice then the introduction of property rights may actually increase poverty levels, particularly in indigenous communities, instead of reducing them.

Self-determination as a human right is derived from the philosophical notion that humans –both as individuals and as peoples – have the equal right to freely control their own destiny. Notably, in conceptualisations of freedom, self-determination has negative as well as positive connotations, as with "freedom from" and "freedom to." "Freedom from" pertains to protection from political suppression, racial discrimination and cultural oppression whereas "free-dom to" with its positive implications refers to empowerment and participatory democracy, allowing indigenous people to make choices with regard to their future (Anaya 1996:75). But self-determination is hardly meaningful without distributive justice. For that to occur, secured property rights, in some instances privileged access to the natural resources that indigenous people depend on, both materially as well as culturally, is a necessary condition for survival be-cause equal access in not synonymous with equitable access. Self-determina-tion is also applicable in terms of resource management decisions; natural re-source management should not put indigenous peoples at the receiving end of management decisions that come from distant state bureaucracies (see chapters by Jentoft, Midré, and Weigård).

Self-determination then is not only and necessarily about statehood (Anaya 1996). In fact, indigenous peoples rarely make such claims when they insist on their natural right to self-determination. At the level of the nation-state, self-determination is more about the right of indigenous peoples to negotiate freely about their political status and representation. Erica Irene Daes (who was the first Chairperson of the working group that drafted the Declaration of the Rights of Indigenous Peoples) asserts that self-determination is basically about "the recognition and incorporation of distinct peoples in the fabric of the State, on agreed terms." Thus, she is "not talking about the assimilation of individu-als, as citizens like all others…", Consequently, she concludes that "(t)he right to self-determination is best viewed as entitling a people to choose its political allegiance, to influence the political order under which it lives, and to preserve its ethnic, historical, cultural, or territorial identity" (Daes 1996:49). Professor Daes finds it "not realistic to fear indigenous peoples' exercise of the right to self-determination" (ibid:54), which many still do, if not always out of fear for the disintegration of the nation-state as out of fear of economic loss when own-ership of land and resources are redistributed.

It would be naïve to think that self-determination is just about governance principles. In real situations, it is also about wealth and power, as indigenous peoples are often without control of the vast natural resources within their ter-ritories (see Barsh in Part II). It is no wonder then that the issue of self-deter-mination has been the most difficult to agree upon in the process within the hu-man rights commission of the UN when working towards a Declaration on the Rights of Indigenous Peoples and had also been resulting in its delay. Indeed, the reluctance to accept the "s" in peoples can largely be explained by reser-vations amongst state negotiators regarding the concept of self-determination as a human right, because it lifts the issue from the level of the individual to the level of the collective or community. But self-determination may involve many issues at different social levels and the mechanisms through which self-determination are instituted may differ from case to case. There is no single approach to instituting self-determination, regardless of context.

Self-determination is complicated by the fact that indigenous peoples are rarely alone within their territories. In many situations, they are also mixed ethnically through inter-marriage. A more recent challenge for indigenous peoples is what self-determination can possibly mean in the age of globalisation. Globalisation undermines the simple dichotomy of internal versus external self-determination, as the internal can no longer be shielded from processes that occur externally. There is no longer a distinct "domestic" and "foreign" relation on which self-determination is exercised. Indigenous politics are, therefore, not only about social and cultural diversity, they are also about how to deal with complexity and interdependency in a globalised, dynamic world. Hence, Anaya (1996:81) argues: "Given the reality of multiple human associational patterns in today's world, it is distorting to attempt to organize self-determination precepts into discrete internal vs. external spheres defined by reference to presumptively mutually exclusive peoples." On issues such as human rights, sustainable development, and resource management, self-determining indigenous peoples would also be subject to intervention from supra-national bodies. They need to relate to and seek support from and try to influence policies that are developed at a global level by institutions such as the FAO and WTO (see chapter of Barsh). Perhaps the greatest challenge facing indigenous peoples in this millennia, is the issue of global warming and requires that indigenous peoples make their voices heard at all levels of society, including the global level. The Intergovernmental Panel on Climatic Change noted pointedly that indigenous peoples are particularly vulnerable to the effects of global warming because their adaptations are based on eco-systems that are often exposed and very fragile.

About the chapters in Part II

In Chapter 8, Jarle Weigård writes that indigenous populations may in many respects live under similar circumstances as other ethnic or national minorities. But it is also a fact that indigenous peoples have both claimed and to some degree have been recognized as having more extensive rights to self-determination than other minority groups. Therefore, the question should be posed as to whether it is possible to give a coherent theoretical justification for why such a differentiation might be legitimate. Most attempts to justify minority rights are based on some sort of benevolent understanding of justice. Considerations related to either equality, impartiality or needs should then explain why minority rights are established, and by the same token, also explain why indigenous peoples have more comprehensive rights than other minority groups. There is theefore a significant reason to demonstrate the possibility that indigenous peoples have suffered more supprepression and therefore are in a weaker position than all other minority groups. In reality, however, this does not always seem to be the case. Yet, there is also the entitlement conception of justice to consider, which states that everyone should be given what they are entitled to. In many cases, this point of departure seems to provide for a better understanding of the uniqueness of indigenous peoples' situation when it comes to both claims for land rights and for political autonomy–due to their long lasting occupation and utilisation of their traditional areas. In general, it seems that a combination of the benevolent view and the entitlement view–the two complementary conceptions of justice– can best capture the specificity of indigenous peoples' circumstances because the two views combined are able to reflect both deprivation and strength as elements of the case for indigenous rights.

In Chapter 9, Svein Jentoft discusses the mechanisms by which global institutions, such as the Food and Agricultural Organisation of the United Nations (FAO) and the World Bank, along with large segments of the academic community, consider secure property rights to marine and coastal resources as essential to sustainable management and development and a necessary part of alleviating poverty among fishers in coastal communities. Securing rights of property and access to marine and coastal resources are also integral to the struggle that indigenous peoples are leading in many parts of the world which is why it was an issue that was raised in the process leading to the Declaration of the Rights of Indigenous Peoples. Whereas the FAO and other global players in natural resource conservation and management tend to emphasize the functional merits of property rights, i.e. property rights as a handy management tool, the latter are more concerned with the justice and equity implications of property rights in this context. Yet, fisheries and coastal management require the full recognition of both concerns, particularly, in indigenous communities, but not exclusively. The approach must therefore be holistic where ecological, social, and cultural aspects are considered in an integrated fashion. Although the recent global move towards ecosystem-based management sponsored by the FAO and other global actors opens up a broader vision of the management challenge, the problems and concerns of indigenous peoples may easily be forgotten. In fact, there is little mention of indigenous peoples in the management policy documents that come out of these organisations. If considerations of justice for indigenous peoples in fisheries and coastal management are given the marginal attention that was typical in the past, then management systems and their inherent property rights may exacerbate, rather than alleviate, poverty in indigenous coastal communities.

In Chapter 10, Georges Midré briefly discusses two concepts of equality,equality of opportunity and equality of distribution– with respect to indigenous peoples and the national states, using Norway and Guatemala as examples. In spite of the fact that the dominant concepts of equality differ in the two countries, the consequences for the indigenous minorities in the two countries have important similarities. The main similarity is that in neither case were policies based on recognition of the particular cultures of the indigenous peoples. The concept of equality of opportunity is then discussed in relation to various concepts of and options for manoeuverability, as well as to Sen/Nussbaum's discussions of capabilities and functionings. Regardless of significant differences between these two countries, in the last decades there have been positive changes in the situations of the indigenous populations. This can be explained by the increased organisational capacity and political strength of indigenous organisations, but also by their links to international developments.

Lina Gaski, in Chapter 11, describes how the Sami political elite are continuously creating and developing the Sami nation in a process whereby the masses are invited into history. However, many of the potentially new Sami voters are hesitant; they live outside the so- called Sami core area where the ethnic border between Sami and Norwegians is blurred, many of them can not speak the Sami language and they do not have the visible cultural traits or knowledge traditionally connected to "Saminess." For this group of Sami, imagining the Sami nation is not obvious and this represents a challenge for developing Sami nationhood. The focus in the chapter is on how Sami identity is constructed in such an ambiguous context; how dominant political actors, by using certain interpretative repertoires in public discourses about territory and place, construct versions of reality, and further, how these discursive practices produce certain categories and identities. The chapter argues that the discourse about territory represents a persistent dilemma that occurs in the Sami endeavour to create nationhood and to demarcate a Sami political community: How should nationhood be constructed, without on the one hand essentialising, or on the other hand compromising the underlying popular assumptions about what constitutes the culture of an ethnic group?

Russel Lawrence Barsh begins Chapter 12 by stating that despite the good work of the UN in stressing the human rights issue as it relates to indigenous peoples there is still a lack of real improvement in their actual living conditions around the world. Although the confidence of indigenous peoples in asserting their rights has improved, there is little evidence of real economic progress; they continue to be in situations characterized by exploitation, marginalisation and poverty. But rather than talking about ways to increase economic assistance, Barsh argues that the economic incentives and terms of trade that tend to displace indigenous peoples and ruin their material conditions, such as their territories and natural resources, must be addressed directly. Consequently, we must examine those institutions through which such mechanisms are defined and determined, such as the Word Trade Organization. He argues that it is also essential that we stop discussing human rights, development and trade as if they are separate issues. On the contrary, with globalisation these issues are indeed closely linked and should be treated as one entity. In his judgement, it is also within the legal framework and in accordance with the mission of the WTO to consider trade in relation to indigenous peoples' rights, for instance related to the issue of subsidies, because at the end of the day it is a social justice issue that cannot be ignored. Seizing indigenous peoples' land and natural resources for economic gain is not only illegitimate, it is also illegal according to the standards of the WTO because it affects prices and hence distorts the trade value of the products that are made from those seized resources. In fact, WTO rules provide an "open window" for indigenous peoples to try their case with the WTO trade panels which will reunite the rights aspects and the economic aspects in a powerful forum. Barsh' chapter provides examples from Canada and the US where this actually happened. Bringing indigenous peoples' interests into the realm of trade and trade policy, would therefore not only be the right thing to do from a justice perspective, it may also be far more effective than any assistance program targeted specifically for indigenous peoples.

Part III: Politics of Knowledge

United Nations Declaration on the Rights of Indigenous Peoples:

Article 31
1. Indigenous peoples have the right to maintain, control, protect and develop their cultural heritage, traditional knowledge and traditional cultural expressions, as well as the manifestations of their sciences, technologies and cultures, including human and genetic resources, seeds, medicines, knowledge of the properties of fauna and flora, oral traditions, literatures, designs, sports and traditional games and visual and performing arts. They also have the right to maintain, control, protect and develop their intellectual property over such cultural heritage, traditional knowledge, and traditional cultural expressions.

Article 33
1. Indigenous peoples have the right to determine their own identity or membership in accordance with their customs and traditions. This does not impair the right of indigenous individuals to obtain citizenship of the States in which they live.
2. Indigenous peoples have the right to determine the structures and to select the membership of their institutions in accordance with their own procedures.

Part III of this book mirrors the wide range of topics and challenges connected with indigenous knowledge, traditional and newly acquired theoretical knowledge, and higher education and research today. Epistemological and methodological considerations with regard to indigenous research are discussed from different points of departure, as well as the persistent questions regarding representativity, authenticity and innovation on traditional ground. As a whole, this section demonstrates different approaches and interests with regard to research on indigenous issues. Several questions are being raised, not least of which the recurring quandary as to whom has the legitimate right to conduct research in indigenous communities, and how should this research be conducted? Do indigenous peoples need institutions of their own in order to benefit from the results of research, or is it possible to envision that national research institutions will take on the responsibility and make the commitment needed to compensate for the historically lacking voices of indigenous peoples' in academia? What will be the best way to gain the interests of indigenous peoples? Would it be to constitute a small minority in a huge national institution or rather to comprise a majority in a small institution that is owned and run by indigenous people themselves? Does research have an ethnic stamp, or is that a problematic idea? Still, it must be conceded that the debate over research policy within indigenous communities also has this side to it, which is discussed in some of the chapters in Part III, although mainly as an in-between the lines subject. As is the case with indigenous politics globally, we also experience the same dilemma concerning research: Who is an indigenous person, and how much indigenousness is needed in order to accept a person's identity as for instance a Sami, an Aborigine or Native American?

On the surface, it is fairly easy to find definitions that most scholars would agree upon, but there are still hierarchal differences within the indigenous groups themselves on the matter of who may speak for whom, and who may claim representativity on behalf of whom. To some extent, this may be viewed as a relic of the traditional respect indigenous people have had for knowledge, as pointed out by Smith, Burke and Ward (2003:22):

> Indigenous peoples have a particular and profound respect for the intellectual and cultural property of others. One manifestation of this is a reluctance to speak on behalf of other Indigenous peoples (…) This profound respect for each other's property is grounded in cultural systems in which this property constitutes an important facet of land ownership, and in traditions of restricted knowledges (…).

This may be one possible reason for the modesty exercised by indigenous researchers in becoming involved in comparative projects that implicate assessments of other indigenous peoples' cultures, since one is really only fully cognizant of one's own culture. In another respect, urbanization has brought about a new perspective about the interconnectedness of indigenous peoples' values and priorities, suggesting that the only way of receiving respect and being heard internationally is to combine efforts and speak up. This also requires that indigenous peoples have some common issues to gather around which are of essential importance to them as representatives of traditional values. This may be even more important today as people begin to deal with challenges facing modern indigenous communities who must cope with altered situations.

"Perhaps the most serious omission from international debates on the future of indigenous cultures is inadequate recognition of the fact that most indigenous people now living in settler states are urban" (Sissons 2005:28). Thus, nation-building, identity and authenticity are key terms for several of the chapters in this section and also raise questions about which direction indigenous peoples themselves are developing their own cultural articulations: Is it towards a fusion of international indigenous artistic expositions or will the tradition of each culture still be the most valued for each group? Is the international indigenous community striving for a cosmopolitan critique of its expressive forms or will there continue to be an emphasis on the insider interpretation? How do critical studies within indigenous scholarship position themselves between indigenist, nationalist, and cosmopolitan approaches to art and knowledge systems?

Knowledge production is often related to power, because the management of research and education has always been linked to power relations and hegemony in society. For the indigenous peoples of the world, for the most part this has implied a situation of alienation towards research and researchers. The results of research have neither been communicated back to the indigenous communities nor has the effect of the research been of much value and use for the researched; the objects of the investigations. Quite the contrary, indigenous peoples by sharing their knowledge, rather, contributed to educating new "experts," who in turn overshadowed and silenced indigenous voices. Even though some became advocates for the indigenous cause, for politicians, bureaucrats and the mass media of the dominant societies, it has always been much easier to use "experts" and to interview those from their own people who could speak "for the Native," although not "as a Native."

Therefore, research and higher education became an early battlefield for the attention of indigenous politics. Initially this was integral to the struggle for recognition of indigenous cultures, but later on it was even more so for the emerging international cooperation that was established through the alternative world politics of the so-called Fourth World. In the past few decades, the presence of indigenous people in academia and the development of their scholarship have presented new questions and challenges for conventional academic scholarship and practice. With references to both First Nation and Maori scholars in this field, Kuokkanen states in her contribution that many indigenous peoples now require that research dealing with indigenous issues has to emanate from the needs and concerns of indigenous communities, rather than those of an individual researcher or the dominant society. The idea of "giving back," of conducting research that has a positive outcome and is relevant for indigenous peoples themselves is built into the reasoning over the perspectives of higher education and research. The focus is changing from conducting research on indigenous peoples into research being conducted by indigenous researchers–as also evidenced by the many contributions in Part III, written by people with an indigenous background and who represent a wide range of approaches to the current status of indigenous research.

Kuokkanen's preferred site for testing out this philosophy is the establishment of a Sami university where the foundations of the institution and the commitments of the researchers will have a decisive impact on how the research is conducted and how it can be productive for the Sami themselves. Vigdis Stordahl's chapter is more sceptical, and asks whether simply naming an institution Sami will in fact stimulate reasearch that focuses upon Sami concerns and preferences. Her examples include how Sami interests have been a battlefield for the rhetoric on the best ways to serve indigenous Sami interests in academia in Norway, where the University of Tromsø has proclaimed itself to be a Sami university. It is because of this that it has met opposition from Sami scholars who have also acted as ethno-politicians. Cojtí Cuxil's example of the universities' role in educating indigenous leaders is from Guatemala, where the number of indigenous students is low compared to the total population of the country. Cojtí is occupied with creating a welcoming environment for indigenous students in higher education in order to establish good learning conditions for collective action. Into this rhetorical battlefield regarding Sami research, Nils Oskal enters with a chapter that problematises the whole question as to whether epistemological arguments are actually the most relevant for legitimizing a specific indigenous scientific knowledge management. He situates himself in a position that accentuates convincing argumentative scientific practice as the basis for social sciences, into which category he seems to be inclined to classify indigenous research.

About the chapters in Part III

Since knowledge is a source of power, as argued by Vigdis Stordahl in Chapter 13, it became a priority for indigenous peoples to get into positions where they can produce knowledge about themselves. One way of producing knowledge that has proven to increase in importance is through higher education and research. Thus, higher education and research are not merely seen as the individual privilege each member of an indigenous group has, as a citizen of a particular state, but also as an integral element of self-determination and nation-building. The chapter focuses on the struggle of the Sami in Norway to get in positions to be able to produce knowledge about themselves; a struggle that has aroused controversies and debates especially in academia. From time to time the debates have created an agonizing professional atmosphere. The chapter analyses the debates surrounding these controversies by applying a frame of interpretation that reflects the specific characteristics as to indigenous peoples and the field of knowledge.

Rauna Kuokkanen's Chapter 14 is a critical analysis of the current status of Sami higher education and research. She employs a comparative analysis that draws parallels to other indigenous peoples' scholarship in North America and Aotearoa/New Zealand. The chapter argues for a distinct, collective vision for the future of Sami studies and research. This vision is based on the central objective of contemporary indigenous discourse and scholarship, that of transforming and decolonizing indigenous societies. Rather than grounding Sami research methodologies and higher education on the discourse of Cultural Studies, this chapter contends that there is a need to move away from the "politics of distraction" to advancing Sami intellectual self-determination.

Vicki Greaves' point of departure in Chapter 15 is the "history wars" in Australia, which was a debate between the western political divisions of "left" and right" over the "true" history of colonial conquest as it played out on the battlefields of Aboriginal history. White historians' efforts to showcase Aboriginal histories obscure the more silent issues around the lack of opportunities for community-based indigenous power in the academy. Greaves' chapter extends the battlefields metaphor to associated issues arising from the hegemony of western sites of knowledge production which makes issues of indigenous identity and authenticity more complex by taking them out of Aboriginal community control and influencing the nature of indigenous knowledge production. Indigenous identity is a contentious and conflicted issue within Australia where indigenous people have recently had to fight for an indigenous identity, against the widely held settler colonial conviction that all Aboriginal people had "died out" and at any rate the culture had been "lost." The adoption of Aboriginal culture-based approaches to research necessitates the indigenous researcher's sound engagement with kin and community, removing confusion over questions of identity and allowing meaningful indigenous knowledge development to occur.

In Chapter 16, Demetrio Cojtí Cuxil, discusses the higher educational system in Guatemala and its actual and potential role for leadership in the Mayan movement in the country. The relative number of indigenous students at the universities is disproportionately low. The possible reasons for this are discussed; the irrelevance of the programmes for indigenous culture and the hostile environment that confronts indigenous students are possible explanations. Furthermore, many of the programmes are of low quality. The situation has improved in the last decade, due to some national programmes, but mainly because of a fairly large number of foreign programmes aiming to support indigenous students. Education and political leadership are connected, even though they often are viewed as separate fields. Traditional leadership at the local level does not require higher education, but a large majority of the most high profile indigenous national leaders do have university degrees or secondary diplomas. Finally, the chapter discusses the role of learning–and the importance of unlearning flawed knowledge in the process of forming collective action.

Chapter 17 by Nils Oskal, takes as its theoretical point of departure the past decade's debate over the introduction of indigenous methodologies. He begins by referring to a central idea of Cartesian philosophy; namely its theory of knowledge and the belief that epistemology is a foundational enterprise. The idea was that epistemology would ultimately make clear just what made knowledge claims valid and the degree of validity they could lay claim to. Validity is something we can generate for ourselves by ordering our thoughts correctly according to methods founded on epistemology. Similar ideas are formulated by defenders of a separate and distinct indigenous methodology in social sciences, in order to justify investigations from a culturally internal perspective. In the meantime, epistemology has lost its reputation since the heyday of logical empiricism and the whole epistemological enterprise is refuted by criticism from different directions. The main arguments of philosophical hermeneutics have been integrated into social sciences after the "interpretative turn," and the problem of the justification of the scientific validity of social sciences is even more precarious. Social sciences stand in danger of collapsing into political moralizing and hollow rhetoric. As an alternative to claims on a priori epistemic superiority the validation of social sciences has to rely on practical argumentation.

In Chapter 18, Harald Gaski formulates another angle to discuss the implications of globalisation for indigenous peoples' artistic expressive forms. Gaski introduces the particularities of the Sami yoik as a traditional art form, and discusses what kind of impact the globalisation process will have on indigenous peoples' traditional music. Over the past decades the yoik has been modernized and introduced to modern instruments, which on the one hand has created an increased interest in the yoik, but on the other hand has also brought about a discussion of authenticity and genuinity with regard to the uniqueness of tradition contrasted to the blend of different music genres, derived from different indigenous cultures. Copyright and safeguarding of traditional artistic expressions may become harder to manage when there is the experience of a continued mix of musical elements from a very diverse combination of indigenous peoples' traditions, in this case exemplified by the story of how the Sami yoik entered the international stage of world music.

The last (19) chapter in this volume is by Arnold Krupat, where he gives an overview of Native American literary criticism. He writes that it may be seen to proceed from either of three overlapping perspectives, all of which the chapter argues, are committed to indigenous culture's contribution to the ongoing fight against colonialism. The perspective of the indigenist foregrounds the epistemological difference to be found in works by indigenous writers. Different ways of seeing and organizing perception are invoked as ways of promoting different ways of thinking and behaving. The perspective of the nationalist invokes the special treaty relation of the Tribes to the dominant nation-state, the US, when referencing the historical sovereignty of Native Nations. Language and culture, rather than perception, are the basis by which greater degrees of independence lie. The cosmopolitan perspective, as it is here understood, is respectful of epistemological, linguistic, and cultural difference, and to the importance of the category of the nation even in the context of globalisation.

Cosmopolitan critics – the author considers himself among them – are also interested in comparativism and the possibilities of anti-colonial translation. Both the comparisons they offer to colonial and postcolonial peoples around the world, and the translations they offer of other visions and histories are meant to support the anti-colonial work of the indigenists and the nationalists.

Concluding Remarks

In a cross-disciplinary manner, the chapters in this book explore cultural and socio-historical dimensions of political mobilisation around indigenous-based claims and grapple with the complex and contentious debate on the global, national and local level of indigeneity, justice and knowledge. As editors, we are convinced that this is the most productive approach to current indigenous scholarship. In this way, the subject field with all its international attention and relevance, is analysed and debated from multifaceted angles. Self-determination, resource and knowledge management, in all their nuances, are the most important issues for the ongoing international debates about indigenous peoples. With the ever increasing literature on indigenous realities within nation-states and common systems of law and governance, the time is due for attempts at a broader comparative approach using developments in one context to pose questions about similar or different trajectories and developments in other contexts: "When indigenous people are gaining political ground there, why are they not here?"

These are also relevant matters for continued comparisons between the development we see in some parts of the world where indigenous issues are gaining ground politically, and other areas where reluctance is being expressed against indigenous interests. It is interesting to observe the current behaviour of the settler states in relation to indigenous people. From originally being among the first supporters of the emerging indigenous global organizing in the 1970s, they have almost totally shifted position into becoming opponents of the ongoing political process. Why is this? Have the premises changed, or does this express a fear among the settler states that the rights of free trade and global enterprises will become limited in indigenous peoples' areas? Does this, in turn, tell us something about the growing influence and power of the indigenous movement, that it has actually grown from being a symbolic issue worth superficial support into an audible political voice that can no longer be neglected and overruled?

The rights of indigenous peoples are not nearly as contested as they used to be. Currently, the discussion focuses on the practical application of these rights, thus there is acceptance that indigenous peoples have distinct rights of their own, and as such are entitled to exercise and enjoy the right of self-determination, which in turn includes the right to decide over their own futures and celebrate life on their own terms. Research and research issues are minor issues in this great picture. Still, research has represented and will most conceivably continue to represent in the future, a defining power of how to interpret, understand and enhance the continued development of the integrity and cultural survival of the world's indigenous peoples. In our view, to say the least, this is presently one of the most interesting academic fields internationally.

References

Altman, J. and M. Hinkson (eds.): *Coercive Reconciliation: Stabilise, Normalise, Exit Aboriginal Australia. North Carltonasa.* Australia: Arena Publications Association, 2007.

Anaya, S.J.: *Indigenous Peoples in International Law.* New York/Oxford: Oxford University Press, 1996.

Beck, U.: *Cosmopolitan Vision.* Oxford: Blackwell, 2006.

Brysk, A.: *From Tribal Village to Global Village: Indian Rights and International Relations in Latin America.* Standford, California: Standford University Press, 2000.

Cant, G., A. Goodall and J. Inns (eds.): *Discourses and Silences: Indigenous Peoples, Risk and Resistance.* Christchurch, New Zealand: Department of Geography, University of Canterbury, 2005.

Daes, E.-I.: "The Right of Indigenous Peoples to "Self-Determination" in the Contemporary World Order". In D. Clark and R. Williamson (eds.): *Self-Determination: International Perspectives,* London: Macmillan, 1993, pp. 47-57.

Ivison, D., P. Patton and W. Sanders (eds.): *Political Theory and the Rights of Indigenous Peoples.* Cambridge: Cambridge University Press, 2000.

Falk, R.A.: *Human Rights Horizons.* New York: Rutledge, 2000.

Haverman, P. (ed.): *Indigenous Peoples' Rights: In Australia, Canada, & New Zealand.* Auckland: Oxford University Press, 1999.

Held, D., A. McGrew, A. Goldblatt and J. Perraton (eds.): *Global Transformations: Politics, Economics and Culture.* Cambridge: Polity Press, 1999.

Kuokkanen, R.: *Reshaping the University. Responsibility, Indigenous Epistemes, and the Logic of Gift.* Vancouver-Toronto: University of British Columbia Press, 2007.

Kuper, A.: "The Return of the Native". In *Current Anthropology*. 2003:3, pp. 398-395.

Kymlicka, W.: *The Rights of Minority Cultures*. Oxford: Oxford University Press, 1995.

Kymlicka, W.: "Theorizing Indigenous Rights." In *The University of Toronto Law Journal*, 1999:2, pp. 281-293.

MacMillan, M.: *Paris 1919: Six Months that Changed the World*. New York: Random House, 2003.

Meynard, J.: *For Liberty and Freedom: Fred Maynard and the Australian Aboriginal Progressive Association*. Aboriginal Studies Pr., 2007.

Minde, H.: "The Making of an International Movement of Indigenous Peoples". In *Scandinavian Journal of History*, 1996:3, pp. 221-246.

Minde, H. and R. Nilsen: "Conclusion", in S. Jentoft, H. Minde and R. Nilsen (eds.): *Indigenous Peoples: Resource Management and Global Rights*. Delft: Eburon, 2003, pp. 297-309.

Nash, K. (ed.): *Readings in Contemporary Political Sociology*. Oxford: Blackwell, 2000.

Robbins, J.: "The Howard Government and Indigenous Rights: An Imposed National Unity?" In *Australian Journal of Political Science*, 2007:2, pp. 315-328.

Sissons, J.: *First Peoples: Indigenous Cultures and Their Futures*. London: Reaktion Books, 2005.

Smith, C. and G. K. Ward (eds.): *Indigenous Cultures in an Interconnected World*. St Leonards, N.S.W.: Allan & Urwin, 2000.

Smith, C., H. Burke and G. K. Ward: "Globalisation and Indigenous Peoples: Threat or Empowerment?" In C. Smith, & G. K. Ward (eds.): *Indigenous Cultures in an Interconnected World*. St Leonards, N.S.W.: Allan & Urwin, 2000, pp. 1-24.

Tauli-Corpuz, V. and J. Cariño (eds.): Reclaiming Balance: *Indigenous Peoples, Conflict Resolution & Sustainable Development*. Baguio City, The Philippines: Tebtebba Foundation, 2004.

Tully, J.: *Strange Multiplicity: Constitutionalism in an Age of Diversity*. Cambridge: Cambridge University Press, 1995.

Walker, R.: *Ka Whawhai Tonu Matou – Struggle Without End*. Auckland: Penguin Books, 1990.

Part I

Indigenous Movements and their Opponents

CHAPTER 1

Indigeneity:
Anthropological notes on a historical variable

Jonathan Friedman

The initial assumption of this paper is that indigeneity is not an absolute term but one that is necessarily relative to a larger hierarchical field. The fact that the legal context of the use of the word has tended necessarily to universalize and absolutize it, must be understood in contrast to its fundamentally relative and ambiguous character. The discourse on indigeneity is prolific in the contemporary world. It is politicized and embattled in forums on rights to resources and it is understandable that it might easily be assumed that it is something quite modern. In this discussion I shall try to situate the relativity of the term within the political representations historical and contemporary worlds.

Theme and variations

An interesting point of reference for understanding the genealogy of indigeneity can be found in the variations of representations of hierarchy in the ethnographic and even ancient historical literature. Political hierarchy in a great many kin based social formations is represented in terms of dualism of autochthonous peoples and their foreign rulers. The relative value of these two terms varies from case to case but the logic of the relation is surprisingly maintained as if a "structure of the long run". A great many myths of the foundation of chiefly and royal polities are based on the following kind of schema.

- in the beginning there were the people. They were politically egalitarian, "ruled" by elders who were generous and caring and whose only status resided in their social age. The political was based on a ritual order for the promotion of the fertility of the land.
- then came the foreign chiefs, from overseas, across the river, from Kahiki etc. They were men, usually young men, that left their home land and came to their new hosts where they killed/subdued the local men and married the local women, establishing an alliance between their warlike function and the peace/fertility function of the local/original people.

The dualism established here corresponds to the following variable configurations:

- autochthones/foreigners
- female/male
- inside/outside
- land/sea
- peace/war
- fertility/destruction
- religious chiefs(priests)/political chiefs (war)
- wife-givers/wife-takers

This series can be found in variations throughout large parts of the world: In Oceania, South America, East and Southeast Asia, for example. But it is also the core of one of Dumézil's famous studies of Indo-European representations that became basis of a well-known article by Sahlins concerning the nature of Fijian chiefship (Sahlins 1985). The structure is one of ambivalence insofar as the political power of foreign conquering chiefs is countered by the ritual power of local priest (chiefs). The ritual of investiture often stresses the power of the autochthonous via the "death" of the chief as "foreign" and his rebirth as a member of the local society (at least in part). The model of Congolese hierarchy is one that stretches from the most rooted (pygmies) to the most foreign, i.e. chiefs and kings, colonial representatives from a distant Europe. This is expressed in the modern context in the representations of power and in ritual activities such as "la sape" (below). But hierarchy may also be contested and even inverted as in the historical examples from Hawaii in which chiefs were ousted or killed, in which their foreignness (descended from Kahiki or Tahiti) is denigrated as opposed to the sacred unity of the ancient social order. In the modern context this is expressed in the assimilation of all the waves of colonization, Kahiki, England, USA, Japan, to a common denominator represented by the first chiefs (Friedman 1992). The people of the land, the *maka'ainana* are here elevated to the representatives of a possible revolutionary reversion to an original state of nature. This is a conflictual strain that cuts across the contemporary Hawaiian movement. Even European societies develop these kinds of discourses of local people and foreign power. This is expressed in the opposition between a people and their aristocrats who are represented as belonging to a cosmopolitan intermarrying elite who in certain periods represent the illegitimacy of rule, what in other circumstances would be called colonialism.

Indigeneity as a relative term can be said to belong to the kind of framework discussed above. While the actual internal relations involved are very different there is a certain logic or representation that is maintained. The indigenous is linked to nature, to historical precedence, to simplicity, equality and harmony, but also to the state of underdevelopment, to savagery, to the state of Warre of all against all and to disorder. These opposing sets of terms are not independent of one another but on the contrary are merely positive vs. negative interpretations of the same position within a larger hierarchy, whether within a single polity, as in kinship based social formations, or between polities or "peoples" as in larger scale imperial orders. The usages of the term can be understood in terms of this more general framework as in the samples that follow here:

- Roger Williams one of the founders of the Baptist movement who lived part of his professional life in the American colonies said in comparing his own home country, "We have Indians at home—Indians in Cornwall, Indians in Wales, Indians in Ireland" (Williams, 1974 [1652]: 200).
- Some years ago the Afrikaners of South African attempted to participate in the Permanent Forum on Indigenous Issues. There was some clearly expressed opposition to this even if no formal decision was made and the Afrikaners were not present in subsequent sessions.
- When my wife and I first visited Hawaii in the late1970's we were told by well known anthropologists that there was little to study in the way of real living Hawaiians, that the indigenous population had been integrated biologically and culturally into American Hawaii and that in cultural terms it would be more interesting to do research on their history. That year we discovered that these same Hawaiians had occupied Sand Island in Honolulu Harbor and were engaged in a number of other actions to gain control over lands that they claimed. We discovered young people on the island of Hawaii who spoke Hawaiian and in our naivety asked them if they had learned it at university. They laughed and explained that they spoke Hawaiian at home. Things have changed since then.
- In large parts of Africa the notion of indigenous is considered an insult to the local population. In Republic of Congo there is hierarchical relationship between categories which is competitive, especially between North and South but which always places the pygmies at the bottom of the scale. The latter are often associated with the first settlers in a cosmology that is common in many parts of the word in which "little" people once inhabited the place where contemporary populations are now located. Often these are people, as in Hawaii, the *menehune*, who are long since gone, but in Central Africa the association is still regularly made accompanied by extreme forms of discrimination. But this is often historically an ambivalent relation, i.e. while politically low ranked they often are said to possess magical powers related to their custodianship of the spirits of the land. Among the *Sapeurs* of Brazzaville, who were so well known for their cult of haute couture, and where "life force" was identical with wealth and health expressed directly in and on the body,

there are invitations to parties in which this relation is made clear.[1] Here the use of the word applies more generally to those of lower status but the linkages are obvious in other contexts.

- The logic of the African situation as in all situations in which the population was divided into colonists and indigenous might be understood as follows: Indigeneity is associated with peoplehood and thus, with the colonized. It is a relative term in an asymmetrical relation of dominance.[2] For the colonists the different "ethnic" groups, "tribes" or "ethnies" were all of the same category, subdivisions of the indigenous (especially in the French context where the word is used formally). In the postcolonial situation the categorization is shifted downward within the formerly colonized population, but at least in the Congolese case there is an older formal hierarchization of groups that encompasses the term indigenous. In politicized situations in which a case is made for the rights of indigenous peoples in Africa it is often vehemently stated that it is "we" who are the indigenes and no one else. But this was often a statement made by white settlers in the not so distant past.
- The logic of this situation is clearly expressed in the ambivalent conflation of indigeneity with colonial identity itself. Thus the dominant white class of colonial Hawaii claimed to be the true Hawaiians.
- A wrong impression has obtained that only those born here of the aboriginal Hawaiian stock are the true Hawaiians. A man born here of white parents who spends his talents and energies for the benefit of Hawai'i is as true a Hawaiian as if his parents were all red, or one red and the other white. Those who benefit this country by their own good character and example and life are the true Hawaiians (Judd 1880).
- And more recently, a documentary film by Karl Slättne showed the mayor of Nouméa proclaiming, "c'est nous les indigènes" (Bergom-Larsson and Slättne 1986).

The "modern" national context of indigeneity

In countries that are themselves nation states or colonial extensions of such states, the logic is somewhat different. Here indigenous refers to the enclaves of minorities who pre-date the formation of the nation state (in general), associated with previous life forms and economies in a situation where the national population makes no claims to indigeneity although there is an interesting difference between immigrant based and non-immigrant based national identities.

---

1 Entrée interdite aux personnes indigènes, car la Société des Ambianceurs et des Personnes Elégantes (SAPE) déteste les indigènes. Venez-voir les superbes étiquettes de la plus prestigieuse haute couture (Zibélé).

2 But this is of course, as we suggest a replication of the general scheme of conquest in which the foreign conqueror is opposed to the local, indigenous population; where indigeneity is a colonial term expressing dominance of the stranger.

In the former indigenous peoples are identified quite easily but in the latter there a deeper ambivalence. In Sweden, for example, there is a strong bond between "ethnic" Swedes and their landscapes and territory. The existence of the Sami represents a contradiction and this has led to interesting paradoxes and even conflicts.

- Many Swedes do not recognize the status of the Sami and the state refuses to grant them such status with rights connected to the ILO convention on indigenous populations.
- Local Swedes in the north of the country claim that they are just as indigenous as the Sami and there are innumerable conflicts concerning land use rights
- The Sami are considered to be an ethnic minority of course, as other minorities who have the status of being official minorities, as opposed to immigrants. These groups include the Roma, the Jews, and the Finnish-Swedish inhabitants of Törnedalen and the descendents of Finnish immigrants. The Sami are referred to as indigenous, but they do not belong to a clearly separate category.

If we compare the above logic with that to be found in the United States or Australia we find significant variations. In Australia the majority population identifies with the past history of the prison colony that was Australia. Here the land itself is represented as foreign, dangerous, not belonging to the population and the Aborigines are thus associated with danger as well as magical powers (negative) just as the nature of the outback in general. Aborigines just as other indigenes were treated abysmally by colonial powers and the post-colonial nation state, but the popular imagination was quite specific.

- Australians do recognize the indigenous status of the Aborigenes, unlike Swedes who sometimes contest that status and provide little in the way of respect. In Australia a combination of fear and will to elimination has been a powerful tendency. In Sweden there has been competition concerning indigenous status, but no more recent will to elimination.
- Australian relations to the indigenous are relations to the foreign and since it is they who are the foreigners, all of Australian Nature takes on a negative hue.
- Australians are immigrants, forced immigrants, with ambivalent status and relation to the land, surrounded by immigrant populations on the coast and indigenous peoples in the inland.

In the United States, an immigrant country like Australia, but not founded as a prison colony, the indigenes are also an ambivalent category but in a different way. They are accepted as indigenous but also low ranked, sometimes as noble savages and other times as barbarians. They were conquered by an expanding population and either killed them off or placed them in reservations where they often suffered major decline in living standards and health conditions.

- Americans recognize the indigenous status of the Indians but as in Australia there is an ambivalence in their association with nature, in this case of a more classical nature, the Noble versus the Ignoble Savage at least in what is called the "popular imagination". The category Indian belongs to Nature here as well, but the latter is not negative and foreign as in Australia.
- Indians were massacred and displaced and finally placed on reservations in the expansion process, but the plural nature of the American "nation" state means that there is no clear association of a particular culture/ethnicity with the definition of the nation. The census is clear on this point. It is impossible to identify as simply an American, only in terms of origins. Only American Indians have been able to identify as Native Americans and this is a category apart rather than that associated with the identity of the state. This has made all ethnic politics rather easy to develop and in the period since the 70's this has been so not only for Red Power for most other "powers".
- The United States, an immigrant society like Australia, maintains a very different structure of identification, one in which the land is said to have been given providentially to the newcomers, in which indigeneity is worth respect and even guilt but where the ambivalence is one in which the indigenous had to make way for progress, as tragic as this might seem, and in which indigenous politics is assimilated to minority politics in general, even if not for the indigenous peoples themselves.

If there is logic to indigeneity it can be suggested that it is within this hierarchical context that it can be fully grasped in its real relativity.

34

Figure 1: Hegemonic cycles and cultural identity

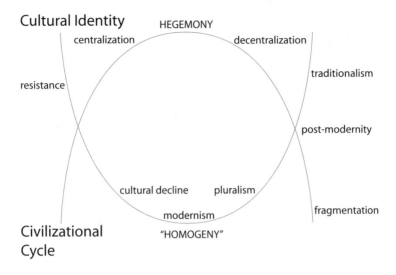

Figure 2: Hawaiian identity in the cycle of Western hegemony

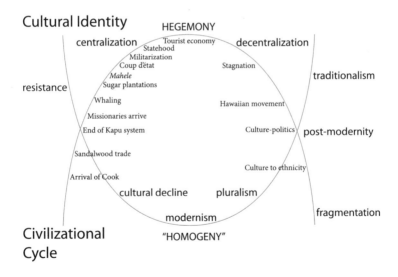

If the category itself can be said to be part of the logic of social hierarchy, it is not always marked, not always even present. It has, in other words, a historical variability that is related to the changing context which, I have suggested, is a global systemic context. The appearance and disappearance of indigenous identity is related to the expansion and contraction of hegemony. In research on the decline and rise of indigenous identity in Hawaii we arrived at a summary statement that follows from the following model.

A very short history[3]

The graph on the left represents the inverse relation between changing hegemony and cultural identity in the world system. In the expansion phase, local social orders are either destroyed or integrated within the larger political and economic field of expanding hegemony and local identities are either weakened or integrated as subaltern categories of a larger imperial order. This schema is applied to the history of Hawaii in the world system in order to trace the specific trajectory of Hawaiian identity and political organization in terms of the larger political-economic context. The penetration the Hawaiian political order in the first decades of the 19th century was a complex set of processes in which demand for sandalwood played a crucial role. The European connection first led to the unification of the islands under the leadership of king Kamehameha I whose success depended upon British supplies of arms and ships. The trade with British and then American merchant vessels led to a rapid depletion of forest and of commoners who were taken out of agriculture to collect sandalwood at the same time as landed chiefs flocked to Honolulu which was the collection point for foreign prestige goods. Following the unification of the islands, the king faced the new problem of control over the trade wealth and the monopoly over relations to the foreigners. The competition for wealth led to a division in the royal house itself and to the introduction of Christianity via one branch of the elite represented by the Maui based queen and wife of Kamehameha, Ka'ahumanu. A short civil war led to a shift in the direction of development, the end of the former political-religious order, referred to as the *Kapu* system and the introduction of Christianity under Ka'ahumanu's leadership.

Demographic collapse characterized the entire period. The sandalwood trade bankrupted the aristocracy and made them increasingly dependent on foreigners a relation mediated by the increasing presence of Calvinist missionaries. The royalty became increasingly linked to a new European-American elite leading to the transformation of the social order, the introduction of private property in 1848 a series of new economies, first Whaling which meant a boom for local production, as well as the transformation of Honolulu into a typical free port saturated with prostitution and gambling, and then the introduction of sugar production. The expansion of sugar plantations became the domain of the missionaries who used their positions to obtain large tracts of land. This led following 1850 to the massive import of foreign labor, Chinese, Japanese, Filipino, being the largest groups. The world sugar market can be said to have

---

3   This section draws in part on the following works, Kirch and Sahlins 1992, Stewart 1970, Kuykendall 1976, McGregor 1989, Kent 1983, Gray 1972, Dougherty 1992, Ekholm Friedman 1998, Friedman,1992, 1994, 1999.

been the major factor driving the politics of the white elite in this period. In order to avoid tariffs there was a constant attempt to arrive at arrangements with the United States but since the latter also had a major sugar economy in the South of the country it was difficult. This combined with the identification of the Hawaiian missionary-planter class with the United States led to increasing conflict with the Hawaiian government/royalty and ultimately to a coup d'état in 1892. The new government demanded to become a territory of the United States but this was rejected by the then President Cleveland and they instead claimed a republic for several years until they succeeded in being annexed by President McKinley's government. This was in the same period as the United States expanded massively in the Pacific and in the Caribbean and Hawaii was strategic for its access to the rest of the Pacific and Asia, lying half way between the continents. In this period Hawaiians who were declining in demographic terms were looked down upon by the white missionary class that had come to dominate the islands, the Big Five, as they were called.

At the end of the century, Hawaiians were a minority in their own islands (40.000). Their culture and language had been forbidden and they were divided into those who populated Honolulu, primarily poor and landless of course, but with a middle class of professionals (doctors and lawyers) connected to the aristocracy in one way or another, and a rural population that had for decades been creating self-isolating enclaves for themselves in the larger landscape of ranches and plantations. There was resistence in the early decades of the 20th century e.g. the Hawaiian party the *Homa Rula* party whose object was ostensibly to regain power over the islands. But this was brief, elites being bought off by the plantation class Republican party. By the 30's with the advent of the American military as part of the geopolitical developments in Asia, Hawaiians were on the way to complete marginalization. After WWII, the plantation economy had decline rapidly as the result of successful and militant unionization and global competition, and the elites had to quickly find what was called "a new kind of sugar" which turned out to be mass tourism, an industry that was the final blow to Hawaiians as even their "culture" was put on display by other Pacific Islanders and Asians while they cleaned the hotel rooms.

Throughout this period, the apocryphal model of adaptation was "marry out, don't speak Hawaiian, but English and integrate into the American world". This was a process of gradual identifying out that was facilitated by the high rate of intermarriage with immigrant groups. Thus part-Hawaiian (an official category) could also be part-Chinese, part-Filipino, part-white (*hapa haole*). In this way Hawaiians virtually disappeared from the ethic map of the United States a rapid fall from having been a kingdom recognized by most states in the world including Great Britain and France. It is noteworthy that when I myself began to work in Hawaii the academic establishment hardly recognized the existence of Hawaiians, except as a marginalized and mixed-origin group at the bottom of American society. Hawaii had become a plural society via the import of foreign labor and throughout the 20th century this is clearly expressed in the combination of ethnically localized residence, the development first of pidgin then of neo-pidgin typical of a colonial order and of an ethnic hierarchy in which there have been shifts in position but no real leveling of or elimination of the rank order itself. Hawaii has been and still is a prime example of what is called structural discrimination in which the institutional practices of the state reproduce an ethnic division of "labor". Japanese-Americans came to dominate politcs and the education sector, Chinese-Americans were more dispersed economically but became major economic players and the wealthiest group in the islands, White Americans were divided between a minority of old and wealthy land-owning families and poorer newcomers, Hawaiians, Islanders and Filipinos gravitated toward the bottom, Filipinos in the sugar and pineapple sectors (now almost defunct), Hawaiians as either unemployed or in menial jobs. Intermarriage was and is most common at the bottom of this society while higher ranked groups, especially the Japanese, have been very largely endogamous. The white elite did make strategic marriages to the Hawaiian aristocracy, but this created, via patriliny, a transfer of land title and often identity in the direction of whiteness. Only the Royalty has maintained a Hawaiian identity in the context of intermarriage, but this is a common elite phenomenon.

In this historical process indigeneity was absent. At the end of the period of hegemonic expansion Hawaiians were simply the remnants (mixed) of a former independent polity. There were, of course, representations of Hawaiian culture, in Museums and in tourist displays, but they were hardly associated with the contemporary Hawaiian population. In the 1970's this process began to reverse itself. Declining American hegemony in and following the Vietnam War and internal opposition were paralleled by the flourishing of identity movements, black and red power. These were primarily ethno-political in character but they implied the elaboration of cultural parameters; history, language and religion. A number of groups emerged in this period making land claims and attempting to stop the advance of the tourist based building industry on what were seen as Hawaiian property (which was legally the case). This was the period of left wing student revolt and the latter groups supported Hawaiian demands, just as they did with regard to other minorities on the mainland. From the mid to late 70's this began to change as Hawaiians decided to go it alone.. As one spokeswoman said, "We don't want socialism. We don't want to be workers! Socialism is simply the continuation of capitalism." They wanted "out". Here the model of a past social existence became central. The "return" to the land as a background figure was a major force and many Hawaiians did return to the land. The Hawaiians were emerging as an indigenous people with a culturally distinct identity that stressed a set of core values opposed to the society of which they were a part. This process has continued since the 1980s. It has become complex with the emergence of different sorts of movements, some royalist, others commoner based. And there has also been a consolidation of a new set of leaders which might be referred to as an elite or congery of elites increasingly connected to the institutional structure of the state, to the media, but where actual class formation is embryonic at most, unlike e.g. the situation in New Zealand.

This very bare sketch is meant to illustrate the process summarized by the above graphs. What occurred in Hawaii occurred in many parts of the Western world. In the Pacific (Maori), in the Americas and in Europe (e.g. Sami) there was a generalized revival of the indigenous. And this was of course categorized as such and institutionalized at a global level within the United Nations with the founding of the World Council for Indigenous Peoples which became an important venue for alliance making and a global construction of identity, at least for those representatives of indigenous groups who became part of the global community). This revival of indigenous identity is paralleled by a broad re-identification in the Western dominated sector of the world system. Where a number of relatively successful struggles have been mounted by various self-identified indigenous groups, "indigeneity" has moved from being a hierarchical classification to a locus of "subaltern" struggle. But it must be understood as always within this hierarchical field.

It can be suggested that indigenous awakening is part of a larger process of indigenization, one that applies to those populations that we usually associate with "real" indigenous but also with many national and other populations. The practice of rooting in general has created a series of parallel intensifications of local identity and it has occurred as part of a generalized ethnicization which generates the following series: indigenous populations, regional minorities, national populations, immigrant minorities. This is expressed in the above graphic as a product of declining hegemony in which the homogeny of national or state based identity dissolves into its fragments, creating the basis of a plural social order which is fraught with internal conflict. Indigenization as practice accounts for the emergence of certain forms of neo-pagan movements, of new American Indian tribes such as the Washitaw (Friedman 1999) who are black, have an internet site, a empress, arms and are allied with right-wing militia groups and for some members of the New Right which is actually multicultural and against the current form of the nation state.

The model suggested here implies as well that while indigenization and ethnicization occur in the West and its dependencies, the inverse process is occurring in South and East Asia where there is certainly conflict and violence, but where the tendency is toward the integration of minorities within larger state units rather than fragmentation. Integration is of course a violent and even bloody process but that which distinguishes it from declining hegemonies is the outcome. Recent study of the Mongolian language issue is revelatory. Here a long struggle for cultural autonomy led to the establishment of Mongolian language and culture at the same time as the generation that had struggled for this liberation began to send their children to Chinese schools. Nothing succeeds like success!

The fact that one can describe such processes as indigenization in general and even global terms, does not mean that indigenous movements are mere inventions as has often been argued. In my own work I have found that the identification process works very much because the images created in such movements resonate with those who participate and that this is because they are grounded in specific shared experiences. The notions of *aloha* and *malama* and *'aina* among Hawaiians are connected to interpersonal forms of sociality in which exchange is denied, in which a kind of community fusion is practiced, in which the experience of broken relations is traumatic if not deadly, and which can all be traced back in time into the 19th century. The formation of closed communities, of an inward looking endosociality etc., these are products of the historical logics of power in Hawaiian society in which commoners built walls around themselves, both literally and figuratively.

I have suggested that the denial of historical continuity by anthropologists is the product of an anthropological vision that would compete with "natives" for the control over culture or the identification process itself (Friedman 1994). Hawaiians have been involved directly in such battles with respect to "inventionists" such as Keesing (1989) and Linnekin (1983; 1992). It pits anthropologists against those that they study in a situation where the latter begin to identify themselves, thus contesting the anthropologist's own power of categorization. Yet this is precisely what could be the object of analysis, and in the approach suggested here it is to be expected that this kind of conflict should arise. The argument for historical continuity in the constitution of indigenous movements is an important recognition that the local really exists and is not a mere product of the global as is often suggested in globalization discourse (i.e. Appadurai 1996) and here there is a significant overlap between the modernism of inventionism and the cosmopolitanism of globalization. In the current situation there is an extreme polarization in which self-identified cosmopolitans or globalizers see fit to criticize indigenous populations precisely on the grounds that they are indigenizing, this is essentialist for such anthropologists and contains the seeds of nationalism and racism (Kelly 1995, Malkki 1992) and which is expressed in an opposition between nomads and autochtones, between cosmopolitans and indigenes.

The globalization discourse refuses the validity of any local identity on the grounds that the latter is a mere global construction, but there is rarely any research to back up such statements. The opposition between those who move and those who don't however is clearly expressed in statements like the following:

Across the globe a romance is building for the defense of indigenes, first peoples, natives untrammelled by civilization, producing a sentimental politics as closely mixed with motifs of nature and ecology as with historical narratives...In Hawaii, the high water mark of this romance is a new indigenous nationalist movement, still mainly sound and fury, but gaining momentum in the 1990's (...) This essay is not about these kinds of blood politics. My primary focus here is not the sentimental island breezes of a Pacific romance, however much or little they shake up the local politics of blood, also crucial to rights for diaspora people and to conditions of political possibility for global transnationalism. (Kelly 1995:476)

The statement seems to suggest that one must choose between natives and diasporas, and the choice is clear. It is best captured in an ideology that in one sense can be said to desire a return to the hierarchical vision of a past in which indigeneity was safe as a mere category rather than an active political force. But this is not a mere question of discourses. The realignment of identities is a real social phenomenon in the contemporary world, one that has led to increased

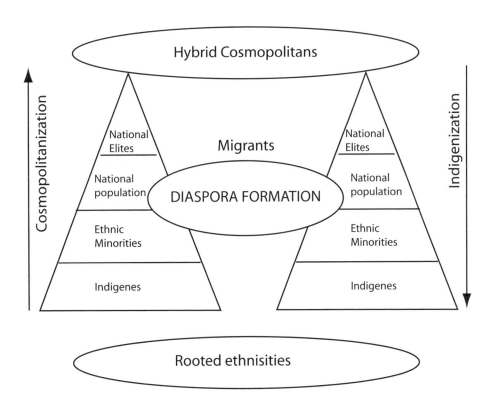

polarization as a process in which indigenization is the complementary opposite of cosmopolitanization, a process that is complicated by the fact that real populations with real histories are implicated in this process. While the global processes involved are indeed powerful, they are articulated with the specifics of local lives and strategies that imply that the latter can never be seen as mere products of the global. To do so is to practice a kind of intellectual imperialism in which local actors are pacified objects who have no strategies of their own. It remakes some anthropologists into latter-day colonialists.

Figure 3: The dialectic of cosmopolitanization and indigenisation
This new alignment is a significant reconfiguration of the arena of representation even if the basic structure is invariant. There is still a cosmopolitan or national top and an indigenous bottom, but intellectuals have been drawn in increasing numbers to the top itself, and the top has become increasingly cosmopolitan just as the bottom has become increasingly indigenized.

A second round: the threat to cosmopolitanism
The conflict that I have described above has taken on explicit qualities in the debate surrounding Adam Kuper's recent onslaught on the notion of "the indigenous" (Kuper 2003; 2006). The argument that the notion is not scientific warrants a discussion in relation to what I have outlined above. The entire discussion hinges presupposition that the notion should have a scientific value as a definition. Kuper links the use of the word "indigenous" to earlier notions of "primitive" and has little trouble demonstrating that the idea is a construction and that in certain respects it can be understood as parallel to earlier constructs in anthropology that have been abandoned. But this overlooks a certain social reality that is crucial in this respect. The indigenous populations of the world are of course constituted in the formation of states and/or of colonial regimes that rank and categorize their inhabitants.

Guha provided important insights into this issue in his subaltern studies of Indian history, where a dominant representation all but eliminated other subjectivities and intentionalities from the understanding of the sub-continent (Guha 1982-7). But real social history demonstrates clearly that such intentionalities have existed, that peoples have been reduced, marginalized and eliminated either culturally or physically by the expansion of hegemonic powers, a story that is as old as civilization, of course and not merely a modern or capitalist phenomenon, nor a mere expression Western culture as some postcolonial thinkers would have it.

It is not necessary to argue for the primordiality of a population in order to accept its status as indigenous although the verbal battles have often been confused. The Sami of Sweden need not argue that they were on the land before the Swedes in order to argue that they had a distinct way of life on the land *before the advent of the Swedish state.* Swedes are defined by the existence of the state in an important way even if there is a strong cultural continuity-in-variation that needs to be taken into account. That there were Scandinavian populations (more precisely: "populations unknown in respect to ethnic identity", see Hansen and Olsen 2004) in the north of the country prior to the Sami does not really contradict the argument if it is enunciated in relation to a state rather than to other populations. It was state power that often in a violent way, marginalized and compartmentalized the population. This is a different kind of argument than that assumed by Kuper.

Of course there are and have always been conflicts between different populations occupying the same territory, but this is not the real issue in the current argument. Nor does it contradict the suggestion made above that indigenisation can be understood as the practice of roots in any population. It is important here to maintain an intellectual distance to these issues in order to understand the mechanisms at work, before taking a moral position, but much of the discussion as been the other way around. That is, it has been imperative to take a stance on weather indigenous peoples should be allowed to speak, what they can say, and whether they should be allowed to exist as self-identified indigenes. One might say the same for all social phenomena, whether class, ethnicity, race, gender. Race is interesting in this respect. While it is trivial that the category has no biological reality, it certainly does in certain societies such as the USA, have a real social existence etc.. Social facts, after all, are not the product of scientific procedure. They are the realities of our investigations. The ensuing debate around Kuper's articles is from the point of view of the current discussion, a confusion concerning the social realities of the terms involved.

The implicit understandings of Kuper's argument are similar to those of Keesing, Linnekin and others. Ingdigeneity is merely a construction that has no reality where the populations concerned no longer live the lives associated with the precolonial existences that they are assumed to have led in the past. Turner, in his reply insists on the fact that it is irrelevant whether or not those struggling for their rights as indigenous peoples practice their traditional life styles or not (Turner 2004). This is also the position that has been taken by IWGIA.[4] Contrary to Kuper, indigeneity does not refer to a particular kind of society or even life style, but to a political identity that is, as we have argued here, a product of the structure of the state itself. Indigenous peoples are not primarily self-defining populations, but categories that have been imposed by colonial orders, at least in the past centuries of the modern state (even if, as has been shown, there are similar categorizations in previous and other imperial worlds). The category is, however, subaltern and it implies thus that claims

---

4   Personal communication with Andrew Gray. He discussed this in relation to Cultural Survival which he criticized for taking a human zoo approach in which indigenous peoples ought to have a "traditional" life style.

can be made in its name, that such populations can claim autonomy of one kind or another. And since it is a socially institutionalized category it can give rise to new identifications and even political claims by "outsiders" to indigenous status (as with the Afrikaners).

Kuper goes much further in his critique than do the previous inventionist anthropologists who merely attacked the authenticity of indigenous movements. He argues that the category "indigenous" is itself a misnomer that should be entirely eliminated. And our answer to this is, likewise, an extension of the earlier argument against the inventionist position, that the category is not an intellectual construct but a political-institutional reality, that has a very strong life of its own. The deconstruction of categories does not imply their elimination, especially when they possess an emic reality. More important for us here is the understanding of the position occupied by this kind of discourse. Kuper has also argued for certain cosmopolitanism in anthropology, one that reveals the relation between his critique of indigeneity and his own self-identification. This is not, I would argue, an example of a particular individual choice, but of a positioning within an already established social order, one described in figure 3, and which implies an opposition to the indigenous by definition.

Kuper's attack on indigeneity appears, paradoxically, to express a certain desire for authenticity, for a lost authenticity of which anthropologists were the masters. The apparent emotional engagement in this argument is related to the feeling of loss, a loss of order. The world that the anthropologists have lost is a world of ordered hierarchy in which the peoples that we studied were positioned clearly in their subservient positions, silenced and on display for our intellectual gaze. This is the heart of the crisis of "ethnographic authority" and of the issue of authenticity, defined as an objective phenomenon. But authenticity is an existential and not a museological issue, something that inventionists, modernists and globalizers consistently overlook. (Friedman 1994).

The recent emergence of indigenous movements is not an intellectual phenomenon but one that is deeply embedded in the lives of individuals. I do not seek here to simply take sides in a debate. It is more important to situate the debate as a whole within the larger structure of Western hegemony and its decline. This might sound alarmist to those who refuse the possibility that such declines can occur, especially now and for us. But I allow myself the opportunity to argue such a position since it does make sense with respect to the current debate. Kuper's quandary is ultimately founded within the larger transformation of western hegemony. The latter's decline with all the occidentalism and self-hate involved, is still an expression of a real loss of authority that is accompanying the decline itself as well as being its principal expression. It is not only some indigenous groups that claim the right to a voice with respect to their social position in the world. The entirety of postcolonial discourse is imbued with this politics of culture. It is in turn reinforced by a culturalization of a former critique of imperialism. Now it is western culture itself that is the core of the problem.. *"Hey Hey ho ho Western culture's gotta go"*[5] as a popular postcolonial campus chant would have it. This embodies a reversal of values or better an inversion of those values that is related in turn to the increasing decentralization of voice and even of real power in the world system. And while this is a piecemeal process it has resulted in some areas in a real inversion of ideology.

This is a significant, even massive, political change within the world order and cannot be reduced the kind of moralizing discourse that seems to have imbued what needs to be understood in terms of "social facts". Kuper is struggling against a real process of change as if it were a mere intellectual error. And he does so from a position that he calls cosmopolitan but which is, even more so, modernist. And it is the latter order which is disintegrating today. If this implies liberation for some minorities if not all, not by any means, it is not reducible to a mere intellectual phenomena. Now one may wish to struggle against what might appear to be intellectual surrender on the part of academics, but this must be understood as a Western intellectual phenomenon and not be confused with the movements of indigenous peoples to which it is linked.[6]

Thus one may readily agree that in a purely intellectual sense, the category of indigenous is an essentialized and non-scientific construct. Durkheim argued something quite similar for the concept of ethnicity, an argument which fit the republicanism of the French state like a glove. This may account for the fact that when his student Halbwachs visited the Chicago School he discovered an ethnic diversity that was the basis of the entire research program of the school and which he contrasted to the homogeneous national societies and especially cities of Europe (Halbwachs 1932). He overlooked, as a demographic sociologist (!), the fact that Marseilles was in many ways the equivalent of Chicago, and that France had a higher percentage of immigrants in the 1930's than the United States (Noiriel 1996). The absence of immigrant ethnicity in France was a state imposed social fact that organized perceptions as well as politics. It might be argued that the nature of the state, including the culture that it produces, has a powerful effect on the way in which people identify, whether they

---

5   This was a slogan chanted by students at Stanford University in the 1980's against the existence of required courses on Western culture.

6   This analysis overlaps in some respects with that of Alan Barnard (2006) but with very different emphasis. He is more focused on the actual debates concerning Ur culture, which are not an issue here even if Kuper does make this an essential part of his argument, assimilating in this way the concept of indigenous to the anthropological concept of the primitive. This is due to his situating of his discussion within the debate concerning the San, i.e. as representatives of a primordial hunter-gatherer social form or a product of a wider regional and even global system of power relations within which they have been forced to specialize.

are regional populations predating the advent of the state or immigrants antedating the advent of the state. Our object of analysis would benefit greatly from a reflective distancing from the categories of political order that in their historical vicissitudes seem to penetrate our own categories of interpretation.

Divided we stand?

Kuper's call for a cosmopolitan anthropology and his onslaught on the category indigenous dovetails with the globalization approaches less modernistic cosmopolitanism. The overlap concerns the politics of native or local identity and the way it threatens the master voice of the anthropologist.

But this threat is very much related to the ethnographic aspect of anthropology, to the mastery of the meanings and actions of indigenous peoples as of all peoples. And the general revolt against this mastery, which applies across the board of emergent identities of all types, ought not to represent the kind of threat that it apparently poses. The threat is a product of the anthropological subject rather than of its subjects, even if the latter have become increasingly empowered. The inventionists reject the authority of those that they study. The globalizers reject the validity and morality of the indigenous populations that get in the way of globalization itself. There is a convergence here toward a modern consensus but it is not equivalent for globalizers and inventionists-modernists. The former see the truly modern as hybrids, as alternative modernities that combine elements of past and present in what is conceived as equivalent to Western modernity, thus the modernity of witchcraft (which means simply the contemporaneity of witchcraft). The inventionists-modernists, claim that indigenous peoples are not real because they are actually modern but refuse to recognize it on political grounds, i.e. instrumental (modernist) grounds. The globalizers oppose indigeneity because it negates the obvious and morally progressive tendency of globalization. The modernists oppose the indigenous on objectivist rather than moral grounds, i.e. that they are not really indigenous at all, but simply playing power politics with their identities. The two positions are also opposed to one another in another sense, at least to the extent that globalizing anthropology is culturalist while modernist anthropology is quite anti-culturalist. Thus the modern for globalizers can contain all kinds of phenomena that inventionists might claim to be false representations.

But the differences recede on closer examination. For both, indigeneity is a false construct, a global product localized by political practice, a dangerous denial of global modernity, dangerous for modernists because a denial of the truth of a false tradition, dangerous for globalizers as a reactionary negation of globalization itself. In both cases anthropology can easily survive this threat by returning to its own tradition of holism in which theory was central, where reality was to be explained rather than engaged by the anthropologist as a participant in a morality play. Even that quintessential politician, Lenin, understood that political action was only conceivable on the basis of scientific understanding of the situations in which we find ourselves.

References

Appadurai, A. (1996): "Patriotism and its futures", in Modernity at Large, 158-177

Barnard, A. (2006): "Kalahari revisionism, Vienna and the 'indigenous peoples' debate'", *Social Anthropology*, 2006, vol. 14, no.1, pp. 1-16.

Bergom-Larsson, M. and Slättne, C. (1986): *Ett ÖGONBLICK av glömska*, Qfilm AB.

Bulag, U. (2003): "Mongolian Ethnicity and Linguistic Anxiety in China", *American Anthropologist*, vol. 105, no. 4: pp. 537-544.

Dougherty, M. (1992): *To steal a kingdom.* 1st ed. Waimanalo, Hawaii: Island Press.

Friedman, J. (1992): "Myth, History and Political Identity", *Cultural Anthropology*, pp. 193-209.

Friedman, J. (1992): "The past in the future: History and the politics of identity" in *American Anthropologist* vol. 94 pp. 837-859.

Friedman, J. (1994): "Will the real Hawaiian please stand: Anthropologists and Natives in the Global struggle for identity" in *Bijdragen tot de Taal- Land- en Volkenkunde*, vol. 147:137-167.

Friedman, J. (1994): *Cultural Identity and Global Process*. London: Sage 1994.

Friedman, J. (1999): "Indigenous movements and the discreet charm of the bourgoisie", *Australian Journal of Anthropology*, vol. 10, no.1

Gandoulou, J.-D. (1989): *Au coeur de la Sape: moeurs et aventures des Congolais áa Paris*. Paris, L'Harmattan.

Gray, F. d. P. (1972): *Hawaii: the sugar-coated fortress*. New York, Random House.

Guha R. (ed.) (1982-87): *Subaltern Studies*. I-V Oxford: Oxford University Press.

Guha, R. and Spivak, G.C. (eds.) (1988): *Selected Subaltern studies*. Oxford University Press.

Judd, A.F. (1880): *The Saturday Post*, Oct. 2.

Halbwachs, (1932): "Chicago expérience ethnique", *Annales d'Histoire Ecoomique et Sociale*, Jan.

Hansen, L.I and Olsen, B. (2004): *Samenes historie fram til 1750*. Oslo: Cappelen akademiske forlag.

Kent, Noel J., (1983): Hawaii, islands under the influence. New York: Monthly Review Press.

Kirch, P. V. and Sahlins, M.D. (1992): *Anahulu : the anthropology of history in the Kingdom of Hawaii*. Chicago, University of Chicago Press.

Keesing, R. (1989): "Creating the past: custom and identity in the contemporary Pacific", *Contemporary Pacific*, 1989 (1), pp. 19-42.

Linnekin, J. (1983): "Defining tradition: variations on the Hawaiian identity", *American Ethnologist*, vol. 10, pp. 241-52.

Linnekin, J. (1992): "On the theory and politics of cultural construction in the Pacific", *Oceania*, vol. 62, no.4, pp. 249-63.

Kelly, J. D. (1995): "Diaspora and World War, Blood and Nation in Fiji and Hawaii", *Public Culture*, vol. 7, no. 3, pp. 475–97.

Kuper, A. (1994): "Culture, identity and the project of a cosmopolitan anthropology", *Man*, vol. 29, no. 3.

Kuper, A. (2003): "The Return of the Native", *Current Anthropology*, vol. 44, no. 3, pp. 389-395.

Kuper, A. (2006): (Discussion), *Social Anthropology*, vol. 14, no. 1, pp. 21-22.

Malkki, L. (1992): "National Geographic: The Rooting of Peoples and the Territorialization of National Identity among Scholars and Refugees", *Cultural Anthropology*, vol. 7. no. 1: 24–44.

McGregor, D. (1989): "Kupa'a I Ka 'aina : persistence on the land: ph.d. thesis, department of History." University of Hawaii.

Noiriel, G. (1996): *The French Melting Pot*. Minneapolis: Minnesota University Press.

Sahlins, M (1985): "The Stranger King or Dumézil among the Fijians" in *Islands of history.* University of Chicago Press.

Turner, T. (2004): (Discussion), *Current Anthropology*, vol. 45, no. 2, pp. 265-266.

Williams, R. (1974): ('An Eminent Person') The Hireling Ministry none of Christs, (London 1652), in Miller, P. Roger Williams: His Contribution to the American Tradition. New York Cited in Williamson.

Williamson, A.S. (1996): "Scots, Indians and empire: The Scottish politics of civilization", *Past and Present*, pp. 46-83.

CHAPTER 2

The Destination and the Journey
Indigenous Peoples and the United Nations from the 1960s through 1985[1]

By Henry Minde

Introduction: Political Developments and Academic Controversies

In the last decades of the 20th century the fight for indigenous peoples and their rights was a story of international success. From being marginalised socially, economically, and politically, with no possibility to be heard in international forums, they have gained direct access to existing bodies and have been directly involved in the development of new institutions in the United Nations (UN) system (Working Group on Indigenous Populations). During these years, indigenous issues grew in political importance. At the turn of the century, they had acquired institutional changes (other working groups and the Permanent Forum for Indigenous Issues) and the adoption of legal norms was on the horizon (the Draft Declaration on the Rights of Indigenous Peoples) all of which would considerably strengthen their political and legal influence both locally and globally.[2] But at the same time as the transnational indigenous movement made progress internationally, especially within the UN system, an ideological and political counterforce was mobilising through the old power structures (Minde & Nilsen 2003). Even when indigenous issues were discussed in the UN system, some African and Asian states, in particular, have been preoccupied with what a clear definition of these terms should entail (see Kingsbury 1998; Saugestad 2001). Criticism culminated in the autumn of 2006, when the

1   This article will also be published in *Gáldu Čála-Journal of Indigenous Peoples Rights*. I want to thank two anonymous referees for their valuable comments on this article. A special thanks to Brita Solvang who made suggestions for improvement and translated the text to English. Thanks also to Ellen Marie Jensen for useful language editing. The article was written during my pleasant stay as a Visiting Scholar at the Ethnic Studies Department, University of Hawai'i at Mânoa. I whish to thank the Department for their great hospitality during my stay. The research upon which this article is based was funded by The Norwegian Science Council and The Resource Centre for the Rights of Indigenous Peoples, Guovdageaidnu, Norway.
2   Cf. articles in *The Indigenous World*, published yearly by the International Work Group for Indigenous Affairs, Copenhagen about Draft Declaration (accessed on 25 April 2007 at: www.iwgia.org/sw160.asp).

Third Committee of the UN General Assembly postponed the adoption of the UN Declaration on the Rights of Indigenous Peoples, a declaration that had already been adopted by the new Human Rights Council.[3]

At this point in time it is appropriate to take a step back and investigate why and how the development of the Declaration on the Rights of Indigenous Peoples found a way into the UN system. This question has mostly been overlooked in the now extensive academic literature on indigenous issues in international law (but see Barsh 1986; Sanders 1989; 1994; Maiguashca 1994; Venne 1998; Dunbar-Ortiz 2006). The mostly North American literature does not take notice of, or has even misrepresented, contributions made by indigenous peoples or states from other regions of the world (see e.g. Coulter 1992). This preoccupation led to the exclusion of the complex and ambiguous cultural and political processes among the indigenous peoples themselves and also of the larger historical context within the UN. For example, only Douglas Sanders (1989) has so far mentioned the importance of the Norwegian government and the Sami organisations for establishing the Working Group on Indigenous Populations in 1982-83.

Lately, some social anthropologists have criticised the indigenous movement and their academic supporters for the way they have defined the term "indigenous." According to the most eager of the critics Adam Kuper, the reasons for his criticism are in short (1) its emphasis on the connection to their ancestors and their way of life, (2) their supposed use of invented presentations of the past, and with that (3) their use of arguments that flirt with the "*Blut und Boden*"–rhetoric from the Nazi regime in Germany and the apartheid regime in South Africa. And in his conclusion, Kuper combines his professional and political objections towards the indigenous movement in this manner:

> [W]hatever the political inspiration, the conventional lines of argument currently used to justify "indigenous" land claims rely on obsolete anthropological notions and on romantic and false ethnographic visions. Fostering essentialist ideologies of culture and identity, they may have dangerous political consequences (Kuper 2003:395).

This type of argument has a long tradition in the political debate on indigenous rights; however it did not have a prominent place in anthropology until Kuper presented it. Still, many anthropologists protested, including Alan Bernard

---

3   The adoption process came to a halt in the Third Committee on Tuesday November 27 2006, when a resolution put forward by the Namibian delegation to defer further debate was supported by a vote of 82 to 67 and 25 abstentions (A/C.3/61/L.57/Rev.1). The process is therefore deferred until the end of the session of the General Assembly in September 2007. The motion is widely viewed as an effort to weaken or undermine key provisions of the Declaration as adopted by the Human Rights Council by a vote of the overwhelming majority of the members of the UN Human Rights Council (resolution 2006/2 of 29 June 2006).

who admitted that the term "indigenous" is a problematic category because the ethnic content varies considerably. According to Bernard, since Kuper attempts to discredit the term itself by using the ethnographic facts and its alleged content, he himself has an essentialist approach when he looks for "real" or "idealised" indigenous people, for example as participants in the UN system. However, Bernard argues strongly that the term "indigenous" is useful as a political and legal category (Bernard 2006:9-12).[4] Yet in the debate that followed, the concepts "indigenous"/ "indigeneity" and "indigenous peoples" were also questioned by scholars who supported the indigenous movement. Some wanted to return to the old term "tribal," while others preferred the term "The Fourth World."[5]

This chapter will follow up on this debate with a historic approach and make an inquiry into questions that up until now have not been posed in social anthropology discourse: Why and how was the term "indigenous" introduced in the international forum and why did it become such a powerful tool in the process for recognition, empowerment and entitlement? My analysis will be linked closely to the study of the process leading to the preparatory work with a Declaration on the Rights of Indigenous Peoples. First, I will demonstrate how participants within the UN and different indigenous organisations used the demand for a Declaration to frame the indigenous–state relationship in new ways. The application of concepts had their background in colonial history, but as we will see, they were marked by the counter-hegemonic discourses linked to the process of decolonisation from the 1960s. Secondly, I will analyse how the category "indigenous peoples" was understood and defined in the UN, and how this term has been strongly connected to the question of self-determination and land rights. The basic principles for a new declaration and the question of definition were provisionally clarified in the UN's Working Group for Indigenous Issues in 1985. In the end of this chapter I will discuss the extent of the influence of the social anthropological discourse of ethnicity in terms of the question of the definition of "indigenous" in the UN. Since the declaration process of indigenous rights in the meeting of 1985 has not been studied properly in its historical context, I will argue that in recent academic and political debate, these issues have become more confusing and misleading than they rightfully deserve.

---

4   See in particular the debates in *Current Anthropology* 2003/2004 and *Social Anthropology* 2006 with main contributions from Adam Kuper (2003) who wants to discard the concept completely and Alan Barnard (2006) who argues for the validity of the concept as a useful political and legal term.

5   See the contributions in this debate by Guenther (2006): and Plaice (2006).

The Period of Reports in the UN

The battle against racism and for decolonisation is the important backdrop for the so-called "re-emergence of indigenous peoples" on the world scene.[6] These political battles were fought within individual states all over the world and they are for the most part well documented (cf. Maiguashca 1994; Minde 1996). Here we will concentrate on how indigenous issues were raised at the global level with the UN being the most important arena.

The struggles for decolonisation and anti-racism

The post-WW II years brought about a global industrial, technological, and welfare colonisation of peripheral areas, which stretched from the tropical rain forests to the Arctic region (Paine 1977; Eidheim et.al. 1985; Brodley 1990). Initially, these developments accelerated the need to assist the most exploited indigenous people on humanitarian and welfare grounds, especially in some countries in South America.

This new stage of colonisation was the backdrop for the question addressed by the International Labour Organisation (ILO), an affiliate agency of the UN. It came to a conclusion in 1957 when the ILO adopted Convention No.107 concerning Indigenous and Other Tribal and Semi-Tribal Populations. In order to protect the material living conditions of these "populations" the convention recognised, in line with the practice in some of the former British colonies, customary rights over the lands which they traditionally occupied. But the main goal was still to integrate and assimilate these populations into the national states (see article 11, cf. Bennett 1978:29-32).

The wave of decolonisation in the Third World had an impact on the situation for indigenous peoples–in the long run. The famous UN General Assembly Resolution 1514 of 1960 reiterated the principle of article 1 of the UN Charter that "[a]ll peoples have the right to self-determination," and this new opinion was stated by including peoples outside the system of Western states who should be free to determine their own social and cultural development. Thereafter the right for "all peoples" formed the basis for the UN covenants of 1966 on Civil and Political Rights and on Economic, Social and Cultural Rights respectively (the common article 1.1). However, the principle of self-determination for all peoples largely bypassed indigenous peoples during the 1960s and 1970s. Because of its state-centred view the decolonisation prescriptions delimited the colonial territory as an integral whole with their colonial boundaries intact (Anaya 1996:43-45; 75-82). A corresponding but much more limited principle was accorded minorities in the mentioned Conventions on

---

6 Douglas Sanders first used this term in his article "The Re-emergence of Indigenous Questions in International Law", printed in *Canadian Human Rights Yearbook*, 1983. The term "re-emergence" points to the debate on indigenous rights among law scholars, a subject of conflict among the European states under the period of the so-called "Great Discoveries."

Civil and Political rights. Article 27 stressed the individual approach by saying that "members of minorities" have the right to "enjoy their own culture /.../ in community with other members of their group."

Nevertheless, the developments within the UN system were an outcome of an international consensus in the 1950s and 1960s that viewed colonial governance as oppressive and condemned race discrimination and apartheid. Both the independence movements in Africa and the Civil Rights movement in the US inspired indigenous movements around the world. And some of the new African leaders openly supported the indigenous peoples cause (interview Leif Dunfjeld; Douglas Sanders).

Reports on discrimination in the 1960s
The UN's Sub-Commission for Human Rights[7], which consisted of appointed experts, began working on several reports concerning different aspects of discrimination against minority groups. The assignment of Special Rapporteurs opened the possibility, within the system, to point to individual states, criticising them for violating human rights; the Secretariat, being expected to be neutral was unable to criticise individual states. Also, the members of the Sub-Commission often refused to criticise other states, themselves being proposed by states, even though they where experts, not diplomats. Therefore, some of the studies where in fact carried out by the Secretariat under the cloak of the Special Rapporteurs.

One of the lawyers in the UN Secretariat in New York, a Guatemalan named Augusto Willemsen Diaz, became particularly interested in indigenous issues while he was working on these reports. In one of the reports depicting how minorities were treated by juridical systems, he mentioned the Sami for the first time in a UN document. Willemsen Diaz was fascinated by Sami reindeer herders' way of adapting to their circumstances since they "brought with them in their nomadic migration two things: the school and the courts." [8] However, the first time that indigenous issues were treated in special chapters was when the Chilean diplomat Hernán Santa Cruz completed a report on the economic, social and cultural discrimination of minorities.[9] Originally Santa Cruz had been unwilling to include indigenous issues in the report but he was most likely influenced by the progress of the socialists in his own country and gradually be-

---

7   The official name is The Sub-Commission on the Prevention of Discrimination and Protection of Minorities. On its history and role in the UN system, see Eide 1992.

8   Cf.: Mohamed A.A. Rannat: *Study of equality in the administration of justice*, United Nations publication, Sales No. F.71XIV.5.

9   Hernan Santa Cruz: *Study on Racial Discrimination in the Political, Economic, Social and Cultural Spheres*. United Nations Publication, Sales number E.71. XIV, chapter IX: "Measures taken in connexion with the protection of indigenous peoples" and chapter XIII, para 1094-1102, "Problems of indigenous populations." The work on this report continued between 1966-1970.

came more sensitive to the living conditions of indigenous peoples in general. The Left Alliance in Chile, led by Allende, supported some indigenous claims to land rights (Interview Willemsen Diaz; cf. Castro Lucic 2005).

Alarming reports from South America made a serious impression on Western public opinion. The results of gold mining, logging and the introduction of farming on indigenous lands were of particular concern. Many social anthropologists who had been doing research in Latin America became advocacy researchers and formed a network that founded the International Working Group for Indigenous Affairs (IGWIA). This organisation has since been an important advocacy organisation disseminating information about indigenous peoples around the world, and contributing support to the development of organisations starting with Latin America (Sanders 1983; Wright 1988).

In the completed Santa Cruz report of 1970, indigenous peoples were described as "Disadvantaged in relation to the rest of the population: in some countries they are the victims of *de facto* discrimination and continue to suffer from prejudice."[10] The report concluded with a recommendation that a new report should be made solely on indigenous peoples; this report should not restrict itself to discrimination but have a focus on individual and equal rights. In the end, Santa Cruz departed from the language used in the drafts written by Willemsen Diaz (interview Willemsen Diaz). First: while Willemsen had used the term "peoples" in reference to indigenous peoples, Santa Cruz changed this to "populations." Secondly: Santa Cruz' last version concluded that the most appropriate policy for the states to adopt was a policy of assimilation. According to this line of thought, such a policy would neutralise differences between groups of peoples, and it would be in tune with statements in the recent UN Declaration on Racial Discrimination (1965). Thirdly: during the discussion on this report in the Sub-Commission in 1970, Santa Cruz created an opening for the possibility that the report on indigenous peoples could be included in a common report on minorities.[11]

A fellow countryman of Willemsen Diaz–Carlos García Bauer–partly came to his side during the meeting in the Human Rights Commission in 1971. García Bauer was highly respected, being one of the fathers of the Declaration of Human Rights. He managed to prevent the new report on indigenous peoples from being included as part of the study on the protection of minorities. In addition, he succeeded at including in the mandate that the study should be:

> a complete and comprehensive study of the nature and extent of the problem of discrimination against indigenous populations and to suggest the necessary national and international measures for eliminating such discrimination (…).[12]

---

10 Ibid, chapter. XIII, para 1094.
11 Resolution 4B (XXIII) of April 1970, Operative paragraph 6.
12 The Economic and Social Council (ECOSOC) adopted the proposal from HRC in Resolution 1589(L) 21 May 1971.

The result was as Willemsen Diaz had wished: the study could be carried out under the supervision of the experts in the Sub-Commission who were more open and flexible for new initiatives than were the diplomats in the Human Rights Commission. Further, the mandate was defined to be comprehensive enough that few limits were required for the work. Even so, the mandate was more concerned with discrimination per se than with the protection of minorities. Thirdly, and most important in the long run, was that minorities and indigenous peoples were to be dealt with separately in the future. At that time, minority rights were viewed as problematic by many governments. The strategy chosen by Willemsen Diaz, therefore, ultimately opened the doors of the UN for indigenous peoples.

The Martínez Cobo Study

The Ecuadorian José Martínez Cobo was given the political responsibility for the study and the report.[13] In reality, Willemsen Diaz completed this mission; it proved to be a permanent task for him throughout the rest of his active working life until he retired in 1984 (cf. Eide 1987:18-21;Coulter 1992:4, Sanders 1994:6). He immediately began to produce preliminary reports for the Sub-Commission. The process of gathering information from states and from the still few indigenous organisations, created a new and informal gravitational field around the UN in Geneva where the Secretariat of Human Rights had moved in 1974. Willemsen Diaz' advice to all indigenous organisations, which by this time had been in contact him, was that they should get together and form into international organisations. The message was that these organisations had to create new organisations in order to meet the requirements of the UN system on how NGOs were admitted into UN meetings.[14]

Willemsen Diaz soon discovered that the Secretariat would have difficulty in obtaining information about indigenous concerns in the traditional UN fashion, i.e. sending long lists of questions to government offices all over the world. With this in mind, Willemsen Diaz at an anti-slavery conference in 1974 in Cambridge aired the suggestion to establish a special working group for indigenous peoples.[15] The winds of favourable change that indigenous questions were experiencing in Western countries opened up the possibility for Willemsen Diaz to formulate a new strategy for the UN when it came to indigenous issues: a special working group could be open for indigenous groups "to en-

---

13 Ibid.
14 Cf. Willemsen Diaz's speech at an international conference in November 1973 published in the report from the conference: North American Conference on the Protection of Human Rights for Indian and Inuit's. Wingspread Conference convened by Commission to Study the Organization of Peace and The Johnson Foundation, November 1973. In the archive of Augusto Willemsen Diaz in Guatemala City, copy on file with author.
15 SO. 234 (18-1) Confidential Note, 23 January 1975, p. 10, the archive of Willemsen Diaz, copy on file with author.

deavour to cover all sectors and shades of opinion and the different problems involved, as well as solutions envisaged as suitable by the indigenous populations themselves."[16] In addition, it should be open for the various indigenous peoples within the global world. In this way, Willemsen Diaz obviously understood that it was possible to avoid the temptation of being paternalistic towards indigenous peoples or to fall into stereotypical attitudes. But the time was not yet ripe for this proposal.

Indigenous as defined in the UN

As we have seen, the question concerning a definition was only superficially addressed in the Santa Cruz report. But for the Martínez Cobo report the task was of greater importance. A decision was made that all states in the UN should be asked to report on the political, social and legal state of indigenous peoples within the states' borders. The Secretariat was convinced that a definition of the target group had to be attached to the request. This type of study anticipated that the national reports were to be compared from a human rights perspective. These considerations were decisive for the tentative definition of the terms "indigenous" and "indigenous populations" in the study.

The result was the working definition from 1972:

> Indigenous populations are (1) composed of the existing descendants of the peoples who inhabited the present territory of a country wholly or partially (2) at the time when persons of a different culture or ethnic origin arrived there from other parts of the world, overcame them and, by conquest, settlement or other means, reduced them to a non-dominant or colonial condition; (3) who today live more in conformity with their particular social, economic and cultural customs and traditions than with the institutions of the country of which they now form part, (4) under a State structure, which incorporates mainly the national, social and cultural characteristics of other segments of the population which are predominant. (Points added by this author.)[17]

I would characterise these requirements for a definition of "*indigenous population*" as (1) historical continuity, (2) experiencing colonisation, (3) social and cultural divergence with the majority populations and (4) economic and political marginality, i.e. lack of adequate control of economic and political institutions deciding on their living conditions. The first two points mainly address a colonial history where the colonisation has come from Europe–across the ocean, "the blue water theory" (Bennett 1978:12f. Anaya 1996:43f). The Martínez Cobo report's commentary in reference to these points assumes that the colonisation which has come "from other parts of the world," culminated in "a

16 Ibid.
17 Preliminary Martínez Cobo Report, UN doc E/CN 4./Sub.2/L.566 (29 June 1972), para. 34.

condition of political, economic and cultural dependence on a 'metropolitan' power which exploited land, goods and peoples to its own advantage." Nevertheless, the study emphasises that even if marginalized groups never have experienced "conquest" they can be considered as indigenous peoples/populations for the following reasons:

- They are descendants of the people who inhabited the present territory when persons of a different cultural background arrived (point 1).
- They have been isolated from other segments of the population in the country and have conserved customs and traditions from their forefathers corresponding with other indigenous customs and traditions.
- They are subordinate to a state structure that expects them to observe the national, social and cultural characteristics that are foreign to them.

The possibility for marginalized groups, other than those that had been conquered, to be included was a consequence of the main objective of the work as it was conceived by the researchers: namely to advance special rights and efforts to protect "non-dominant groups" against a "non-neutral" State (point 4).[18] We shall later see that the Sami who had been subjugated by the expansion northward by the Norwegian, Swedish, Finish and Russian states, were the first people in this category who could then be recognized internationally as "indigenous peoples."

The first draft of a definition must be understood in the historical context: the preoccupation in the UN system with decolonisation and racism, and its practical purpose. An international human rights perspective was addressed by the fact that formulation of the three first points of the draft were taken from article 1 (b) in ILO-convention No. 107, the only international treaty on indigenous rights in existence at the time. The changes made in the Martínez Cobo study moderated the one-sided weight on conquest and colonisation in the ILO Convention and removed its use of the terms "tribal and semi-tribal."

The next step in the process of formulating a definition came in 1975 when the Secretariat had received the land reports. Fifty-seven states had answered, and of them only fourteen confirmed that they had an indigenous group within their borders. Official information from an additional five states was received.[19] This was the basis for Willemsen and the Secretariat when they made a listing of the criteria that were used for a definition (in a compressed form here): [20]

---

18 Ibid, paras. 35-45.
19 Preliminary Martínez Cobo Report, UN doc E/CN 4./Sub.2/L.622 (17 July 1975), paras. 12 and 16.
20 Ibid, paras. 31-227.

- Occupation of ancestral lands, common ancestry with the original occupants of these lands and residence in certain parts of the country.
- Culture in general, or in specific manifestations such as religion, membership within a community, dress and means of livelihood.
- Language as the most important cultural trait.
- Group consciousness and acceptance within the indigenous community.

The Martínez Cobo report has been criticised later for the different working definitions. On this background I will now draw attention to two circumstances: first of all, the criteria used by the report are found in older ethnography and in more recent social anthropology. Descriptions of indigenous peoples' material and cultural characteristics are used here. However, from the very beginning the Martinez Cobo report argued against a strict definition and emphasized the aspects of positions, relations and identity (confirmation from others). This demonstrates that the first version of the Martínez Cobo report was already influenced by the paradigm shift of the concept of ethnicity introduced by the Norwegian anthropologist Fredrik Barth in 1969 with the book "Ethnic Groups and Boundaries" (cf. Saugestad 2001:306; Bernard 2006:6-9).

Secondly, it has been suggested that the weight on "ancestral" and "ancestry," i.e. the requirement of continuity, links the definition to the conception of "*Blut und Boden*" (Béteille 1998, Kuper 2003; 2004). On one hand, one has to distinguish between criteria that were in fact used around the world and documented in the report, and on the other hand what is in fact recommended in the report. This distinction is described in the report in this way: the criteria in different countries are "ranging from factors which are exclusively or almost exclusively 'racial' to considerations which are purely social and cultural."[21] The report further refers to and criticises the popular understanding of "pure racial groups" and governments' use of blood quantity as a criteria in deciding who is "indigenous."[22]

International Indigenous Movement: Becoming Visible

The UN studies were in progress around 1970 at the same time as indigenous movements appeared–and reappeared–all around the world. It might seem odd that these often local and socially deprived organisations were immediately engaged in international cooperation. This was the result of an historic "push-and-pull"–effect: their territories all over the world became attractive for big development projects threatening their basis of existence. Indigenous peoples were therefore forced into action. At the same time they had discovered that the UN could offer them an attractive platform. Their concerns and aspirations could now be addressed in solidarity on a global stage.

21 Ibid. para. 32.
22 Ibid. paras. 33-75.

World Council of Indigenous Peoples (WCIP)

The immediate background for the first initiative to form a global organisation for indigenous peoples was the political battle in Canada about indigenous issues around 1970. The new liberal Trudeau government aimed at including First Nations in Canadian society in order to expunge all special rights, including the Indian Act, the reserves and the treaties and to transfer all welfare matters affecting the Indian population to the Provinces. When this programme was launched in June 1969, spontaneous militancy ensued and Canada experienced an unexpected and remarkable growth in organisations and institutions amongst all First Nations peoples as they began to call themselves. This growth culminated the establishment of a federative structure; in 1969 they founded an umbrella organisation for Indians, *National Indian Brotherhood* (Weaver 1981:171-189).[23]

The Shuswap chief George Manuel was the leader of the new organisation (McFarlane 1993). In Manuel's youth, the Canadian authorities had obtained a firmer grasp on the everyday life of the people in the interior of British Columbia where his home reserve is located. Manuel was convinced that this was the cause of the difficulties that he experienced in his lifetime. However, he mastered both his people's way of knowing the world, and those of modern society (Manuel and Poslun 1974; McFarlane 1993).

As the leader of the NIB, George Manuel was invited to travel with cabinet ministers in delegations, among others, to a significant environmental conference in Stockholm in 1972. This gave him the opportunity to realise his dreams about a worldwide organisation of indigenous peoples, ideas he had shared with Vine and Sam Deloria. During these travels he built a network of organisations and individuals from New Zealand, Australia, and the Nordic countries (Minde 2003).

George Manuel's deliberate ambition was to offer a new political vision for indigenous peoples around the globe. For this purpose, he used his biography to publish a manifesto in the book "The Fourth World" (Manuel and Posluns 1974). In a dedication he made to the Sami, Aslak Nils Sara, he explained the metaphor in this way:

> The "Fourth world" means the co-existence of mankinds based on mutual respect for each other's Culture, Social, Economic & Political Institutions. It means that Indigenous Peoples of the world, gain control of their Cultural, Social, Economic and Political Institutions. Within our own Indigenous Communities. Guaranteed by legal and constitutional safe guards to protect our Environments and our Indigenous lands.[24]

---

23 NIB underwent a major restructuring in 1982, and changed the organisation's name to its current title of Assembly of First Nations.

24 The book is in family possession, copy of the dedication on file with author.

Manuel maintained that the strong connection to Mother Earth was the main shared value of indigenous peoples. "The land from which our culture springs is like the water and the air, one and indivisible" (Manuel and Posluns 1974:6). Indigenous peoples had lost control over their traditional lands. On this point, Manuel believed that there was a division between indigenous peoples and other minorities. In order to rectify these injustices and discrimination, indigenous peoples had to be compensated for "the fruits" of colonial history. In contrast to nationalism and a public assimilation policy, Manuel underlined that the movement was "a global village" where the indigenous peoples and the States could not "go entirely our separate ways" (ibid: 221; 224 ff.). He therefore dissociated himself from secessionist rhetoric, probably because he realised that "the Aboriginal World is almost wholly dependent upon the good faith and morality of the nations of East and West within which it finds itself." (ibid:6).

Contrary to some current post-modern thought, he reminded the oppressed peoples not to forget the colonial history of recent centuries that had resulted in unjust distribution of political power and economic resources that accompany it. The history is important not in order to underscore stable and permanent ethnic identities –or an "Eternal Resting Place" as Manuel called it–but in order to demonstrate the need for social and political change–through "a Long March." Manual concluded that the only solution for indigenous peoples is to have self-determination, or in his own terminology "decision-making autonomy" (ibid:246; 261).

The WCIP was formally founded at the meeting held at Port Alberni on the west coast of Canada, in October 1975. The meeting gathered around 260 people from nineteen countries. They chose to have a structure where there would be one elected leader and an elected board based on regions. All of these were elected every third or fourth year which meant there would be a great turnover in the leadership. The ambition behind this structure was to have it so that everybody would feel like they had a voice and that they would be heard. The intention was that the board should mirror that this was a global organisation (cf. Sanders 1977).

Bearing in mind the communication technology at that time and deficiencies in administrative capacity, the ambitions to have continuous activity could not be fulfilled. The General Assemblies were therefore used as political and cultural workshops, drawing the course for the future. In the first years the WCIP was admitted to UN bodies through credentials obtained by the NIB in February 1974, under an agreement that they were trying to establish an international organisation. It was not until 1979 that the WCIP obtained consultative status in the UN. The Second General Assembly was held in Kiruna (Sweden) in August 1977. At this meeting, while he was still a member of the Sub-Commission, Martínez Cobo was invited to provide information about the ongoing work on the UN reports. Documented breeches of human rights vis-à-vis indigenous peoples, especially in Latin America were a serious concern at this meeting. The meeting demanded, in general expressions, that the UN system should now recognise indigenous rights, among them the right of self-determination.[25]

International Indian Treaty Council (IITC)

The radical urban American Indian Movement (AIM) began in1974 with an international branch called the International Indian Treaty Council (IITC). This initiative was a result of the vulnerable position of AIM after confrontations with the authorities at Wounded Knee (Pine Ridge Reservation, South Dakota) in 1973. In the confrontation, gunshots were exchanged and Indians and US federal agents were killed (Smith & Warrior 1996:171-268). The leaders of AIM hoped that international opinion would soften the federal authorities' stance to the extent that they would stop the prosecution of Indians and submit enough to give acceptable concessions and fulfil old treaties, especially regarding land rights (Means 1995:356, 365, 371-2). This was the so-called "policy of embarrassment," an international strategy that has been used on different occasions by indigenous peoples when all other possibilities had been exhausted in their own countries (Dyck 1985, Jhappan 1992:64; Minde 1996).

Every year, the IITC arranged open conferences for Indian nations and indigenous groups from all over the Americas, including Hawai'i and Latin America. They reported that between 2000 and 4000 people attended these conferences (cf. Means 1995:356, 365, 371-2). The organisation started a bulletin to keep the members posted on the initiatives and results. The IITC was influenced by the political culture in AIM; they refused to accept any funding from governmental sources, they did not believe in written statements of intent, and they worked mostly with special causes and ad-hoc actions. Since the member organisations in the WCIP actively applied for funding from governmental sources, the IITC often considered them identical to organisations that were suspected of receiving funding from the CIA (see Treaty Council News 1977; no.9).

The main objective for the IITC was to gain recognition of treaties between Indian "nations" and the United States government as international treaties—treaties that could not be set aside by politicians or legal authorities. The IITC soon set up an office on the premises of the World Council of Churches in Manhattan, directly opposite the UN building. They attained UN consultative status in 1977 and in that same year they had their own representative in Geneva working with international issues. In contrast to the WCIP, the IITC never had the intention of establishing a representative structure in the organisation, despite the fact that the organisation gradually included groups from Meso- and

---

25 Information based on communication between the WCIP headquarters in Canada and the Nordic Sami Council. From the archive of Sami Council. Copies on file with author, and the report: World Council of Indigenous Peoples Second General Assembly, Helset/Helsinki, 1978.

South America. The leadership was for a long time dominated by engaged and militant activists like Russell Means and his brothers. This was the reason why the IITC during the time period at the end of the 1970s was the most visible of the indigenous organisation in the UN (Weyler 1982, chapter 1 and 7; Coulter 1992:6; Sanders 1994:16; Dunbar-Ortiz 2006; cf. Means 1995:356, 365, 371-2).

The IITC obtained a key role in the preparation of a conference in the autumn of 1977 that has later been referred to as "indigenous peoples' first meeting with the UN." The official organizer was the Special NGO Committee on Human Rights, created by NGOs in consultative status in the UN.[26]

The connecting link for these contacts was Jimmie Durham, a Cherokee and a successful sculptor and artist, who had lived in Geneva during the late 1960s and early 1970s. At the time of the siege at Wounded Knee, Durham was heading back to the US and participated in founding the IITC, which he was the leader of the following years (Dunbar-Ortiz 2006).[27] The title of the conference suggested which indigenous people were invited: "Conference on Discrimination against Indigenous Peoples of the Americas." George Manuel was certainly invited, being the leader of the pan Canadian Indian organisation (NIB), but when he wanted to speak in the capacity of being the leader of the indigenous peoples of the world (WCIP), he was ignored (Coulter 1992:4-6; Sanders interview). Despite such skirmishes between some of the organisations, the Geneva meeting in 1977 was a success. According to the report from the conference, 82 of about 250 participants were representing indigenous organisations.[28] The whole group gained a lot of attention in the media when they appeared in demonstrations and ceremonies inside and outside the UN buildings dressed in their Indian outfits.

The conference adopted a declaration based on the ideology of IITC, claiming that indigenous peoples should be recognised as "nations" and as such should be accepted as independent legal subjects under international law (Article 1). On this basis, they claimed that indigenous peoples had the right of self-determination (Article 7). But how could claims like these be realised?

---

26 The chairman of the conference was Edith Ballantyne who was General Secretary of the Women's International League for Peace and Freedom. See Report of International NGO Conference on Discrimination against Indigenous Population in the Americas – 1977. On file with author. Also published in: *American Indian Journal of the Institute for the Development of Indian Law*, 1977:3.

27 Jimmie Durham is the main informant in the film *Indian Summer in Geneva* produced by Volkmar Ziegler in 1985. It is available in a CD-ROM version from Indigenous Peoples' Center for Documentation, Research and Information (doCip), Geneva.

28 Divided in these categories: "International organisations": 3 (from NIB), "Indigenous peoples delegation" further divided in different countries and Six Nations: 41, "Observers": 38 (mostly from IITC). See Report of International NGO Conference 1977.

The conference agreed on a plan of action where Augusto Willemsen Diaz' idea of a UN working group for indigenous issues was raised, once more, and they demanded that such a working group should be established (cf. Coulter 1992:8-9; Dunbar-Ortiz 2006:65).

Who was recognised as indigenous?
For good reasons, it was never discussed which groups could call themselves "indigenous peoples" in the IITC. The peoples of the Americas were the prototype of "indigenous" according to "the blue water" theory.[29] But this question came to the table for the WCIP because they tried to establish an international organisation. Nobody questioned that Aboriginal Australians and the Maori were indigenous. But what about the Sami who had not experienced traditional colonisation from overseas? For 2000 years, the Sami had intermingled with– and had been marginalized by–the Nordic and Finnish peoples.

Before the founding meeting of the new organisation, three criteria were agreed upon which would be used as the basis for invitations.[30] In order for an indigenous group to be accepted, it was stipulated that:

- It should comprise a people living in a land with a population consisting of different ethnic and racial groups.
- They should be the descendants of the original group of people who lived on the land.
- They do not have control over the leadership and administration of the lands they live in.

Despite the rather strict requirement of historical continuity, the American Oglala Sioux-Indian, Sam Deloria, who proposed the definition at the meeting, remarked that on reflection it was extremely broad. He noted that it was difficult to make the definition any narrower without shutting out groups of people whom one might wish to have included. He specifically had the Sami in mind who were citizens of welfare states. Deloria was concerned that it could be read as if "indigenous people" felt themselves, by definition, to be under-represented and dissatisfied with the state government. On the contrary, he claimed that it was necessary to include groups of indigenous peoples such as the Sami because they could be put up as examples to the others. Deloria's proposal was carried by the interim committee and ratified at the foundation meeting (Minde 2003:79-85).

---

29 However, even in the North American context this theory mingles ideas of decolonization with features of the definition of "indigenous." E.g. according to the current law, the First nations have no right to decolonization since they are not separated from the settler population by blue water.
30 The following account is built on "International preparatory meeting of the Indigenous Peoples' Conference," Minutes from meetings hold on 8 and 9 April 1974. Document in the archive of Sami Council. Copy on file with author.

* * *

The statements and action plans from the WCIP's General Assembly in Sweden and the International NGO conference in Geneva in 1977 made a significant impact on the activity of indigenous peoples in the UN in the years to come. The declarations from these conferences were used as important frames of reference for the Martínez Cobo study and laid the foundation for subsequent recommendations in the report.[31]

At the same time, the relationship between the IITC and the WCIP was strained. Originally, many Sami activists were appalled by the way the US authorities were handling the Wounded Knee conflict. A statement of disgust was handed directly over to the American embassy in Norway by a small protest march initiated by the Oslo branch of The National Association of Norwegian Sami.[32] In light of this, many Sami activists were disappointed by the cold relations between the IITC and the WCIP and tried to improve the situation. Two members of the Nordic Sami Council, Ole Henrik Magga and Leif Halonen, both delegates to the WCIP, were in New York in March of 1980. They attempted to meet the leaders of the IITC to settle the differences but when they arrived on the premises, the IITC leaders did not show up and the staff said that they "knew (…) nothing about WCIP." After this unsuccessful attempt at reconciliation, Magga and Halonen joined the IITC-critics in the WCIP.[33] This cold relationship lasted until both organisations were drawn into the negotiations of declarations and conventions in the mid 1980s (interviews Dunfjeld; Ibarra).

Institutionalisation
Here we will see how indigenous issues formally were adopted as a concern for the UN. This began during the World Conference to Combat Racism and Racial Discrimination in 1978. The programme of action that was approved there opened the possibility for the establishment of a special UN body for indigenous issues. A new working group was to give attention to the evolution of standards concerning the rights of indigenous populations. Principles for this work were mainly agreed upon in the working group meeting in 1985.

---

31 UN doc. E/CN.4/Sub.2/476, Add.5 (17 June 1981; UN doc. E/CN 4/Sub.2/1983/21/Add 8 (30 Sept. 1983).

32 The letter to the US Embassy was handed over by the leader of the Oslo branch, Ole Henrik Magga, later the first leader of UN Permanent Forum for Indigenous Issues. (Personal information from Johan Klemet Kalstad).

33 Report to Nordic Sami Council by Ole Henrik Magga, 1980. The archive of Sami Council. Copy on file with author.

The UN declaration of 1978: The connection to Sami issues
Despite the presence and international activity of the WCIP and the IITC, there was still no formal, high-level decision that had been made to address indigenous concerns in the UN. The Human Rights commission was awaiting the Martínez Cobo study, which at that time remained unfinished. The political breakthrough came under the World Conference to Combat Racism and Racial Discrimination that was held in Geneva in 1978. The final statement from the conference included the following passage (Article 21): [34]

> The Conference endorses the right of indigenous peoples to maintain their traditional structure of economy and culture, including their own language, and also recognizes the special relationship of indigenous peoples to their land and stresses that their land, land rights and natural resources should not be taken away from them.

This article was followed up by a programme of action recommending states to recognise the rights of indigenous peoples in many fields: for instance the right to the maintenance and use of their own language, the right to freely express their ethnic and cultural characteristics and the right to form their own representative organisations.

Two paragraphs in the plan of action indigenous peoples were given special consideration:

- To carry on within their areas of settlement their traditional structure of economic and way of life; this should in no way affect their rights to participate freely on an equal basis in the economic, social and political development of the country.
- The Conference further urges States to facilitate and support the establishment of representative international organizations for indigenous peoples, through which they can share experiences and promote common interests. [35]

With these objectives in the concluding statement from the conference on racism, the status, living conditions, and rights of indigenous peoples were now a concern for the work with human rights in the UN. [36] In order to understand the extent of this statement we need to take a closer look at the events during the Geneva negotiations.

---

34 United Nations Declaration and Programme of Action to Combat Racism and Racial Discrimination, Geneva, 1978. The Declaration is printed in Bodley 1990:217-218.

35 Ibid.

36 A controversial wording in the declaration on the relationship between Zionism and racism made many countries, among them Norway, not signatories of the Declaration. These countries nevertheless declared themselves committed to the other parts of the Declaration, which were commonly agreed upon.

In the Norwegian state delegation we find Thorvald Stoltenberg as a leader. At that time he was Secretary of State in the Norwegian Foreign Office.[37] The leader of IWGIA, Helge Kleivan, who had close contact with Stoltenberg, had proposed that the government should include the Sami, Aslak Nils Sara, in the Norwegian state delegation, since he was so engaged with the WCIP.[38] In addition, a Human Rights expert, Asbjørn Eide, also participated in the delegation. At the conference, Sara chose to separate indigenous questions from general minority issues. He was given the opportunity to air his views to Stoltenberg, who asked him to first address the issue in the Norwegian delegation. Nobody in the delegation had any objections to his proposal after they had heard him speak (interview Sara). On behalf of the Norwegian delegation, Sara moved the proposal into a working group about minority issues. This working group was chaired by the Greek professor Erica Irene Daes. Sara recalled that Eide "helped me in formulating my speeches and proposals in English and now and then he would speak on behalf of the Norwegian delegation." Further, Sara got the impression that the chairperson Daes was gradually becoming more interested in the question. One could assume that because she "came over to us to collect more information" (interview Sara).[39]

As a result of this conference, from then on indigenous peoples and minorities were treated separately in the UN system, not only in studies but also in policy, a distinction that Willemsen Diaz had introduced. The main reason that Sara's proposal was adopted in that working group was that it was possible by that time to use *lege ferenda* arguments in order to keep indigenous issues separate from minority rights. The Caportorti report, the Sub-Commission's study of minority rights, had been submitted in 1976.[40] This report recommended that indigenous issues should be kept separate from minority issues, firstly for practical reasons (the complexity of the issue); secondly, because international rules of law might have different consequences for minorities than for indigenous peoples.[41] Also, because the Caportorti report had been addressed in the Human Right Commission, the Norwegian delegation was familiar with it during the conference on racism (cf. Eide 1987:21; 1992:219-222).

---

37 Thorvald Stoltenberg later became Norway's Minister of Defence (1979-1981) and after that the Minister of Foreign Affairs (1987-1989 and 1990-1993).
38 "Intervention by Mr. Thorvald Stoltenberg," attachment to the report from Foreign Office from the Conference on Racism in Geneva 1978, in the archive of Nordic Sami Council, copy on file with author.
39 Foreign Office report from the Conference on Racism in Geneva 1978, "Vurdering av konferansen: urbefolkningene" (Aslak Nils Sara), in the archive of Nordic Sami Council, copy on file with author.
40 E/CN.4/Sub.2/384.
41 For example Article 2(2) in the Declaration on Racial Discrimination from 1965 could be interpreted as a dismissal of indigenous peoples' local self-government and special rights (cf. Sanders 1983:22).

For the international indigenous movement, Aslak Nils Sara was in the right place at the right time. He seized the opportunity when it came to introduce the hopes and aspirations of indigenous peoples into the UN agenda. An important trigger for the historical process was the Sami struggle for land rights in Norway during the Alta conflict from 1979-1982. The Norwegian authorities proposed to dam the Alta River for hydroelectric power in some of the Sami core areas. A Sami action group engaged in a short, but important, hunger strike in the autumn of 1979 in a Sami tent just outside the Parliament in Oslo. As a result, the Norwegian Labour government postponed the construction of the dam and started comprehensive studies on Sami matters. However, the majority in the Parliament, including the Labour party caucus, forced the government to continue the construction. This led to an escalation of the conflict surrounding Sami rights. In January 1981, the government used substantial police force and military equipment to remove demonstrators engaged in civil disobedience from the front of the construction machinery and they forcibly removed Sami hunger strikers from the National Parliament building in the capital city (cf. Minde 2005).

The force that the Norwegian State had used to remove the protesters attracted international attention and was strongly criticised from i.a. the WCIP and the IITC, and some NGOs sent resolutions of disgust through the media and through diplomatic channels. The conflict had attracted so much attention that it reached the Human Rights Committee, the monitoring body for the International Covenants on Civil and Political Rights (1966). For the first time in history, Norway was questioned by the UN about the legal position of the Sami people in Norway. The Norwegian state was set to lose its positive reputation in the indigenous and human rights groups (Minde 2003). The embarrassing situation this represented for the Norwegian state triggered initiatives that sped up the inclusion of indigenous peoples into the UN system.

Even prior to the Alta case, Sami issues had become controversial in Norway; the Norwegian Foreign Ministry had taken the initiative to establish a Nordic group of senior civil servants with the main goal "to advance the interests of indigenous peoples." Many of the people in the ministry who were working with human rights had a positive attitude towards indigenous issues in general. As discussed earlier, this was already observed during the conference on racism. In the autumn of 1979, the Norwegian Foreign Ministry, through its special adviser on human rights issues, Knut Sverre, unofficially took important initiatives while working together with the Sami organisations. Observers from Canada and Australia were invited to participate in the Nordic group from autumn of 1980 on, because they, according to the Norwegian understanding, were "countries who had experienced problems with regard to indigenous questions which they tried to resolve in a positive way. They are also influential and useful partners in the UN connection."[42] The Nordic countries, with Norway as the most active, planned to take initiatives vis-à-vis the UN human rights bodies; the invitation to Canada and Australia has to be seen in view of this plan.

In the winter of 1981, while the Alta case dominated Norwegian media and the political system, the Nordic countries were planning a resolution for a working group on indigenous populations in the UN. The proposal took its starting point from some of the nearly completed parts of the Martínez Cobo report.[43] In order to speed up the process, the Nordic countries proposed that some of the recommendations in the report should be acted on immediately.[44] The resolution was moved in the meeting of the Human Rights Commission in the spring of 1981. Norway maintained that the report "was the most general accepted basis for further progress"[45] But the Human Rights Commission was not easily moved. It decided that the case first had to be discussed in the Sub-Commission that had the direct political responsibility for the Martínez Cobo report, but for a set of reasons this was a short postponement.

The Working Group on Indigenous Populations (WGIP)

High Politics: The Creation and the Mandate
The time was now ripe for the United Nations to create a working group for indigenous issues. The international backdrop was in the wake of the Vietnam War and the Helsinki process. The USA, under President Carter, promoted a human rights agenda in their competition with the Soviet Union (Smiths & Walker 2004; Soares 2006). In relation to indigenous peoples, this policy had two momentums.

Firstly, after a few months in office, President Carter signed the UN covenants from 1966, the one on civil and political rights as well as the other on economic and cultural rights. Even if the US Congress never ratified the latter, the convention on civil and political rights included articles on self-determination for "all peoples" (article 1) and the right of individuals to "enjoy their own culture (...) in community with other members of their group" (article 27). These articles were to be the foundation for the negotiations of the Draft Declaration.

Secondly, the Carter administration encouraged Latin American peoples to demand their political rights (Soares 2006). In compliance with this rhetoric,

---

42 Knut Sverre, speech at a seminar in Kautokeino, Februar26 1981 on the possibility of Norwegian ratification of ILO-convention Nr. 107, copy in the archive of Royal Commission on Sami Rights (Samerettsutvalget), Nr. 90:6. Instead of a convention, the Nordic Countries proposed a declaration, meaning that a convention "probably would be too ambitious" Ibid: 5.
43 E/CN.4/Sub.2/476.
44 See note 37:6.
45 Ibid, p.5.

the US government at the 1977 International NGO Conference enunciated that they supported the United States' participation at the conference out of its "conviction that vigorous efforts must be made to eliminate grievances at home as well as abroad." Related to the question of creating a working group, the US government delegation stated that they were "encouraged by the possibility of the establishment of an international organisation of indigenous peoples of the Americas–one that would go beyond the borders of the U.S. to include all of the Western Hemisphere."[46]

The mutual accusations of human rights abuses between the East and the West, created a greater scope for manoeuvring on indigenous issues. The Carter administration could not deny that indigenous peoples had unsolved problems. In addition, the hopeless situation of indigenous peoples in Latin America was frequently revealed by human rights organisations. Therefore, when the Soviet Union and Eastern Block countries criticised the human rights records of the West regarding indigenous peoples, they embarrassed the US and other Western countries, including Norway.

In 1979, the Soviet intervention in Afghanistan immediately escalated the tension of the Cold War. Simultaneously, the left-wing Sandinista movement in Nicaragua came to power, this triggered corresponding rebellions against military regimes in Central America. Since the guerrilla soldiers often were recruited from indigenous areas, the autocratic governments retaliated by sending soldiers to comb through entire villages, which in many cases ended in massacres. In social terms, the repressive regimes implemented war against indigenous peoples, most significantly in Guatemala.[47] After the 1980 election in the US, the incoming Reagan administration went to remarkable lengths to defend the violation of human rights in these autocratic regimes.

Under the leadership of the Dutch director of the Division of Human Rights from 1977, Theo van Boven, the human rights mechanisms were developed (Eide 1992). As a response to the violation of human rights in some Central and South American countries, the Division managed to get approval to form a group to work on the problem of kidnappings and disappearances. Argentina and the Reagan administration strongly disapproved of the work carried out in this group and of the director's role. Therefore, they sought to have van Boven ousted from his position in 1982 (Guest 1990: especially 323).

In this sort of atmosphere, Theo van Boven had nothing to lose when in his policy address to the Sub-Commission on August 17, 1981; he illustrated the problem facing indigenous peoples in the following statement:

---

46 See Report of International NGO Conference on Discrimination against Indigenous Populations in the Americas – 1977.

47 83 % of fully identified victims were Maya, according to findings by the Guatemalan "Truth Commission" submitted on 25 February 1999. See *Guatemala Memory of Silence*. Report of the Commission for Historical Clarification. Conclusions and Recommendations, p. 17.

Whatever their size, situation or location, indigenous peoples may be counted among the most vulnerable groups in today's world. They are, for the most part, unorganised, that is to say that they have not been able to organise themselves into lobby groups in their respective countries. They often are unable to participate in the institutions, which affect their lives. They often have no voices to speak for them whether at the national or at the international level. Fortunately, in recent years, some organisations of indigenous peoples have been established which have worked nobly to make the world aware of the plights of these peoples. Nevertheless, the majority of the world's indigenous peoples remain silent sufferers whose voices are rarely heard, while they continue to suffer inhumanity, degradation, violation of their rights and while they continue to approach the very frontiers of their continued survival." (van Boven, quoted in Ramcharan 1989:207).

In 1981, the staff of the Human Rights Division, with the director in the lead, warmly supported the Martínez Cobo study's proposal to create a working group. In addition, the Nordic countries had been promoting this proposal at the level of the state the previous year in the Human Rights Commission, as discussed earlier. A contributing factor in keeping this proposition alive was the successful Norwegian campaign to have the human rights expert, Asbjørn Eide, chosen as a member of the Sub-Commission from 1981. These people, together with a few representatives from indigenous groups (all of them representing IITC), and other NGOs in Geneva, helped Augusto Willemsen Diaz to elaborate a draft for a mandate and a strategy for guiding the issue through the UN system.[48]

The mandate of the working group consisted of two parts. Firstly, the working group was to review whether human rights and fundamental freedoms were secured with regard to indigenous peoples. In a sense, this was the general task for the Sub-Commission. But the mandate underlines that the world community interprets the situation for indigenous peoples as dramatic with regard to these values. The other side of the mandate instructs the working group to:

(…) give special attention to the evolution of standards concerning the rights of indigenous populations, taking account of both the similarities and the differences in the situations and aspirations of indigenous populations throughout the world.[49]

---

48 Personal information from Roxanne Dunbar-Ortiz who was one of the indigenous lobbyists: e-mail 28.03.2007, on file with author. See also interview with Bertrand Ramcharan, in The Human Rights Tribune, autumn 2001, vol. 8, no. 2. See internet acceesed on 25 April 2007: http://www.hri.ca/tribune/viewArticle.asp?ID=2624. He was at that time one of van Boven's closest adviser.

49 This wording from Resolution 2 (XXXIV) from 8 September, 1981 was adopted by EC-COSOC, in resolution 1982/34 from 7 May 1982.

When the mandate was discussed in the Sub-Commission, those supporting it, strongly disagreed at the last minute as to whether or not to include the prevailing reference "human rights and fundamental freedoms" in the second part of the mandate. The reference was not included, and for this reason the mandate was more open for *special* rights for indigenous peoples, for example in terms of historical and collective rights (interview Willemsen Diaz). In addition, the working group could later argue that they had been invited to not only demonstrate the current status of the law, but also to *develop* human rights.

Thus, at the meeting of the Sub-Commission in August 1981, the proposal to establish a working group for indigenous issues in the UN was unanimously supported. In spite of scepticism from some states, this time the supporters were able to pilot the idea quickly through the UN system.[50] The *Working Group for Indigenous Populations* (WGIP) formally consisting of five members who were chosen from among the experts of the Sub-Commission had their first meeting on August 9th, 1982. In recognition of Norway and Eide's achievements during this process, Eide was chosen as the first Chairperson of the Working Group.[51].

Owing to the mandate and the background, the Working Group was positioned under the UN Sub-Commission of Human Rights, i.e. at the lowest level in the UN hierarchy. Nonetheless it has been maintained that it was fortunate for the indigenous movement to have their issues addressed at this level from the beginning (Lâm 2000:76 ff.) for the following reasons:

- The indigenous groups were still able to create space between the super powers. In this respect, the field of indigenous peoples issues was the only field within the human rights system where something "was going on" in the 1980s and 90s. The premise was that the indigenous movement avoided going into alliance with any of the sides in the Cold War. For many organisations, this led to a difficult balance between criticising their home country in public on the one hand and the loyalty their home countries demanded from "their" indigenous peoples on the other.
- The leaders in this period were Asbjørn Eide from Norway (1982-83) and later Erica Irene Daes from Greece (1984-2002), both of them representing the "Western" region successively in the Working Group. Indigenous and state delegations respected them for their independent, but

---

50 Seven states abstained from voting: Brazil, Bulgaria, Cuba, Belarus, the Philippines, Poland, The Soviet Union, i.e. two from Latin America, four from Eastern Europe and one from Asia.

51 In the North American literature the focus has been on the NGO conferences 1977 and 1981. But the NGO conference in 1981 took place September 15-18, i.e. two weeks after the meeting in the Sub-Commission 8 September, when they moved the resolution to form a working group.

engaged, leadership. Also, the experts representing Eastern Europe and Latin America were active, even if the Yugoslav Ivan Tosevski, (1982-1985), was sceptical about treating indigenous peoples and minorities separately. The other members in the Working Group were not very interested in indigenous issues (interview Eide; Daes). Many of them were from countries that said they did not have indigenous peoples. Accordingly, the leaders in cooperation with the Human Rights Secretariat conducted most of the work and had responsibility for the activity within the Working Group (Sanders 1989:408; 410, Lâm 2000:76 ff.; Dunbar-Ortiz 2006:70).

- By far the most important fact was that at its first meeting, the Working Group in 1982 decided to open up its meetings for any indigenous groups who could send delegates to Geneva. This was pushing the rules of the ECOSOC accreditation. But regardless, the decision was approved in the UN's higher levels. Simultaneously, a voluntary UN fund was established in order to support travel costs for a number of delegates who needed funding.[52] Once again, one of Willemsen's proposals was now realised and which was expressed in his own words: "To let the indigenous peoples come to speak through their throat what is in their hearts and minds" (interview Willemsen Diaz).

The first proposals for new legal standards

The first concrete proposal for international standards concerning indigenous peoples was addressed at the WCIP General Assembly in Australia (Canberra) in May 1981. Douglas Sanders, a Canadian law professor, had been the special adviser for George Manuel for many years. He had been studying the development of indigenous rights both domestically and internationally and had seen progress only when concrete proposals were on the table. As part of his teaching curriculum on indigenous rights at the University of British Columbia, he developed a draft for an international convention (interview Sanders). The starting point for the draft was the right of self-determination, further it addressed civil and political rights, and economic, social, and cultural rights. In keeping with the idea of self-determination, the draft assumed that the convention had to be ratified by states and by indigenous peoples; a permanent commission for indigenous rights should be established and states, as well as indigenous peoples, should decide on the members of this commission.

---

52 Report of the Working Group on Indigenous Populations on its first session. UN document E/CN.4/Sub.2/1982/33, paras. 111-112. The final decision on establish a voluntary fund, was made by the General Assembly, by Resolution 40/131 of 13 December 1985. By adoption of this resolution the General Assembly accepted the "open door policy" of the Working Group.

This draft (henceforth "Canberra 1981") was presented in one of the groups at the WCIP meeting in Canberra.[53] Because it had not been distributed in advance, and due to the legalistic language, few delegates took the floor on the matter. The Norwegian human rights adviser Knut Sverre expressed that the document was interesting, but probably overly ambitious, even for the friendliest of states.[54] The board decided that the draft was to be distributed to the member organisations as a working document. Aslak Nils Sara had been elected Vice President and he undertook the task of co-ordinating the work with a convention for the next General Assembly that was to be held in Panama in the autumn 1984. Many of the organisations had by then sent their commentaries for the working document and indigenous and human rights groups in Canada had discussed it (Sanders1983: 29).

On Sara's initiative, a Nordic expert panel was established (6 out of 10 were Sami). This group made a careful revision of Sanders' text (henceforth "Nordic Sami Council 1984").[55] The Nordic Sami Council then brought this revised text to the General Assembly of WCIP in Panama. Still, the understanding here was that the proposal had been insufficiently prepared in the member organisations so they were unable to come to a unanimous resolution. At this point of the discussion, the representatives from the Nordic Sami Council suggested that their version could be used as a declaration of principles. This declaration of principles, with seventeen articles in all, was then adopted (Lasko 1984:29). At the meeting it was decided that this declaration of principles could be used in the upcoming work in the UN. When the Sami, Leif Dunfjeld, began his commission as a WCIP lobbyist in the UN a few months later, the most important document he brought with him was the Panama Declaration of principles (henceforth "Panama 1984").[56]

*   *   *

The establishment of WGIP became a watershed for the indigenous movement. The "open door policy" introduced by the Working Group, increased their chances of gaining political participation and influence. The number of delegates coming to the meetings started to dramatically increase. Around one hundred people attended the first meeting in 1982, thirty-two NGOs, twelve states and a few academics. Twelve years later, in 1994, when the Working Group completed the Draft Declaration, the level of participation had reached 790 delegates, representing 267 NGOs and twenty-eight states.

53 International Covenant on the Rights of Indigenous Peoples, Draft /March 20, 1981, Copy on file with author.
54 Author's notes from the meeting.
55 International Covenant on the Rights of Indigenous People, Draft/March 1984, Notes from Sami Institute, copy on file with author.
56 UN doc. E/CN.4/Sub.2/1985/22 Annex II.

These numbers demonstrate that the indigenous movement underwent a transformation in these years. Every self-respecting indigenous organisation on earth aimed to participate with their delegates in the events in Geneva. The yearly meetings in the WGIP under the UN umbrella became the most important meeting place for the movement and its political think tank. But the constant influx of new organisations changed the indigenous movement into a mixed group with differing objectives. This development undermined the WCIP, the most international and democratically oriented organisation. On the other hand, the IITC, which was more oriented towards special cases and had centralised leadership, adapted more easily to the new situation. However, by establishing this new UN body, the indigenous movement began to transform from a weak international movement to an influential transnational movement.

Towards a Declaration

The standard-setting process moved into a new phase in the first half of the 1980s. The Martínez Cobo report was completed in 1983 and many of its most important recommendations had already been implemented. Its status of being a white paper in the UN system was confirmed when the Human Rights Commission and ECCOSOC stated that the 1,400 page report was to form the foundation for the future work on a declaration.[57] But this extensive study remained inaccessible, and as Douglas Sanders pointed out: it was gradually "overtaken by events" (1989:408).[58]

The input from the indigenous movement and its experts was becoming a dominating factor in the UN system, and this development complied with the very intention of the Martínez Cobo report. We have seen that groups who participated in and around the WCIP ended up deciding on declaration of principles in Panama 1984, which was used in the strategy discussions of the indigenous caucus gathered in Geneva before the WGIP meeting in 1985 (Barsh 1986:380-381; Weissbrodt 1985). Groups that had been prepared to support the Panama declaration, moved their own proposal for a declaration of principles instead (henceforth "Six NGOs 1985").[59] It will be shown that there is a continuing line drawn from Sanders' first draft at the Canberra meeting in 1981 to the proposal of the six indigenous NGOs in 1985.

---

57 ECCOSOC decision 1985/137 of 30 May 1985.

58 From January 2007 UNPFII has published the conclusions and recommendations on the internet, accessed on 25 April 2007 at: http://www.un.org/esa/socdev/unpfii/en/spdaip.html

59 UN doc. E/CN.4/Sub.2/1985/22 Annex III. The Six NGOs were: Indian Law Resource Center, Four Directions Council, National Aboriginal and Islander Legal Service, National Indian Youth Council, Inuit Circumpolar Conference and International Indian Treaty Council.

<u>Land rights</u>
Regarding land rights for indigenous peoples, the Martínez Cobo report concluded as follows:[60]

- It is essential to know and understand the deeply special relationship between indigenous peoples and their land as basic to their existence as such and to all their beliefs, customs, traditions and culture.
- For such peoples, the land is not merely a possession and a means of production. The entire relationship between the spiritual life of indigenous peoples and Mother Earth, and their land, has a great many deep-seated implications. Their land is not a commodity, which can be acquired, but a material element to be enjoyed freely.
- Indigenous peoples have a natural and inalienable right to keep the territories they possess and to claim the land of which they have been deprived.

The rights of indigenous peoples to land and water are emphasised, as well as its special relation to their historical development, collective character and emotional connectedness. The demands made by the indigenous organisations in their declarations of principles had thus received full support in the final report.

The wording of various initial proposals from the indigenous organisations have stated their rights to traditional lands "of which they have retained or which have never been transferred out of their control" (Canberra 1981:3.1) and that the content of this right is "surface and subsurface rights, full rights to interior and coastal waters and rights to adequate and exclusive coastal zones" (ibid: 3.1). The size of the tract of land and the content of the rights were specified and strengthened in the drafts to follow. For example, the Nordic Sami Council (1984) proposed that land could be surrendered "only with the consent of the authorities of the indigenous peoples concerned" (13). If land had been taken from indigenous peoples without their consent, the WCIP maintained in the Panama declaration, "such land and resources shall be returned" (9). The six NGOs added more specific demands in 1985. They proposed that the theory of *terra nullius* [61] could no longer be used as a legitimate basis for states to claim

60 UN doc. E/CN.4/Sub.2/1985/22, paras 196-198.
61 This theory does not imply that the territory was devoid of people. On the contrary, the presence of indigenous peoples was accepted, but according to this theory, these peoples were considered to be so inferior both in culture and organisation, that they were not capable of possessing land, and neither did they have any concept of land rights. About the development and practice of this theory in North America, see Williams (1990) and corresponding in Australia, see Reynolds (1987). The term *terra nullius* (in Norwegian"ingenmannsland") has been applied in reference to Sami areas, see for example volume 4 in the highly regarded work *Norges historie* from 1977 (Imsen og Sandnes 1977).

the territories of indigenous peoples (6), and that no states could take territories from indigenous populations for military use without their consent, (8) and in addition, that treaties made between states and indigenous peoples should be recognised as international treaties (15-17).

In the report from the Working Group meeting in 1985, they stated as a matter of fact, that the most common reason to begin the standard setting process "was deprival of the territorial base and land rights, including all the surface and sub-surface resources which come with the land and which form so essential a base of the indigenous way of life."[62] Thus, we are able to maintain that the entire indigenous movement was united in the demand for land rights. In this way, the local and historical experience of indigenous peoples became important for the international negotiations that would involve the entire movement. They were conscious that the claims they were submitting for land rights and resources were going to be controversial and provocative for many states (Barsh 1986:380) as well as some of the formulations and strategies used in connection with negotiations. Therefore, it was important to have a certain level of tolerance in order to be open for compromises. But how could, at the very beginning, the indigenous movement have any legitimacy to negotiate with states? It is in this historical context that the question of self-determination became such an important issue, not only in terms of reality, but also in terms of strategy.

Self-determination

The experience of the indigenous movement was that the framework for general human rights and for special minority rights were unable to deal with issues connected to territories and collective rights. Because of this, it became important for the movement to create a distance from the ongoing work in the UN concerning minorities.

From the end of the 1970s, one could suspect that the term self-determination also came to include indigenous peoples. Firstly, the International Court of Justice in 1975 issued an opinion in a case concerning a nomadic tribe in West Sahara where they rejected the theory of "*terra nullius*." On the contrary, the court claimed that the nomads possessed legal rights to land and self-determination.[63] Secondly, the Sub-Commission had initiated an investigation into the implementation of self-determination, which in 1980 concluded that this principle had relevance for "peoples" in all countries.[64] However, the UN bodies did not adopt this conclusion, but it was nonetheless an indication of greater flexibility in this area.

---

62 Report of the Working Group 1985, UN doc. E/CN.4/Sub.2/1985/22 27 August 1985, para. 61. The land rights issue was the main issue on the WGIP meeting in 1984, see UN doc. E/CN.4/Sub.2/1984/20 8 August 1984, paras. 27-53.

63 I.C.J.Reports 1975, p. 6.

64 Hector Gros Espiell: Self-Determination: Implementation of United Nations Resolutions, FN dok. E/CN.4/Sub.2.405/Rev.1 (1980).

The Martínez Cobo report concluded that self-determination "must be recognised as the basic precondition for the enjoyment by indigenous peoples of their fundamental rights and the determination of their own future."[65] And it adds:

> In essence, it constitutes the exercise of free choice by indigenous peoples, who must, to a large extent, create the specific content of this principle, in both its internal and external expression, which do not necessarily include the right to secede from the State in which they live (…).[66]

Since the UN bodies did not dissociate themselves from these parts of the Martínez Cobo report, there seemed to be an opening for indigenous peoples to expect greater acceptance of their right to self-determination. They could do so because the report did not set up a choice between minority rights, on one hand, and the right to self-determination on the other. Instead the Martinez Cobo report pointed out that indigenous rights were indigenous rights – a separate category from either.

The indigenous organisations submitted this claim with more and more strength. The convention proposal from the Nordic Sami Council was cautious on this point. They proposed to limit self-determination to "internal autonomy" (1) and it should be interpreted within the framework of article 27 in the International Conventions on Civil and Political Rights (6).[67] The WCIP's Panama declaration returned to Sanders' draft (Canberra 1981) and maintained that the right of self-determination was to "freely determine their political status and freely pursue their economic, social, religious and cultural development" (1). This statement was strengthened even more in the statement from the Six NGOs in 1985. They emphasised there that the right to self-determination involves "whatever degree of autonomy or self-government they choose" and the right to "determine their own membership and/or citizenship, without external interference" (2, see also 3). This involves indigenous peoples being recognised as "subjects of international law" (15).

Self-determination was not on the agenda at the WGIP meeting in 1985 as a separate point, but the issue was commented on in different contexts.[68] What was most surprising was the support that the indigenous movement received

---

65 Martínez Cobo 1987: *Conclusions*, para. 580.

66 Ibid, para. 581.

67 We have to underline that the Nordic Sami Council's reading of Article 27 here was based on a maximalist interpretation of this provision that was protecting the resource base (Eide 1987:23-24). This interpretation was adopted by the Norwegian Parliament when they created The Sami Parliament and in a new paragraph in the Norwegian Constitution (see Minde and Nielsen 2003:305-306).

68 See the official report from the meeting: UN doc. E/CN.4/Sub.2/1985/22, paras. 48-52, 65-66, 79-83. The report can be compared with a professionally commented upon account by one of the participants: Barsh 1986.

from the Vatican, which for the first time had sent an observer to the meeting in Geneva. Rome's observer gave an account of a speech held by Pope John Paul II to Canadian Indians at Fort Simpson, where he emphasised "self-determination in your own lives as native peoples" (Barsh 1986:382). It was even more remarkable when the Vatican opposed Latin American state delegations that maintained that self-determination for indigenous peoples would be backwards. In contrast to these predominantly Catholic states that were still ruled by military juntas, the Vatican claimed that "to preserve their own identity does not mean wanting to remain rooted passively in the past," and that they were convinced that the indigenous peoples were motivated "by the spirit of openmindedness and progress." Also at this meeting, the expert from Africa (Ghana), Kwesi Simpson, referred to their own experiences in his support for drafting a declaration on indigenous rights. He stated that the Working Group should draw inspiration from the influence of the General Assembly resolution of 1960 since "millions of people all over the world now lived in freedom and independence."[69]

Simultaneously, there were strong warnings against the demand for self-determination. The leader of the Working Group, Asbjørn Eide, in 1983 urged moderation for two reasons: (1) Fear of the states closing down WGIP and (2) that international organs had great difficulty in defining "peoples" in connection with self-determination.[70] At the WGIP meeting in 1985, the delegate for the Reagan administration expressed their concern over the proposal from the Six NGOs involving the right to decide political status and citizenship. The USA stated that such a proposal would result in the right of secession for "indigenous populations." Supposedly, arguments of this kind were used in order to maintain the status quo, or as in this case, used as a threat to close down the WGIP.

The experts in the official Working Group were painfully aware that self-determination would be one of the most difficult issues to be resolved, given the claims made in 1985. The great challenge would be to create an extensive declaration covering the enormous variation in economic, social and political circumstances for indigenous groups. It was in this perspective that the connection between self-determination and the definition of "indigenous" and "peoples" was routinely discussed.

The necessity of a definition
The claims coming from indigenous groups for land rights and their positioning with regard to self-determination would necessarily have an impact on the debate as to understanding the category "indigenous peoples." The UN had established a group for "indigenous populations" with a mandate to develop legal

---

69 Ibid, para. 15, cf. Barsh 1986:378.
70 UN doc. E/CN.4/Sub.2/1983/22, para. 100.

standards. Because of this development, different states immediately developed special interests concerned with how to limit the number of beneficiaries. At the time of the establishment of the Working Group, only the Nordic countries, the settler states,[71] and an increasing number of Latin American countries acknowledged that they had "indigenous populations" within their borders. However, the transnational indigenous movement from Africa and Asia had gained very little access to the UN system,[72] considering that support groups such as IW-GIA, Survival International, and Cultural Survival assumed that there exists a total of 5000 indigenous groups spread out over approximately seventy states all around the globe, and that altogether they amounted to 250-300 million people (Burger 1990). In this period, when the rivalry between the Western–and the Eastern block dominated the UN, we can maintain that the Western countries supported every initiative to make indigenous issues into a global affair, while the Eastern block and most countries in Asia and Africa wanted to limit the issue and to persistently stick to "the blue water theory" (Sanders 1989:412-418).

The backdrop of high politics made attempts to define the group into "an extremely complicated, difficult and delicate task" as it was formulated in the conclusion of the Martínez Cobo report.[73] This question was intensely discussed in all the WGIP meetings up to 1985. Before we begin to analyse this debate, we will briefly study the claims made by the indigenous organisations. In the first draft from the WCIP in 1981, the convention would apply to indigenous people who: "are descendants of the earliest population living in the area and who do not as a group control the national governments of the state within which they live." (1.2)

These relatively strict requirements of historical prerogative were identical to the requirements used by the WCIP towards the member organisations. Nevertheless, this definition was slightly more flexible than the working definition used in the Martínez Cobo study. Even if Sanders referred to the decolonisation declaration in the paragraph on self-determination, we can see that he used the term "indigenous people" in the singular form. The Nordic Sami Council was particularly keeping watch that the term "indigenous people" would include peoples not necessarily colonised by conquest, and they found no reason to change the wording in Sanders' draft (2). The two declarations of principles to follow, drafted by indigenous organisations, not surprisingly, had no provisions on who could benefit from the usage. But we can see in the Panama declaration, where there was vacillating between the use of the singular form "people" and

---

71 The phrase "settler states" concerning indigenous peoples is often used about former British colonies, which are in this context US, Canada, Australia, New Zealand and South Africa.

72 The first indigenous peoples organisation from Asia that attended a WGIP meeting was the Chakma People from the Chittagong Hill Tracts in Bangladesh.

73 Martínez Cobo 1987: *Conclusions*, para. 363.

the plural form "peoples," the wording from the Six NGOs was consistently "peoples" or "nations." If we return to the debates in the WGIP, we can observe that the lack of a definition is connected to the fact that the indigenous organisations focused increasingly on self-determination and correspondingly focused less interest on a definition.

The first important debate concerning the definition of the term "indigenous" in the Working Group came in 1983. Countries from Asia and South America argued for a comprehensible and restrictive definition, whereas many indigenous representatives and other NGOs were arguing that this concern should be handed over to the indigenous themselves to decide on, based on the right of self-determination.[74] The disagreement over the need for, and also the content of a definition, was so intense that the chairperson Eide asked the Human Rights Secretariat to clarify the problem in the next meeting.

This is how the challenge returned to the author of the UN working definition from 1972/75, Augusto Willemsen Diaz, who had also written the conclusions and recommendations in the Martínez Cobo report. Willemsen Diaz had a certain reluctance to express more than what was already in the definition from 1972/75. However, when he proposed a revised definition for the use in international law, Willemsen Diaz underlined that this definition should be understood as a working definition: a point of departure for criticism and modification. Nevertheless, this definition has been used in the years to come as a kind of official definition in UN matters:

> Indigenous communities, peoples and nations are (1) those which, having a historical continuity with pre-invasion and pre-colonial societies that developed on their territories, (2) consider themselves distinct from other sectors of the societies now prevailing in those territories, or part of them. (3) They form at present non-dominant sectors of society and (4) are determined to preserve, develop and transmit to future generations their ancestral territories and their ethnic identity, as the basis with their own cultural pattern, social institutions and legal systems (numbers added by this author).[75]

This version is more general and flexible than the 1972 version regarding the claims for historical continuity (point 1), colonisation (point 2) and distinctness (point 3). But still the same historical factors as before (see the above analysis of the 1972/75 version) were added. What is new in this version is the weight put on the subjective intentions of indigenous groups, their intentions to be in existence as peoples with regard to culture, social institutions and legal systems, and especially with regard to the right to their ancestral territories (point 4). At last we can see that what is no longer to be defined is "population," but "com-

---

74 E/CN.4/Sub.2/1983/22 23 August 1983, paras. 109-119.
75 Martínez Cobo 1987: *Conclusions*, para. 379.

munities, peoples and nations." This includes the right of indigenous peoples to decide freely who is to be included in an indigenous community. This right was spelled out in the following paragraph in the report:

> On an individual basis, an indigenous person is one who belongs to these indigenous populations through self-identification as indigenous (group consciousness) and is recognized and accepted by these populations as one of its members (acceptance by the group).
>
> This preserves for these communities the sovereign right and power to decide who belongs to them, without external interference.[76]

Moreover, we can observe that the term "tribal" was again left out of the definition. The term was "buried" at the Working Group meeting in 1983, partly because some of the indigenous representatives warned of the use of the term due to its strong colonial and authoritarian connotations, and partly because the ILO observer, Lee Swepston, informed the meeting that the term "tribal" was added at the last minute during the development of ILO 107 in 1957, "to take into account peoples living in the same situation as those who were "indigenous" strictly speaking."[77] Also, the term "The Fourth World" which George Manuel had publicised, met the same fate when the indigenous peoples themselves became engaged in the legal battle linked to the terms "indigenous population" or "indigenous people(s)." In addition, the term "Fourth World People" was in a way connected to socialistic rhetoric and many indigenous groups from Latin America wanted to remain neutral in the state of civil war their countries were living under.

Conclusions
The fourth session of the WGIP in 1985 demonstrated that the serious work on a draft declaration on indigenous issues now had begun. The years from 1985 to 1994, when the draft declaration was finally sent from the WGIP upwards in the UN system, were characterised by a higher degree of juridification of the process and by a shifting of roles between the indigenous groups. The more important the question of self-determination became in the Working Group, the more they doubted the usefulness of continuing to define indigeneity. All of the unsuccessful attempts at defining "minorities" in the UN had made an impression on the process. Instead, there was a will to use time and energy on more substantial issues (interview Eide). Many speakers reminded the audience that the terms "minorities" and "peoples" had never been exhaustively defined; yet these groups en route had achieved substantial rights in international law.

---

76 Ibid, paras, 381-382.
77 Ibid para. 116.

In these cases, the different countries were granted the responsibility to outline the meaning of the terms.[78]

After having studied the context of the origin of the definition, we can conclude that some of the participants in the current academic debate on the interpretation of the working definition of "indigenous peoples" have been generalising on a fragile contextual and historical basis. As mentioned before, the author of Martínez Cobo report, Augusto Willemsen Diaz, emphasises further the term's relational and positional aspects, a parallel to the modern concept of ethnicity introduced by Barth and other social anthropologists around 1970. This has its contextual explanation. This modern approach was used by anthropologists in the Sami context from the very beginning (see especially Eidheim 1971). In the course of the long debate surrounding the development of the Alta River, it also became common knowledge, not only in academia but also by the Sami elite. Through his work on the final Martínez Cobo study, Willemsen Diaz had insights into Sami issues through literature on ethnicity. This interest became even stronger when, as leader of the Prevention of Discrimination Unit by the Human Rights Centre, he cooperated closely with the Norwegian Asbjørn Eide, who was the first leader of WGIP. The "up-to-date" perspective of ethnicity was therefore not only used in the Martínez Cobo report, but was also evident early on in the minutes from the WGIP proceedings.

This suggests that the participants in the current anthropology debate underestimate the importance of their own discipline and because of this some of them exaggerate the essensialist elements in the report. We have also seen that when ethnographical or biological criteria of the concept was brought into the discussion by some states, that Martínez Cobo report in order to refer to the actual use of such criteria, included them into the definition of "indigenous". Nevertheless, the report rejected criteria based on racial factors, for example the demand for a certain blood quantum, as still is used in the USA today. The strongest critic, Adam Kuper, has from a historic perspective misinterpreted the emphasis on content and form in the UN definition. The last version of the definition which the Martínez Cobo report proposed was more in line with modern anthropology than Kuper maintained. And if racial criteria are still used, it is a historical legacy not from Nazi Germany, but from colonial mechanisms of control used against indigenous peoples in South Africa as well as in the USA, for example.

Up until the 1960s, the outcome of governmental policy imposed from above and from the outside decided the global destiny of indigenous peoples. This was the background for the rise of the international indigenous movement, its objective being to formulate specific political demands and aspirations that derived from injustices suffered. The indigenous movement and their supporters picked up the term "indigenous peoples," a term that in the colonial context had been

---

78 E/CN.4/Sub.2/1985/22 27 August 1985, para. 52.

82

condescending both socially and politically. Nonetheless, they aimed at turning the words into something positive for those affected; they were often–but not always–the most marginalized groups in society. The most successful attempt was made within the framework of the World Council of Indigenous Peoples, with George Manuel, who had created a vision with a global appeal.

The modern indigenous movement, which came into existence in the settler states, the Nordic countries, and in Latin America after World War II, was part of the global struggle against racism and colonisation–in other words, these trends strongly dissociated themselves from the rhetoric of essentialist dogma that had lost its legitimacy during the war. In the years following the war, when the human rights system was developing, the most obvious and most strategically promising for the indigenous movement was to forge a connection to and participate in developing a legal system in connection with existing rudimentary doctrines about "indigeneity." The issues raised by the indigenous movement were naturally addressed under the UN's institutions for human rights. In the political climate of those days, their issues could gain support from many different circles but for different reasons.

The countries in the Third World, in alliance with the Eastern block, pursued the development of social and economic rights within the UN system. At the same time the old Western colonial powers were pressured by domestic indigenous organisations. These countries' moral double standards, when it came to "equal rights," had over the years led to grotesque differences between indigenous peoples and the rest of society. This even applies to countries that are considered welfare states and rank high on the UN barometer for quality of life, such as Canada and Australia. When the ecological state of the earth was introduced to the agenda in the 1970s, the pressures on the Western countries increased. They were now also expected to respect indigenous resource management and their close connection to the use of land and water.

The result was complicated and intense negotiations in order to bring forth a UN declaration, a declaration that could secure the vital necessities for indigenous peoples and at the same time provide them with the opportunity to actively participate and to influence the outcome.

The indigenous movement gradually dissociated itself from a definition of "indigenous" because they feared that it could be misused by the states. China and the Soviet Union interpreted the term in a way that excluded their own "national minorities" and "small nations," and many African states have maintained "we are all indigenous peoples." The term "indigenous" can have different uses, the understanding of the term has developed over time and the interpretation of how it should be defined has been (and is) an ongoing political struggle. This historical study has demonstrated that the indigenous movement has left behind a discourse simply based on essence, at least on international level, to a discourse on "positioning" (cf. Hall 1998:226).

The existence of peoples outside the Americas who considered themselves indigenous and who made common cause with the First Nations peoples, as the Sami had in the late 1960s, made the question of a definition more complex and delicate. When the peoples themselves took the floor, the term "indigenous" became more exclusive in relation to other minorities and simultaneously more extensive within the larger context of the political battle. In practice, the indigenous movement denied that the term should be reduced to a question of academic or political definitions. They used the term as a positive category, in a continuous political and moral struggle that questioned the necessity for a definition altogether. Therefore, the emergence of a new form of global indigenousness became less dependent on essentialist arguments, which were often the products of legal straitjackets. Instead, indigeneity turned out to be re-envisioned to develop a discursive weapon to be used against entrenched states and a powerful tool in the ongoing process of the Declaration in the years to come.

Interviews[79]

Augusto Willemsen Diaz (b, in Guatemala City, Guatemala, August 22, 1923), interviews on recording tape November 11, 1996, and on videotape November 25, 2004.

Leif Dunfjeld (b. in Namskogan, Norway, April 1944), interview on recording tape July 29, 1995.

Mario Ibarra (b.in Temuco, Chile 1954), interview on recording tape July 31, 1997.

Asbjørn Eide (b. in Norway, 1933), interview on recording tape December 2,1998.

Douglas Sanders (b. in Edmonton, Alberta, Canada, February 8, 1938), interview on recording tape April 12, 1997.

Aslak Nils Sara (b. Karasjok, Norway March 2, 1934-d. January 1996), interview on recording tape October 8, 1995.

References

Anaya, S.J.: *Indigenous Peoples in International Law,* New York/Oxford: Oxford University Press 1996.

Barsh, R.L.: "Indigenous People: An Emerging Object of International Law", *American Journal of International Law*, vol. 80, 1986, pp. 369-385.

Barsh, R.L.: "Indigenous Peoples in the 1990s: From Objects to Subject of International Law", *Harvard Human Rights Journal* 1994:1, pp. 33-86.

Barnard, A.: "Kalahari revisionism, Vienna and the 'indigenous peoples' debate", *Social Anthropology*, 2006:1, pp. 1-16.

Barth, F.: "Introduction", in F. Barth (ed.): *Ethnic Groups and Boundaries.* Oslo: Norwegian University Press, 1969.

Bennett, G.: *Aboriginal Rights in International Law.* Royal Anthropological Institute of Great Britain, Occasional Paper no. 37, 1978.

Bodley, J.H.: *Victims of Progress.* Mountain View, CA.: Mayfield Publishing Company, 1990 [1982].

---

79 From the author's collection of interviews.

Burger, J.: *The Gaia Atlas of First Peoples*. New York: Anchor Books, 1990.

Castro Lucic, M.: "Challenges in Chilean Intercultural Policies: Indigenous Rights and Economic Development", *PoLAR*, 2005:2, pp. 112-132.

Coulter, R.T.: Recollections of the Early Years of Indian Involvement in the International Community, 1974-1983. Copy on file with author. This manuscript was translated to French and published in *Destins Croisés*. Bibliothéque Albin Michel/UNESCO, Paris 1992.

Dunbar-Ortiz, R.: "The First Decade of Indigenous Peoples at the United Nations", *Peace & Change*, 2006:1, pp. 58-74.

Dyck, N.: "Aboriginal Peoples and Nation – States: An Introduction to the Analytical Issues", in Noel Dyck (ed): *Indigenous Peoples and the Nation-States*. ISER, Memorial University of Newfoundland, 1985.

Eide, A.: "United Nations Action on the Rights of Indigenous Populations", in Thompson, R.: *The Rights of Indigenous Peoples in International Law: Selected Essays on Self-Determination*. University of Saskatchewan, Native Law Centre 1987, pp. 11-33.

Eide, A.: "The Sub-Commission on Prevention of Discrimination and Protection of Minorities", in Alston, P. (ed.): *The United Nation and Human Rights: A Critical Appraisal*. Oxford University Press 1992, pp. 211-264.

Eidheim, H.: *Aspects of the Lappish Minority Situation*. Oslo-Bergen-Tromsø, 1971.

Guenther, M.: "Discussion: The concept of indigeneity", *Social Anthropology*, 2006:1, pp. 17-19.

Guest, I: *Behind the Disappearance: Argentina's Dirty War Against Human Rights and the United Nation*. Philadelphia: University of Pennsylvania Press, 1990.

Hall, S.: "Cultural Identity and Diaspora", in J. Rutherford (ed.): *Identity, Community, Culture, Difference*, 2nd printing, London: Lawrence and Wishart, 1998.

Imsen, S og J. Sandnes: Avfolkning og union 1319-1448. In Knut Mykland (red.): *Norges historie*, bd.4, Oslo:Cappelen, 1977.

Jhappan, R.: "Global Community?: Supranational Strategies of Canada's Aboriginal Peoples", *Journal of Indigenous Studies*, 1992:1.

Lâm, M.C: *At the Edge of the State: Indigenous Peoples and Self-Determination*. Ardsley, New York: Transnational Publishers, Inc. 2000.

Manuel, G. and M. Posluns: *The Fourth World: An Indian Reality*, Ontario: Collier-Macmillan, 1974.

Maiguashca, B.: *The Role of Ideas in a Changing World Order: The International Indigenous Movement 1975-1990*. CERLAC Occasional Paper, York University, June 1994.

McFarlane, P.: *Brotherhood to Nationhood: George Manuel and the Making of the Modern Indian Movement*. Toronto: Between The Lines, 1993.

Means, R. with M. Wolf: *Where White Men Fear to Tread. The Autobiography of Russel Means*. New York: St. Martin Griffin, 1995.

Minde, H.: "The Making of an International Movement of Indigenous Peoples", *Scandinavian Journal of History*, 1996:3, pp. 221-246.

Minde, H.: "The Challenge of Indigenism: The Struggle for Sami Land Rights and Self-Government in Norway 1960 – 1990", in S. Jentoft, H. Minde, R. Nilsen (eds.): *Indigenous Peoples: Resource Management and Global Rights*, Eburon Delft 2003, pp. 75-104.

Minde, H.: "The Alta case: From the local to the Global and back again", in G. Cant, A. Goodell and J. Inns, (eds.): *Discourses and Silences: Indigenous Peoples, Risks and Resistance*, Christchurch, New Zealand 2005, pp. 13-34.

85

Minde, H. & R. Nilsen: "Conclusion", in S. Jentoft, H. Minde, R. Nilsen: *Indigenous Peoples: Resource Management and Global Rights*, Eburon Delft 2003, pp. 297-310.

Paine, R. (ed.): *The White Arctic*, Memorial University Press of Newfoundland, 1977.

Plaice, E.: "Discussion: The concept of indigeneity", *Social Anthropology*, 2006:1, pp. 22-24.

Kingsbury, B.: ""Indigenous peoples" in International Law: A Constructivist Approach to the Asian Controversy", *The American Journal of International Law*, 1998:3, pp. 414-457.

Kuper, A.: "The Return of the Native", *Current Anthropology*, 2003:3, pp. 398-395.

Kuper, A.: (Discussion), *Social Anthropology*, 2006:1, pp. 21-22.

Lasko, L-N.: "Urbefolkningsrätten i förvandling", *Samefolket*, 1984:11, pp. 28-32.

Sanders, D.: *The Formation of the World Council of Indigenous Peoples*, IWGIA Document No. 29, 1977.

Sanders, D.: "The Re-Emergence of Indigenous Questions in International Law", *Canadian Human Rights Yearbook 1983*, pp. 3-30.

Sanders, D: "The Working Group on Indigenous Population", *Human Rights Quarterly*, vol. 11, 1989, pp. 406-433.

Sanders, D.: "Developing a Modern International Law on the Rights of Indigenous Peoples", Report for the Canadian Royal Commission on Aboriginal Peoples. (Manuscript) December 22, 1994 (on file with author).

Saugestad, S.: "Contested Images: 'First Peoples' or 'Marginalized Minorities' in Africa?", in A. Barnard and J. Kenrick (eds.): *Africa's Indigenous Peoples: 'First Peoples' or Marginalized Minorities'*, Centre of African Studies, University of Edinburgh, 2001.

Schmitz, D.F and D. Walker: "Jimmy Carter and the Foreign Policy of Human Rights: The Development of a Post-Cold War Foreign Policy", *Diplomatic History*, 2004:1, pp. 113-143.

Smith, P.C. and R.A. Warrior: *Like a Hurricane: The Indian Movement from Alcatraz to Wounded Knee*. New York: The New Press 1996.

Soares Jr., J.A.: "Strategy, Ideology, and Human Rights: Jimmy Carter Confronts the Left in Central America 1979-1981", *Journal of Cold War Studies*, 2006:4, pp. 57-91.

Reynolds, H.: *The law of the land*. Penguin Books, 1987.

Venne, S.: *Our Elders understand our Rights: Evolving International Law Regarding Indigenous Peoples*, Penticton, BC: Theytus Books Ltd. 1998.

Weaver, S.: *The Hidden Agenda 1968–1970*, University of Toronto Press, 1981.

Weyler, R.: *Blood of the Land*. Everest House 1982.

Weissbrodt, D.: "Indigenous Workings: The Geneva Story Continued", *Aboriginal Law Bulletin*, 1985, no. 16, pp. 10-12.

Williams, Jr. R.A.: *The American Indians in Western Thought*. Oxford University Press, 1990.

Wright, R.M.: "Anthropological Presupposition of Indigenous Advancy", *Annual Review of Anthropology*, Vol. 17, 1988, pp. 365-390.

CHAPTER 3

Between the Global Movement and National Politics: Sami Identity Politics in Finland from the 1970s to the early 1990s

JUKKA NYYSSÖNEN

Introduction

Entering the international venue and gaining victories from national governments through the use of international law has been presented in research as a liberating and empowering experience for indigenous peoples. In the same manner, the strengthening of Sami identity through participation in the indigenous peoples' movement has been celebrated in research conducted in Norway on Sami history. It can be highlighted that from the Alta dispute onwards, there has been some successful use of the global rights discourse in landownership cases. The global legal discourse has challenged the autonomy of state law (Minde 2005; Niezen 2000; Nyseth and Pedersen 2005). In spite of many similarities, such a narrative cannot be written from the Finnish Sami experience. In Finland, the cautious minority policy of concessions and conflict avoidance changed to a more hostile policy after the internationalization of the Sami movement.

Legal scholar Lennard Sillanpää made a positive remark about the Finnish administrative organs, which were moving away from a controlling mode to a more conversational mode regarding Sami politics. A later development, identified by Seija Tuulentie, reveals a grimmer undercurrent: a great difficulty granting the Sami special rights, especially with regard to the land rights issue. These trends emerged in the discussion of Sami rights in the 1990s, but they revealed an enduring dominant discourse of citizenship securing formal equality for all individuals, including the Sami. The discourse of citizenship subordinates the discourses of justice and indigenousness. Researchers in Finland have noted that Sami complaints to judicial organs have been met with poor success and have been granted few improvements in regulatory agency (Hannikainen 1996, 323-4; Sillanpää 1994; Tuulentie 2001). Incorporating the Sami into citizenship can be viewed as an inclusive and exclusive act. It is a constitutive discursive categorization, which grants a status to the Sami that preserves the society's status quo and hierarchies (Fowler 1980, 64). Granting individual rights and inclusion into the welfare society leads to the exclusion of alternative forms of citizenship and rights claims based on collective forms of social organization (Lawrence 2005).

This chapter will focus on the tension that internationalization created in the Sami movement and in the political space in which Finnish and Sami actors operated. How did the Sami movement and discourses change when Sami activists from Finland entered the global indigenous peoples' movement? How were the new discourses received in the Finnish national context? Could the new discourses and institutions challenge the discourses of citizenship and formal equality? If not, why? What impact did environmentalist discourse have on the Sami issue's receptiveness? The questions are posed within the timeframe beginning approximately from the internationalization of the Sami movement in the 1970s to the end of the Kessi dispute in 1990, which could be regarded as the first test case for the global rights discourse in Finland.

The theoretical framework for this presentation is modestly constructivist. Identities are processes–both invented and constructed–and culturally conditioned, not only in the sense that they assume different meanings in different historical contexts, but also that they are based on historical/social processes of intra-group negotiation. Identities are not voluntary nor are they totally conditioned by history, let alone by biology or race (Hall 1998, 223ff.; Thuen 1995 4ff.). The construction of cultural and ethnic identity is an argumentative process of identification linked to political and territorial loyalties, which sets the limits for minority peoples' articulation of ethnic identity.

Articulation is not only based on a "politics of difference," that is on the recognition of the differences between minorities and the majority, but is also a deliberate attempt by the ethnic elite to launch a mobilising ethnic identity. This occurs in identity politics, defined here as political projects, which are founded on a shared identity and not on abstract ideologies launched in order to gain legitimatisation and recognition as an ethnic group. The ethnic elites operate on supralocal, intercommunal, and global levels, and also have connections to the national level. The elite try to incorporate the ethnic identity building process on the local level and at the same time they negotiate public stereotypical imagery. Ethnic identities are products of power, of hegemonic processes of articulation, and are reproduced in the discourses of power (Anttonen 1996, 17ff.; Levi and Dean 2002, 15; Thuen 1995, 4ff.; Tuulentie 2003, 74).

The Sami Movement and Global Contact and Impulses–Historical Context and Counter Imagery

The national and international political-cultural context had some positive features for the Sami in the 1970s. The "progressive" ideological atmosphere of the 1970s, as well as a new phase of the Cold War, marked by "bilateral" accusations of violations of internal human rights, seemed to ease the access of indigenous NGOs into the UN-system, even though rights were not yet implemented (Minde 2000a, 234; Minde 2002, 67). The rights of minorities were an issue in Finnish political culture, where defending the powerless and speaking from an oppositional stance was a powerful and popular position (Alasuutari 1996, 65-6). In the 1970s and 1980s, Finnish Sami politics and legislation recognized the distinct Sami cultural community and their claims to positive action; this goodwill materialised mostly in legislation concerning education (Lewis 1998, 29ff.).

The poor reputation of the Forest and Park Service[1] was cemented in the increasing number of articles about ecologically unsound logging practices and the office's attitude of superiority (Paltto 1973, 34). In terms of identity politics, the demonization of the Forest and Park Service finally gave Sami activists an opponent against which imagery could be built. Unlike the "silent state"–which mostly practiced politics of minor concessions and conflict avoidance–the Forest and Park Service in damaging the reindeer pastures of Inari had a highly physical presence. Consequently, the imagery of the Sami as ecologically-sound people could easily be constructed because the criticism of the Forest and Park Service had a mostly ecological orientation.

The counter-imagery[2] in the Finnish public sphere was mostly positive towards the Sami. At first they were represented matter-of-factly, but when the Sami began to voice exclusive demands then a paternalistic undercurrent ensued which absorbed the Sami into the Finnish national whole by referring to the formal equality that citizenship provided. In the 1980s, the representation of Sami as agents of sustainability enjoyed a brief moment of hegemony. It was typical to deal with the Sami as a cultural entity and their livelihood was viewed as a cultural marker. Thus, the imagery was cultivated of the Sami as a people practicing a sustainable way of life.

In the late 1980s and 1990s a new trait in Finnish minority politics was identified: a rhetoric of fear emerged in official and unofficial statements regarding separatism and disintegration of the nation-state. Similar to views in Norway, cultural differences were viewed as belonging to nationality whereas ethnic diversity was viewed as more threatening to national cohesion. This kind of rhetoric was infrequent, but it was part of the national discourse becoming more openly critical to the radicalising group-rights demands of the Sami. The ethnic-based encroachments against the territorial integrity of the state of Finland–the natural and unquestioned frame of identification–enjoyed low legitimacy, which was evidenced in the increased resolve of the land rights issue (Thuen 1995, 62; Tuulentie 2001, 71ff.).

The Finnish authorities have traditionally been concerned with landownership and management of resources, but a new feature of land discussions was introduced in the 1970s which gained attention. Environmentalist discourse

---

1   Forest and Park Service is the institution responsible for forestry and conservation of state owned land in Finland.
2   The chapter on counter-imagery is based on press-sources presented in the reference list and is a part of my thesis on Post-war Sami identity politics in Finland.

brought new actors and ideas to the home areas of the Sami. This both global and national discourse was based on western hegemonic scientific practices. The discourse disturbed the legitimacy of national actors and institutions at the local level and to some extent marginalized local indigenous issues. The environmentalist discourse appeared in Finland in the 1970s but gained full momentum in the 1980s, when Finland was characterized as being a "thoroughly ecologized"[3] nation; the discourse encouraged everyday environmentalism and national policies. Finnish environmentalist thought was somewhat supportive of deep ecological thought, which stressed the intrinsic value of "the untouched nature."

The Finnish wilderness-thinking was twofold: one sector, consisting of old established conservationist organizations and also a new wave of environmentalists, stressed the value of the disappearing "untouched" forests. The other sector, consisting of state institutions responsible of resource management, stressed its potential usage, including reindeer herding and forestry. Both of these views differed from the Sami perceptions of wilderness, which had been represented as a combination of both cultural/natural landscape and as a resource, where the legacy of previous Sami generations was visible. These contesting views were mobilized in the Kessi dispute over what was regarded as the "last wilderness-forests of Finland" (Heikkilä 2004, 138-46; Kahelin 1991, 252; Länsman 2004, 99; Nyyssönen 2000, 155ff.; Rannikko 1994, 20). The national discourses evolved from a (stereotypically) friendly to a more hostile tone when it came to the Sami cause. The national discourse became stern on the issue of property rights and on alternative forums new ecologies were introduced that competed with the local and industrial ecologies.

Internationalization of the Sami movement: Entering the Global Indigenous Peoples Movement

The Sami in Finland may have been informed about the initial phases of the international indigenous peoples' movement from the unofficial contacts that the Sami in Norway had made in the early 1970s. However, public discussion among the Sami about entering the movement was not comprehensive; nonetheless, the Sami from the Nordic countries entered the emerging global indigenous NGOs simultaneously. The Finnish Sami were not as active in the founding phases of the World Council of Indigenous Peoples (WCIP), where the initiative was found in contacts between George Manuel, Aslak Nils Sara and Tomas Cramér (Jernsletten 1997, 289; Minde 2000a, 230-1; Minde 2000b, 30-3; Minde 2005).

The first signs of a new global bond in Finnish public sphere emerged in June 1972, when Samuli Aikio, representing the Society of Promoting the Lappish Culture, and Kaarlo E. Klemola, from the Forest and Park Service, participated

---

3   Unless otherwise noted, all quotations are my own translations.

in the Environment Forum, a shadow meeting of the Conference on Environmental Conservation in Stockholm. In the conference, Sami from Sweden and representatives from two native tribes from North America made comparisons between the Sami situation and their own. There were many parallels: both were oppressed minorities with diminishing resources and polluted lands and neither of the minorities aimed to dominate nature, but rather lived in harmony with it. The consequences of forestry and the Lokka reservoir[4] were presented in an exhibition at the forum (*Lapin Kansa* 13.6.1972, Aikio ja Klemola saamelaisten puolestapuhujana). The self-representation of the Sami as a people practicing ecologically sustainable lifestyles began to be more widely cultivated, as a result of more frequent contacts with other indigenous groups.

The Sami entered the global movement at the Arctic Peoples Conference in Copenhagen in November 1973. One of the themes of the conference was to define indigenous peoples and identity. Pekka Aikio presented the idea of "original inhabitants," Tomas Cramér discussed "national indigenous minorities," while Aslak Nils Sara used the term "autochthonous peoples." The final term ended up in the resolution, which stressed the integral and firm connection between autochthonous identity and the lands and domiciles of the people. The term possessed potential for two kinds of representation–building on legalist discourses and the other building on primordial imagery and discourses.[5] The demands of the first resolution constructed the indigenous or autochthonous peoples as legal claimants; they required acknowledgement as equals with the dominant cultures and also recognition of indigenous peoples' collective ownership of their domiciles.

Pekka Aikio used both potentials in his lecture. The premise was that "[e]ven today the Lapps still get their main income in livelihoods closely connected with nature." He continued by reflecting on the work that the Sami committee was doing at the same time: "The draft law on Lapp affairs includes regulations that secure the position of these tradings." This meant that the Sami lacked full rights in the context of the nation-state of Finland. The legitimation of these "indisputable" rights to the areas resources was in the status of the Sami as being "original inhabitants of their area."[6]

---

4   Lokka and Porttipahta reservoirs in Sodankylä municipality were built in the late 1950s and were filled in the late 1960s. 600 people, both Sami and Finns, had to relocate in the process.

5   Compare with Paine 1984, 212-213. Paine defines the autochthonous peoples in relation to majority people, in the context of colonised first-comer domiciles within the nation-states (a legalist potential). The autochthonous people are colonised and marginalised and yet keeping alive their cultures and identities.

6   The archive of professor Henry Minde, Programme and lectures from the Arctic Peoples' Conference, Copenhagen 1973: Lecture "A report on Lapp Committee work in Finland" by Pekka Aikio and lecture "Sámi Institut`ta, Kautokeino" by Aslak Nils Sara and lecture "National Indigenous Minorities" by Tomas Cramér.

The first meeting of WCIP, with Aslak Nils Sara in the founding committee, took place in Port Alberni, Canada, in November 1975 (Minde 2000b, 34). The Sami conference in 1974 had chosen Pekka Lukkari, Nils-Aslak Valkeapää and Esko Palonoja as "Finnish" representatives and participation has been steady ever since.

It has been estimated that the global cooperation was of great significance. The landownership claim became dominant in the Sami discussion, where there was an ongoing shift from stressing immemorial usage rights and the status of a national minority to the status of indigenousness. The Sami movement was influenced by the notions of equality based on their own development premises (Lehtola 2005, 38; Minde 2000a, 231-2; Minde 2000b, 33-4; Seurujärvi-Kari 1994, 178ff.).

Internationalization marked the beginning of a paradigm shift in Sami identity politics. It was inspired by the native people of Canada's reaction to the White Paper (1969) which aimed to dismantle special legislation and treatment of native tribes by establishing standards of (formal) equality and "non-discrimination" in the relationship between Natives and the Trudeau government. Native Canadians demanded direct participation, equitable treatment, and that special rights and grievances concerning lands and resources be honoured. The Red Power Movement also took hold in the US, where many tribes reasserted claims to their ancestral lands and resources. Claims for autonomy and self-government were also made. Many Sami activists were inspired by this struggle, which was communicated through personal contacts and literature in Sami conferences arranged by the Sami Council. The Sami emerged in conferences as an ethnic group seeking the right to self-rule and in the Snåsa conference of 1974 they finally emerged as an indigenous people (Johnson 1996, 135ff; Minde 2005; Weaver 1981, 3-11).

For Sami activists, the global discourse meant both coherence in building ethnic boundaries as well as transformations and diversity in identity-politics. The new global bond required sustaining the imagery of "natural people," which was undertaken in cultural forums by Sami outside the official Sami Delegation (from here on the "Independents"). The ongoing paradigm shift towards land-ownership claims signalled a need for disengagement from the radical identity politics practiced in the global cooperation, which in its extreme forms denied the possibility of land-ownership for indigenous people. There was a need for a firmer judicial foundation for their rights claims. The institutionalised Sami elite, working under the mandate of the Sami Delegation (est. 1973), chose the global rights discourse. The quest for a firmer foundation took almost two decades before it became established, and there was always a more radical, more "primordial" identity political strategy pursued alongside.

The Era of the most Exclusive Identity Politics: Enter the Colonized Sami

The "Independents" sustained a non-inclusive self-imagery and hostility towards the Finnish majority. A history of Sami colonization was constructed and inspired by global impulses. Author Kirsti Paltto and poet Nils-Aslak Valkeapää, relying on *Johti Sabmelažžat* (JS)–a newly established radical Sami association–represented the settlement of the Lappmarks as a history of plunder and violence which caused poverty and hunger. It was represented as deportation and conquest and not retreat, which resulted in a colonialist policy in the 17th century as the spheres of interest were negotiated between states and national borders were arbitrarily imposed. In the process of Christianization, many aspects of vernacular culture were totally destroyed. The Sami had to adopt agriculture because of the narrowing niche for their traditional livelihoods. Paltto agreed with the notion that landownership was foreign to the Sami. The Sami adaptation to agriculture led to an increasing gap in wealth and to disputes between the *dalolas* (permanently settled Sami) and the *badjeolmmos* (reindeer herding Sami) as well as to disputes between Sami reindeer herders and Finnish settlers (Paltto 1973,13ff.).

According to Paltto, the Sami were an oppressed, colonized and exploited people and were not treated as equal citizens of Finland. The reservoirs built by the hydro-power company, Kemijoki Oy, confirmed that that there was a colonial attitude towards the Sami. The efficient forestry was shaking the ecological balance of the Sami domicile. The Sami were underdogs in the meeting between the minority and majority cultures and the adaptive measures (for example those of dalolas-Sami) were viewed as assimilation. Isolating the reindeer herding Sami from majority impulses would be the only guarantee for the Sami culture to survive (Paltto 1973, 42ff.).

The self-imagery of a colonized people and the cultivation of an indigenous brotherhood and pride continued in the cultural sphere. In the case of Finland, this occurred most notably in the cultural exchanges occurring between the circumpolar peoples in the 1970s. The Finnish Sami sent cultural delegates to Alaska, Greenland and Canada. In Finland, the *Davvi Suvva Festival* (Breeze from the North) was a venue for expressions of indigenousness and an arctic sense of communion. The festival was arranged by WCIP, the Finnish branch of the Sami Council, Karesuvanto Sami Society (Gárasavvona Sámiid Searvi) and JS. It presented traditional expressions of circumpolar indigenous cultures and stood in opposition to the "standardized technical culture" and majority political institutions (*Vuovjoš* 1/1977, passim).

Nils-Aslak Valkeapää was active in *Davvi Suvva* and in indigenous cultural cooperation. He was also one of the most audible Sami in Finland, due to his appointment as provincial artist of Lapland in the years 1979-1983. He produced and coined self-representations which came to be associated with Sami identity in general and in the majority's representations of the Sami in years to come. In his representations the Sami did not have a word for "war" in their language; they have a rich vocabulary for snow, weather and reindeer in their language; the Sami were not enclosed by national borders, but integrated by nature; and the borders and states are unknown to the Sami; Valkeapää was also eager to draw parallels to other indigenous peoples suffering from ecological deprivation.

As the "Independents" were eager to adopt the "natural people"-imagery, the development of policies was one of abandoning this imagery in institutionalized Sami politics. Enclosed in the state machinery and its political procedures, the Sami Delegation grew increasingly suspicious about the "primordial" imagery.

Applying the Global Discourses: Identity Politics of the Sami Delegation[7]

The Sami Delegation was established in 1973 as the first self-governing organ for the Sami in the Nordic countries. The first phase of an institutionalized identity politics of the Sami Delegation was relying heavily on the "natural people"-imagery. In a statement on tourism in Sami areas in 1975, the premise was that the Sami were dependent on and an integral part of nature. Subsistence in traditional ways had been weakened for reasons out of their control. "The Finnish society, with ideals based on maximising profits, has changed and raped nature in the Sami home area with logging, ploughing, building reservoirs, regulating the waters etc". The Sami would be forced to change their way of life, unless areas were reserved for their use. The Sami had little agency, they were conditioned by nature, and threatened by Finnish modes of production.

Within two years time a change in representational strategies occurred. In a statement concerning trekking routes in May 1977 the rhetoric was toned down and the use of identity as a political tool more cautiously asserted. The Sami were represented as the original population of the land, "/.../who gain their livelihood mostly from traditional means of living". Nature was essential in relation to their livelihood and to Sami culture, which was founded in the Sami forms of subsistence. We witnessed the birth of an identity-based political tool with the longest continuity and the most widely used in the years to come (f.ex. Helander 1991, 64-5). In the new representation, nature is still viewed as a basis for Sami culture, but not the only one: the Sami were also cultural subjects and their traditional livelihood also contributed to creating their culture and iden-

---

7 The next three sections, unless otherwise noted, are based on archive sources, the annual reports from the Sami Delegation of Finland from the period 1977-1992 in the archive of Sami parliament, Inari, Finland. All of the quotes were originally in Finnish and are this author's translations.

94

tity. The Sami were no longer waiting for fatal Finnish intervention. The representation allowed more room for the Sami to have agency. The Sami culture has been continuously developing and they have created societies which were not conditioned by, but integrated into nature. Having a deep connectedness to nature meant that disturbances to nature would have an immediate impact on Sami trades and culture, forcing them to change their way of life.

The identity politics of Matti Sverloff, the chairman of the Sami Delegation, was deeply integrated into the "natural people"-imagery. Sverloff's policies constituted an exception from the emerging self-representation. In a statement from a committee report regarding reindeer herding legislation from 1977, he intertwined reindeer herding–as "the oldest mode of human functioning"–and Saminess and he argued that reindeer herding had always been "inseparable from the Sami way of life" and "a constitutive economic factor for the Sami culture." Further, reindeer herding was based on an "almost equal relationship" between reindeer and man and that "reindeer is a social partner to man, a source for nutrition as well as for many-sided production and means of transport, the human being has supported reindeer in many situations important to the animal, such as preventing the predator-menace, digging nutrition under the snow and regulating the use of reserve pastures etc."[8] The way in which Sverloff places the human being in the social life of a reindeer is unique in Sami self-imagery. He made a reference to the increasing problems in the pastures as a result of herding becoming part of the market-economy, which threatened the livelihood that was "traditionally stable and secure, a means of living intertwined with the way of life."

In order to secure the productivity of reindeer herding, the Sami delegation demanded conservation and maintenance of winter pastures, the condition of which was viewed as the most vital precondition for reindeer herding. Integration with nature was not referred to in statements based on judicial reasoning. The inconsistency reflects the tension between the Matti Sverloff-led "primordialists" and the Sami politicians who were more suspicious of the "nature people"-imagery. This group was led by three figures: researcher and Sami politician Pekka Aikio, teacher and lawyer Heikki Hyvärinen, and Nils Henrik Valkeapää who was also a Sami politician and teacher. Hyvärinen and Valkeapää had been active in researching the judicial aspects of the settlement history of Lapp-marks. For example in a statement concerning the water district boundary issue (*vesipiirirajankäynti*), the state claim to lands was denied on the basis that the collective and non-sharable common ownership of the *siida*

---

8   The archive of the Sami Parliament, Inari, Statements/initiatives 1974-1986, statements 1975-1980, *Annual report* 1977, appendix, Saamelaisvaltuuskunnan lausunto poronhoitola-kitoimikunnan mietintöön (1976:26) Maa- ja metsätalousministeriölle, 1977. Sverloff used the term "vaihtolaidun" (literally "exchange-pasture"), which I translated as reserve pasture. This is not a literal translation, as I do not know the function of a "vaihtolaidun" in Skolt Sami reindeer herding.

(Lapp Village) was never handed over to the state. The establishment of state lands was based on false assumptions of *terra nullius.*[9]

The 1980s and Streamlined Identity Politics of the Sami Delegation

One can detect an increasing dissatisfaction with the "natural people"-self-imagery among some members of the Sami elite. A shift towards legal discourse is evident also in Sami conferences in the 1970s: the rhetoric of the Sami being in danger of losing their judicial position was used in the resolution from the Sami conference in Inari in 1976, as well as in the Sami trade and social policy program given in the Arjeplog conference in 1978. These resolutions still relied on the self-representation of indigenous people as agents of sustainability. But by the time of the Tromsø conference in 1980, a change had occurred. Nils Henrik Valkeapää spearheaded the Finnish Sami opposition by referring to his own study of judicial history and demanding a more factually-based judicial foundation for the landownership claims. According to him, "political programmes" were not enough, only litigation would be sufficient. Landownership based on immemorial usage rights could only be settled with reference to Sami genealogy. The legal discourse became dominant in the Sami Political Programme, a statement drafted and disseminated at the conference. According to the Programme, the Sami became legal claimants, legal subjects and no longer just people living close to nature: indigenousness was transformed from cultural emblem to a judicial status (Nyyssönen 2006:77|).

In the 1980s, Pekka Aikio became a major actor in formulating Sami identity politics. He was the chairman of the Delegation in 1980-1981, and again from 1988 onwards (Lehtola 2005, 197-209). In the 1980s, in statements concerning reindeer herding, man and reindeer are again separate and a more scientific discourse around reindeer became prevalent. Herding was no longer regarded as the only means of Sami livelihood that was constitutive of Sami identity and the focus shifted to the legislative and social organization of the subsistence, rather than the ecological organization that had been stressed by Sverloff.

Aikio was consistent in using self-representation, coupled with a cultural component, which he had already mobilized in the Copenhagen meeting in 1973. He argued that the Sami were a people whose livelihood was based on traditional means which were dependent on the natural environment remaining in an undisturbed state. A disturbance in the natural environment would lead to a change or disturbance in the Sami economy and subsistence. To preserve or conserve nature meant to preserve the Sami culture and livelihood. In 1980 Aikio suggested the establishment of "a protection area for Sami culture, where the Sami – the right holders of the Lapp villages – can practice and develop

---

9   Terra nullius means land, which is declared/seen as "no man's land," i.e. which is not owned by anyone.

/.../ their traditional, hereditary means of living, which are nature-based".[10] The self-representation utilised both the legal potentials and the "natural people"-agency, while the former was toned down in a sense that its inclusiveness was greater ("/.../ getting *most* of their livelihood from the traditional means of living /.../" [my italics]). Nature no longer overwhelmed Sami agency–they were represented as people who were developing and practicing sustainable culture.

Another typical representational strategy was to represent western industrial forms of land-use as being far less sustainable than Sami the forms of Sami land-use. This was a widely accepted notion in the Finnish public sphere. Traditional Sami livelihood was poorly protected under the legislative conditions of the time regarding the unaltered property rights situation of state owned lands. What is also evident is that identity politics became more matter-of-fact, clearer, and more systematic by the beginning of the 1980s. Such representation was used on many occasions to legitimize giving the Sami access to planning and resource management.

Test Case for Global Rights Discourses: The Kessi-Dispute and Beyond

The conflict in Kessi was fought over logging in eastern Inari in the late 1980s. It was part of a series of Finnish disputes over forestry and conservation of the environment, which began in the 1970s with criticism of efficient forestry. Disputes were local, but they mobilized national actors, and some, for example in Kessi, mobilized international actors. Ideologically, the disputes marked the growing international, national and local scepticism of industrialization and modernisation, the motor of which was the wood industry in Finnish imagery. At the time of the dispute the environmentalist movement had become fragmented. The deep ecologists had entered the movement, and had defended the untouched forest-nature by using civil disobedience. In a not so radical language in environmental thinking, the idea of "sustainable development"–trying to connect concerns for the environment with economic growth, made environmentalism more accessible and popular in Finnish context. Institutions supporting the logging were the Forest and Park Service as well as some of the local community members of Inari who were concerned with employment. Those who were against the logging included members of the Sami community and the Sami Delegation, the local informal conservationist front as well as national environmentalist and conservationist organizations. On one level, the dispute was about the relationship between forestry and reindeer herding. On another level an issue taken up by the Sami delegation–which never dominated the public discussion–was landownership in the Sami home area. In addition, the Kessi

---

10 The archive of Sami Parliament, Inari, Statements/initiatives 1974-1986, Statements 1975-1980, Annual Report 1980, appendix, Quote in Saamelaisvaltuuskunnan lausunto Sisäasiain-ministeriölle valtakunnallisesti merkittävistä virkistyksen intressialueista, 3.10.1980.

dispute denotes the beginning of the still unresolved series of disputes between Sami reindeer herders and the Forest and Park Service (Heikkilä 2004, 139; Järvikoski 1991, 168; Pekurinen 1997, 56-63;Väliverronen 1996, 49).

The logging in Kessi was compensation for the Koilliskaira nature conservation project, which was disputed over in the 1970s and resulted in the establishment of the Urho Kekkonen National Park in 1982. The Forest and Park Service lost the battle in Koilliskaira, which made them determined to log in Kessi, as the area reserved for logging had diminished significantly in Inari because of the national park. An old Aanaar Sami settlement in the area was not particularly dense, but it was a pasture area for the mostly Skolt Sami herding cooperative of Vätsäri, which for example had a reindeer round-up area nearby (Nyyssönen 2005, 252-7).

There were three different strategies used by the Sami in the dispute. First, the official "Sami front"–the Sami Delegation–used a strategy based on rights claims and avoided the "natural people"-imagery in their self-representations. Second, the "Independents" practised more radical representations and points of departure. In these representations, the Sami were agents of sustainability under ecological exploitation facing a colonialist economy. The third strategy was to support the logging in order to secure possibilities for employment which was voiced most audibly by the Skolt Sami from the village of Nellim (Nyyssönen 2005, 258ff.).

In the dispute, the Sami Delegation was consistent in making their argumentation scientific while toning down the "natural people"-imagery. The Delegation referred to international covenants (article 27 on the International Covenant on Social and Political Rights), unsolved landownership and usage rights questions, studies on law, pasture ecology, and judicial and settlement history. The study most widely used was the doctoral thesis of Kaisa Korpijaakko-Labba, where the Sami landownership was verified with reference to 17th and 18th century court procedures. It was estimated that the Sami traditional livelihood and its sustainability had been lost under the process of "Finnicization." The Sami Delegation had no inhibitions about representing the Finnish forms of industrial land use as ecologically unsound, but they did not use references to a strong relationship to nature, or that the Sami had an identity forged by the wilderness. They also refrained from using references to indigenous peoples' traditional ecological knowledge (Nyyssönen 2005, 259ff.).

Was the global rights discourse legitimized in the national context? The Finnish Parliament expressed doubt as to the legal founding of state ownership of the lands, but this was exceptional. The Wilderness Committee (est. 1987) did not engage in solving the Sami landownership question. The chairman, Professor Martti Markkula, referred to the aim of "commonly acceptable suggestions" in the formulation of the committee's task, which was not likely to be achieved in the landownership matter. The committee concentrated on finding a balance between conservation and (obviously favoured) use of the established wilderness-areas. Great effort was made to account for sustainability of forestry, which is where there was the greatest tension, not on issues of the Sami.

The committee assigned to the Sami the status of indigenous people. They had a traditional livelihood, they were attached to nature and mostly practiced reindeer herding. Their judicial agency was constructed using the status of the old Lapp village-system and through reference to the emerging claim to their domicile. A statement by Pekka Aikio was included as an appendix in the committee report, which accounted for the recognition of Sami landownership and it repeated familiar legal statements from the Sami Delegation. In accordance with the committee, Aikio had to rely on the dominant imagery of wildernesses in the natural state, without roads, as a foundation for Sami culture and reindeer herding. The collective Sami identity was thus constructed through the Finnish definition of the wilderness! Sustaining the viability and productivity of the wilderness guaranteed the survival of the Sami culture, while stressing "productivity" left loop-holes for the possibility of other uses as well (Erämaakomitean mietintö 1988:39, 12ff.).

The freedom to manoeuvre was greater in the identity politics pursued by the "Independents". The entire discourse was ecologized. The unofficial Sami statements mainly concentrated on the fate of their livelihood, based mostly on reindeer herding, which was viewed as a cornerstone for sustaining Sami language and culture. The Sami were indigenous people under ecological exploitation. The cultural and economic sphere of the forest Sami had been changed into an area reserved for forestry. The district of Inari was logging on the lands formerly owned by the Sami *siidas*, which threatened ecological balance for decades to come. The Kessi-dispute was not only an economic and rights issue, it was also an environmental issue. The northern natural environment was exploited and the indigenous people faced colonialist economy and a way of thinking which was only possible to dismantle by allowing the Sami Delegation to enter into resource management.[11] The critique by the "Independents" was built with sharpened tools for identification (reindeer herding as a bearer of Sami culture), sharpened judicial reasoning (blaming colonization) and sharpened environmentalist reasoning (blaming the ecological colonization and questioning the rationale behind the western relationship with nature).

How was the ecologized self-imagery by the "Independents" met by other actors? The nature conservationist movement and the Sami had been cooperating from the early 1980s onwards. In Kessi, the nature conservationists drew a parallel between the conservation of Kessi as a wilderness and the survival of Sami culture and the future of their traditional livelihood (Pekurinen 1997, 58). The conservationists were supportive of the Sami claims, but by focusing

---

11 This chapter is based on articles from *Lapin Kansa* 1987, *Sámieana/Pohjoiskaira* 1987, and *Sápmelaš* 1978-1989.

on reindeer herding and hunting the conservationists did not fully succeed in building a shared imagery and only with the "Independents." The Sami were living closely connected to land and could only survive in relation to land. This imagery along with the ecological reputation of the Sami reindeer herders was strongly refuted by environmentalists. The most visible deep ecologist in Finland and in the Kessi-movement, Pentti Linkola, blamed the conservationists for romanticising when encountering the Sami who were "deprived by forestry." Consequently, the Sami were thus blamed for exhausting pastures with large herds, and accused of the same kind of despotism over nature as the Forest and Park service (Linkola 1988, 156-7).

The imagery of being close to nature is an example of a self-representation which was borrowed from dominant western discourses. The "primitive" features have long been viewed in western thinking as being of lower status than those of civilized, culture-nations, but the "primitive" had increased value in various anti-modernist and anti-industrial ideologies. The problem with such self-representation is that "modernizing" can be viewed by the majority as "unnatural" and fraudulent; the expectation is that indigenous people are the gentlest users of the environment, and modernizing goes against the romanticizing and stereotypical expectations of the majority. The "fraud" committed by the modernizing Sami becomes even more profound as nearly every form of land use is seen as misuse.

The breakthrough in environmental thought in Finland gave rise to the wilderness obtaining positive connotations, but mostly in relation to the intrinsic value of nature itself. The aggressive majority representations of the Sami as being hostile to their own environment have been viewed as an effort to cope with unfulfilled expectations and with the crisis of modernity itself, where old concepts do not correspond with the new fluidity of Sami identities (Kramvig 2002, 126; Lehtola 1999, 15-6; Schanche 2002, 156ff.; Torp 2001, 108-9). The trap hidden in essentialising imagery sprang in Finland. The new discourse was fatal for the Sami cause. The Kessi dispute, in contrast to the Alta dispute, appeared as a forestry dispute with the central dispute being employment versus forest ecology, which never fully evolved into a landownership or self-governance dispute. In Kessi, the Sami in Finland were not capable of the demonstration of power and unity that the three Sami organizations in Norway, NRL, NSR and the delegation of the Sami Council had when initiating the Committee for Sami Rights 1980 in the wake of the Alta dispute. There was not any re-evaluation of the state-Sami relationship as there had been in Norway (Berg 1997, 122-8; Eidheim 1992, 22). If viewed from the perspective of the state of Finland, the considerable issues of self-government (establishment of the Sami Delegation in 1973) and landownership (establishment of the state owned lands in the Forest Law 1883) were already resolved. The dispute ended in a compromise with the establishment of "Wilderness-areas," often interpreted as a defeat to the Sami because limited logging was still allowed in the region.

Conclusion

The Sami in Finland have not been able to harness the full extent of the empowering possibilities of globalization. One reason for this is the early institutionalization of the Sami movement, which bound the Sami movement to the national political frame. Due to this concession instead of using the global rights discource efficiently, the Sami were forced to try "politics of embarrassment" against national organs, which they themselves were part of and which were not receptive to radicalising demands. Goodwill towards the Sami cause on the part of the majority was eroding. The legal arguments were ignored just as the Sami Delegation had gotten their representational strategies together at the time of the Kessi dispute. As the "Independents" chose to ecologize the discourse, it was stripped of legitimacy in the Finnish public sphere. This was due to other global impulses, in particular to the environmentalist discourse that infiltrated Finnish society in a way that the Sami discourse never achieved.

The silent discourse of formal equality and citizenship became audible and remained dominant. In addition, policies of deliberate exclusion of indigenous issues can be highlighted, for example in the case of the Wilderness Committee. One consequence of the inclusiveness of the equality discourse is that it allows the state to view partial concessions as sufficient (Lawrence 2005). The third attempt to legislate the Sami Law[12] in the early 1990s was renounced by referring to the "sufficient" existing legislation (Tuulentie 2001, 130ff.), which concerned welfare measures, for example. The Sami institutions voice different legal discourses; international conventions and local customary usage rights are still relinquished by national law.

In addition to the discourse of citizenship/equality and environmentalism, the discourse of legalism deserves mention, rooted in the Finnish nation-building project of the 19th century and its bureaucratic stance. The discourse developed from the pressures of "Russification," where the rational policy, in order to secure the status of a nation was to stress the integrity of the existing law, rather than creating new laws. Legalism and stressing the need to obey existing law was reinforced in the independent state of Finland due to the violent rupture of the civil war of 1918. This discourse bound actors in the political procedures, argumentation and praxis in different ways. After institutionalization, the Sami have adopted, a professional, legal approach to claims and argumentation, but it is in this context that they meet the strongest resistance. In Finnish institu-

---

12 In vernacular thinking the Sami law, which has not yet come into existence in Finland, was meant to settle the land-ownership question in the Sami domicile. The two earlier attempts were made in connection to the Sami committees, which distributed reports in 1952 and in 1973.

tions, justice is built on existing legislation and legal tradition, not through common moral values. Even if Sami claims were to be taken more seriously and negotiated, the argumentation as well as the proof needed to make changes in legislation would need to be indisputable and scientific. In the Finnish context, this demand has backfired: *siida* ownership of their land could not be fully proven according to the statement made by the legal scholar, Juhani Wirilander. The basis for ratification of the ILO 169 weakened, as the question of the land and water rights remained unresolved (Nousiainen 1998, 24-25; Ruotsala 2002, 221; Stenius 2003, 348-9; Tuulentie 2001, 123; Wirilander 2001). This discourse and its rigid practical consequences constitute a major obstacle for the Sami land rights claim in Finland.

Regardless of the obstacles, some minor victories can be demonstrated. At best, the Parliament of Finland could recommend that the Sami be treated as indigenous people in claims and to pursue *equality in relation to other groups of citizens*.[13] The state of Finland has tried to continue its policy of partial concessions, particularly with regard to "soft" cultural issues. Cultural autonomy was granted to the Sami in 1995, which acknowledged them as a cultural community and claimant. The greatest victory has been the recognition of the status of indigenous people in the Finnish constitution, but this has not led to changes in the situation of landownership. The state of Finland clings to the current legislation securing landownership with the state.

References

Alasuutari, Pertti: Toinen tasavalta, Suomi 1946-1994. Tampere: Vastapaino, 1996.

Anttonen, Pertti J.: Introduction: Tradition and Political Identity. In Pertti J. Anttonen: *Making Europe in Nordic Contexts*. Jyväskylä: Gummerus, 1996.

Berg, Bård A.: Næring og kultur, Norske reindriftsamers Landsforbund 50 år (1947-1997). Karasjok: Davvi Girji OS, 1997.

Eidheim, Harald: Stages in the Development of Sami Selfhood. Working Paper no. 7 (1992), Dept. of Social Anthropology, University of Oslo.

Erämaakomitean mietintö 1988:39 (official publications).

Fowler, Roger: Power. In Teun A. von Dijk: *Handbook on Discourse Analysis, Vol. 4, Discourse Analysis in Society*. USA: Academic Press, 1980.

Hall, Stuart: Cultural Identity and Diaspora. In Jonathan Rutherford: *Identity, Community, Culture, Difference*. 2nd printing. Trowbridge: Lawrence and Wishart, 1998.

Hannikainen, Lauri: Position of Indigenous Peoples, Especially the Scandinavian Sámi, in Decision-Making Processes. In Manfred Lange: *Proceedings in the Arctic Opportunities Conference September 12-15, 1994, Rovaniemi, Finland*. Rovaniemi: Arctic Centre, University of Lapland, 1996.

Heikkilä, Lydia: Saami reindeer herding confronted with modern environmental management. In Lars Magne Andreassen: *Dieđut 5/2004, Samiske landskapsstudier, Rapport fra et arbeidsseminar*. Kautokeino: Sámi instituhta.

---

13 The archive of Sami Parliament, Inari, Annual report 1992, appendix, Asiantuntijalausunto HE:stä n:o 192 laiksi poronhoitolain 4 pykälän muuttamisesta, 12.10.1992.

Helander, Johannes: Suomen saamelaisväestö ja heidän elinkeinonsa. *Dieđut 2/1991*. Sami Instituhta.

Jernsletten, Regnor: Reindrift, samevenner og samisk etnopolitikk i Norden 1945-1975. In Bjørn-Petter Finstad et.al.: *Stat, religion and etnisitet, Rapport fra Skibotn-konferansen, 27.-29. mai 1996.*(eds). Tromsø: Senter for samiske studier, 1997.

Johnson, Troy R.: Roots of Contemporary Native American Activism. *American Indian Culture and Research Juornal*, 20:2, 1996.

Järvikoski, Timo: Ympäristöliike suomalaisessa politiikassa. In Ilmo Massa, Rauno Sairinen: *Ympäristökysymys, Ympäristöuhkien haaste yhteiskunnalle*. Helsinki: Gaudeamus, 1991.

Kahelin, Juhani: Marginaalisesta ympäristöpolitiikasta ekokulttuuriin. In Ilmo Massa, Rauno Sairinen: *Ympäristökysymys, Ympäristöuhkien haaste yhteiskunnalle*. Helsinki: Gaudeamus, 1991.

Kramvig, Britt: I kategorienes vold. In Harald Eidheim: *Samer og nordmenn, Temaer i jus, historie og sosialantropologi*. 2nd impression. Oslo: Cappelen akademisk forlag, 2002.

Lawrence, Rebecca: Sámi, citizenship and non-recognition in Sweden and the European Union. In Garth Cant et.al.: *Discourses and Silences: Indigenous peoples, Risks and Resistance*. Christchurch: Department of Geography, University of Canterbury, 2005.

Lehtola, Veli-Pekka: Aito lappalainen ei syö haarukalla ja veitsellä, Stereotypiat ja saamelainen kulttuurintutkimus. In Marja Tuominen et.al.: *Pohjoiset identiteetit ja mentaliteetit, osa 1, Outamaalta tunturiin*. Rovaniemi: University of Lapland/Kustannus-Puntsi, 1999.

Lehtola, Veli-Pekka: Saamelaisten parlamentti, Suomen saamelaisvaltuuskunta 1973-19995 ja Saamelaiskäräjät 1996-2003. Inari: Saamelaiskäräjät, 2005.

Levi, Jerome M. and Dean, Bartholomew: Introduction. In Bartholomew Dean and Jerome M. Levi: *At the Risk of Being Heard: Identity, Indigenous Rights and Postcolonial States*. Ann Arbor: University of Michican Press, 2002.

Lewis, Dave: Indigenous Right Claims in Welfare Capitalist Society: Recognition and Implementation, The Case of the Sami People in Norway, Sweden and Finland. Rovaniemi: Arctic Centre, University of Lapland, 1998.

Linkola, Pentti: Ihminen ja Kessi. In Tapio Osala: *Pohjoinen erämaa Kessi-Vätsäri*. Vaasa: O & G kustannus, 1988

Länsman, Anni-Siiri: Väärtisuhteet Lapin matkailussa, Kulttuurianalyysi suomalaisten ja saamelaisten kohtaamisesta. Inari: Kustannus-Puntsi, 2004.

Minde, Henry (Minde 2000a): Alkuperäiskansojen kansainväliset liikkeet: historiallinen näkökulma. In Irja Seurujärvi-Kari: *Beaivvi Mánát, Saamelaisten juuret ja nykyaika*. Helsinki: SKS, 2000.

Minde, Henry (Minde 2000b): Samesaken som ble en urfolkssak. *Ottar* 4/2000.

Minde, Henry: Mot rasediskrimering, for urfolksretter - to sider av samme sak? Et historisk perspektiv på samiske rettsspørsmål. In Harald Eidheim: *Samer og nordmenn, Temaer i jus, historie og sosialantropologi*. 2nd impression. Oslo: Cappelen akademisk forlag, 2002.

Minde, Henry: The Alta case: From the local to the global and back again. In Garth Cant et.al.: *Discourses and Silences: Indigenous peoples, Risks and Resistance*. Christchurch: Department of Geography, University of Canterbury, 2005.

Niezen, Ronald: Recognizing Indigenism: Canadian Unity and the Movement of Indigenous Peoples. *Comparative Studies in Society and History* 42(1), 2000.

Nousiainen, Jaakko: Suomen poliittinen järjestelmä. 10th revised impression. Helsinki: WSOY, 1998.

Nyseth, Torill, and Pedersen, Paul: Globalization from below: the revitalisation of a Coastal Sámi community in northern Norway as part of the global discourse in Indigenous identity. In Garth Cant et.al.: *Discourses and Silences, Indigenous Peoples, Risks and Resistance*. Christchurch: Department of Geography, University of Canterbury, 2005.

Nyyssönen, Jukka: Murtunut luja yhteisrintama, Inarin hoitoalue, saamelaiset ja metsäluonnon valloitus 1945-1982. Unpublished licentiate thesis, University of Jyväskylä, 2000.

Nyyssönen, Jukka: Mikä on ihminen suhteessa metsään? Tapaus Kessi identiteetti-poliittisena kiistana. In Heikki Roiko-Jokela: *Metsien pääomat*. Jyväskylä: Minerva Kustannus oy, 2005.

Nyyssönen, Jukka: "The use of Settlement history in Sami Identity Politics in Finland – From indigenous People to Landowners". In Lars Elenius: *The Use and Abuse of History in Barents Region I*. Luleå: Luleå University of Technology, 2006.

Paine, Robert: Norwegians and Saami: Nation-State and Fourth World. In Gerald L. Gold: *Minorities and Mother Country Imagery. Social and Economic Papers* No. 13, Institute of Social and Economic Research, Memorial University of Newfoundland, 1984.

Paltto, Kirsti: Saamelaiset. Helsinki: Tammi, 1973.

Pekurinen, Mika: Elämää metsässä ja metsästä, Metsäkonfliktien kahdet kasvot. In Heikki Roiko-Jokela: *Luonnon ehdoilla vai ihmisen arvoilla? Polemiikkia metsien suojelusta 1850-luvulta 1990-luvulle*. Jyväskylä: Atena, 1997.

Rannikko, Pertti: Ympäristökamppailujen aallot. In Ari Lehtinen et.al: *Pasilasta Vuotokselle, Ympäristökamppailujen uusi aalto*. Helsinki: Gaudeamus, 1994.

Ruotsala, Helena: Muuttuvat palkiset, Elo, työ ja ympäristö Kittilän Kyrön paliskunnassa ja Kuolan Luujärven poronhoitokollektiivissa vuosina 1930-1995. *Kansatieteellinen Arkisto 49*, 2002.

Schanche, Audhild: Meahchi - den samiske utmarka. In Svanhild Andersen: *Dieđut 1/2002: Samiske landskap og Agenda 21: kultur, næring, miljøvern og demokrati*. Kautokeino: Sámi Instituhtta.

Seurujärvi-Kari, Irja: Saamelaiset alkuperäiskansojen yhteisössä. In Ulla-Maija Kulonen et.al.: *Johdatus saamentutkimukseen*. Helsinki: SKS, 1994.

Sillanpää, Lennard: Political and Administrative Responses to Sami Self-determination, A Comparative Study of Public Administrations in Fennoscandia on the Issue of Sami Land Title as an Aboriginal Right. Helsinki: Commentationes Scientiarum Socialium 48, The Finnish Society of Sciences and Letters, 1994.

Stenius, Henrik: Kansalainen. In Matti Hyvärinen et.al.: *Käsitteet liikkeessä, Suomen poliittisen kulttuurin käsitehistoria*. Tampere: Vastapaino, 2003.

Thuen, Trond: Quest for Equity, Norway and the Saami challenge. St. John's, Newfoundland: ISER, 1995.

Torp, Eivind: "Rädda vargen - skjut en same". In Audhild Schanche: *Dieđut 2/2001, Naturressurser og miljøverdier i samiske områder: forvaltnings- og forskningsutfordringer*. Kautokeino: Sami Instituhta.

Tuulentie, Seija: Meidän vähemmistömme, Valtaväestön retoriikat saamelaisten oikeuksista käydyissä keskusteluissa. Helsinki: SKS, 2001.

Tuulentie, Seija: For and against the rights of the Sami people: The Argumentation of the Finnish Majority in the Debate on the Sami Rights. In Svein Jentoft, Henry Minde, Ragnar Nilsen: *Indigenous Peoples: Resource Management and Global Rights*. Delft: Eburon, 2003.

Väliverronen, Esa: Ympäristöuhkan anatomia, Tiede, mediat ja metsän sairaskertomus. Tampere: Vastapaino, 1996.

Weaver, Sally M.: Making Canadian Indian Policy: The Hidden Agenda 1968-1970. Toronto: University of Toronto Press, 1981.

Wirilander, Juhani: Lausunto maanomistusoloista ja niiden kehityksestä saamelaisten kotiseutualueella. 2001

Wirilander, Juhani: Lausunto maanomistusoloista ja niiden kehityksestä saamelaisten kotiseutualueella. 2001. <http://www.om.fi/uploads/0r7qisigbqn6t1.pdf> (accessed on 1 February.2004)..

CHAPTER 4

The Dynamic and Multifaceted Character of Pan-Mayanism in Guatemala

KAY WARREN

This chapter examines the dual urban and rural contexts in the development of the Pan-Maya movement in Guatemala, and the challenge that its multi-faceted politics presents to anthropologists who seek to represent indigenous opposi-tional politics. Since the early 1980s, the "culturalist" wing of the movement has sought to transform Guatemala's mono-cultural imaginary of the nation-state to a multicultural one that makes possible full citizenship without ethnic assimilation for indigenous Guatemalans.[1] The culturalist agenda targets violent racism on the part of non-indigenous Guatemalans as the root cause of inequal-ity. It advocates the expansion of indigenous rights, the recrafting of democratic participation to include indigenous voices and politics, and new imaginaries of self-governance and autonomy. By contrast, the "popular left" current of Pan-Mayanism channels its activism into a class analysis of economic exploita-tion and political repression in Guatemala and the global face of neoliberalism. The relation of these two currents of activism has been marked by moments of both heightened tension and rapprochement over political goals, tactics, and the place of non-indigenous Ladino activists in these movements. Anthropologists have long debated how to understand this complex political formation and rep-resent the social contexts that have incubated the quest for Maya cultural and political recognition. Scholars have sought to weigh the impact and efficacy of cultural rights, class-based, and liberal constructions of identity politics.

This analysis focuses on the dynamic character of Guatemala's Pan-Maya movement from its formative community and regionally focused period in the 1970s to the emergence of transregional movements in the 1980s and the inten-sification of national organizing in the late 1980s and mid-1990s during Gua-temala's peace process and its immediate aftermath. While this chapter places greater emphasis on the culturalist wing, the analysis systematically illustrates

---

1   My thanks to Henry Minde for the invitation to the highly stimulating Tromsø conference and the exemplary involvement of Maya activists and scholars on these panels. I am especially grateful for the feedback of George Lovell and Abigail Adams on earlier drafts of this chapter (see Warren 2005) and to Henry Minde for his insightful questions and encouragement to de-velop this longer engagement. With a collaborative commitment to making scholarly works widely accessible, Ellen Marie Jensen did an excellent job editing this chapter.

the mutual influence of the popular left and the culturalists. The chapter also discusses the passage of the 1995 indigenous rights accord, the 1999 referendum on indigenous rights, and the current Maya assessment of the peace accords' impact at its tenth anniversary in 2006.

At issue in analyzing Pan-Mayanism in its full diversity is how to portray its often clashing views of identity politics, injustice, and political strategies for social transformation. Most anthropologists now see the frontier between the Maya "culturalist" movement which supported cultural revitalization and the Ladino-Maya[2] "popular left" movement which supported labor and land struggles as a flexible boundary under constant negotiation. The extreme violence of the counterinsurgency war from the late 1970s through the 1980s, which endangered all activists, was central to the development of both currents of Pan-Mayanism. During this period, leftist rebels fought a revolutionary war in the predominately indigenous western highlands to overthrow the state, and the Guatemalan army responded by militarizing the countryside, invading rural communities, and engaging in genocidal violence to inhibit a wider uprising (CEH 1999).

The 1985 democratic transition marked the gradual opening of new political space, the opportunity for some leaders to return from exile, and the emergence of urban-based leadership. As the peace process regained momentum in the early 1990s, possibilities emerged for alliances across groups and consensus over a national agenda of rights issues that included the reframing and recognition of indigenous politics on the national level. The primary analytic goal of this chapter is to discuss the challenges of representing these dynamics–rather than reducing Maya activism to a single legitimate or authentic form of political engagement–over the complex decades of Central America's Cold War, peace process, and reconstruction.

---

2   In Guatemala, "Ladinos" see themselves as non-indigenous Guatemalans with special ties to urban national Hispanic culture, whereas indigenous Guatemalans are seen as the rural cultural offspring of a large linguistically diverse Maya culture and several much smaller minority cultures. See Charles Hale (2006), Carol Smith (1990), Demetrio Cojtí (1991, 1994), and Warren (2002b) for discussions of history, identity, and interethnic relations. In many rural communities in the western highland, these relations have generally involved ethnic hierarchy with cross-cutting economic stratification. For regional and comparative considerations of identity politics, see Watanabe and Fischer (2005). For other accounts of historical and intergenerational activism in Guatemalan communities, see Falla (2001), Lovell (1988), Carmack (1995), A. Adams (1999, 2002), Carleson (1997), Wilson (1995), Stoll (1993), Fischer (2001), McAllister (2003), and Manz (2004).

The Pan-Maya Movement's Dynamic Agenda for Social Change

Guatemala's Pan-Maya Movement[3] has offered alternative analyses of the sources of poverty and marginalization, different visions of a just society, and a variety of public intellectuals and activists. *Culturalistas* have sought to create a Maya *pueblo*[4], a unity of interests across Maya language groups with respect for their internal diversity. The culturalist political critique has advocated autonomy and self-determination to redress the social and economic discrimination faced by the Maya *pueblo*. This political project has emphasized collective cultural rights (including the official recognition of Maya languages, religious freedom, and school reform), political rights (such as the civil and political rights enjoyed by other citizens, freedom from racism, administrative self-determination, and the inclusion of Mayas in the government and all major social institutions), judicial reforms (such as the recognition of Maya customary law and the transformation of the court system so that Mayas have adequate legal representation), and land rights (including support to challenge those who have illegally acquired Maya lands).[5] One can see the "culturalist" movement as a vehicle for wider agenda of institutional, political, and economic issues. It is important to recognize that its agenda has been much wider than conventional understandings of "culture" but the term is often used as shorthand for this movement which has also focused on the revitalization of Maya culture and cosmology in local communities, the schools, and the media.[6]

For their part, Pan-Mayanism's *populares* have had a long history of focusing on land and labor issues with a class-analysis that importantly cross-cuts the Ladino-Maya divide.[7] Their strategy has been to organize local activist groups by economic class and sector rather than uniquely by cultural identity. They have a long history of protesting the exploitation and mistreatment of Guatemala's plantation laborers, pressing for land reform in a country where much of the land is controlled by a few powerful families, and denouncing government repression and the human rights abuses. During the Cold War, this movement supported the revolutionary vision of the rebel left and their goal of toppling the

---

3   On the Maya movement, see Bastos and Camus (1995, 1996, 2003), Esquit Choy and Gálvez Borrell (1997), Fischer and Brown (1996), and Fischer (1996).

4   Pueblo is a versatile Spanish word with a variety of meanings, including "community," "town," and "people."

5   For discussions of the details of these rights, see COMG (1991, 1995) and Saqb'ichil/ COPMAGUA (1995).

6   For culturalist literature, see Cojtí Cuxil (1987, 1991, 1994. 1995, 1996, 1997), Sam Colop (1983, 1991, 1992), Rodríquez Guaján (Raxché) (1989), Otzoy (1988, 1990), Tay Coyoy (1996), CECMA (1992), ALMG (1993), Instituto de Lingüística (1997), Pop Cal (1992), England and Elliot (1990), Montejo (2003, 2005), Fischer and Brown (1996), Rancancoj (1994), and Velásquez Nimatuj (2005a, 2005b).

7   See Bastos and Camus (1995, 1996, 2003), Manz (2004), McAlister (2003), Jonas (2000), Arias (1990,2007), Smith (1992), II Encuentro Continental (1991), and Menchú (1985).

state and establishing a new Marxist socialist order in the country.[8] Guatemala's counterinsurgency war ended after years of on-and-off negotiations in a UN brokered peace accord in 1996 (ASIES 1996) which demobilized the rebels and encouraged them to channel their activism into the political party system, human rights NGOs, and municipal politics.

As the war waned and the negotiations progressed, it became common for individual Maya leaders to move across the *popular/culturalista* divide. Many *culturalistas* admired the *populares* for their bravery in facing the violence of wartime Guatemala and organizing to meet people's needs through grassroots left organizations like CUC, CONAVIGUA, and GAM.[9] Maya *populares* who critiqued ethnic hierarchies and divisions of labor within their bi-ethnic organizations decided to form splinter groups (such as CONIC[10]) that directly promoted indigenous issues within the left. Others extended the critique of racism to the rebel forces. As a result, there came to be more room for maneuver under the umbrella of Pan-Mayanism.

The Peace Accords, specifically the 1995 Accord on Identity and Rights of Indigenous *Pueblos*, gave a wider public exposure to demands for Maya cultural, civil, and political rights (COMG 1991, 1995; Saqb'ichil/COPMAGUA 1995). The *Asamblea de Sociedad Civil* (ASC), which drew representatives from the *populares* and *culturalistas* in addition to other social sectors, became the key channel for civilian input into the peace process. With strong backing from the international community, the ASC successfully pressured the army and government on these issues. Regional autonomy and agrarian reform, however, did not receive as much attention in the final accords as many had hoped. Activists were aware, however, that the decisive language of the accords and the optimistic official time-line for articulating reforms badly underestimated the difficulty of constitutional reform, the ambivalent political will for change, and limited sources for funding the implementation of the accords. As we will see in the treatment of the 1999 referendum on the indigenous accords later in this chapter, the political parties were not really convinced of the merits of multicultural conceptions of Guatemalan society.

---

8 In the post-Cold War, this continues a critique of capitalism and neoliberalism. Of course beyond this schematic history of Pan-Mayanism is a more complex social and political history of the leadership. Today the meanings of these labels and the agendas pursued by different local groups and coalitions in community affairs are fabulously complex and variable, as Tim Smith has demonstrated in his studies of Sololá.

9 CUC stands for Comité de Unidad Campesina (Committee for Campesino Unity), CONAVIGUA for Coordinadora Nacional de Viudas de Guatemala (National Coordinator for Guatemalan Widows), and GAM for Grupo de Apoyo Mútuo (Mutual Support Group of the families of the disappeared).

10 CONIC stands for Coordinadora Nacional Indígena y Campesina (National Indigenous Campesino Coordination, a Maya-identified group with strong *popular* roots which focuses on land issues).

Histories of Political Activism in Rural Communities

So far, this account has focused on a history of inter-group involvements in the development of the Pan-Maya movement without considering the important role that rural indigenous activism played in the history of these communities. This issue has important implications for bottom-up understandings of the politicization of indigenous identity. In fact, the rural-urban axis of activism has been a crucial dimension in the development and the reception of transregional movements in the countryside. Anthropologists have contested each other's representations of rural leaders, the role of cultural versus material concerns in rural communities, and the connection between urban movements and rural communities.

This analysis argues that public intellectuals have a longer history in Maya communities than some anthropologists are willing to acknowledge. Carol Smith (2005), for example, associates "*non*-literate" with "*non*-intellectual" in rural indigenous towns. This construction acts to heighten differences between the interests of Pan-Maya intellectuals–who span the rural-urban divide–and Mayas living in rural communities. Such a framing sets the stage for descriptions of culturalist disengagement with the rural poor and the poor's alienation from "cultural" issues in general (Warren 2005). In contrast, one can argue that rural communities in the western highlands have a history of indigenous public intellectuals who were *seen by their communities* as gifted in alternative Maya ways of knowing and valued as important producers of knowledge and social criticism.[11] By recognizing this variety of leaders, anthropology helps challenge degrading stereotypes of Mayas conventionally propagated in the media and circulated in the wider society. In this context, I want to introduce ethnographic materials from my early research in San Andrés Semetabaj, a dominantly Kaqchikel-Maya county (*municipio*)[12] of 3,500 persons in the Department of Sololá where I did extended field work in 1970-72 with continuing visits in the late 1980s and 1990s (1978, 1998). While no one rural community can represent the whole, this history of generational change has important echoes in other parts of the highlands.[13]

---

11 Montejo is the Maya who has written most eloquently on the ties between local cosmology and Pan-Mayanism (2005).

12 I draw the San Andrés Semetabaj ethnography from Warren (1978, 1998, and 2002). Municipios are country-like administrative units in Guatemala, often with a market center and outlying hamlets and regional plantations.

13 Smith's (2005) emphasis on the differing economies of Maya communities is very much to the point on this issue. Moreover, there are interesting cross-cutting ties between communities with different economic bases. Totonicapán's Maya community, which overcame limited arable lands by developing a strong commercial and artisanal economy at the expense of regional Ladinos, sent some of its surplus population to communities along the routes of its traveling merchants. In fact, some indigenous migrants from this region settled in San Andrés and became Catholic Action activists and corn farmers. It is interesting that in both communities parents valued the education of their children so that they might represent their families in wider affairs.

In 1970, the elder generation in this *municipio* had little or no formal education; most, in fact, were illiterate. Some of the most respected traditionalist religious elders were landless illiterate day laborers. Neither the traditionalist *k'amöl b'ey* "knower of the way" who acted as a human archive of Maya ritual knowledge and cosmology, nor the *aj q'ij* diviner who used the Maya calendar to engage in shamanic ceremonies and healing rituals, needed to be literate (or speak Spanish) to do their cultural work. In the early 1970s, a highly respected elder that everyone turned to as the head (*cofrade*) of an important saint society was one of the poorest men in town. As many people explained, it was not particularly important that the public knew the details of Maya cosmology or ritual action but that someone who was respected did. Traditionalist public intellectuals were notables in this cultural world.

San Andrés represented wider trends in the 1970s highlands, including local activism in the cooperative movement, the emergence of Catholic Action with wider social agendas for transformative change, and struggles with local Ladinos over land and power in the local government–all before the Pan-Maya movement emerged. *Popular* movements were not as active here as in other areas of the highlands, although community members were certainly aware of class-based politics and groups like CUC had a presence in outlying hamlets.[14]

The first generation of a new wave of indigenous leaders emerged in the 1960s as priests trained young men to be Catholic Action catechists. In their early twenties, these day laborers with at best three years of schooling eagerly pursued every opportunity for non-formal education through the workshops offered by the Catholic Church. The importance of these opportunities is clear from the collections of workbooks that they still had years later.

Members of Catholic Action self-consciously pursued community activism to demonstrate their religious faith. Young leaders created new paths of local leadership. As parents, they sought school reform such as the abolition of school fees that kept poorer children out of public school. They were also major supporters of the agricultural cooperative movement because it gave poor farmers like themselves access to credits for fertilizer so they could increase yields on their micro-plots and aspire to be independent corn farmers instead of seasonal laborers on others' farms and coastal plantations. Finally, they challenged the system of onerous, unpaid service in the municipal government and traditionalist religious system, which channeled access to communal land.

Both the traditionalists and catechists were consulted by the wider community. All functioned as intellectuals in the sense that they interpreted the world for the community, engaged in social criticism, and kept important kinds of knowledge alive. Their tactics, however, were distinctive, with the traditional-

14 It is important to note that youths during the 1980s counterinsurgency years were well aware of the rebels' social and economic critiques.

ists working to create separate cultural spaces for the celebration of a sense of community distinctive from the ever-present bi-ethnic social life and work places where Ladinos dominated most public affairs. Within their separate space, Maya religious practice and belief articulated a moral critique of Ladino racism. By contrast, the young Catholic Action members criticized traditionalist ethnic separatism arguing, instead, for a tactic of local activism to confront social and economic discrimination in a variety of public settings. At this time, however, they did not make their claims in the discourse of rights.

There were moments of high tension between the traditionalists and catechists on religious and tactical grounds. Catholic Action preached against indigenous religion, processions, and the saint societies because they did not practice sacramentally oriented Catholicism or recognize the control of the official church authorities. Shamans faced a government crusade in the 1960s and 1970s that stigmatized them as witches (*brujos*), marginalizing them in the eyes of many, until the Pan-Maya revitalization movement called for a rethinking of Maya culture and cosmology. A deeper engagement with the localized history of indigenous activism in San Andrés Semetabaj reveals complex patterns of resistance, distinctive formations of religious leadership, and outside interventions in community affairs that attempted to undermine traditionalist leadership from a variety of directions.

In 1970 Guatemala, many highland *municipios* such as San Andrés offered only three years of elementary school and had no indigenous teachers. Rural poverty seemed intractable. Ladino elites owned the major stores in the municipal center and almost all large tracts of land, including the dairy, wheat, and corn farms that employed day laborers in the fields surrounding the municipal center. Most indigenous adults were laborers, domestic servants, and subsistence agriculturalists on mirco-plots of land. Many migrated seasonally to coastal plantations for a pittance in wages until chemical fertilizers were introduced to the community along with the agricultural cooperative in the late 1960s. Then more agriculturalists could make a living in their home region.

At that point, the formally recognized local government was dominated by Ladinos, with a non-official but well organized local hierarchy of indigenous officials that handled their community's affairs as long as they did not impinge on the other ethnic group or the national police and court system. Elite Ladinos monopolized jobs that required literacy, specialized training, and driving skills. Given this ethnic division of labor, adolescent boys had to pass as non-indigenous Ladinos away from home in urban centers like Guatemala City to find better jobs —something that frightened their elders who felt that it threatened the integrity of families and communities. Girls could leave the community to become indigenous maids in urban homes.

Catholic Action's diverse activities were not seen by the San Andrés community as "*popular*" tactics as this word was used in the early 1970s when it signaled a grassroots leftist involvement in plantation labor organizing or later when there were diversified *popular* causes involving solidarity with the rebels. Rather, community members saw this early activism as *religious* action that flowed from Catholic Action's commitment to equality in this world that mirrored the equality of souls in the spiritual world. The young catechists strongly believed that their actions in the community should reflect their religious beliefs.

I am not convinced that it is particularly useful to draw a fixed line between "cultural" and "material" agendas, and labeling material claims as uniquely "*popular*," as some observers have.[15] Clearly what some analysts might see as the "hybridity" of the young catechists' religious and economic goals was perceived by the catechists as a coherent set of religious activities in their community. That these catechists were unable to achieve their greater economic equality through the vision of equal access was an important lesson from their activism. They learned the limits of liberal individualism in the practice of their agrarian cooperative memberships in a situation where histories of discrimination and exploitation had left significant numbers of indigenous families without land and unable to take full advantage of the agricultural services offered by the cooperative. The failure of this political model to achieve parity between *ladinos* and *indígenas* in the community contributed to a growing openness to other political movements in the following years, especially among the youth.

As becomes evident from the ethnographic study of San Andrés, "the base" is a complex and dynamic entity, with histories of competing groups and their leadership, shifting sources of work, and a variety of local tactics for defining community needs and responding to outside interventions. It is important to note that Catholic Action did not spawn only liberal, anti-communist visions of religious action in the highlands. In some communities further to the north in the department of Quiché, for example, Catholic Action was appropriated by radical priests who advocated a more politicized reading of religious action, informed by the theology of liberation, which was used by *popular* groups that operated in solidarity with the rebels. Once again, one sees the multiple readings of religion and political action.

From Rural Communities to the Pan-Maya Movement
Given Guatemala's ethnic hierarchy, poverty, and the widespread political repression in the 1970s, it was hard to anticipate that growing numbers of Mayas–including some from San Andrés–who would become teachers or gain positions in regional and national government organizations and NGOs in the late 1980s and 1990s. In the mid-1980s and 1990s, a small but increasing number of

---

15 On the interplay of cultural and material issues, see Warren (1978). The argument I am evaluating here appears in Smith (2005).

Mayas originally from highland communities gained access to university training in education, linguistics, law, communications, history, and anthropology,
and contributed to the emerging field of Maya Studies through publications and
newspaper commentaries. These changes in a country of back-breaking poverty
and corrosive prejudice against the indigenous majority set the stage for a new
generation of indigenous leadership. Their voices added to the clamor for Maya
civil, political, and cultural rights in the 1980s and 1990s and to appeals for the
transformation of Guatemalan institutions and political culture to reflect the
"pluri-ethnic, multilingual, and multicultural" reality of the country so that all
Guatemalans might be represented in their society's basic institutions.[16] Activists were challenging the national *status quo* of ethnic relations among Mayas,
Ladinos, and the tiny stratum of Guatemalans of European descent that stand at
the apex of Guatemalan society.[17]

My ethnographic research on the culturalist movement on the national and
regional levels focused on the experience and media of activism and the difference that individual activists and the proliferation of new organizations made in
the early phases of the Pan-Maya movement in the mid to late 1980s (Warren
1998). At issue were the concerns that were debated behind closed doors and
the questions raised by young people in early consciousness-raising meetings.
The early culturalists were compelled by the profound effect of structural racism and discrimination in perpetuating the country's hierarchical ethnic division
of labor, and the impact of prejudice in shaping people's views of themselves.
Activists had to confront public views that indigenous people were inherently
inferior and lacked intelligence, modern culture, and fully developed language.
At issue for the movement was the internalization of these racist views by indigenous people. Activists explored the scars of racism in their communities
(see especially Sam Colop 1991, González 1992, and Cojtí Cuxil 1994, 1995).
In public, these activists pursued projects of cultural and historical recovery.

The emphasis on "cultural" issues for the culturalists of the Pan-Maya
movement had been a safer route for activism during Guatemala's genocidal
counterinsurgency violence. This was an echo of earlier generations that had
sought safe haven for their activism in religious groups–from the saint societies to groups like Catholic Action. Across these generations, leaders and com-

---

16 One of my goals in writing Indigenous Movements and Their Critics twenty years after the
    community study The Symbolism of Subordination was to describe the emergence of Guate-
    mala's multi-faceted indigenous movement with its complex local and national histories. Af-
    ter the dean of Maya activists, Demetrio Cojtí Cuxil, published the path breaking Ri Maya' pa
    Iximulew: El Movimiento Maya (en Guatemala) (1997a), I felt that I could publish my own
    anthropological study of the movement. Non-indigenous analyses of the movement include
    Bastos and Camus (1996, 1996, 2003), Hale (1994), Watanabe (1994, 1995), Wilson (1995),
    Nelson (1999), Fischer (2001), Fischer and Brown (1996), Smith (1991, 1992, 2005), and my
    own work.

17 See Casaús Arzú (1992) for this history.

munity members found the opportunity in unexpected places to imagine a just world with some measure of self-determination and a culturally grounded sense of moral worth. During the war, however, indigenous leadership and activism were targeted as subversive, kidnappings and assassinations were common, and many community leaders were forced into silence for their own survival. Ironically, the cooperative movement and Catholic Action were seen as threatening sources of rural leadership despite the fact they had been fostered by the U.S. government and its conservative Guatemalan allies in the Catholic Church and government to compete with militant leftists who were struggling for the hearts and minds of impoverished *campesinos*. In the anti-communist climate of the Cold War, many leaders were suspect, not just the armed rebels.

Culturalist activism spanned revitalization activities, education projects, and the quest for cultural, civil, and political rights through the country's peace process. In the 1980s and 1990s, a few culturalists tried their luck at seeking regional or national political office. Most saw the political party system through cynical eyes, noting that the rural population was courted during election campaigns only to be ignored after vote tallies. Bypassing the political party system, some culturalists sought public office through *comités cívicos*,[18] a strategy that Rigoberto Quemé Chay successfully pursued on the mayoral level for Quetzaltenango, Guatemala's second largest city. Others pursued local power by creating slates of candidates for municipal office that were more in tune with indigenous concerns.

Reflections on Education and Urban-Rural Relations
New educational opportunities have been critical for the development of the national Pan-Maya movement with its urban educated base of operations, hundreds of workshops for local and regional leaders throughout the country, and policy groups that meet with government officials on a range of issues. Beyond these activities and their active programs for elementary, secondary, and university studies, culturalists have been interested in disseminating their message to wider publics through newspapers, the radio, and general interest books in Maya Studies. Clearly social movements seeking greater equality need an educated leadership, so it should not be surprising that Pan-Mayanism would do the same and advocate for wider educational reforms in the process.

There are obviously important "power knowledge" issues at the interface of urban and rural communities. Just as we can see continuities in the old and new patterns of leadership and admire culturalist commitments to work in their home communities on the weekends in addition to their urban jobs during the week, it is important to recognize the power differences between these social worlds. Differences in financial support and institutional access, opportunities

---

18 Civic committees organize their own slates of candidates separate from the political party system.

to disseminate their message, and the advantages of a privileged position in urban society, despite its ambivalence about high-achieving Mayas, place urban activists in a powerful position to assert the authority of their vision of culture and change. These differences were intensified as international funders pressured Pan-Mayanists to create standardized representations of Maya culture in preparation for projects to promote Maya customary law as an alternative to the existing court system, which hears cases in Spanish and largely ignores Maya norms for dispute settlement. Such legal reforms would mark a profound recognition of Maya norms which differ procedurally as well as substantively from the national legal system (CECMA 1994). It would also benefit rural Mayas who cannot represent themselves in Spanish in the existing court system. Yet, one question regarding the state's standardizing of customary law as a formally recognized written legal system remains. What are the costs of a national system for the moral authority of local community leaders who had long operated with their own oral norms tied to the particular histories of their communities as expressed in their local dialects of indigenous languages?

There have been lines of resistance to the thought of growing powers for urban movements. There are predictable tensions between Pan-Mayanists' dream to forge a unified Maya *pueblo* to pursue a national agenda for change and local peoples' deep sense of loyalty to community, sacred space, local language, and their ancestors. Pan-Mayanism, itself, is diversified into many separate organizations by their own tactical design.[19] Interestingly enough, new national policies and the culturalists own programs for change have reinforced these counter-currents to urban power. Neoliberal policies of decentralization, mandated by the government in accordance with the demands of the international development community have given rural parents a new voice in monitoring public schools–which have long been notorious for high rates of teacher absence. Unfortunately, this has been an inadequately funded mandate for many communities.

It is also important to acknowledge community skepticism of groups that rural communities viewed as "external" whether they were religious, governmental, political, or social movements. San Andrés had a long history of involvement with all kinds of organizations. During peace time, the community was able to respond to these interventions largely on their own terms and with their own tactics. However, national organizations that sent outsiders to organize quick workshops and events–no matter what their politics or rhetoric–were often seen as distant and hard to fathom, even by community leaders. This reac-

---

19 This organizational form reflected the decentralized origin of these interest groups which focused on different issues in different communities. The tactic of independent organizing was used during the counterinsurgency war when centralized organizing or wider groups became magnets for state suppression. Culturalists had their own parables that spoke to the issue of not confronting enemies head on (see Warren 1998: 148-162).

tion jibes with the experience of more remote communities which saw culturalists, popular left activists, and human rights promoters as people from other
cultural worlds. These outsiders were well dressed, perhaps well meaning, and
certainly well connected, yet they spoke in terms that were difficult to really
comprehend. It was hard for locals to see these people as advocates.

Clearly the flows of power across the urban-rural interface and the complex history of Maya activism deserve serious ethnographic and historical study
rather than a structuralist analysis. One direction this study takes is to trace
diverse kinds of activism and counter-activism across the period of the indigenous rights accord in 1995 and the national referendum on indigenous rights
in 1999.

The Defeat of the National Referendum on Indigenous Rights and the Politics of Numbers

Guatemala's Peace Accords, negotiated though a United Nations brokered process to formally end the bloody civil war, brought together wartime protago-
nists–the government, army, and guerrillas–rather than civilian bodies. The one
exception was the ASC, a small body appointed after a grassroots uproar that
civilians had been left out of the peace process; however, the ASC had no formal power or ties to elected bodies in the government. Composed largely of
popular activists with a few culturalist representatives, it was able to lobby
for reforms including the special Indigenous Rights Accord issued in 1995.
The full Peace Accord document, which dealt with demilitarization, postwar
reconstruction, and democratization, was formally signed in 1996. It included
a timeline for reforms, yet it did not have the force of law for these aspirations.
Rather, accords were calls for further discussion, congressional legislation, and
constitutional reform. Agreement was needed in order to begin to operational-
ize reforms, and referendums or constitutional assemblies were needed to ratify
the move toward implementation. While the disarming of the guerrilla forces
occurred rapidly and successfully as a result of the Peace Accords, many other
reforms including those that dealt with democratization raised highly controversial issues–over and above the question as to how reforms would be funded.

Three years short after the celebration of the peace accords, a national referendum was scheduled on wide ranging reforms. In theory, this moment of
feedback from the wider public was designed to measure consensus for constitutional change, a key step toward the eventual implementation of the accords.
It was also seen as a barometer of citizen support for the implementation of the
peace process. In practice, however, the 1999 referendum was seen as a test of
public acceptance of ethnic-based rights as outlined in the 1995 Accord on Indigenous Rights. A "yes" vote, argued indigenous rights supporters, would re-
affirm the goal of widespread official recognition of indigenous identity in state
affairs. It would add momentum to the creation of a "pluri-ethnic, multilingual,

A flyer handed out in the streets of Quetzaltenango as part of the "dirty campaign" against the 1999 Referendum on Indigenous Rights

and multicultural" national society through the transformation of the dominant monocultural Hispanic construction of the nation in the schools, courts, congress, and government bureaucracies. It would affirm the legal recognition of indigenous groups and their cultures, the officialization of indigenous languages, the recognition of indigenous religion, culturally inflected educational reforms of the school system, wider indigenous representation at all levels of the government and the recognition of indigenous customary law. A "no" vote was seen by the opposition to the referendum as a rejection of the indigenous rights accord and its model for reformulating the nation-state.

The 53% to 47% national defeat of the referendum was seen as a devastating blow to the indigenous rights movement. Neither the popular left nor the culturalists were able to mobilize sufficient supporters in a country where

119

indigenous rights groups routinely argued that Mayas made up the majority of the population.[20] What did this vote tally actually measure? What are the politics behind these numbers in voting systems that are viewed by international policy makers to be the ultimate measure of democratic participation? What were the repercussions of this loss for the Pan-Maya movement, the government, the implementation of the peace accords, and international donors that had financed the indigenous rights agenda as the framework for an inclusive multi-cultural democracy?[21]

A strong case can be made that the referendum was structured by bureaucrats, national politicians, and key economic elites so that it would fail. First, the referendum was held in the summer, rather than along with the 1999 national elections, which virtually guaranteed a low turnout rate. In fact, a national average of only 18 percent of the registered voters went to polling sites, which for rural populations were located at municipal centers often at a substantial distance from their outlying homes and often impossible to reach for migrant laborers. Low voter turnouts are common for referendums in Guatemala. In fact, general election voting rates by department in the western highlands in the hotly contested presidential primaries held the same year were more than 30% higher than the referendum rates.

Second, the actual text of the referendum was agreed upon by contending political parties in the congress just two months before the vote through a strategy of "piling on" each interest group's choice of issues into what become four heterogeneous packets of articles. The result was a complex document in convoluted language that was difficult for even educated Guatemalans to fathom. Third, none of the political parties or their major political players came out in favor of the referendum during the short period before the vote. President Arzú's PAN party gave little support and prohibited government agencies from taking a position on the reforms; Ríos Montt's FRG opposed the referendum; and CACIF, which represents business elites, came out at the last minute supporting the "no" position (Ríos de Rodríguez 1999). Forth, there were very effective dirty campaigns to polarize and mobilize the urban electorates. Various groups were targeted to oppose the reforms as counter to their own personal interests. Advertisements and talk shows condemned "special rights" and cultivated fears of national fragmentation and violence if the referendum passed.

Playing by these rules, Maya congressional representatives, with support from the Maya umbrella organization COPMAGUA and leftist coalitions in the party system, pushed for a set of reforms dealing with "the national and social rights," including:

---

20 See Tzian (1994) on the politics of numbers.
21 See Warren (2002) for more information on the referendum including regional voting patterns, illiteracy rates, and outcomes by question of the referendum.

- The recognition of Guatemala as a multiethnic, multilingual, and pluricultural nation
- Access to sacred sites for Maya descendants
- Consultation with indigenous people concerning laws that would affect them
- State recognition of twenty-five indigenous languages
- Congressional formation of a language officialization committee[22]

Indigenous issues were predominately, though not exclusively, allocated to packet #1 in the referendum. Other unrelated issues were added to packet #1, including free health care, government employee compensation reform, and compulsory military or social service.

The referendum's three other packets included reforms for the "legislative branch," "executive branch," and "judicial branch." Voters had to vote "yes" or "no" to each color coded packet–which forced those who were literate in Spanish to decide what to do if they had different opinions on the 10-19 "articles" within a given packet. Illiteracy rates in the heavily Maya departments ranged from 26 % to 58 % of the population which meant that many voters could not read the text of the articles even if they spoke Spanish in addition to their indigenous language.

In many communities, there were no effective get-out-the-vote campaigns or organized transportation to the polls. In isolated rural areas there were reports of voters who wondered if casting ballots would be seen as support for the military or for the guerrillas. It was clear that voter outreach to explain the referendum never got off the ground in distant communities. Moreover, activists in Pan-Maya organizations reported that they found it impossible to vote their interests given their strong but conflicting judgments about different articles within each packet.

One might ask how packet #1 faired in the western highland departments with higher Maya populations. In fact, Mayas who decided to vote and made it to the polls tended to support indigenous rights. By my calculations, departments with over 40% indigenous inhabitants represented 38.1% of the nation's voters. These heavily indigenous departments produced a "yes" vote that ranged from 54% to 75 % of their voters, with the exception of Quetzaltenango, the country's second largest city, where the "yes" vote was 42 %. This outcome was very important to culturalist leaders who, in trying to make the best of the loss, noted that the voting patterns revealed "a truly Maya map of an indigenous nation within the nation."[23]

---

22 It is interesting to note that in the political process of prioritizing, the land issues from the Indigenous Accords disappeared from the referendum.

23 This regionalized support mirrors Richard Adams's observations (1996) that over

Ladinos were not won over by the project to include them in multicultural state building. The opposition to the referendum mounted a very effective dirty campaign of graffiti and leaflets in Quetzaltenango to cast reforms as a zero sum game in which Ladinos would lose by any change in the *status quo*. Different markets were targeted with different messages: evangelicals were told that the protection of Maya spirituality would promote paganism; urban Mayas were told they would be forced to speak indigenous languages even if they were monolingual Spanish speakers; Ladinos were told their children would be forced to dress in indigenous clothing and speak Maya languages or that Mayas would enjoy special rights at their expense. Poster graphics pictured Guatemala as becoming a dangerously fragmented country if the referendum won.

Estuardo Zapeta, a forceful and energetic independent culturalist with a pro-business line and conservative support for his daily radio show and frequent newspaper columns, ran a sophisticated campaign that took on the Pan-Maya agenda issue-by-issue. He argued that identity issues are, in effect, private social concerns not constitutional issues; cultural rights are "special rights," and the nationalist position on the referendum calls for the rejection of plural legal systems. He criticized foreign donors for intervening to "buy" Maya leaders and the national government by pouring funding into development projects on reforms, rights, democratization, and language policy–all for one ethnic community. Zapeta's arguments for national unification were cleverly designed to undercut the power of Maya culturalist experts, to take cultural issues out of the arena of public debate and national policy, and to privatize identity as a personal concern.

Zapeta's liberal agenda refused to see Maya politics as a collective endeavor or indigenous communities as a locus of rights. Rather, for him, the nation is rightfully a transcendent non-ethnic entity and haven for liberal individuals who should reject the foreign economic interests behind foreign donors' largess. This discourse stood diametrically opposed to the collective subjectivity of culturalist Pan-Mayanists who argue for the incommensurability of Maya and Ladino cultures, languages, and spirituality which serve as the basis for a federalist and collective solution to injustice and racism.

One can see the defeat of the referendum as a failure of the Pan-Mayanists to mobilize voters around indigenous rights issues connected to their daily lives and a failure to get out the vote in May 1999.[24] Yet the defeat was also the re-

the 20th Century, departments in Guatemala with higher Maya populations have become increasingly indigenous while other departments have lost Maya-identified populations with the assimilation of younger generations into the national Ladino "mainstream."

24 This is not to say that the Pan-Maya movement was detached from electoral politics. In fact, major Maya organizations routinely had election forums, see CEDIM (1992), and published studies on the flaws of Guatemala's ethnically stratified political system (see de Pax 1993).

sult of political strategies by the government and economic elites. They short circuited the power of the peace process and undercut democratic participation by creating a referendum where the choices were unclear and confusing. Their time frame limited opportunities for voter education to advocate for the legitimate role of identity issues in democratic politics and citizenship. In this case, the savvy dirty campaign in Quetzaltenango and Zapeta's clever use of the media in Guatemala City made for effective counterpunches to Pan-Mayanist attempts to promote the transparent good of cultural rights and the benefits of collective recognition, anti-racism activism, and self-determination.

While the defeat provoked post-mortems and reevaluation of activist strategies, what is most fascinating is the way that Pan-Maya leaders responded by accepting invitations to join political parties that needed Maya leaders to fill out their slates for government appointments. In what they judged to be a risky but important experiment, culturalist leaders, such as Demetrio Cojtí Cuxil, Demetrio Rodríguez Guaján, Otilia Lux de Cotí, and Miguel Angel Velasco Bitzol among others decided to work in the system after 1999.[25] Prominent culturalists joined popular left leaders from older grassroots organizations with a longer history of working within the system in congress.

Culturalist leaders who accepted appointments in conservative parties, especially those whose leadership was tied to counterinsurgency governments during the war, knew they were taking a highly controversial step. In spite of their goal of expanding Maya political representation and gaining political power to pressure the state from within for wider Maya goals, these leaders often faced harsh criticism and charges of having sold out. This collaboration with the state tapped a profound Maya disenchantment with national governments that marginalized indigenous concerns despite their promises, and inevitably descended into patterns of pervasive corruption (Montejo 2002, 2005). Some culturalists felt like social pariahs after their adopted party lost power and another took its place. One can argue that these political parties, none of which had progressive track records on indigenous issues, used Pan-Maya leaders for their own ends. The question continues to be how Mayas could respond to international pressure that democratic participation means more than social movement activism, that the real measure of power is party politics. How might there be more options for indigenous leaders in the future. In today's politics, the struggle has become intense to keep indigenous issues on the national agenda when there are many other pressing issues such as the assassination of candidates running for office during this year's elections and the widespread violence and corruption brought with Guatemala's current status as a key drug trans-shipment point between Colombia and the U.S. and European markets.

---

25 For some, this was the first time they had worked in the party system; others had served primarily in educational positions or on Guatemala's Truth Commission. This time, however, the decision was seen as a particularly charged one.

Conclusions

There are complex patterns of politicization and depoliticization in this history of identity politics. James Ferguson's work (1994) is useful here. He characterizes "depoliticization" as taking issues outside the realm of public debate and decision-making. In the case of international development, he examines this process by bureaucratic means, although one could imagine other arenas in which this process would play out. It is clear that the Pan-Maya movement has *re*politicized many issues–cultural difference, conventional forms of social hierarchy, and inequality; diversities in plain view that challenge Guatemala's self-perception as a monocultural contemporary society. These issues had been off the screen in public debate before the culturalist movement went public in the late 1980s.

The culturalists have done this at a cost, given the power differentials between rural and urban social worlds and the contrast between Pan-Maya salaries and the greater vagaries of rural incomes. One can see "power knowledge" issues in the movement's role as an authenticator of Maya language and culture, the risk of Pan-Mayanism displacing elders who have their own local knowledge, and the privileged access to social positions and resources that the urban base maintains. The question is what does the culturalist movement give back to rural communities and can it find coalitional opportunities with other Pan-Mayanists to reach more of the rural poor?

It no longer makes sense to see those who live in the countryside far from urban centers as the uniquely authentic Mayas. Pan-Mayanism has made the case that there are many ways of being Maya in order to free their identity from the racist equation of "indigenous" with inferiority. Abigail Adams, in personal communication, describes vibrant culturalist practices in the region of Alta Verapaz. Maya leaders have occupied a range of posts in President Berger's ministries and regional state bureaucracies. There was, in fact, substantial interest in running for office in the 2007 elections. A new generation of teachers, young married couples, and parents are active in Maya spiritual events. Urban women are now taking on leadership positions in Maya organizations, and university students are writing their theses on topics like Maya spirituality and community mental health issues. The legitimacy of Maya spirituality with its deep connection to the land is publicly recognized in towns, schools, and Catholic and Protestant ceremonies. Here one sees how culturalist activism–both secular and spiritual–has developed deep regional roots and a new generation of practitioners across rural and urban spaces.

In this chapter, I have tried to accomplish a careful if partial reading of the politics of the Pan-Maya movement and its production of culture, social criticism, and new social organizations over a critical period in its development and in Guatemala's history. One could write companion studies to this one which would focus on the *popular* wing of the movement and show how rural Mayas across generations in other parts of the highlands see the dynamics of their communities and their social, economic, and cultural concerns. Engaged researchers stand to benefit a great deal from reading across the different urban and rural views of Maya politics and their patterns of politicizing and depoliticizing issues. Scholars like Velásquez Nimatuj (2005b) have written a new generation of studies that deal with the politics of inequality in the countryside, tensions and subdivisions among elites and impoverished Maya populations, and current popular Maya struggles.

From my analysis in this chapter, one would judge the culturalist movement as successful in attracting international support and helping to transform the terms in which cultural diversity and rights are debated nationally. Maya schools offer innovative classes and subsidized meals for rural children and evening courses for adults. The movement has generated professionals in a range of new fields breaking through the conventional ethnic division of labor. Just as *popular* groups were pressured by their Maya members to be more responsive to indigenous issues and the previously unexamined hierarchies of authority in their bi-ethnic groups, culturalists confronted the fact that the racism of some Ladinos was fueled by corrosive poverty that cross-cuts the ethnic divide. As a result, Pan-Mayanism has become a broader umbrella for Guatemala, with members who have learned to practice more coalitional politics than in the early days.

Clearly Pan-Mayanism is now facing daunting challenges: How will the movement adapt to changing circumstances, such as the trailing off of international support as donors move on from the post-war reconstruction in Central America to international crises in Africa and the Middle East? How will it successfully attract young Mayas from another historical generation of activism with deep commitments to *popular* political and economic issues? How will it appeal to youths with more materialist values? How will Pan-Mayanists deal with growing income gaps and the persistent poverty of the countryside? Will the culturalists find more effective ways to work within the national government? What are the possibilities for new coalitional politics that overcome some of the limitations of the culturalist framing of politics? These are open questions for *culturalistas* and *populares* alike.

On the class issue, Pan-Mayanism itself has been part of a complex process of rural and urban middle class transformation that began in the 1970s and was further consolidated across Guatemala's democratic opening and the peace process.[26] There has been increasing Maya access to high school and university study. Mayas have gained new jobs in teaching at all levels, in state bureaucracies, in development projects for international NGOs and multi-lat-

---

26 One might also add the remittance economy generated by the country's political and economic refugees who now work in other countries, although I do not take on this issue in my work.

eral groups, and in Maya rights organizations. I have argued that this mobility has resulted in the growth of *parallel* middle classes due to the corrosive racism that previously forced Guatemalans of Maya descent to pass as Ladinos if they sought better work in the nation's capital.[27] Pan-Mayanists have created another strategy–one of actively revitalizing their indigenous identity and fighting for their rights as Mayas–to violate the old grammar of ethnic hierarchy. Not surprisingly, there are new tensions and debates with these transformations in the context of economic uncertainty and growing income gaps.[28]

One issue that is clear from the Pan-Maya assessment of the Indigenous Accord on its tenth anniversary is that, rather than abandoning the state, the movement is appropriating a more sophisticated empirically based analysis of the government's inner workings (Cojtí Cuxil, Son Chonay, and Rodríguez Guaján 2007). In some ways, Pan-Maya leaders have used their recent engagement with the state as participant-observer research which they have extended through a series of studies with indigenous and non-indigenous collaborators to measure the human cost of discrimination, racism, and intolerance. They have developed new tactics to hold the state accountable for the aftermath of the defeat of the referendum.

The Cojtí Cuxil, Son Chonay, and Rodríguez Guaján analysis (2007) focuses on the ways that the Guatemalan state responded to international pressures to keep momentum going on indigenous rights with the defeat of the 1999 referendum and consequent failure to achieve constitutional reforms. These Pan-Mayanists note that over time the Guatemalan state has developed a wide range of legislative decrees and governmental and ministerial agreements dealing with such issues as the elimination of ethnic and gender discrimination in the schools, language recognition, and indigenous rights. Although these decrees and agreements may not have the force of constitutional reforms, they have been commonly created with references to international law.[29] The emergence of this normative paradigm across separate decrees and agreements is an important achievement from the movement's point of view.

---

27 It is striking that some American and European anthropologists continue to be so ambivalent about the issue of economic mobility across generations in countries with frightening economic gaps and entrenched structural violence. Viewed across the four generations in the Maya families I know, this mobility has been an achievement of great family pride. It has been built on the desire to superarse (to get ahead) that was often the topic of family discussions as poor parents struggled to save small amounts of money to keep their children in school in the 1970s.

28 One tension has come from urban Ladinos who, during the peace economy, found themselves competing for jobs with Mayas whose language expertise had suddenly become a key form of cultural capital. Another tension, according to Victor Montejo (2005), is the upwardly mobile Maya preoccupation with being *nivelado* (catching up and being even) with Ladino professionals in the world of material status markers.

29 For instance to Convention 169 of the ILO.

Yet everyone recognizes that there have been very weak efforts to implement reforms. The Pan-Maya response that Cojtí Cuxil, Son Chonay, and Rodríguez Guaján advocate (2007) has been to study the gaps between Ladino and indigenous *pueblos* in rates of malnutrition, years of schooling, earnings, and other quality of life issues–all with a concern for gender and age differences. Then the magnifying glass is turned on the government to reveal the institutional reasons why existing policies to address inequality are often not implemented. Pan-Maya critiques include an exposé of the "most notorious deficiencies" on the part of the government to implement the spirit of the Indigenous Accords. For example, a governmental accord to enhance primary education by establishing new bilingual schools and training bilingual teachers was signed in 2005. The question is how much of this plan was actually carried out since only 5.7% of the national education budget went to indigenous areas of the country in that year. The increased allocation in the 2006 national budget for extra payments to 13,512 bilingual educators never reached its goal. A good part of this funding was diverted to the renovation of Guatemala's international airport. At the root of some of these problems is the bureaucratic tension between the Ministry of Education and the Consultative Commission for Educational Reform (Cojtí, Son, and Rodríguez 2007: 50-59).

Through their analysis one sees how in the field of education national policies are in tension with the indigenous paradigm with its emphasis on bilingual intercultural education. The organization of the state into departments bureaucratically complicates policy implementation because regional indigenous language distribution is not congruent with the territorial subdivisions of the state. Competing government entities that deal with education have led to aborted reforms for creating bilingual intercultural schools and training new staff, paying bilingual teachers incentives for their added duties, and adequately staffing the national DIGEBI office, which is in charge of education and language issues on the primary and secondary levels, so it can deal with bilingual programming in the nine major languages (including eight of the largest indigenous linguistic communities and Spanish). In addition, the analysis is candid about cases, such as plans for creating a Maya university, in which indigenous groups were unable to coordinate their efforts contributing to the project's lack of success (Cojtí, Son, and Rodríguez 2007: 61-62).

What is most notable, the Pan-Maya authors observe, is that most of the government's efforts on indigenous rights have produced additional governmental entities with few resources that actually meet the needs of the indigenous *pueblo*. Indigenous participation in Guatemala's elite-driven state has not grown substantially. At the celebration of the first decade of the Indigenous Rights Accord, the pressing issue has become options beyond monocultural liberalism for Guatemala. These Pan-Maya leaders, including Son Chonay, a young activist who interweaves culturalist and popular issues in her work, have several suggestions. One would be to look for ways to bring national and international anti-discrimination court cases. Another would be to find new alliances with non-indigenous sectors that are democratic and multicultural. And the third solution, advocated by Cojtí Cuxil, would be to create a federalist state that makes room for increased decentralization along with self-governance that includes the protection of minorities. This Multicultural State would incorporate collective rights, the possibility of multiple nations within the state, and indigenous political parties on the regional level (Cojtí, Son, and Rodríguez 2007: 80-83, 89-92,181).[30] These options represent the current Pan-Maya replies to Zapeta's advocacy of the liberal state in which cultural identity becomes a private social issue. One sees in these paths for activism a concern not just with the recognition of indigenous rights but also with the appropriate institutional bases to realize them.

If one looks at indigenous movements in Latin American as a whole, it is clear that activists are quite astute in appraising and responding to the shifting sands of national and transnational politics and the media (see Warren and Jackson 2002; Jackson and Warren 2005). One only has to follow the recent history including the rise of the Evo Morales presidency and struggles over national energy policy in Bolivia after years when most activism was focused on intercultural education and school reform to see important new issues that are clamoring for attention on indigenous agendas in the Americas. Or one can follow attempts by Hugo Chávez in Venezuela to create a new Pan-Latin Americanism. The options for activism at this historical moment seem to multiply, though it is telling that many currents of political innovation are focusing on creating a new Latin American left. One wonders how Pan-Mayanism in its diversity will negotiate the boundaries of this newly emerging period of transnational political activism.

References

Adams, Abigail. 1999 "World, Work, and Worship: Engendering Evangelical Culture Between Highland Guatemala and the United States." Unpublished Ph.D. Dissertation, Department of Anthropology, University of Virginia.

Adams, Abigail. 2001 "The Transformation of the Tzuultaq'a: Jorge Ubico, Protestants and Other Verapaz Maya at the Crossroads of Community, National and Transnational Interests," *Journal of Latin American Anthropology*, a special edited volume.

Arias, Arturo. 1990 "Changing Indian Identity: Guatemala's Violent Transition to Modernity," In, Carol Smith, ed., *Guatemalan Indians and the State, 1540-1988*. Austin: University of Texas Press, 230-57.

Arias, Arturo. 2007 "The Maya Movement, Postcolonialism and Cultural Agency." *Journal of Latin American Cultural Studies* 15 (No. 2, August): 251-262.

---

30 The multicultural state as a federalist formation is a political model that Cojtí Cuxil has been refining for more than fifteen years (1991, 1994, 1995, and 2005).

ASIES (Asociación de Investigación y Estudios Sociales). 1996. Acuerdo de Paz Firme y Duradera: Acuerdo sobre Cronograma para la Implementación, Cumplimiento, y Verificación de los Acuerdos de Paz. Guatemala: ASIES.

Bastos, Santiago and Manuela Camus. 1995 *Abriendo Caminos; Las Organizaciones Mayas desde el Nobel hasta el Acuerdo de Derechos Indígenas*. Guatemala: FLACSO.

Bastos, Santiago and Manuela Camus. 1996 *Quebrando el Silencio; Organizaciones del Pueblo Maya y sus Demandas*. Guatemala: FLACSO.

Bastos, Santiago y Manuela Camus. 2003 *Entre el Mecapal y el Cielo; Desarrollo del Movimiento Maya en Guatemala*. Guatemala: Flacso and Cholsamaj.

Carlsen, Robert S. 1997 *The War for the Heart and Soul of a Highland Maya Town*. Austin: University of Texas Press.

Carmack, Robert. 1995 *Rebels of Highland Guatemala: the Quiche-Mayas of Momostenango*. Norman: University of Oklahoma.

Casaus Arzú, Marta Elena. 1992 *Guatemala: Linaje y Racismo*. San José: FLACSO.

CEDIM (Centro de Docmentación e Investigación Maya). 1992 *Foro del Pueblo Maya y los Candidatos a la Presidencia de Guatemala*. Guatemala: Editorial Cholsamaj.

CECMA (Centro de Estudios de la Cultura Maya). 1994 *Derecho Indígena; Sistema Jurídico de los Pueblos Originarios de América*. Guatemala: Serivprensa Centroamericana.

Cojtí Cuxil, Demetrio. 1987 "La Educación Bilingüe: Mecanismo para la Uniformidad o para el Pluralismo Lingüístico?" *Boletín de Lingüística* Year 1, No. 5, August.

Cojtí Cuxil, Demetrio. 1991 *Configuración del Pensamiento Político del Pueblo Maya*. Quetzaltenango, Guatemala: Asociación de Escritores Mayances de Guatemala.

Cojtí Cuxil, Demetrio. 1994 *Políticas. para la Reivindicación de los Mayas de Hoy*. Guatemala: Editorial Cholsamaj.

Cojtí Cuxil, Demetrio. 1995 *Ub'aniik Ri Una'ooj Uchomab'aal Ri Maya' Tinamit; Confirguración del Pensamiento Político del Pueblo Maya*. 2da. Parte. Guatemala: Seminario Permanente de Estudios Mayas and Editorial Cholsamaj.

Cojtí Cuxil, Demetrio. 1996 "The Politics of Mayan Revindication", in, Edward Fischer and R. McKenna Brown, eds., *Mayan Cultural Activism in Guatemala*. Austin: University of Texas Press, 19-50.

Cojtí Cuxil, Demetrio. 1997 *Ri Maya' Moloj pa Iximulew; El Movimiento Maya (en Guatemala)*. Guatemala: Editorial Cholsamaj.

Cojtí, Waq'i Q'anil Demetrio, Ixtu'ulu Elsa Son Chonay, and Raxche' Rodriguez Guaján. 2007 *Ri K'ak'a' runuk'ik ri Saqamaq' Nuevas Perspectivas para la Construcción del Estado Multinacional: Propuestas para superar el incuplmiento del Acuerdo sobre Identidad y Derechos de los Pueblos Indígenas*.

COMG (Consejo de Organizaciones Mayas de Guatemala). 1991 "Derechos Específicos del Pueblo Maya; Rujunamil Ri Mayab' Amaq'." Guatemala: Editorial Cholsamaj.

COMG (Consejo de Organizaciones Mayas de Guatemala). 1995 *Construyendo un Futuro para Nuestro Pasado; Derechos del Pueblo Maya y el Proceso de Paz*. Guatemala: Editorial Cholsamaj.

CEH (Comisión para el Esclarecimiento Histórico). 1999 *Guatemala: memoria de silencio*. Washington, D.C.: American Association for the Advancement of Science.

de Paz, Marco Antonio. 1993 *Maya' Amaaq' xuq Junamilaal; Pueblo Maya y Democracia*. Guatemala: Seminario Permanente de Estudios Mayas and Editorial Cholsamaj.

England, Nora C. and Stephen R. Elliot, eds. 1990 *Lecturas Sobre la Lingüística Maya*. Guatemala: Centro de Investicaciones Regionales de Mesoamérica.

Esquit Choy, Alberto, and Víctor Gálvez Borrell. 1997 *The Mayan Movement Today: Issues of Indigenous Culture and Development in Guatemala*. Guatemala City: FLACSO.

Falla, Ricardo. 2001 *Quiche Rebelde: Religious Conversion, Politics, and Ethnig Identity in Guatemala*. Austin: University of Texas Press.

Ferguson, James. 1994 *The Anti-Politics Machine: "Development," Depoliticization, and Bureaucratic Power in Lesotho*. Minneapolis: University of Minnesota Press.

Fischer, Edward. 2001 Cultural Logics and Global Economics: Maya Identity in Thought and Practice. Austin: University of Texas Press.

Fischer, Edward and R. McKenna Brown, eds. 1996 *Mayan Cultural Activism in Guatemala*. Austin: University of Texas Press.

González, Gaspar Pedro. 1992. *La Otra Cara*. Guatemala: Ministerio de Cultura y Deportes, Serie Miguel Angel Asturias.

Hale, Charles R. 1994 "Between Che Guevara and the Pachamama: Mestizos, Indians, and Identity Politics in the Anti-quincentenary Campaign." *Critique of Anthropology* 14(2): 9-39.

Hale, Charles R. 2006 *Más que un indio=More than an Indian: Racial Ambivalence and Neoliberal Multiculturalism in Guatemala*. Santa Fe: School of American Research Press.

Instituto de Lingüística, Universidad Rafael Landívar. 1997 *Primer Congreso de Estudios Mayas*. Guatemala: Editorial Cholsamaj.

Jackson, Jean and Kay Warren. 2005 "Indigenous Movements in Latin America, 1992-2004: Controversies, Ironies, New Directions." *Annual Review of Anthropology* 34: 549-573.

Jonas, Susanne. 2000. *Of Centaurs and Doves: Guatemala's Peace Process*. Boulder: Westview Press.

Lovell, W. George. 1988 "Surviving Conquest: The Maya of Guatemala in Historical Perspective." *Latin American Research Review* 23 (No. 2): 25-58.

Manz, Beatriz. 2004 *Paradise in Ashes: A Guatemalan Journey of Courage, Terror, and Hope*. Berkeley: University of California Press.

McAllister, Carlota. 2003 "Good People: Revolution, Community and Conciencia in a Maya-K'iche Village in Guatemala." Ph.D. Dissertation, Department of Anthropology, Johns Hopkins University.

Menchú, Rigoberta con Elizabeth Burgos, ed. 1985 *Me llamo Rigoberta Menchú y así me nació la conciencia*. Mexico: Siglo Veintiuno Editores.

Montejo, Victor. 2002 "The Multiplicity of Mayan Voices: Mayan Leadership and the Politics of Self-Representation." In, Kay Warren and Jean Jackson, eds., *Indigenous Movements, Self-Representation, and the State*. Austin: University of Texas Press, 123-148.

Montejo, Victor. 2005 *Maya Intellectual Renaissance: Identity, Representation, and Leadership*. Austin: University of Texas Press.

Nelson, Diane. 1999 *The Finger in the Wound: Ethnicity, Nation, and Gender in the Body Politic of Quincentennial Guatemala*. Berkeley: University of California Press.

Otzoy, Irma. 1988 "Identity and Higher Education Among Mayan Women." Unpublished M.A. Thesis, Department of Anthropology, University of Iowa.

Otzoy, Irma and Enrique Sam. 1990 "Identidad Etnica y Modernización Entre los Mayas de Guatemala." *Mesoamérica* 19 (June): 97-100.

Pop Caal, Antonio. 1992 *Li Juliisil Kirisyaanil ut li Minok ib'; Judeo Cristianismo y Colonización*. Guatemala: Seminario Permanente de Estudios Mayas and Editorial Cholsamaj.

Rancancoj A., Víctor. 1994 *Socioeconomía Maya Precolonial*. Guatemala: Editorial Cholsamaj.

Rodríguez Guaján, Demetrio [Raché]. 1989 *Cultura Maya y Políticas de Desarrollo*. Guatemala: Coordinadora Cakchiquel de Desarrollo Integral, Departamento de Investigaciones Culturales.

Sam Colop, Luis Enrique. 1991 "Jub'aqtun Omay Kuchum K'aslemal: Cinco Siglos de Encubrimiento." Seminario Permanente de Estudios Mayas, Cuaderno No. 1. Guatemala: Editorial Cholsamaj.

Sam Colop, Luis Enrique. 1983 "Hacia una Propuesta de Ley de Educación Bilingüe." Unpublished thesis for the Licenciatura en Ciencias Jurídicas y Sociales, Universidad Rafael Landívar, Guatemala, 1983.

Saqb'ichil/COPMAGUA, Coordinación de Organizaciones del Pueblo Maya de Guatemala. 1995 *Acuerdo sobre Identidad y Derechos de los Pueblos Indígenas*. Punto 3 del Acuerdo de Paz Firme y Duradera. Suscrito en la Ciudad de México por el Gobierno de la República de Guatemala y la Unidad Revolucionaria Nacional Guatemalteca. Guatemala: COPMAGUA.

II Encuentro Continental. 1991 *Documentos y Conclusiones*. Guatemala: Secretaria Operativa del Segundo Encuentro Continental.

Smith, Carol, ed. 1990 *Guatemalan Indians and the State: 1540-1988*. Austin: University of Texas Press.

Smith, Carol. 1991 "Mayan Nationalism." NACLA, *Report on the Americas* 25(3): 29-33.

Smith, Carol. 1992 "The Second 'Encuentro Continental.'" *Guatemala Scholars Network News*, April: 1-3.

Smith, Carol. 2005 "Acerca de los movimientos mayas en Guatemala." Guatemala: *Mesoamérica* 47 (enero-diciembre): 114-128.

Stoll, David. 1993 *Between Two Armies in the Ixil Towns of Guatemala*. New York: Columbia University Press.

Tay Coyoy, Alfredo. 1996 *Análisis de Situación de la Educación Maya en Guatemala*. Guatemala: Editorial Cholsamaj.

Tzian, Leopoldo. 1994 *Kajlab'aliil Maya'iib' Xuq Mu'siib': Ri Ub'antajiik Iximuleew; Mayas y Ladinos en Cifras: El Caso de Guatemala*. Guatemala: Editorial Cholsamaj.

Velásquez Nimatuj, Irma Alicia. 2005 "Entre el cuerpo y la sangre de Guatemala." Guatemala: *Mesoamérica* 47 (enero-diciembre): 105-113.

Velásquez Nimatuj, Irma Alicia. 2005b "Pueblos indígenas, estado, y lucha por tierra en Guatemala: Estrategias de sobrevivencia y neogociación ante la desigualdad globalizada." Unpublished Ph.D. Dissertation, Department of Anthropology. Austin: University of Texas.

Warren, Kay. 1978 *The Symbolism of Subordination: Indian Identity in a Guatemalan Town*. Austin: University of Texas Press.

Warren, Kay. 1998 *Indigenous Movements and Their Critics: Pan-Mayan Activism in Guatemala*. Princeton: Princeton University Press.

Warren, Kay. 2002a "Voting Against Indigenous Rights in Guatemala: Lessons from the 1999 Referendum." In, Kay B. Warren and Jean E. Jackson, eds., *Indigenous Movements, Self-Representation, and the State*. Austin: University of Texas Press, 2002, pp. 149-180.

Warren, Kay. 2005 "Los desafíos de representar los movimientos panmayas: respuesta a Carol Smith." Guatemala: *Mesoamérica* 47 (enero- diciembre): 139-150.

Warren, Kay and Jean Jackson. 2002 "Introduction: Studying Indigenous Activism in Latin America." In, Kay Warren and Jean Jackson, eds., *Indigenous Movements, Self-Representation, and the State*. Austin: University of Texas Press, 1-46.

Watanabe, John. 1994 "Unimagining the Maya: Anthropologists, Others, and the Inescapable Hubris of Authorship." *Bulletin of Latin American Research* 14(1): 25-45.

Watanabe, John. 1995 "Neither as They Imagined Nor as Others Intended: Mayas and Anthropologists in the Highlands of Guatemala since 1969." In, John Monaghan, ed., *Supplement to the Handbook of Middle American Indians*. Vol. 6. Austin: University of Texas Press.

Watanabe, John and Edward Fischer, eds. 2004 *Pluralizing Ethnography: Comparison and Representation in Maya Cultures, Histories, and Identities*. Santa Fe: School of American Research Press.

Wilson, Richard. 1995 *Mayan Resurgence in Guatemala: Q'echi' Experiences*. Norman: University of Oklahoma Press.

CHAPTER 5

Reconciliation and its Denunciation[1]

Henry Reynolds

The Sydney Bridge Walk 2000

We arrived early for the march across Sydney harbour Bridge on Saturday the 29th of May 2000. But as we walked up to the crest of the roadway we saw that in front of us the bridge was already densely packed with those who had gone before us. When we returned to the city-end of the bridge three hours later the marchers were still coming and they continued to stream across the roadway and down into the city until well into the afternoon. It was estimated that a quarter of a million people crossed the bridge that day in support of reconciliation between indigenous and settler Australians. It was one of the most significant political mobilizations in the country's history. The Sydney march was followed by comparable rallies in the major cities over the following weeks. Crowds were comparable even if the bridges were not. It was a euphoric moment for supporters of the cause. For a moment, it seemed as though anything was possible. Looking back five years later, prominent Aboriginal leader Jackie Huggins observed:

> The emotional triumphs of the bridge walks gave some people the sense that reconciliation had arrived. But the reality was that, significant as they were, the walks masked the harsh reality of a lot of what we call unfinished business.[2]

The enormous effort, the manifest goodwill–achieved so little. The great marches, it increasingly appears, marked the end of an era of reform, not the opening of a new one. But to understand the politics of race in Australia it is necessary to consider the reconciliation movement and where it had come from.

The Colonial Era

The Australian colonies gained control of Aboriginal policy in the middle of the 19th century in New South Wales, Victoria, Queensland, South Australia and Tasmania with the British Colonial Office maintaining that authority in Western Australia until 1897. Throughout the colonial era, individuals agitated against the treatment of the Aborigines. They were often missionaries, clergymen or

---

1   This chapter is based on lecture Henry Reynolds gave at the Center for Sami Studies, University of Tromsø 19 September 2006.
2   Reconciliation News, no.1, April 2005, p.1.

evangelically inspired laymen. They wrote letters, drafted petitions, delivered sermons and wrote to The Aborigines Protection Society in London seeking to exert pressure on the assorted Australian governments which in turn insisted that Aboriginal policy was a purely domestic matter. It remained in the hands of the states after the federation of the colonies in 1901.The new Commonwealth Government only became involved in 1912 when it took control of the Northern Territory from South Australia.

There was an upsurge of political activity in the 1920's stimulated in part by the ideas of trusteeship promoted by the League of Nations. At the same time, the Anti-Slavery Society in London took up the cause with renewed vigour. Australian governments suddenly became aware of the rapid growth of mixed race communities and were confronted with the realization that the comforting idea of a dying race was redundant. The 1920's and 1930's saw the first Aboriginal organizations which grew up in Perth, Melbourne and Sydney. After the Second World War the national government became directly involved in co-ordinating Aboriginal policy for the first time under the guidance of Paul Hasluck, a persistent and persuasive advocate of assimilation.

The Federal Council for Aborigines and Torres Strait Islanders

Hasluck's national policy advocacy stimulated the development of community organizations with a comparable continent-wide reach. The Federal Council for Aborigines and Torres Strait Islanders (FCAATSI) was founded in 1958 with one eye on national developments and the other on the expectation of being able to take their case to the United Nations which was showing increased interest in indigenous communities given the growing membership from Africa, Asia, the Caribbean and the Pacific.

FCAATSI began as a predominantly white reformist organization but it had Aboriginal members from its foundation and they became increasingly prominent during the 1960's. Faith Bandler, who became the best known advocate, was the daughter of a Malaitan recruited to work in the Queensland cane fields. FCAATSI agitated persistently for the removal of the remaining discriminatory laws, both federal and state, and for the recognition of traditional land rights, a cause also taken up by Aboriginal communities in the remote areas of North and Central Australia

But FCAATSI's great achievement was the campaign to change the federal constitution by the required means of a referendum. To begin with, it was necessary to persuade the conservative Liberal-Country party coalition to put the question to the people, and then to mount a long and highly successful campaign to win the support of a large majority of the electorate–an unusual event in the long history of failed referenda proposals. The two targeted clauses in the constitution did not in themselves seem all that important–one stipulated that Aborigines were not to be counted in the national census; the other effec-

134

tively prevented the federal government from legislating on Aboriginal matters. In practice the referendum result paved the way for an increasing role for the national government in Aboriginal affairs and symbolically intimated that Aborigines and Islanders were accepted as citizens with all the rights of white Australians although it took considerable legislative reform in both state and federal spheres to effect that goal in practice.

The success of FCAATSI was due to a number of factors. It was a co-operative enterprise bringing together both white and black activists. The leadership was able to deal persuasively with politicians and the public alike. Above all it conducted a precisely targeted campaign to bring about specific changes which were amenable to political action.

From the Northern Territory Land Rights Act to Reconciliation Movement

FCAATSI did not survive long after its successful campaign. It was overtaken by demands for Aboriginal control and then outflanked by the reforming Labor Party government of Gough Whitlam which came to power in 1972 and set in train a process which culminated in the Northern Territory Land Rights Act of 1976.

The prospects for further reform seemed propitious when the Labor party returned to power in Canberra in 1983 with commitments to national land rights legislation and the implementation of measures to achieve indigenous self-determination. The drive to achieve land rights soon faltered and was eventually abandoned in the face of opposition from State governments and a vociferous and well funded campaign by the mining industry. The Department of Aboriginal Affairs was transformed into the Aboriginal and Torres-Strait Islander Commission (ATSIC) with commissioners elected from regional electorates all over the country. ATSIC was given control of service delivery in health, housing, education and legal aid. But it remained an anomaly–part government department, part representative institution, and part political organization, all the while dependent on the goodwill and annual grants from the government.

Demands for a treaty between Aboriginal and Settler Australians were articulated during the 1970's and 1980's by both white and black activists. It was firmly, albeit briefly, impressed on the national political agenda when the Prime Minister R.J. Hawke accepted the so-called Barunga Statement at a cultural festival in the Northern Territory in June 1988 which included a demand that the Australian parliament 'Negotiate with us a Treaty or Compact recognizing our prior ownership, continued occupation and sovereignty and affirming our human rights and freedoms'.[3] Mr. Hawke's enthusiasm for the negotiation of a treaty soon waned once he had left the heady atmosphere of the festival.

---

3   Cited by Attwood & Marcus (eds.) 1999:317.

135

His activist Minister for Aboriginal Affairs, Robert Tickner, launched the idea of reconciliation late in 1990, and legislation to establish a Council for Reconciliation was passed in June 1991. The council of prominent Indigenous and Settler Australians was given the task of initiating a decade-long process of discussion, advocacy and education. Among the aims defined in the legislation were promotion of a deeper understanding of the history, past dispossession and continuing disadvantage of Indigenous Australians and to consult widely on whether a document or treaty would advance the cause of reconciliation.

The mass marches of 2000 were a fair indication of the widespread enthusiasm which had been generated by the movement. Less obvious, but equally impressive , was the work of many small, local Reconciliation Committees which sprang up all over the country–in urban and rural areas alike. They initiated local historical research and soul-searching about race relations in their own communities both in the past and the present. There is no doubt that the movement drew many people into the campaign who had never been involved before, certainly more than were part of the referendum crusade of 1965-67.

Why did it Fail?

But when viewed objectively, the Reconciliation movement failed to achieve much of lasting significance. The most important developments of the 1990's came from elsewhere–the land rights cases in the High Court–Mabo in 1992 and Wik in 1996, and the inquiry into the removal of Aboriginal children by the Human Rights Commission resulting in the best selling report: 'Bringing them Home'.

The length of the process presented serious problems. Cynical observers viewed it as a delaying tactic but it is fair to assume that Minister Tickner believed that a long period of debate and education was required. But the greatest difficulty was that the Labor Party government was defeated in 1996 half way through the decade and the in-coming conservative co-alition under J.W. Howard was antagonistic to many of the aspirations implicit in the movement. Conservative hostility increased with time, particularly after further electoral victories in 1999 and 2002.

While clearly feeling unable to directly repudiate reconciliation, members of the new government adopted a policy of what became known as 'practical reconciliation' with an emphasis on programmes directed to the most obvious areas of indigenous disadvantage. While welcome, these commitments had little to do with the core issues of reconciliation. In all other respects, the conservative co-alition has returned with obvious enthusiasm to the ideas of assimilation last so openly espoused in the 1950's.

The government gave no support to the idea of a treaty or 'document of reconciliation' and in its international dealings has strenuously opposed the idea of indigenous self-determination while generally expressing hostility to the

United Nations and any criticism from the Human Rights Commission.

Australia's growing conservatism owed much to international developments but also to the sudden and quite unexpected arrival of Pauline Hanson on the political stage. She entered federal politics in1996 winning a hitherto safe labor seat with a massive swing having been dis-endorsed by the Liberal party for racist remarks. Her maiden speech contained savage attacks on both Aborigines and migrants. Her instant popularity stunned the mainstream parties and the political commentators. At the Queensland elections in 1998, her party, now called One Nation, won a staggering 23% of the vote. It was enough to unsettle national politics and shatter the implicit, but extremely important, consensus on questions of race and migration. With over a million potential supporters the One Nation vote became an irresistible target for the conservative co-alition which moved quickly to the Right and began to promote policies which they had previously eschewed, adopting hard line attitudes towards both Aborigines and refugees.

Central to the Aboriginal engagement with Reconciliation was a desire to gain acceptance of their view of the nation's history, not with the intention of promoting guilt on the part of whites but to receive acknowledgment of their loss and suffering. This was the theme of innumerable speeches and comments made by indigenous spokesmen during the decade of Reconciliation. Prime-Minister Howard took particular and deeply personal offence at this view of the past–'Black-Arm Band History'–as it was called by a legion of conserva-tive commentators. He expressed a strong preference for a positive view of the past, declaring on many occasions that there was too much emphasis on past violence. He personally welcomed the emergence of a school of revisionist historians and especially the work of Keith Windschuttle whose controversial book 'The Fabrication of Aboriginal History' was published in 2002.

The Return to Policies of Assimilation and Re-assertion of Nationalism

The drive to return to policies of assimilation has picked up in the last few years. There has been a concerted attack on traditional law and a declaration that it should no longer be given any consideration by the courts, although the State and Territory governments–all currently in the hands of the Labor Party–have not responded to federal demands. The use of indigenous languages in education has been denounced by federal ministers as hampering Aboriginal advancement. The small outstations on traditional land have been condemned as anthropological museums or alternatively as small soviets and Ministers are currently threatening to cut off their funding. ATSIC and its regional councils were abolished in 2005 with few lamenting its passing as scandal enveloped se-nior office bearers. It has been replaced by a Consultative Committee appointed by the Prime Minister and whose deliberations are never made public.

Ranged behind all these developments is the strong re-assertion of nationalism, persistent attacks on the idea of multi-culturalism, anxiety about cultural difference, and the harsh treatment and incarceration of asylum seekers. Self-determination and treaty-making have virtually no support from the major political parties and have completely disappeared from the political agenda.

The Aboriginal Issues in Australian Politics

What of Aboriginal politics in this environment? Prominent individuals have absorbed much of the contemporary mood-looking to the private sector for assistance and calling into doubt the capacity of government to effect change, even eschewing politics itself and calling into doubt the value of what has become pejoratively termed "the human rights agenda'.

Aboriginal politics became, for a generation, almost totally dependent on government funding which circumscribed action and sapped the spirit of dissent. The struggle for land rights has been completely absorbed by the judicial process which gives the leading role to lawyers. There are still innumerable indigenous organizations confined to particular localities and focused on specific tasks. But there is no national indigenous political movement and seemingly no plans to establish one. If there is one clear lesson to be drawn from the current circumstances, it is that dependence on government may provide real benefits when it is sympathetic but there is nowhere to turn when the national political climate changes, as it did so dramatically in Australia in 1996.

At the same time, much of the media attention once given to indigenous politics is focused on the parlous condition of communities as they sink into despair, substance abuse and violence.

At the moment of writing this, the Labor Party opposition under the new leader Kevin Rudd has made a strong comeback in the polls. They will, if elected, return to some of the policies of the 1980's and early 1990's. They are committed to the re-introduction of an elected indigenous assembly. But Aboriginal issues have a much lower priority than they did when Labor was last in power and the new government would be very cautious about such issues as a treaty or agreement and would downplay any but the most pragmatic of reforms. Human rights activists will not find much encouragement in the immediate future. Many of them, no doubt, feel like Sisyphus and will have to prepare to recover lost ground before there can be any new achievements. But many Australians look forward to a renewed commitment to reconciliation.

References

Aboriginal and Torres Strait Islander Social Justice Commissioner: *Social Justice Report.* Published yearly from 1993. Webside: http://www.humanrights.gov.au

Attwood, B.: *Rights for Aborigines.* Sydney: Allan & Unwin, 2003.

Attwood, B. & A. Marcus (eds.): *The Struggle for Aboriginal Rights*, Allen & Unwin: Sydney, 1999 p.317.

Haebich, A.: "The Battlefields of Aboriginal History", in Martyn Lyons and Penny Russell: *Australia's History: themes & debates.* Sydney: UNSW Press, 2005.

Robbins, J.: "The Howard Government and Indigenous Rights: An Imposed National Unity?", in *Australian Journal of Political Science*, 2007:2, pp.315-328.

Russell, P. H.: *Recognizing Aboriginal Title: The Mabo Case and Indigenous Resistance to English-Settler Colonialism.* University of Toronto Press, 2005.

Weaver, S.: "Australian Aboriginal Policy: Aboriginal Pressure Groups or Government Advisory?", in *Oceania*, Part I, 1983:1, pp. 1-22, Part II, 1983:2, pp. 85-108.

Weaver, S.: "Self-Determination, National Pressure Groups, and Aborigines: The National Aboriginal Conference 1983-1985", in Michael D. Levin: *Ethnicity and Aboriginality: Case Studies in Ethnonationalism.* University of Toronto Press, 1993.

CHAPTER 6

After the Change
The Opposition against Indigenous Movements
in Hawai'i

ULF JOHANSSON DAHRE

The Indigenous Rights Revolution

Since the end of the 1960s indigenous peoples' movements have been salient factors on international and national political agendas. Indigenous peoples in Hawai'i and elsewhere have become increasingly politicised in the hope of changing their relationship with the states within which they live. The political arguments of indigenous peoples has been centred around the concept "First Nations" whose collective and inherent rights to self-determination were never extinguished, but prevail in international and national law as a basis for constitutional concessions, political self-determination or affirmative action. This claim has primarily been based on a historical perspective that addresses the special relationship indigenous peoples have with the state based on a unique set of entitlements acknowledged throughout political history.

In western countries, considerable energy has been spent among governments and parliaments in redefining indigenousness as a distinct social and political category with a corresponding set of characteristics and delegated powers deriving from the acknowledgement of their historically based status of being "nations within." Political observers called the changes in policy in the 1990s towards indigenous peoples in Western democracies "the silent revolutions" (Werther, 1992). However, in recent years the general recognition of indigenous claims in Western democracies have also ignited a strong current of critique and opposition that have led to considerable changes in political and legal attitudes, as well as in public opinion regarding constitutional and legal concessions for indigenous peoples. In the same way that dramatic pro-indigenous changes swept over Western democracies in the 1980s and 90s, the critique and opposition to indigenous movements are now sweeping across those same states.

The Opposition against the Indigenous Revolution

Why is the opposition against indigenous claims suddenly so strong, heated and explicit after a period of seemingly public and political tolerance, respect and legal concession? The case of the opposition against the Hawaiian sovereignty movement provides some clues. As indigenous peoples have been challenging the legitimate political power and control over resources in the islands, the issues of indigenous peoples were bound to meet resistance. There is much at stake, both politically and economically. In a public debate in Honolulu in 2005, the nature of the issues that led to confrontations between the Hawaiian sovereignty movement and the opposition became clear. Thurston Twigg-Smith, former editor of *The Honolulu Advertiser* and in the front of the opposition against the Hawaiian movement, pointed out the economic side of the opposition: "We are barely making it economically as a state. And if we divide into two competing governments, what will happen?" Another participant at the debate voiced his concerns over the control of resources and political power when he described the situation of indigenous rights and self-government as "…a great sucking vacuum that could take land and resources vital to the state's economy without the say of taxpayers" (*Honolulu Star-Bulletin*, July 18, 2005). The claims and rights of indigenous movements have become threats to states or, at least, they are perceived to be threats.

The opposition against indigenous claims can thus be found in the development of central political issues. Discussions and concessions between indigenous peoples and states since the 1960s have been focused around issues such as land rights, control of natural resources, intellectual property, and political self-determination. The claims of indigenous peoples have forced many states to rethink basic assumptions regarding individual and group rights and the basis of rights in political society. Democracies adopted policies that in a strict sense violated the liberal constitutions based on the principles of equality and individual rights. Indigenous movements during the 1980s and 90s, particularly in the West, with the aid of historically based arguments influenced considerable political changes in this constitutional doctrine. Individual human rights were part of the concessions, but more controversially, it was collective rights and self-determination that were central parts of the political agenda which for some time were more or less a question in many political arenas of how far states would go in granting self-determination to indigenous peoples. States such as Canada, New Zealand, Hawai'i and Norway are cases where the claims of indigenous movements led to the creation of new political relations and self-governing political institutions.

I studied the political change in Hawai'i in the 1990s (Johansson Dahre, 2001). The focus of the study was on how and why the changes in the state constitution, legislative concessions and policies came to be and what strategies the Native Hawaiian sovereignty movement used in that process. I argued that the changes in Hawai'i were part of a global movement and change, where indigenous peoples using argumentative tools, such as history, morality and legality, were able to dramatically change international and national landscapes concerning their relations to states over a period of thirty years. At the end of that research period I also witnessed the growing political opposition towards

Hawaiian rights in the end of the 1990s. It became clear that the opposition was part of a broader global opposition to all kinds of affirmative action policies and special rights for indigenous peoples.

The Revision of the Relationship between States and Indigenous Peoples

Until the end of the 1990s, it appeared as if the issues of indigenous peoples in international and national politics were going to be settled in a relatively progressive way from an indigenous perspective. For instance, representatives of the Hawaiian movement talked about rolling back the policies of racism and discrimination for good. Some politicians were even convinced that the old days of exclusion and derogatory views of the Native Hawaiians were never to return to the political agenda. The same views were expressed in many other countries around the world. The governments in Canada, Finland, New Zealand, Norway and Sweden apologized for past atrocities and established policies and mechanisms of reconciliation and self-government. In Hawai'i, according to many of the elected representatives in the state congress, the main question was whether they should agree upon moving towards indigenous self-government step-by-step through political reforms, or enter into completely new and unknown territory. Some more outspoken independence-minded groups within the Hawaiian movement, of course, did not agree to step-by-step reform politics, as the congress had wanted, and many still have a goal of complete Hawaiian separation from the USA. However, in conversations with Native Hawaiian leaders at the end of the 1990s, it became clear that the political and legal support they had gained for their claims was a basis for further political developments regarding sovereignty, land rights and other issues up for discussion at the time.

The idea that indigenous rights were to be a permanent part of international politics and law was also a rather widespread opinion in the corridors of the United Nations in Geneva. There were, of course, critical voices among the diplomatic representatives on the frequent use of the concept of self-determination for indigenous peoples. But even the controversial self-determination issue seemed likely to be solved at that time with reasonable compromises for both governments and indigenous nations. The 1990s saw a dramatic shift in international politics from hardcore state opposition against the use of the concept of self-determination, to a softer approach where states actually proposed to discuss some new perspectives on self-determination in the context of indigenous peoples. Some countries even suggested that the UN should change its language from *Indigenous People* to *Indigenous Peoples* with the 's' at the end signalling the general concept of peoples in international law; 'peoples' have the right to self-determination according to the two United Nations Human Rights Covenants of 1966. Even if it was confined to the realm of political rhetoric, it is well known that the 's' issue has followed the indigenous rights debate over the last couple of decades and that is not simply a small political change of language.

In 1998 when the centenary of the American annexation of Hawai'i was celebrated by some, and mourned by others, few in the political leadership had in mind (at least not publicly) a different roadmap. The role and history of Hawaiian culture was celebrated, while behind the scenes of seemingly widespread political agreement, the opposition against indigenous rights was nevertheless simmering. The opposition towards Native Hawaiian rights emerged on a wider scale after the 1995 PASH-case, which was considered by many observers as a landmark case in changing legal and political concessions of native rights in Hawai'i. Concluded by the Supreme Court of Hawai'i, the PASH-case concerned access to land for Native Hawaiians, and was the last of a series of legal cases Native Hawaiians had won since the beginning of the 1980s. After the PASH-case, private landowners began talking about indigenous rights being an obstacle to tourism development and a threat to property value. Landowners argued that they did not even have control over their own land anymore. And it was also the PASH-case that triggered landowner Harold Rice to legally challenge the whole system of a self-governing entity for Native Hawaiians called the Office of Hawaiian Affairs (OHA). OHA was established in 1978 after an amendment to the Hawaiian state constitution. It was from the beginning a semi-state institution as it was funded both by government funds, and from compensations from the use of Native Hawaiian land by the state.

Beside the opposition from landowners and tourism developers, critique also emerged from other economically powerful interest groups. Just a few weeks before the commemoration in 1998 of the American annexation of Hawai'i, one of the most prominent and public oppositional writers against Hawaiian rights, Thurston Twigg-Smith, a grandson of one of the leaders who overthrew the Hawaiian kingdom in 1893, published a book called *Hawaiian Sovereignty: Do the Facts Matter?* (1998). The book was a passionate critique of what he called the history revisionism conducted by the Hawaiian sovereignty movement, with the aid of some local politicians, regarding the overthrow of the Hawaiian kingdom in 1893. In the book Twigg-Smith sought to argue that "much of the current version of Hawaiian history of the revolutionary period is wrong..." (Twigg-Smith, 1998:xvi) based on historical facts around the overthrow of the Hawaiian kingdom. The 1893 incidents have for a long time been at the centre of the Hawaiian movement's use of history as a strategy to change contemporary politics in Hawai'i. Even though history has been used as a political instrument, it does not mean that the movement falsified or revised historical facts. On the contrary, there are many historical facts that are in favour of the views and arguments of the Hawaiian movement. The validity that this was the case was also politically acknowledged in 1993, when the U.S. Congress and President Bill Clinton in a public law apologized for the American involvement in overthrowing the Hawaiian kingdom (U.S. Public law, 103-150). Twigg-Smith consequently called the apology "a travesty" (Twigg-Smith, 1998:271).

The emergence of opposition against indigenous rights in Hawai'i was part of an international tendency at the end of the 1990s. In countries like Australia, Canada, New Zealand, Norway, and Sweden, opposition and critique began to take more organized forms. In Australia, the leader of the One Nation Party, Pauline Hanson, attacked what she called "the aboriginal rights industry" (Hanson, 1996). According to Hanson, the Australian state had conceded too many rights and resources to a small and scattered minority group; a system which she argued, threatened the very existence of an integrated Australia. In Sweden, local politicians and interest groups began talking about "ethnic war" if the Swedish government decided to ratify the International Labour Organization Convention 169 on the Rights of Indigenous People. When I visited northern Sweden in 1999, people said they were fed up with the talk of strengthening the rights of the Sami people–"It is we, the Swedes, having the problems"–was a fairly widespread opinion among groups living close to Sami communities. Non-indigenous people in British Colombia, Canada, started to feel uneasy with what they perceived as the overly public flirtation between the government and indigenous peoples. In other countries like Denmark, Norway and New Zealand things were not going smoothly on the topic either. Further, it did not take long before the heated discussion on the cultural and political status of indigenous peoples returned to the pages of anthropological journals in the beginning of the new millennium (Kuper, 2003).

Despite the emerging opposition against Native Hawaiian claims and concessions, the beginning of the new millennium looked much like the end of the last one. To many observers of the politics of indigenous movements, the opposition against indigenous rights were viewed as being part of a normal discussion in any democracy. This view was also confirmed by a legal battle that began building momentum. In 1999, the U.S. Federal Court of Appeals of the Ninth Circuit dismissed the claims of Harold Rice that the OHA was discriminating against the majority population of Hawai'i. Rice claimed that the political process in the OHA, which from the beginning was designed to be a self-government entity for Native Hawaiians, was unconstitutional and a violation of the Fourteenth and Fifteenth Amendments to the U.S. Constitution, which prohibits racial discrimination in political processes. These amendments constitutionalized color-blindness in American law and politics. Rice, not satisfied with the decision, appealed to the U.S. Supreme Court. However, few among the observers of the Hawaiian dispute expected a change in the legal view on the matter. The Indians and the Inuit already had similar rights and limited political self-determination and the Federal Court of Appeals highlighted that fact in its 1999 decision. The Native Hawaiian side was legally defended by the Governor of Hawai'i, who was officially part of the dispute. The expectation among observers in Hawai'i was therefore that there would be continued legal and political support for indigenous self-government. But things were soon going to change. Before analyzing the changes in attitudes, it is necessary to evaluate the anatomy of the basic arguments forwarded by the opposition against indigenous rights. I claim that these arguments have relevance, not only to the Hawaiian case, but to most of the contemporary national disputes concerning indigenous rights in Western democracies.

The Arguments against Indigenous Rights

In the book by Twigg-Smith and in the general critique of indigenous claims, the issue was not only about whether there is an objective history to recount. It was also a perspective that presented how democratic societies should be organized and on what political assumptions they should be based. For Twigg-Smith, the democratic society should always and only look forward into the future. He claims that history is important in his "attempt to untangle revisionism," but not as a basis for claiming rights on historical atrocities and discriminatory policies. For the Hawaiian movement, on the other hand, the future only makes sense if there is historical continuity. According to the debate, it is therefore clear that the opposition and the Hawaiian movement view history and the kinds of political and legal concessions that should follow from the historical facts, in two completely different ways. Twigg-Smith, for instance, argues that the 1893 overthrow of the Hawaiian kingdom was not caused by the U.S., rather, he argues, that it was a revolution by members of the Hawaiian government. The Hawaiian movement, on the other hand, argues that the incidents in 1893 were an act of war committed against Native Hawaiians by some Hawaiian politicians with American ancestry who had the help of the U.S. ambassador and the military, which was based on ships anchored in the harbour of Honolulu.

Twigg-Smith and others argue that indigenous rights claims are unlawful cultural relativism when the government is turning away from universal standards of equality and individual rights and emphasize rights based on ethnicity and histories of minority groups (Twigg-Smith, 1998: 6-16). For the Hawaiian movement, on the other side, it is cultural relativism when politics is side-tracking the rights and history of the Hawaiian culture and when political emphasis is placed on formal universal rights, like equality and individual rights. For some of the groups in the Hawaiian sovereignty movement, the American presence on the islands is the result of unlawful occupation and colonization. While Twigg-Smith argues that history should be left behind, the Hawaiian movement emphasizes history and its decisive influence on politics and social relations in contemporary Hawaiian society. These are, of course, arguments stemming from two different theoretical directions. Twigg-Smith argues that the government should maintain strict neutrality between various normative statements, while the Hawaiian movement argues that there is no such thing as neutrality,

146

not even in a human rights context; there are only different theoretical perspectives.

Considering the contemporary importance of the human rights doctrine, it might seem clear that the best way for a democratic society is to commence with equal and universal standards. All special rights for indigenous peoples deviate from the universal standards, argues Twigg-Smith (1998:301-310, 323-328). The logic of universal principles generates strong anti-indigenous rights action. Indigenous rights are called reverse discrimination by the majority population. It is the same theoretical perspective and logic that made Kuper (2003) argue that indigenous rights activists and movements are on the same level as extreme right-wing groups as the National Front, Ku Klux Klan or neo-Nazis. The problem with Twigg-Smith and Kupers' arguments is not that they dismiss history and the cause of present-day politics, but that they dismiss political and social reality by removing the usual measures by which we label one act objectionable and another commendable and then substituting these measures by questioning if these display reverse discrimination against the majority population. The arguments against indigenous rights is thus about political power because the questions posed by indigenous rights critics are asked in such a way that it is not possible to answer. For instance they ask:, Are indigenous rights in line with the intent and expressions of liberal and democratic constitutions? Taken from this perspective, it is easy to answer "no" and thereby dismiss the whole project of indigenous rights. But my position is that this analysis is oversimplified and does not reflect correctly the causes of the social and political situation of indigenous peoples. A better alternative is to ask questions regarding indigenous rights such as: Do indigenous rights work? Are there any better alternatives? Does the benefit of indigenous rights exceed the costs? Rather than making indigenous peoples violators of constitutions, we must recognize what caused of the system of indigenous rights in the first place.

The opposition against indigenous rights are structurally and politically powerful and they are blaming the victims for the current conflicts, and therefore we should analyse the content of their critique, which is usually framed within the four arguments to follow.

The first critical argument that has been forwarded in the current oppositional movements against indigenous rights is that special rights for the protection of indigenous peoples are not needed. This argument actually comes in two versions: (1) indigenous rights are not needed because discrimination is already illegal and nothing more is required, and (2) indigenous rights are not needed because perspectives have changed after years of granting rights to them. It is argued that democracies can not handle any more special rights regimes and still call themselves democratic states adhering to equality for all. The first version has validity in terms of the illegality of discrimination through human rights standards and constitutional concessions in many countries today, but to

147

claim they are not needed is to be blind to the empirical reality that systematic discrimination and racism keep indigenous peoples at the lowest level of the social and economic ladder, in Hawai'i and elsewhere. The second version is not true because the legal concessions granted to these groups have yet to change anything. Have majority populations lost anything due to indigenous rights? It would be interesting to know if there is such a case anywhere in the world.

The second argument against indigenous rights is based on the view that these rights are not working because the problems of the underclass have more to do with economics and social problems, like alcoholism, homelessness, suicide or lack of education, than with ethnicity. This might be true, but if it is the case that there are multiple problems concerning indigenous peoples as an underclass, then a multiple strategy to come to terms with the problems would make sense. To propose indigenous rights does not necessarily mean that economics, a class analysis or any other analysis of social problems are abandoned.

The third major argument is that indigenous rights are reverse discrimination. That was the argument of the U.S. Supreme Court in the Rice-case in 2000. This argument is based on simple logic which may seem relevant at first glance: If it was wrong to discriminate against the Native Hawaiians, is it not equally wrong to discriminate against the majority population by giving the natives special rights that the rest of the citizens in a state do not have access to? The argument seems compelling, but it works only if the two different practices of discriminations are removed from their respective historical contexts. According to this argument, those who support indigenous rights are on the same level with, for instance, the extreme right. The peculiar thing with this argument is that those who propose such an idea like for example Adam Kuper (2003) and Thurston Twigg-Smith, do not make a distinction between the motives behind the actions taken. It is only when being blind to history that one can conclude that indigenous rights lead to discrimination in the same way as earlier state policies that were genocidal in their consequences. State policies sometimes set out to extinguish indigenous peoples. It is important to be reminded of the assimilation and termination policies in many Western democracies as late as in the 1960s. The International Labour Organization's policy promoted assimilation until 1989, when convention no. 107 was revised; indigenous rights are hardly intent on extinguishing majority populations. In other circumstances, it seems easy to differentiate between causes and consequences; it should also be so in politics.

The fourth argument against indigenous rights is that it provokes conflicts. The argument is another blame-the-victim strategy. If indigenous peoples did not claim special collective rights, it is argued that we would have a more peaceful world without ethnic conflicts. As in argument three, this argument also mistakes cause for consequence. Most observers realize that racism towards and discrimination of indigenous peoples antedates indigenous rights regimes, which is a response to its effects. What the proponents of this argument actually are saying is that if indigenous peoples dare complain, they will be beaten again. And that is exactly what happened after the Rice-case, when the lobby groups behind Rice supported other anti-indigenous rights activists in Hawai'i and elsewhere.

The Rice Case

Let us now turn to the Rice case in Hawai'i for the sake of explaining the present dilemmas facing the Hawaiian movement and to some extent also the general problems of indigenous movements in Western countries. In 1996 Harold Rice attempted to vote in the state- wide elections for the OHA trustees and was denied the right to vote. Since the establishment of the OHA it had been limited to residents of Hawai'i, who by blood quantum or Hawaiian ancestry met the definition of Native Hawaiian or Hawaiian. Rice sued the state of Hawai'i for racial discrimination. The case was concluded by the U.S. Supreme Court in February 2000, and concerned the constitutionality of having a self-governing political entity, like the OHA, as a political entity for Hawaiian residents with native descent. Rice and his legal advisors, *The Campaign for a Color-Blind America*, argued that this political entity, established by the State of Hawai'i in 1978, violated the racial discrimination prohibition of the Fourteenth and Fifteenth Amendments to the U.S. Constitution. The U.S. Supreme Court ruled that this was racial discrimination. The rest of the population of Hawai'i, approximately eighty percent, were also the victims. Accordingly, the U.S. Supreme Court ruled that in denying Rice the right to vote in the OHA trustee elections, the state of Hawai'i violated the Fifteenth Amendment's guarantee that a citizen's right to vote shall not be denied on account of race, color, or previous condition of servitude by enacting race-based voting qualifications.

The critical concept in the case was race, which in this context means descendants of the people who lived on the islands when Captain Cook arrived in 1778. This group can be called a race, even if race today is a slippery concept because of more than 200 years of interracial contacts. But as governor Cayetano of Hawai'i argued in the court, this group can also be a political entity which has been colonized and deprived of their sovereign nation. The difference is a question of history and its processes. There is nothing natural about either race or nation; both can be said to be social and political constructions. Hence, when the Court says that the constitution requires equality between the races, it actually does not say anything about the historical context in which the differences in the concepts emerged. They can imply nothing, but can be made to imply anything. The concepts are empty and the political conflicts in this field are about filling them up with content.

So what happened? When a concept is detached from its historical, political and social context, it can mean anything to anyone. The Court said it was doing its work, applying a neutral principle of non-discrimination; we are all, as equal citizens, proceeding down the same path and should thus be treated in the same way. The prohibition against racial discrimination rules that everyone is equal. One of the dissenting opinions in the Rice case tried to argue that it was necessary to take into account why there was a separate governmental agency for Native Hawaiians. The political solution represented by the OHA came from the fact that the United States had committed discriminatory acts against the Native Hawaiians and at a certain time, in 1978, the majority of the population in Hawai'i agreed to address these acts. When considering this historical process one can, of course, conclude that it is an easy step to consider non-discrimination as a neutral principle which favours no one, and does not support any specific culture. In emphasizing non-discrimination as a neutral principle, it becomes easy to ignore the historical reasons that the political institution for Native Hawaiians was established in the first place. The Court was not interested in historical motives but rather argued that group rights are reverse discrimination. The concept of discrimination implies that any action which can be race-related is by definition discriminatory. However, this makes sense only if history is neglected; because history still influences social and political relationships in Hawai'i. The Native Hawaiians could have been seen as a colonized nation instead of a "whining racial group."

The Akaka Bill: From Sovereign Hawaiians to Native Americans?
The Rice decision had extensive political consequences for the Hawaiian sovereignty movement and for the whole issue of indigenous rights because the majority on the Supreme Court in the decision concluded that Hawaiians did not have status as an indigenous people in the United States equal to that of Indian and Inuit peoples. The self-government of the Hawaiians was viewed by the Supreme Court as racial discrimination towards the majority population in Hawai'i. However, most Indian and Inuit peoples have politically and federally recognized limited self-determination. The question soon became: How could Hawaiians be granted the same political status and did they really want to have the same status? The different opinions on the effects of federal recognition immediately became a divisive issue among the different groups in the Hawaiian sovereignty movement.

It was shortly after the court's ruling in the Rice case that Daniel Akaka, U.S. Senator of Native Hawaiian ancestry, in an effort to bring back political initiative to the sovereignty movement, formed a "Task force on Native Hawaiian issues" with the immediate goal of clarifying the political relationship between Hawaiians and the United States. The initiative, later known as the "Akaka Bill," proposed that the United States should federally recognize Hawaiians as an indigenous people who, like Indian and Inuit peoples, have a special relationship with the United States and a right to self-determination under federal

150

law. The idea of the bill was to lay the foundation for a "nation-within-a-nation" model of self-determination, similar to that of over five hundred federally recognized American Indian and Alaskan Inuit nations. This model would in the same way as the other indigenous groups have the structure of a domestic dependent nation under the full plenary powers of the U.S. Congress. Akaka himself argued that this model could also be seen as a reconciliation effort, which was outlined in the 1993 Apology Law (Public law 103-150).

Some of the groups in the Hawaiian movement began to take the position that federal recognition could be used as a basic guarantee and opportunity for different sets of programmes that would enable them to have self-government and affirmative action. It would also be a necessary step toward stopping the multiple lawsuits that challenge almost all of the rights and concessions Hawaiians have been granted by federal and state governments, such as lands, assets, and institutions like the Hawaiian Home Lands, the Office of Hawaiian Affairs (OHA) and the Kamehameha schools, which is an educational institution only for Hawaiians. Representatives of these institutions and an extensive number of organizations in the Hawaiian community support the idea of federal recognition.

Others in the movement interpreted federal recognition as the final assault of the United States towards the Hawaiians. The sceptics argued that federal recognition would finally recognize the right of the United States to colonize the islands and there would be no turning back after such a decision. The proposed federal recognition was viewed early on as a violation of Hawaiians' inherent right to sovereignty and self-determination. It was argued that to recognize Hawaiians as "Native Americans" with a political trust relationship to the United States would compromise the distinctiveness of Hawaiian claims. Many groups since the Akaka Bill was presented have persistently and consistently rejected the application of U.S. Federal Indian Law that would make Hawaiians a domestic dependent nation under the full powers of the U.S. Congress.

Many Hawaiian groups also see the Akaka Bill as undermining claims already acknowledged by the U.S. Congress, like the 1993 Apology Law that states Hawaiians have not given up their claims to inherent sovereignty and self-determination: "[Native Hawaiians] never directly relinquished their claims" to sovereignty or their lands, which were taken without consent or compensation. In the groups working against the adoption of the Akaka Bill, the main argument is that: "We were illegally invaded and occupied by the United States, and we were and still are a separate people and nation," (Informant, February, 2006). This argument is to say that Hawaiians are not "Native Americans," and some of them have no intention of becoming like natives either.

The Akaka Bill has also met forceful resistance among the republicans in the U.S. Congress. The bill has been seen as yet another attempt to establish affirmative action, a policy that is out of fashion in contemporary national U.S. politics. However, Senator Akaka has made several attempts to get a majority vote on the bill, but has not succeeded in this effort so far. In January 2007, the bill was renamed "Native Hawaiian Government Reorganization Act" in another attempt to persuade political opponents—both in Congress and among his fellow Native Hawaiians—that this is the necessary guarantee against legal and political challenges of the majority population in the United States against the concessions granted to Hawaiians. For those resisting the Akaka Bill, some see that the current struggle actually began already with the protest petitions in 1897-98 against American annexation (Silva, 2004). It is just a continuation of the same colonial conflict.

The Rhetorical Battle on Equality and Indigenous Rights

The political opposition against indigenous rights, claims and movements, during the last ten years or so have altered the policy landscape, not only in Hawai'i, but also in many other places. The feature of indigenous policies in many Western states from the 1970s until the end of the 1990s was a relatively progressive political development that granted rights and concessions to indigenous groups. Indigenous claims were being considered legitimate in light of historical experiences of discrimination, oppression and marginalisation. The dramatic changes of the indigenous policy debate in the beginning of the 21st century present observers with some cause for concern. We know that closing gaps, or aiming towards statistical equality via mainstreaming, can be incompatible with the claims of cultural and political difference. While there are few that would deny that equitable needs-based mainstream services should be provided to indigenous peoples as citizens of respective states, most would probably add that this does not mean that they also must share mainstream values.

The opposition against indigenous rights and concessions shows that there is no easy way for them or any other group to challenge political power and control over resources. The reaction and the cultural conflict that indigenous groups now find themselves, demonstrates that they can have support for their claims in the wider society, as long as the claims are not seen as too far-reaching. And the most important part of this counter-reaction to indigenous movements is that groups like The Campaign for a Color-Blind America, United States Justice Foundation, The Manhattan Institute and Americans Against Discrimination and Preference, use the very same human rights language as indigenous peoples themselves. Terms like equal opportunity, color blindness, anti-discrimination and justice have been appropriated by these groups to fight those peoples that used those very same concepts to change policies of racism and discrimination (Fish, 1999:312). The question we finally have to ask is: Why has this been possible? How is it possible that the concepts of human rights and social emancipation now work against indigenous rights?

152

The answer seems to lie in the definition of equality. If one just says "equality" no one will really know what is meant by this. Is it equality if everyone has the same opportunities or is it equality if everyone has a level playing field? Sooner or later it must be decided what is meant by equality, because otherwise it will mean or change nothing. When indigenous peoples began to demand equality for everyone without consideration of race and color in the 1960s, this was meant as an effort to level the playing field. It was a concept of social emancipation and justice. States should see to it that indigenous peoples have the same preconditions and possibilities to be beneficiaries of equal rights. Today however, equality means "equal opportunity," and that means that we have the benefit of rights if we are able to or have the opportunity to use them. It used to be a reality that people in this world did not have the same opportunities, depending on different social, economic, political or cultural backgrounds. Now these different backgrounds should not be taken into consideration if some people are able to use their equal opportunities at all.

The opposition against indigenous rights have been able to drastically change the definition of the concept of equality. Human rights and indigenous rights are fields of political conflict and in the centre lies the meaning and definition of the concepts themselves. Human rights are sometimes said to be outside the sphere of political dispute. Who with any sense can be against human rights? But the disputes concerning the rights of indigenous peoples demonstrate that human rights, like any other political concept, are subjected to political power disputes. This point is not insignificant. In any dispute within the public arena, the battle is not won by force, but by the ones who have the possibility to define the concepts, as Stanley Fish argues (1999:312); that is, what the opposition against indigenous rights have managed to do with concepts like equality. By creating policies that ignore history, culture, and politics, is it not then possible that powerful groups can describe society and political relations in any way they please? This occurs by using language that most people are sympathetic to, so it is possible to change the meaning and definition of those concepts without people even realising the change of the content, because it is the same concepts indigenous peoples themselves used.

Conclusions

This chapter has demonstrated how and why the opposition against indigenous movements and their rights claims emerged in the end of the 1990s. Two factors lie at the centre of this current opposition and critique of indigenous movements:

- *Political power*. Since the 1960s, indigenous peoples have been challenging the legitimate political power in states and they have been arguing that there

153

should be a division and delegation of political power. Some indigenous peoples, like in Hawai'i, even make a claim for separate statehood.

- *Control of resources.* The political challenges put forth by indigenous peoples strike at the heart of national politics concerning control and distribution of resources including access to natural resources. The opposition towards indigenous peoples today is to a great extent based on the fear that those in control of the state will loose control over significant resources.

The rolling back of indigenous claims has been achieved through certain political methods that can be called the politics of rhetoric. When the U.S. Supreme Court handed out its decision in the Rice case in 2000, many were amazed. It became clear that Hawaiians did not have the same political status as other Indigenous peoples in America, even if the historical context of all these peoples are pretty much surrounded by the same historical processes. I have argued in this chapter that the critique of indigenous rights and movements have taken another turn since the 1990s due to the fact that the opposition have successfully reversed the arguments of history and its social and cultural consequences.

The reversal has taken place in two steps. First, the present day indigenous politics have been cut off from the historical context that gave indigenous rights its meaning. The U.S. Supreme Court and others argue that everyone is walking on the same road of equality. The second step has been to freeze history and one perspective of it. This step concludes that regardless of how we got to the present situation it should not have any consequences for the policies of today. This strategy of segmenting society and placing all the political focus on the pieces is useful whenever one wants to deflect away from the greater social and historical picture. Because if we do not reflect upon history, then to give concessions that are based on historical circumstances and processes will appear strange in a society that strives for equality for all. Those who are against indigenous rights reject arguments from history, but those historical patterns of discrimination have specifically impaired life's chances for indigenous peoples as a group and are still an impairment today. There has been a rhetorical change in the concept of equality that few have noticed until it was too late. Since equality nowadays means equal opportunities and not equal preconditions, it has been possible to criticize and dismantle policies for indigenous rights and re-name these policies reverse discrimination.

154

References

Akaka bill, (2007), "Native Hawaiian Government Reorganization Act", U.S. Senate Bill No 310.

Fish, Stanley, (1999), *The Trouble with Principle*. Cambridge, Mass.: Harvard University Press.

Hanson, Pauline, (1996), "Wake Up Australia!". Speech to the Australian Federal Parliament, September 10.

Honolulu Star-Bulletin, July 18, (2005), "Debating the Issue".

Johansson Dahre, Ulf (2001), *Det förgångna är framtiden: Ursprungsfolk och politiskt självbestämmande i Hawai'i*. [The Past is Prologue: The Indigenous People of Hawai'i and the Conflict on Political Self-Determination] Lund: Department of Social Anthropology.

Kuper, Adam, (2003). "The Return of the Native." *Current Anthropology*, vol. 44, No 3, pp. 389-395, 400-402.

Silva, Noenoe K., (2004), *Aloha Betrayed: Native Hawaiian Resistance to American Colonialism*. Durham: Duke University Press

Supreme Court of Hawaii, (1995), (Pash-case), Public Access Shoreline Hawaii v. Hawaii County Planning Commission, *Hawai'i Reports*, vol. 79, p. 425.

Trask, Haunani-Kay, (1991), "Natives and Anthropologists: The Colonial Struggle." *The Contemporary Pacific*, vol. 3, No 1, pp. 159-167.

Twigg-Smith, Thurston, (1998), *Hawaiian Sovereignty: Do the Facts Matter?* Honolulu: Goodale Publ.

U.S. Public Law 103-150 "Apology Law", November 23, 1993.

U.S. Supreme Court, (2000), Rice v. Cayetano, Governor of the State of Hawai'i. February 23, 98-818, 146 F.3d 1075.

Werther, Guntram F.A., (1992), *Self-Determination in Western Democracies: Aboriginal Politics in a Comparative perspective*. Westport, Conn.: Greenwood Press.

CHAPTER 7

Beyond the 'Columbus Context'
New Challenges as the Indigenous Discourse is
Applied to Africa

SIDSEL SAUGESTAD

An examination of indigenous discourses is an invitation to review the diverse developments that indigenous peoples have undergone in their internal relations as well as in their relations to their respective nation states and to trans-national expression. The indigenous rights movement is an attempt to give voice to local injustices in a universal language, and reflects the increasing legitimacy of human rights regimes and ideologies. The strength of the indigenous movement is in the sense of unity between indigenous peoples, following from both the striking similarities in their historical experiences and in their current structural relations with their respective nation states (Minde 1996, Muehlebach 2001, Niezen 2003, IWGIA 2004). This is all the more remarkable considering the backdrop of different continents, different adaptations, and different forms of colonialism that indigenous peoples have endured. By the beginning of the 1990s, this movement had consolidated itself, as manifested in interest and solidarity organisations, consultations and standard-setting exercises, as well as venues in both Geneva (WGIP) and New York (UNPFII). The objective of this chapter is to look at the ways this discourse–as expressed in organisations and trans-national structures–has affected and interacted with indigenous peoples of Africa.

The chapter makes a perhaps obvious but still important point: when African organisations became involved in the international movement during the 1990s, they joined a process that was already well underway. Due to this background, the way the discourse has developed in Africa, and the agenda adopted, followed a different trajectory. As African organisations began to emerge in the early to mid-1990s, their challenges were new and different from those that the pioneers of the movement had experienced in the 1970s and 80s. African organisations and discourses should be understood in the context of this particular history, as well as in the context of the nature of the global process underway at the particular time when they became involved.

The African Context

Among all continents suffering from European domination, exploitation and racial discrimination, the African experience was particularly gruelling and the effects most devastating. The congruence between a numbers of dichotomies: white–black, coloniser–native, economic domination–subjugation created a political climate where, upon liberation, African states were to be particularly unreceptive to the subtle distinction between discrimination and affirmative action. This provides some of the explanation as to why indigenous activism began there later than on all other continents (Veber et al.1994, Hodgson 2002a, Hitchcock and Vinding 2004, ACHPR 2005).

My own personal experience in Botswana may help illustrate this point. As a NORAD expert in 1992-93, I was seconded as a research facilitator to a programme within the Botswana Ministry of Local Government, called Remote Area Development. 'Remote Area Dwellers' was a euphemism for the country's geographically and socially marginalised indigenous minority, called San, Bushmen, Basarwa or in their own languages Ju|'hoansi, Naro, G|ui, as well as a dozen or so other names. The attitude in Botswana was and still is that all people born in a country are indigenous. Botswana wanted to distance the country as far as possible from its neighbouring apartheid South Africa. The constitution adopted at independence in 1966, and the policies that followed, rejected any recognition of distinct cultures, traditions, or languages. The result was not a country *without* culture, tradition or language; but the hegemony of *one* majority culture, *one* dominant tradition and *one* national language of instruction. The national culture is taken to be synonymous with the majority Tswana culture that provides a neutral all-embracing identity, and serves as the yardstick against which citizenship and adequate performance are measured (Saugestad 2001a). As philosophers have demonstrated and indigenous peoples painfully know (Nthomang 2004), this way of implementing equality results in a *de facto* discrimination of those not fitting into the majority mould.

By the early 1990s there was no public discourse on indigenous issues in Botswana or Namibia, and South Africa was still under Apartheid. In Botswana, like in most post-colonial states, there were no laws or regulations that explicitly discriminated against the indigenous minority, but discrimination was there in its more subtle forms, played out in person to person encounters. The most striking fact was the lack of recognition, or 'misrecognition' as Taylor (1994) puts it, as poverty and remoteness became the politically acceptable labels for addressing the problems of an indigenous minority. The contrast to the activism one could observe in other parts of the world was striking. The level of activism by Native Americans, Australian Aboriginals, Maori, and the Saami organisations is nicely summed up in the title of a conference held in Tromsø 1993 (the First UN Year of Indigenous Peoples) *Becoming Visible* (Brantenberg et al. 1995).

Within the first UN Decade (1995-2004) these different initiatives had inspired the beginning of indigenous activism in Africa. The making of an international movement of indigenous peoples is well documented (see introduction to this volume). Here I will emphasise only one point: those who took the first steps and initiated the movement were all (with the exception of the Saami who were geographically adjacent to the incoming Norse) victims of the 'blue-water' colonialism that began with Columbus in 1492 and continued from there. This 'Columbus context' of the earlier part of the movement had an impact on how the concept of indigenous was defined. An emphasis on *first come* was natural in contexts where it was unambiguous who was there first and who arrived later. This remains part of the original conceptualisation of the term indigenous. I will return to the implications of this aspect for the African context.

The consolidation of the Indigenous Peoples' movement in the 1990s implied a global perspective. The ILO Convention 169 from 1989 and the Draft Declaration on the Rights of Indigenous Peoples from 1994 provided documents that summed up this understanding. The UN Working Group on Indigenous Populations did more than produce the Draft Declaration. Throughout the 1980s its annual meetings in Geneva provided a "site of particular discursive intensity" (Muehlebach 2001:415), providing a venue and a favourable environment for hundreds of indigenous activists. They arrived as individuals or groups, meeting with supporters and researchers and the odd politician. In the plenary sessions there were moving reports about people's experiences of assault and harassment, and there was plotting and policy-making in the corridors.

When African indigenous peoples got involved in the global process, this is where they began. Right from the beginning they were pulled into the process at the 'top' transnational level, and into a discourse on indigenism that was shaped by the experiences of those who had been subjected to European settler colonialism. It may be useful to reflect on the challenges this has represented for African indigenous peoples. How were they received and how did they experience the Geneva/WGIP process?

Seats to be Taken
Both metaphorically and in reality, indigenous peoples have been claiming–and are increasingly occupying–seats around conference and negotiation tables. Such positions require a process of delegation, as indigenous peoples meet as *representatives* of groups, organisations, regions or continents. This meant that African indigenous peoples also needed to get organised.

It is important to recall that when African indigenous peoples started to attend the WGIP meetings in Geneva, they joined a process that was well underway. They came with the same background of discrimination and oppression, but in contrast to some of the other groups, they came without the experience of several decades of organisation building. Facilitated by support and advocacy organisations, they came into the process by leaps and bounds, and they encountered indigenous 'brothers and sisters' who were well organised, who could report on achievements, and were vocal in their formulation of claims. The movement had gone through stages in a prolonged process, during the 1970s and 80s dominated by identity politics and self-representations, gradually including legal issues and questions of land rights and resource control in the 1990s, and then maturing into an international arena of global conferences with indigenous participation.

The first UN Year of Indigenous Peoples in 1993, and the Decades that followed, introduced a number of international conferences, among them was the first that addressed and involved African indigenous peoples directly, organised by the International Working Group for Indigenous Affairs (IWGIA) in Denmark (Veber et al. 1994). It also heralded the establishment of a solidarity fund that facilitated the attendance for fledgling organisations lacking the means to travel. The first African indigenous group to attend the WGIP was the Maasai from Kenya in 1989, by the 1990s onward Twa from Rwanda, San from Southern Africa, and increasing numbers of Maasai attended.

In order to meet with these new opportunities as they were unfolding, African indigenous peoples needed to come together, to form a caucus, and develop a coherent voice. An important step was the establishment of the Indigenous Peoples of Africa Coordinating Committee, (IPACC), in 1997 (IPACC 2005). It has been argued that this is not a truly indigenous grass-roots organisation because it began in Geneva (see Borchgrevink 2005:17). Coming together in the meeting rooms of the Palace of Nations may be as far as one can get from the bush and the savannah. But the very nature of the process that the 'pioneer' organisations had set in motion from the World Council of Indigenous Peoples first meeting in 1975 and onwards was directed towards this global, all-embracing, structure. There was a space in Geneva that needed to be occupied, using the term Geneva not only to denote a place, but also metaphorically for the web of transnational organisations.

IPACC provided a meeting place for delegates that had made it to Geneva from different parts of Africa. Much of its mandate during the earlier period was to facilitate participation in UN and other international fora, and also to bridge the Francophone–Anglophone divide, which represents a serious barrier to communication across the African continent. Pragmatically, the presence of a large number of indigenous representatives provided the opportunity to hold Annual General Meetings with no extra travel costs accrued.[1] Its found-

---

1   The Annual General Meeting in Geneva 2005 approved a motion to dissolve the Geneva-based meeting and to convene sub-regional elections in Africa. This was meant to increase the participation of members in the electoral process, by not only having to rely on those who were able to go to the UNWGIP.

ing organisations came mainly from East Africa, where the Maasai had taken the lead, and from the far northern (Amazigh, Tuareg) and southern (San) part of the continent. Being an umbrella organisation, the legitimacy of IPACC depended on the status of its participating organisations, most of which had only recently been developed.

It was the *need* for a pan-African organisation of this type, more than a solid basis in well established national organisations, which brought IPACC into existence in the firsts place. Attention is increasingly focused on developing advocacy capacity in each region of the continent, and to strengthen participating organisations at the grass-roots level (Crawhall 2004). The momentum of the trans-national movement, and the new opportunities and challenges it created, explain this somewhat inverse trajectory. Once the process had begun, other trans-national organisations emerged, such as the Organisation for Indigenous People of Africa (OIPA), with its strengths in East Africa, and the Working Group of Indigenous Minorities in Southern Africa (WIMSA).

The Martinez Report 1999

One of the first issues that came up in the WGIP which called for an African response was precisely the issue of *inclusion*. What necessitated a response was when Special Rapporteur Miguel Alfonso Martinez presented his *Study on treaties, agreements and other constructive arrangements between States and Indigenous populations*. An 'unedited version' was made available in July 1998; the official version was debated the next year (E/CN.4/Sub.2/1999/29).

The study had been commissioned in 1989 with a broad mandate to examine:

- the origins and practice of concluding treaties, agreements and other constructive arrangements between indigenous peoples and states;
- the contemporary significance of such instruments;
- and the potential value of all those instruments as a basis for governing the future relationship between indigenous peoples and States (Martinez 1999, para. 17)

In this report–to the surprise of many peoples–Martinez links the identification of indigenous with the method of colonisation. The emphasis of the report was on situations where "the category of indigenous peoples has been established beyond doubt" (para. 69, 85), and suggested that the "overseas colonial undertaking" differed completely from the more common phenomenon of "expansion into adjacent territories" at the expense of their neighbours. Martinez' argument was that indigenous rights flow from the treaty and agreement process at the time of conquest, and the term indigenous should be reserved for those who were subjected to such 'blue-water' colonialism.

The overseas colonial undertaking differed completely from the very common phe-nomenon of expansion into adjacent territories (at the expense of their neighbours) practised by the peoples in those 'new' territories before the arrival of the European colonizer. The inherent nature of the colonial undertaking, the exploitative, dis-criminatory and dominating character of its 'philosophy' as a system, the methods employed, and the final results it had on very dissimilar societies mark the differ-ence. (para. 175)

This more restricted use of the concept indigenous had direct implications for peoples Martinez referred to as 'state-oppressed peoples' and 'minorities' in the particular context of present-day African, Asian and Pacific States (para. 67). "In these countries, the process of decolonialization brought about a radical change in the qualifier 'indigenous.' This was a result of a new political context characterised by the emergence of new States, established under contemporary international law." Thus, Martinez considered it necessary to "re-establish a clear-cut distinction between indigenous peoples and national and ethnic mi-norities" (para. 68).

In sum, the Martinez report clearly and explicitly proposed a division among the indigenous peoples attending the UNWGIP: those that had treaties should stay; the others should take their grievances to other fora, in particular, the Working Group for Minorities.

The immediate reactions to his draft report presented in 1998 were mixed. The mention of African and Asian minorities was only a small part of the re-port, and many groups–Native Americans in particular–were pleased with the main focus of the report and that it emphasised that treaties should be honoured, which was viewed "as a valuable step forward." Only two speakers from Africa argued otherwise. Judge Guisse, from Senegal, and one of the five members of the expert Working Group noted dryly that "the Special Rapporteur has chosen not to find indigenous peoples in certain areas, in particular on the African continent/.../if one looks a little deeper one can say that indigenous communi-ties do, in fact, exist" (UNPO Monitor July 40, 1998, day 4, Afternoon ses-sion: 2). [2]

Whatever other merit the Martinez report might have had, by the time of the debate on the final document in 1999, the main attention was on the perceived attempt to exclude African and Asian representatives from the working group. Opposition was more organised, and it was submitted in writing. Joseph Ole Karia, Chair of IPACC read a statement:

---

2   Of the 18 comments from the floor, 14 were from Native Americans or Hawaiians and they
    endorsed the treaty, those against were two African, one Asian and one from Greenland Home
    Rule (UNPO Monitor July 40, 1998, day 4, Afternoon session).

It is clear that [Martinez] proposes in essence, that indigenous peoples of Africa and Asia are to be sidelined from this working group. I think that the WGIP will not be complete without African and Asian Indigenous Peoples.

We regard the recommendations relating to Africa and Asia as being flawed. In principle, they are divisive in extreme and we reject them totally. Solidarity in the indigenous peoples movement is of the utmost value.

Many state representatives supported this position. Denmark's representative stated:

My delegation strongly believes in indigenous peoples' general right to self-identification. Therefore indigenous peoples, indigenous rights, indigenous issues, cannot and should not be defined in any specific historical, geographical or other context. We therefore neither share nor support the views expressed by the Special Rapporteur in among others para. 83, 90 and 91 on an alleged exclusiveness of the term 'indigenous', nor do we accept the consequences he draws for dealing with indigenous issues within the framework of the United Nations.

I have evaluated this report and the ensuing debate in some detail because it illustrates a very general controversy. In fact, Martinez gives an eloquent voice to attitudes and ways of reasoning that is found persistently among African heads of states. He goes far in conjuring up the image of 'balkanisation' and warns against the possible 'sedition' from the 'weak new states' (para 89). However, the final outcome was a broad rejection of this position. His report has, on the whole, not been treated as a significant document. The event was important, because it exposed the need for the African Caucus to stand together and present a united front. And equally important, the *plenary* of the UNWGIP affirmed its inclusiveness and insisted on African and Asian groups as legitimate participants.

United Nations Permanent Forum for Indigenous Issues (UNPFII)

Another event calling for some degree of unity and collaboration among African indigenous peoples was the process leading up to the establishment of the United Nations Permanent Forum for Indigenous Issues in 2002. The processes again exposed the wide difference between the well organised indigenous organisations that had argued, lobbied, and eventually secured the establishment of the Forum,–with Ole Henrik Magga, a Norwegian Saami, as a highly competent candidate for the presidentship–and the diverse and fairly disorganised African groups. The eventual composition of the Forum allocated one IP representative seat and one state seat to the African continent. This was the logical consequence of applying a global perspective on the formula for distributing seats/representation.

So far, the UN Permanent Forum is the peak of the International Indigenous Movement. Its origin was truly 'grass roots based' and built from the 'bottom-up.' The development was a process that began with local groups, which gradually joined together into national and regional groups, and was supported by a unique combination of activists, support organisations, and legal advisers which were provided by some of the more sympathetic states.

By the beginning of this century two global processes affect indigenous peoples in Africa:

1) The indigenous movement has manifested a certain–many would say considerable–success through the establishment of transnational meeting places, and a number of standard-setting declarations that are beginning to take effect, though obviously in a very random manner. "Indigenism" argues Niezen (2003:9) "is not a particularized identity, but a global one/…/It sets social groups and networks apart from others in a global 'we-they' dichotomy. It identifies a boundary of membership and experience… [and] links local, primordial sentiments to a universal category."
African groups were latecomers in joining this 'universal category.' They have travelled a long road, translating individual experiences of discrimination and marginalisation into a framework that helps them to see the underlying structure of this discrimination. The driving force here is self-identification, and a sense of commitment and communality.

2) At the same time, outside pressure on indigenous communities has become more forceful. Not only the encompassing states, but also the logic of globalised economies are increasingly threatening the subsistence base of indigenous peoples. In the Congo basin it is mining companies and logging, in East Africa it may be wheat farms. Nature conservation, in itself an excellent idea, leads to expulsion of indigenous peoples from remote but attractive wildlife areas which are gazetted as National parks and Game reserves: the Hai‖om from Etosha Namibia, the G|ui and G‖ana from the Central Kalahari Game Reserve in Botswana, the Maasai and Barabaig from Serengeti and Ngorongoro in Tanzania and Kenya, and the Batwa from most of the parks in the Great Lakes area (Crawhall 2005:21, see also Bolaane 2004). These problems call for protection and preservation from states that are often indifferent or hostile towards indigenous peoples.

This brings us back to the precarious position of indigenous peoples in Africa. Their position is related to the postcolonial situation and the challenges of nation-building. To some degree, the attitude of the encompassing state can also be related to a negative view of certain 'indigenous' ways of making a living, and the land-use conflict that this entails.

Who are the Indigenous Peoples of Africa?

With the tremendous natural and cultural diversity of the African continent, including more than half of all languages spoken in the world and the oldest evidence of human settlement, it may seem futile to single out some ethnic groups as being more indigenous than others. However, in exchanges and meetings since the early 1990s, communality has been recognised in relation to a shared history and background among individuals and groups who identify themselves as indigenous.

The following cluster of characteristics expands on the working definition most commonly used in the UN system:[3]

- Priority of occupation, but not necessarily in a strict sense[4]
- Political and economic marginalisation rooted in colonialism
- For those attending school, educational material ignoring or belittling their culture and language
- De facto discrimination based often on the dominance of agricultural peoples in the State system and often denigrating stereotypes and unequal exchange relationships
- Particularities of culture, economy, identity and territoriality that link hunting and herding peoples with their home environments in deserts and forests , i.e. some of the most remote and inaccessible parts of the continent (From IPACC 2005)

Taken together, these characteristics are predominantly associated with hunter-gatherers and nomadic or transhumant pastoralist herders, in other words groups that move around physically without leaving monuments that mark ownership of territory. In Africa and elsewhere, there is a tendency that settled food producing societies look down on those who move around (as also experienced by the Rom and Gypsies in Europe). James Woodburn (1997) describes the ideological basis for local discrimination against hunter-gatherer minorities

---

3   WGIP brings out four principles to be taken into account in any possible definition of indigenous peoples:

   (a) priority in time, with respect to the occupation and use of a specific territory;

   (b) the voluntary perpetuation of cultural distinctiveness, which may include aspects of language, social organisation, religion and spiritual values, modes of production, laws and institutions;

   (c) self-identification, as well as recognition by other groups, as well as State authorities, as a distinct collectivity; and

   (d) an experience of subjugation, marginalisation, dispossession, exclusion or discrimination, whether or not these conditions persist. (E/CN.4/Sub.2/ACV.4/1996/2).

4   The Maasai are the best example of a pragmatic application of the 'first come' criteria, having occupied their present territories for about two centuries. The San/Bushmen, on the other hand, have been in the area they now inhabit as far back as archaeological records go.

in sub-Saharan Africa in terms of negative stereotypes, denial of rights, and segregation. Negative stereotypes are reinforced by political and organisational weakness, which conjures up notions of uncivilized backwardness, that they are eaters of revolting foods and child-like in their behaviour.

Stigma associated with a specific livelihood often lingers after the activity has been abandoned. Woldeselassie (2001) has analysed a small group in Ethiopia, the Weyto, who in addition to hunting, gathering and fishing, also had hunted Hippopotamus until this was prohibited in the 1950s. Fifty years or so after this activity ended they are still categorised derogatorily as 'Hippopotamus eaters,' referring not only to a special form of hunting but also to the breaking of a food taboo that set the Weyto apart from the encompassing society.

The Role of Minorities in the New Nations

While most African states may have some core territory that links the current state formation with traditional occupation, colonialism left countries with boundaries that were accidental and unnatural. There is little or no congruence between 'states' as territories and 'nations' as units with cultural and linguistic communality. Hence, all major indigenous populations are spread over several state territories: the Amazigh in Algeria and Morocco; the Batwa in Rwanda, Congo, and Cameroon; the Maasai in Kenya and Tanzania; and the San in Botswana, Namibia, South Africa and Angola.

Davidson describes how the 'new nationals' embraced the concept of the nation-state:

> Striving to transform colonial territories into national territories, they would find Africa's wealth of ethnic cultures both distracting and hard to absorb into their schemes. They would fall back into the colonial mentality of regarding it as 'tribalism,' and as such, retrogressive. (Davidson 1992:99)

The new African states predominantly pursued a policy which in the name of national unity dismissed cultural differences as tribalism and a threat to the sovereignty of the state. Tribal conflicts have left their mark on national politics in a way that makes indigenous organisations–with their need for 'special treatment'–particularly vulnerable to accusations of being divisive, even secessionist. Or alternatively, the claim has been made that *all* Africans are indigenous. The dominant position of white colonial forces left all of black Africa in a subordinate position that in many respects was similar to the position of indigenous peoples in other parts of the world. In relation to the colonial powers *all* native Africans were (a) first comers, (b) non-dominant and (c) different culturally from the white intruders. Thus, the dominant black/white dichotomy in Africa could be used to reinforce a notion that all native Africans were 'indigenous.'

By any standard, indigenous peoples are generally poor. In African states that reject 'indigenous' as a relevant category, donors and supporting NGOs often find it easier to provide assistance to indigenous people because they are poor, as a form of humanitarian relief, rather than to argue for any kind of 'special treatment' or 'affirmative action.' The danger has been that a focus on poverty alleviation addresses the *symptoms*, not the *causes* of the processes that lead to marginalisation. The international process has introduced, at least in theory, a concept of rights that builds on collective rights and restorative justice.

Changes Underway

Indigenous peoples are exposed to global environmental problems of the 21st century not only as victims of progress; they may also have a role to play as custodians of traditional knowledge. In many respects, the impact of modernisation, the globalisation of the market economy, and the growing environmental crisis converge in Africa, and it may be more than a coincidence that many recent major UN conferences were held on African soil. On each of these occasions there has been a significant indigenous caucus that argued strongly that a new paradigm must be adopted in protected areas that incorporate a respect for indigenous rights.[5] Some examples are the following:

The African Commission. In November 2003, the African Commission on Human and Peoples' Rights (ACHPR) adopted the report of the African Commission's Working Group of Experts on Indigenous Populations/Communities. Mandated by a previous resolution on the Rights of Indigenous Populations/Communities in Africa, adopted in Benin 2000, the report analyses the human rights situation of indigenous peoples and communities in Africa, the African Charter on Human and Peoples' Rights and its jurisprudence on the concept of 'peoples,' and examines the concept of indigenous peoples and communities in Africa (IWGIA 2004:456).

The African Commission defines Human Rights not just as Political and Civil, but also as Economic and Social.

Indigenous peoples and communities experience a range of human rights violations that ultimately boil down to a threat towards their right to existence and to the social, economic and cultural development of their own choice. *Articles 20 and 22* of the African Charter emphasize that all people shall have the right to existence and to the social, economic and cultural development of their own choice and in conformity with their own identity. Such fundamental collective rights are to a large extent denied to indigenous peoples. (ACHPR 2005:107)

---

5   The World Summit on Sustainable Development, held in Durban 2000, The Conference on Racism and Xenophobia, Johannesburg, 5th World Park Congress 2003 in Durban.

The African Commission report is an important step forward. Like other documents of this kind, its effects are slow to come and hard to measure, but it provides a 'window of opportunity.' With the adoption of the report and the resolution, indigenous peoples in Africa now have an instrument that may shed light on the situation in Africa, and help to lobby African governments to recognise indigenous peoples, their human rights concerns, and their particular needs.

Summing up the UN Decade, Cape Town December 2004. The end of the First UN Indigenous Peoples Decade was summed up for Africa with a review held at the Iziko Museum in Cape Town. The venue was well chosen. It was formerly the South Africa Museum, and was notorious for its display of Bushmen figures, cast in plaster and displaying 'authentic' Bushmen life. The display was a typical example of the objectifying, and essentialising exposition of the primitive 'other.'[6] By December 2004, those figures had been removed, and the programme displayed activities that celebrated '10 years of struggle, 10 years of courage, 10 years of change, 10 years of tears, 10 years of work for justice.'

The first Decade failed to bring about the adoption of the Draft Declaration, and in other parts of the world there has been strong feelings of resentment that that the Decade did not bring much change.[7] However, the African celebration conveyed a strong feeling that for them, who more or less started from scratch, there had been real changes. One of the speakers, Cecil le Fleur, put it this way: "For Africa the decade has been a success. We have become part of a movement that has established ties across this continent, and brought us in touch with the rest of the world." Commenting on political changes within African states he was less satisfied, but: "At least we can say it has been a greater awareness." A common thread through the presentations was the opportunities that the decade had created, through its various events, for Africans to share in the experiences of other groups on the continent, and globally.[8]

---

6   The display was challenged by an exhibition in 1996 at the South African National gallery, called 'Miscast. Negotiating Khoisan History and Material Culture.' The exhibition examined the types of relationships that were established between the Khoe-San communities and the Europeans that came to occupy their land. Using photographs, documents and other artefacts, the story was told of how the Bushmen were "stuffed, flayed, scarred, marked, dispossessed, displayed, exploited, scrutinised, hunted, exposed, measured, and controlled" (Skotnes, ed 1996:364, see also Saugestad 1996).

7   The disappointment with the failure of the UN member states to significantly advance towards the adoption of the Declaration was expressed in numerous press releases and demonstrations, including a ceremonial hunger strike and spiritual fast in Geneva, December 2004.

8   See reports on Indigenous-to-Indigenous- Cooperation between the First people of the Kalahari and OIPA with the Saami Council, in Jensen and Saugestad (eds) 2004.

Representation and the Problems of Reification

As indigenous peoples become more visible, as a result of these international processes, their status as indigenous peoples have also been challenged in new ways. As noted earlier, while political systems have preferred to dismiss indigenous claims as irrelevant or unnecessary, academics and advocates (among others) have explored the 'politics of representation' and have noted the ways that groups intentionally manipulate, project, and regulate their public images in a way that is in accordance with 'western stereotypes in order to seek recognition and demand rights' (Hodgson 2002a).

There is an obvious ambivalence inherent in any self-representation that is based on images of traditional adaptations. In some respects it is actively encouraged: exotic, photogenic and colourful cultures sell. The same African states that may ignore indigenous claims for rights will use Bushmen with bows and arrows and stately Maasai in brochures to entice tourists.

The ambivalence lies in the fact that traditional cultures provide the repertoire of material and symbolical traits that indigenous peoples use to communicate their own distinctiveness and to contrast themselves with others. At the same time, traditional cultures are undergoing significant changes, and traditional terms are not necessarily accurate descriptions of a people's current livelihood.

However, while it may appear to be a paradox that identities are based on pasts that can not be recreated, this is to a large extent a question of how definitions are used. This conceptual debate, which addresses the essentialising implications of the term indigenous, is strikingly parallel to the distinction made by Fredrik Barth in 1969 when he introduced what one could call the 'modern' concept of ethnicity. He argued for a shift of focus in ethnic studies, from *group characteristics* to aspects of *social process* (Barth, ed 1969).

According to an 'old' concept of ethnicity, ethnic groups were seen as social entities possessing certain fixed cultural properties, often reinforced by popular folk taxonomies. Linking ethnicity to overt cultural traits lead to endless questions regarding the relationship between definition and reification, the nature of ethnic markers, and how much change could take place without it being construed as a 'loss' of ethnicity (Saugestad 2001b:306). The processual approach, with an emphasis on the socially significant *interface* between groups, rather than content, has made it possible to account for ethnic phenomena with less reification of culture.

The same understanding can be applied to discourse on 'indigenousness.' Indigenous peoples are historically situated in an empirical context, in a relationship between a given group and the encompassing nation-state. It is this particular relationship, as expressed in the recognition–or rather, *the lack of recognition*–of the distinct background and therefore distinct needs of the indigenous population, which make up the core of the indigenous predicament. Scheinin, as quoted by Niezen (2003:20) notes "There must be another ethnic group and a power relationship involved before the descendants of the original inhabitants are understood as indigenous in the legal meaning of the term."

Such a 'processual' and 'relational' understanding of the indigenous situation–in contrast to a 'static' and 'essentialising' understanding–is necessary in order to recognise that the dramatic changes that occur in people's mode of production also affect indigenous people. Sylvain (2002) notes how some of the San in Namibia retained their 'authentic' culture through the segregationalist policies of apartheid rule, while San in other parts of the country found their land taken over by commercial farmers leaving them as assimilated farm workers on their old territories. She raises the important point that the current agenda of the San who were able to remain on their land and retain their language is easily recognised as analogous to those of other indigenous peoples, while the recognition of the assimilated San is far more complicated. This is even more the case in South Africa, where the deconstruction of the previous apartheid category of 'coloured' has revealed a large group of KhoeKhoe or Khoe-San people who claim indigenous status even though they lost their language and hunting or herding adaptation more than a century ago (Bredekamp 2002, Hitchcock and Vinding 2004).

Identities may be based on the past, but must allow for change. The important question is who controls the process. In the legal case between the Government of Botswana and a group of San who claimed rights of residence in their traditional territories now gazetted as the Central Kalahari Game Reserve, the government argued that the inhabitants that were relocated did no longer hunt in the traditional manner, and moreover that many preferred to move closer to modern facilities (Saugestad 2004).[9] Both assertions are true, but they are missing the 'indigenous' point, which is the right to determine how, when and at what pace, such change shall take place.

A few academics also seem to be missing this point when they twist indigenous claims for collective rights to traditional territories to appear as if this were a new form of racism, simply because membership in indigenous communities are closely associated with descent. Kuper (2003) expresses a legitimate concern for the complexities of implementing 'collective rights,' and notes examples of both excessive romanticism and unfortunate opportunism. However, his analysis is not informed by factual knowledge about the activities, events, and documents that underpin the indigenous struggle. Thus, a seemingly 'apolitical' academic exercise feeds into the political position of regimes that look

---

9   In a judgement delivered December 2006 the applicants were granted the right to return to the Game Reserve, and it was ruled that they had lawfully occupied the land. However, the government was not instructed to provide services inside the reserve, and the right to return was restricted to 189 of the original applicants and their minor children. (Saugestad 2006)

for arguments that may support a dismissal of indigenous claims (Kenrick and Lewis 2004).

Conclusion: Both Progress and Backlash

To expand on the note of celebration expressed in Cape Town in 2004, other encouraging events may be noted: in 2002 a forty year ban on the Amazigh language was lifted in Morocco and the Royal Commission on Amazigh Language and Culture was created. In 2004 the South African Cabinet adopted a 'policy tool' that is expected to pave the way for recognition of Khoe and San peoples. In the same year, Cameroon adopted a policy on indigenous peoples.

In 2005 Burundi adopted a constitution that accepts the rights of indigenous people, and Gabon has adopted an Indigenous Peoples development Plan for its National Forestry and Environmental Sector programme, which will guide the governmental intervention in forest areas of Gabon within the next five to ten years (Crawhall 2005, personal communication).

What exactly is the driving force behind such changes? With the possible exception of South Africa, we can probably not attribute these changes to strong national organisations that have succeeded in persuading their governments. Rather, we can increasingly observe the effect of the indigenous discourse being taken up by actors on a level that controls financial capital (World Bank, IMF) or moral capital (the African Commission). Put even more bluntly, some countries in search of loans may come up with a policy on their indigenous populations, because the World Bank directive 4.20 requires it.

Success also leads to backlashes. It is to be expected that real or anticipated gains by indigenous peoples would be counteracted, not only by conservatives adhering to different principles, but by people who feel that their own possessions are threatened. In many cases, indigenous land claims are a zero-sum game: there is only so much land, and any rights upheld or reaffirmed for indigenous peoples means correspondingly less to other stakeholders.

The 'pioneer' indigenous organisations, through decades of debates, lobbying and coercion, have been instrumental in creating a new and innovative transnational structure. African indigenous peoples came into this process at a later stage than other indigenous groups, and they were initially beneficiaries more than initiators. However, the very ideology of the indigenous movement has been inclusive and all-embracing, on a global scale. This has benefited African indigenous groups, who probably needed the financial, logistical and unifying support more than most other groups. The nature of the events and venues that were made available for participation was such that the process for the selection of representation became considerably more 'top-down' in this last decade than the distinctly 'bottom-up' process of the previous decades.

The optimistic notes of the celebration in Cape Town should not be taken without some reservations, and much work remains within the local level constituencies in order to be recognised as partners in dialogue with the states. Nevertheless, it may be fair to conclude that for Africa, the international indigenous movement has provided some much needed support and encouragement, although the main benefits of the movement may still be in the future.

References

ACHPR – African Commission on Human and Peoples' Rights. 2005. *Report of the African Commission's Working Group of Experts on Indigenous Populations/Communities*. Copenhagen: IWGIA

Barth, Fredrik. 1969. *Ethnic Groups and Boundaries. The Social Organisation of Cultural Differences*. Oslo: Scandinavian University Press

Bolaane, Maitseo. 2004. *Wildlife conservation and local management: the establishment of Moremi Park*. PhD thesis, St.Antonys, University of Oxford

Borchgrevink, Axel. 2005. 'Indigenous to Indigenous' Development Cooperation: Review of the Saami Council Projects in Africa. Oslo: The Norwegian Institute of International Affairs.

Brantenberg, T., J. Hansen and H. Minde. 1995. *Becoming Visible*. University of Tromsø.

Bredekamp, Henry. 2002. "Khoisan revivalism and the Indigenous Peoples issue in post-apartheid South Africa: A question of self-identity?" in A. Barnard and J. Kenrick (ed) *Africa's Indigenous Peoples: 'First Peoples' or 'Marginalised Minorities'?* Centre of African Studies, University of Edinburgh.

Crawhall, Nigel. 2004. "The Rise of Indigenous Peoples Civil Society in Africa 1994-2004". *Indigenous Affairs* No. 3,

Crawhall, Nigel. 2005. African Hunter-Gatherers: Threats and Opportunities for Biodiversity Knowledge Maintenance. Draft manuscript

Hodgson, Dorothy. 2002a. "Introduction: Comparative Perspectives on the Inidgenosu Rights Movement in Africa and the Americas" *American Anthropologist* 104(4):1037-1049

Hodgson, Dorothy.2002b. "Precarious Alliances: The Cultural Politics and Structural Predicament of the Indigenous Rights Movement in Tanzania" *American Anthropologist* 104(4):1086-1097

Hitchcock, Robert and Diana Vinding (eds). 2004. *Indigenous Peoples' Rights in Southern Africa*. Copenhagen, IWGIA Document no. 110.

IPACC. 2005. Information leaflet

IWGIA- International Work Group for Indigenous Affairs. 2004. *The Indigenous World 2004.* Copenhagen.

Jensen and Saugestad (eds). 2004. *Forum for Development Cooperation with Indigenous Peoples Conference 2004: Indigenous Rights and Gendered Representations*. Centre for Saami Studies: University of Tromsø

Kuper, Adam. 2003. "The Return of the Native. *Current Anthropology*, No 3, 2003

Kenrick, Justin and Jerome Lewis. 2004. "Indigenous peoples' rights and the politics of the term 'indigenous'." *Anthropology Today* 20(2):4-9

Minde, Henry. 1996. 'The Making of an International Movement of Indigenous Peoples' *Scandinavian Journal of History* 3(21)

Niezen, Ronald. 2003. *The Origins of Indigenism*. University of California Press: Berkeley

Martinez, Miguel Alfonso. 1999.*Study on treaties, agreements and other constructive arrangements between States and Inidgenosu populations*. UN, E/CN.4/Sub.2/1999/29

Mackey, Eva. 2005. "Universal Rights in conflict. 'Backlash' and 'benevolent resistance' to indigenous land rights." *Anthropology Today* 21(2):14-20

Muehlebach, Andrea. 2001. "'Making Place' at the United Nations: Indigenous Cultural Politics at the U.N. Working Group on Indigenous Populations" *Cultural Anthropology* 16(3):415-448

Nthomang, Keitseope. 2004. "Relentless colonialism: the case of the Remote Area Development Programme (RADP) and the Basarwa in Botswana" Journal *of Modern African Studies* 43(3)

Saugestad, Sidsel. 1996. "Setting History Straight. Bushmen Encounters in Cape Town" *Indigenous Affairs*, No.4, 1996

Saugestad, Sidsel. 2001a.. *The Inconvenient Indigenous. Remote Area Development, Donor Assistance and the First People of the Kalahari.* Uppsala: Nordic Africa Institute.

Saugestad, Sidsel. 2001b. "Indigenous Peoples in Africa, 'First Peoples' or 'Marginalised Minorities' ?" in A. Barnard and J. Kenrick (ed) *Africa's Indigenous Peoples: 'First Peoples' or 'Marginalised Minorities'*? Centre of African Studies, University of Edinburgh.

Saugestad, Sidsel. 2005. "'Improving their lives.' State Policies and San Resistance in Botswana". *Before Farming* no 4.

Saugestad, Sidsel. 2006. "Notes on the outcome of the ruling in the Central Kalahari Game Reserve case, Botswana." *Before Farming* No 4.

Skotnes, Pippa (ed), 1996. *Miscast. Negotiating the Presence of the Bushmen.* University of Cape Town Press: Cape Town.

Sylvain, Renée. 2002. "'Land, Water and Truth': San Identity and Global Indigenism" *American Anthropologist* 104(4) 1074-1085

Taylor, Charles. 1994. "The Politics of Recognition" in A. Gutmann (ed) *Multiculturalism*. Princeton University Press.

Veber et al. 1994. *Never Drink from the Same Cup.* Copenhagen: IWGIA

WIMSA - Working Group of Indigenous Minorities of Southern Africa. 2004. *Report on Activities April 2003 to March 2004.* Windhoek.

Woldeselassie, Zerihun Abebe. 2001. Minority Identity and Ethnic Politics in Ethiopia: The Case of the Weyto in Lake Tana Area. National Discourse and Local reality. Mphil Thesis, Department of Social Anthropology, University of Tromsø.

Part II

Self-determination, Social Justice and
Natural Resources

CHAPTER 8

Is There a Special Justification for Indigenous Rights?

JARLE WEIGÅRD

Introduction

Over the last decades, the issue of minority rights has moved more to the forefront of the human rights debate. At the time of the adoption of the Universal Declaration of Human Rights (1948) the general understanding was that human rights ought to be interpreted as *individual* rights only. However, from the 1960s onwards it has gradually been more accepted that the interests of people belonging to ethnic minorities can sometimes only be effectively protected by protecting their cultural environment (Freeman 2002:114–115). To achieve this goal, various types of minority rights have been suggested and also implemented.

Depending on the form and content of such minority rights, from a liberal point of view, this has often been seen as a controversial political move. The reason for the controversy is that it involves dividing a state's citizens into different categories–the majority population and one or more minorities–with unequal rights. Thus, this policy is seemingly in violation of the liberal principles of equal treatment of all citizens and "colour-blindness" towards their racial or cultural differences (Kymlicka 1989; 1995). Will Kymlicka, among others, nevertheless argues that there are ways to justify such unequal treatment–in the name of justice and equality. But the problem widens if states have to differentiate among various minorities and award some more extensive rights than others.

Indigenous peoples around the world have long made claims not just to be treated the same as other ethnic minorities, but also that they should be given a special status, firstly because they are *peoples/nations* and secondly because of their indigenousness or aboriginality. How can such a claim be justified, if at all? Attempts in this respect have been made (Anaya 1996)–and criticised (Kymlicka 2001). I will discuss this problem with special reference to the situation in Norway, where an indigenous people, the Sami, and several national minorities are recognised with different rights statuses by national authorities. I will argue that whether one views this kind of rights differentiation as legitimate or not depends partly on one's understanding of the concept of justice and partly on what kind of minority rights one has in mind.

The Situation Regarding Minority and Indigenous Rights

The concept of minorities and minority rights is at present well established in international law. It had its first expression in Article 27 of the International Covenant on Civil and Political Rights from 1966, and in 1992 the UN elaborated on these rights when adopting the Declaration on the Rights of Persons Belonging to National or Ethnic, Religious or Linguistic Minorities. In addition, after the end of the Cold War the Organisation on Security and Co-operation in Europe (OSCE) and the Council of Europe have also implemented new conventions and other instruments for the protection of minority rights (Hannum 2000:282–285). On the basis of the Council of Europe's Framework Convention for the Protection of National Minorities (1994), Norwegian authorities defined–in addition to the indigenous Sami people–five 'national minorities' in Norway: *Kven*,[1] *Forrest Finns*,[2] the Romani People (Travellers), the Roma (Gypsies), and Jews (Ministry of Foreign Affairs 1999–2000).

The concept of indigenous peoples has primarily attained international recognition through the International Labour Organization Convention 169 on Indigenous and Tribal Peoples (ILO 1989). This convention aims at stopping the discrimination of indigenous peoples in work and social life, i.e. securing their equal human rights within their respective countries. The most radical aspect of the convention is that it grants indigenous peoples the right to their traditional lands or territories and to the natural resources of the land. From an indigenous point of view, the limitations and weaknesses of ILO 169 are two-sided. On the one hand, only eighteen countries[3] have ratified the convention so far, which obviously restricts its universal significance. On the other hand, it does not raise the issue of political autonomy for indigenous populations and the acknowledgment of their status as colonised peoples. Still, this convention has played a major role in the Sami demands for indigenous rights, and for the Norwegian authorities accepting, in principle, these demands.

The main indigenous claim today is the right to *self-determination*, which includes the rights "of self-government, autonomy, territorial integrity and exclusive enjoyment of their own lands and resources" (Daes 2000:302; cf. Freeman 2002:123–127). The indigenous movement has tried to achieve this goal through the long ongoing work on a Universal Declaration on the Rights of Indigenous Peoples in the human rights system of the United Nations. A small breakthrough was reached when the declaration was adopted by the new Human Rights Council in June 2006. But after many years of adjustments and negotiations it still has not received a final and official adoption by the Gen-

---

1 The *Kven* ("kvener") are people of Finnish descent living scattered around in many communities in Northern Norway.

2 The *Forrest Finns* ("skogfinner") are people of Finnish descent living relatively concentrated in a border area of Southern Norway/Sweden.

3 These are: Norway, Denmark, the Netherlands and Spain in Europe, Fiji in the Pacific and thirteen countries in Latin America (cf. http://www.ilo.org/ilolex/english/convdisp1.htm).

eral Assembly. The main reason it has taken this long seems to be that many governments (especially African and Asian) have proven unwilling to commit themselves to these kinds of protections for indigenous peoples' rights (cf. Daes 2000; Freeman 2002:123; Scherrer 2003:213–214).

The Concept of Justice

Justice is a concept that is so central to moral reasoning (at least as it has been conceived in the Western philosophical tradition) that it is hard to conduct a normative debate without referring to it, although its precise content is controversial and difficult to interpret. Aristotle (1976) maintained that justice means to treat equal cases equally and unequal cases unequally, and few would deny that the principle of consistent, equal treatment is the fundamental aspect of justice. This is hardly enough to formulate an operational definition of the concept, for as Aristotle (1957:195–196/207–208) himself points out, the divisive question is often: What are the relevant criteria according to which two cases should be treated as either equal or unequal?

If some good is to be distributed among a group of people, how should this be done in order to claim that it has been done in accordance with justice? This is the fundamental question of distributive–or social–justice, where opinions are split into many schools of thought. However, it is possible to roughly group these schools into two main directions. The first seem to have what we might call a *benevolent* understanding of justice. Although most people seem to agree that *equality* has something to do with justice, they do not necessarily agree on the exact relationship between them. For some, justice is linked to equality only in its strict formal sense. They believe the same rules should apply to everyone or that everyone should have their rights equally respected, although these rights may well prescribe unequal treatment for different people. For others, just equality means that everybody should either receive the same amount of a good, or that everybody should have the same *chance* of receiving a fair amount of the good, or that they all should *end up* with the same amount of the good (Heywood 2004). It is only these last views that we would call an egalitarian conception of justice, at least in the domain of distributive justice.

It is fair to say that equality considerations figure highly in John Rawls' (1971; 1993) theory of justice, as it does in the theory of Ronald Dworkin (1977; 1985; cf. Miller 1999:230–231). Some scholars, however, prefer to label Rawls' theory by its own term: justice as *fairness* (Swift 2006:21–29), and others see it as a justice theory which employs *impartiality* as its basic principle (Barry 1989, 1995), a concept that should well describe all theories which are based on a Kantian form of justification. However, the common denominator for all these conceptions of justice is that they view justice as closely related to a benevolent or compassionate attitude, that justice is about distributing goods in a way that makes life as favourable as possible for everyone. Without a doubt the same can be said about the last 'school' in this category: justice as distribution according to *needs* (Heywood 2004:295–298; Miller 1999:203–229), perhaps most clearly expressed by Karl Marx in his "Critique of the Gotha Programme" (2001:15–21) as a guideline for the coming communist society: "From each according to his ability, to each according to his needs!" (Marx 2001:20).

The other main direction views justice more as a matter of people getting what they can rightfully claim as their own; it might be called the *entitlement* conception. "Justice, in short, is about giving each person what he or she is 'due'." (Heywood 2004:173) The most well-known modern entitlement theory of justice is probably that of Robert Nozick (1974). This theory is based on the demand for respect, in his view, for people's fundamental *rights*, in reality the inviolable right to private property. Thus, we might as well call it a *rights* theory of justice (cf. Heywood 2004:298–300). Another equally well-known conception is that justice is about giving everyone what he or she *deserves* (Heywood 2004:300–303; Miller 1999:131–155; Olsaretti 2003a; Swift 2006:39–47). The desert theory of justice basically holds that people should get in return relative to what they have put in–for example in the amount of effort or work or money they contributed. Sometimes it is difficult to draw the line between justification based on rights and justification based on desert. This seems to be the case when it comes to John Locke's arguments regarding the rightful acquisition of property (Locke 1924:129–141).

Both of these approaches share common ground, however, in that they both represent a more formal, "legal," and in many respects, clearer and stronger interpretation of justice than does the benevolent view. Distribution of goods should be according to who has the firmest rightful claim, not according to what gives the most humane social result–"all things considered." The entitlement view, therefore, is much less likely to favour social redistribution of goods than does the benevolent view. In some respects these two perspectives give competing interpretations of what justice is and should be. At the same time, the perspectives and their various "schools" each contribute different aspects to a comprehensive conception of justice: in this sense they also supplement one another more than they contradict one another.

Kymlicka's Justification for Minority Rights

Will Kymlicka is a theorist who is firmly placed in the tradition of egalitarian liberalism (or liberal egalitarianism) alongside, e.g., John Rawls and Ronald Dworkin. His basic argument for minority rights is also a Rawlsian one: that membership in a cultural community is a type of good that everyone needs and that everyone has a right to demand. Thus, it should be included in the list of *primary goods*. Kymlicka argues (1989:166/177–178) that when Rawls does not realise this, it is because Rawls wrongly assumes that there is an identity between political community and cultural community, and therefore cultural membership is never a problem. As soon as we realise that nation states are in fact multicultural, it will be apparent that the value of liberty dictates the introduction of minority rights in order to secure cultural membership for everyone.

Kymlicka begins his argument with the assertion that our culturally transmitted perspectives shape our understanding of reality. Without cultural membership we would not *have* any perspectives and without perspectives we would not have a background against which we could make meaningful personal choices (Kymlicka 1995:83). The difference between members of majority and minority communities is that for the first group cultural membership is more or less guaranteed, while the members of minority cultures very often risk losing their cultural membership because their culture is threatened with extinction. Therefore, the principle of equal treatment demands that appropriate steps are taken to make it possible for group members to *prevent* their culture from disintegrating. To Kymlicka (1995:26–33), these "appropriate steps" should come in the form of a "differentiated citizenship" or certain rights that apply only to minorities and not to other groups of citizens.

Clearly, his most important argument for minority rights is based on *equality* considerations (Kymlicka 1995:108–115): if we really want to treat people as equals we must take into account that they are different and want to remain different, and then try to make it possible for cultural groups to keep their uniqueness. Because circumstances give people unequal opportunities to hold on to the cultural characteristics that make them different, real treatment as equals implies that the state seemingly must treat its citizens *unequally* and give some groups rights that do not apply to others (cf. Dworkin 1977:227).

Kymlicka does not make a distinction in principle between indigenous peoples and other national minorities. Although his argument primarily refers to the situation of North American indigenous peoples, he does not believe that Inuits and Indians fall into another category than, e.g., French Canadians in Quebec with regard to status as national minorities. He finds that both the rights claims they are making (self-government rights) and the justification for these claims are similar for indigenous and non-indigenous minority groups. He does acknowledge, though, that the tendency in recent international lawmaking seems to be to treat them as separate categories (Kymlicka 2001:120). On the other hand, Kymlicka does make an important distinction between "national minorities" –which are groups/communities with long historic traditions in an area or a country–and what he calls "ethnic groups"–which consist of individuals (and their descendants) who have immigrated to a country in relatively recent times (Kymlicka 1995:11–17).

Kymlicka (1995:27) argues that national minorities have a right to autonomy; that is, they have a right, as far as possible, to keep their traditional social institutions intact and to govern themselves. Ethnic groups, on the other hand, cannot claim a right to–and do not normally want to–rebuild their traditional institutions in their new country, and they have no right to political autonomy. They must be allowed, however, to continue their cultural practises as long as they want to and are able. But even if assimilation is rejected, people who come as immigrants to a new country will in most cases, Kymlicka (1995:15–16) argues, play out their traditional cultural particularities within the institutions of mainstream society and become more and more integrated into that society.

His point is that nobody should be *forced* to exchange their culture for another one, as members of national minorities would be doing if their cultural community was simply allowed to perish. Switching between cultures is nevertheless *possible*, (Kymlicka 1995:84–86), and when people decide to move from one country to another, they do make a personal choice which they have to realise will involve adapting to a new culture. And because this is a choice they presumably have made freely, immigrants have no reason to demand protection against or compensation for these consequences.

Kymlicka discusses two arguments for minority rights, in addition to the argument based on equality. One of them is based on the fact that some national minorities at some point in history entered into agreements with a country's authorities that specified the terms under which they would accept these authorities and/or to become citizens of the state (Kymlicka 1995:116–120). The claim is that even today, by virtue of such agreements, minorities can hold the state accountable and demand that their rights be fulfilled. For example, many American Indian tribes entered into these kinds of treaties. Kymlicka's judgement is that this argument is valid, as far as it has relevance. One limitation is that most national minorities do not have these kinds of documents to present to the state. In addition, even if they have such documents, what was agreed upon long ago does not necessarily have any relevance today, nor did the circumstances under every negotiation warrant a fair and just agreement.

The other additional argument considered by Kymlicka (1995:121–123) is based on the claim that promotion of cultural diversity through the introduction of minority rights would be beneficial to the majority as well as to the minorities (just as biological diversity in nature enriches the whole planet). This is not an unusual line of argument, but is still a problematic one, as Kymlicka views it, because it considers the matter from the perspective of majority *interests*, not from the perspective of minority *justice*. Whether or not a culture should be protected through minority rights must, then, be decided on the basis of how important the majority finds it for the overall cultural pluralism in society. The rights of minority cultures should be evaluated on the basis of the legitimacy of the claims made by their members, not on the basis of folkloristic value, for example.

Discussion of Kymlicka's Justification

I interpret Kymlicka's theory of minority rights–like Rawls' theory of justice–to be a theory of distribution according to needs, combined with an equal-treatment justification. In these theories there is no obvious connection between contribution and reward and unlike in Nozick's theory, the distribution does not follow from a pre-existing "natural" right. Rather, Kymlicka lets the establishment of rights follow from what he deems necessary in order to get a fair distribution of vital social goods.[4] This is much the same as when Rawls, according to Nozick (1974:208), introduces an ideal end situation and then distribute resources based on where needs are greatest in order to realize this ideal goal.[5]

It is doubtful, however, whether or not Kymlicka's theory is absolutely consistent at this point regarding his differentiation between the rights of national minorities and the rights of ethnic groups. Based on his own claim that membership in a cultural community is a fundamental good that no one should be forced to renounce, it could well be argued that the loss of one's cultural context is not necessarily experienced more painfully by members of national minorities than it is by members of ethnic groups. On the other hand, it could also be said that people who make the decision to migrate to another country choose to give up the human rights to their traditional cultural environment and must, of course, also face the consequences of this decision. In fact, this is how Kymlicka defends his position. One problem with this idea is that many immigrants today have not necessarily moved "voluntarily." Another problem is the situation of second-generation immigrants who might experience an equally severe cultural void as do members of a national minority who witness their traditional culture disintegrating. Still, Kymlicka is not theoretically prepared to grant second-generation immigrants the same extensive cultural rights as national minorities, despite the fact that they (unlike their parents) cannot be held personally responsible for their own situation because *they* did not make the decision to migrate.

As mentioned before, Kymlicka does not make a clear distinction between the rights of national minorities and the rights of indigenous peoples. He has chosen to emphasise the similarities rather than the differences between the two groups. Does this mean he believes that no such distinction can be morally justified? Actually, Kymlicka is not that categorical either, on the contrary, he

---

4   In fact, this is also how Kymlicka himself sees it. When discussing indigenous land claims he makes it clear that his theory does not aim to rectify historical wrongs done to indigenous peoples through a principle of compensatory justice, but to give these peoples what they need to survive as distinct groups through a principle of distributive justice. "These compensatory aims actually fit more comfortably with Nozick's libertarian theory of entitlement than with a liberal egalitarian theory of distributive justice" (Kymlicka 1995:220).

5   It is exactly this aspect of Rawls' theory which is most vigorously criticised by Robert Nozick (1974:208): it is an "end-result" or "patterned" theory.

seems to agree that as far as it can be proven that indigenous peoples' fundamental rights to self-determination have been more systematically violated than have the rights of other national minorities, they would be more vulnerable and therefore need stronger protective measures today (Kymlicka 2001:127). The objective of "real equal treatment" could then be viewed as justification for a more comprehensive set of self-determination rights for indigenous peoples than for national minorities.

Apparently, this also seems to have been part of the reasoning behind much of the international legislation on indigenous rights. When indigenous peoples are singled out as a special group in the work on minorities, the underlying justification is their needs for extra protection. Even if ILO Convention 169 does not make a direct comparison between indigenous peoples and other minorities, it is evidenced from the processes behind both this document and the Draft Declaration on the Rights of Indigenous Peoples that indigenous peoples' generally exposed and vulnerable situation has been an important argument for the widely accepted necessity of providing them with more comprehensive rights.

It is, however, still a disputed question as to which groups should be regarded as "indigenous peoples." This partly has to do with the fact that circumstances are so different around the world that it is difficult to find one set of descriptions or criteria that would cover every relevant group everywhere. Kymlicka (2001:122) points to the criteria that while what he calls "stateless nations," [6]generally speaking, were contenders yet losers in the process of European state-formation, indigenous peoples were entirely isolated from that process until very recently. But to understand why indigenous peoples always found themselves in that situation, it is necessary to focus on another characteristic –also mentioned by Kymlicka– which appears to single them out from other peoples in most instances. That is that relative to other peoples they encountered they retained a pre-modern way of life, at least until well into the twentieth century. In most cases they had not developed strong political structures and generally speaking, from a modern perspective, they represented entirely distinct "civilisations" (Kymlicka 2001:128–129). This is not the case with most other stateless nations.[7]

---

6   Kymlicka (2001) splits 'national minorities' into two subsets: indigenous peoples and stateless nations. He thereby seems to overlook at least one other national minority situation, that is when some members of a people who has their own nation state live within the borders of another state. There are countless examples of this world over, like German speaking peoples living in Poland, Hungary, Romania, Italy, France and Denmark, Hungarians in Slovakia and Romania, and Turks in Bulgaria, to mention just a few examples from the European area. The cause of this situation is that borders of nation states not always follow (and for practical reasons not always *can* follow) ethnic and language borders. I believe this kind of national minorities are often seen as having weaker claims for political autonomy than both indigenous peoples and stateless nations.

7   Castellino and Gilbert (2003:168) points to another characteristic feature of indigenous peoples: "First, it is central to the definition of indigenous peoples that they have a specific rela-

In economic terms most indigenous peoples found and often still find their livelihood from hunting and gathering or, in some cases (like the Sami), from nomadism, while neighbouring peoples had or have agricultural or industrial cultures. A characteristic of both hunter and gatherer and of nomadic cultures, is an extensive utilisation of land resources, which makes it both attractive and easy for groups with more intensive forms of land use to infringe on the formers' traditional domains. Another consequence of these typical indigenous forms of adaptation is that they do not necessitate nor is it natural for them to develop concepts of private ownership of land.[8] Due to this and because of their weaker political structures, other cultures that have developed such concepts because they have cultivated the land, may perceive indigenous peoples' territories as no man's land and thus unimpeded make use of that land for their own benefits.

Based on this description, it is fair to say that indigenous peoples constitute groups which have the potential to be rather culturally vulnerable and thus have a great need for protective rights. But if this is true as a general statement, it is a more complex picture when looking at specific examples. When examining the situation in Norway and comparing the conditions for the indigenous population, the Sami, with those of groups that are "only" recognised as national minorities, it is in no way apparent that the Sami are the most culturally vulnerable of these groups. Therefore, it is not at all certain that the conclusion should be that the Sami are in need of the strongest protection through minority rights. On the contrary, I believe that the claim would be well founded that groups like the Kven, the Forrest Finns and the Romani currently find themselves much closer to a state of cultural extinction than the Sami, and historically, a group like the Romani People has surely experienced even harsher discrimination, prejudices and direct infringement than the Sami.[9]

If one takes Kymlicka's emphasis on the equality and needs aspects of justice as the only point of departure, it would be difficult to justify why the Sami should have a more comprehensive special rights scheme than other minority groups in the Norwegian context. Nevertheless, it seems that a large portion of the Norwegian population has a sort of intuitive sentiment which accepts that

---

tionship to a defined territory. In this sense indigenous peoples are sometimes referred to as 'territorial minorities.' This point is central to the notion of indigenousness, since one of the core elements of the indigenous discourse is to ensure that indigenous peoples have a right over their ancestral territories."

8 This is not to say that indigenous societies never have any regulatory mechanisms regarding utilisation of their territorial resources. An example of this from the Sami reindeer nomadism is the so-called *Siida* system, which is the traditional form of regulation of who's reindeer herds have pasture rights where.

9 Kymlicka too agrees that generally speaking indigenous peoples have been worse treated than most other groups. But he also points to exceptional cases like the Crimean Tatars as an example of a stateless nation which has been even worse treated than most indigenous peoples (Kymlicka 2001:128).

the Sami *should have* a special status; that many Norwegians find it reasonable that the Sami have their own parliament, without the Kven, the Gypsies or the Pakistani immigrants having claims to the same sort of treatment. Is there a logical basis for such sentiments? Can it be that other dimensions of the concept of justice are better suited to capture the unique side of the situation of the Sami and other indigenous peoples, dimensions which Kymlicka has been less willing to consider?

An Alternative Justification, Based on Entitlement

Clues to an answer may be found in the other main group of justice theories, the one referred to earlier as the entitlement conception. In his second Treatise of Government (1690), John Locke offers an explanation on the origin of private property. His starting point is the principle of self-ownership; he assumes that each individual is the rightful owner of his/her own person, thereby also owning one's ability to work and the fruits of that work.

> Though the earth and all inferior creatures be common to all men, yet every man has a "property" in his own "person." This nobody has any right to but himself. The "labour" of his body and the "work" of his hands, we may say, are properly his. Whatsoever, then, he removes out of the state that Nature hath provided and left it in, he hath mixed his labour with it, and joined to it something that is his own, and thereby makes it his property. In being by him removed from the common state Nature placed it in, it hath by his labour something annexed to it that excludes the common right of other men. For this "labour" being the unquestionable property of the labourer, no man but he can have a right to what that is once joined to, at least where there is enough, and so good left in common for others (Locke 1924:130).

By harvesting from the gifts of nature or processing the things one finds there, people take them into their possession and make use of them for their own welfare. In the same way someone can appropriate a piece of land by cultivating it and taking care of it. Such actions give them exclusive property rights that nobody else can question, according to Locke, because by mixing one's labour with the resources of nature one becomes the deserved owners of these things.

In his book *Anarchy, State, and Utopia* (1974), Robert Nozick continues Locke's line of reasoning and develops it further into a theory of justice based on what he calls the principle of "entitlement." He underscores that this kind of theory is based on a "historic" principle, i.e., the justice or injustice of a certain distribution of property must be evaluated on the basis of the legitimacy of the process that has produced it. He contrasts this to theories of justice of the Rawlsian type, which he calls "end-result" or "patterned" theories and where the legitimacy of a property distribution is evaluated on the basis of its proximity to a certain pattern or ideal end-result. The basic principles in his own theory are

186

that everyone is the legitimate owner of things that s/he acquires which nobody else is the rightful owner of already. And secondly, that someone who is the rightful owner of a thing may legitimately transfer the ownership of that thing to whomever and in whatever way (through sale, gift, inheritance etc.) they choose (Nozick 1974:150–151). Paraphrasing Marx, Nozick (1974:160) states: *"From each as they choose, to each as they are chosen."*

Discussion of the Entitlement Justification

Nozick's entitlement theory is best known as a statement of the libertarian position. His interpretation of the right to property as absolute led him to attack (almost) all taxation and the principle of social redistribution, which constitutes the foundation of the welfare state. This has, of course, made the theory highly controversial politically. But one does not have to accept all these more or less questionable interpretations in order to accept that there is something intuitively reasonable in the way both Locke and Nozick argue for property rights. It can hardly be denied that most of the social order is based on respect for the principle of property–that we accept that other people get an exclusive right to own a thing because they have acquired the possession of it before anyone else, or because someone in a legitimate way has transferred their own property to them. Therefore, what people often seem to think constitutes a just distribution of goods is when each gets what they are entitled to or in other ways deserves (cf. Miller 1999:61–92; Swift 2006:39–47).

Respect for ownership also lies at the heart of the argument as to why indigenous peoples should be singled out as a group entitled to stronger special rights than national minorities. Typically, indigenous peoples are those who came first to an area and took the land and its resources into possession or use for their own purposes. Through the long and continuous use of the land we must assume that they have developed (collective) ownership of it, although this has not always been legally acknowledged because their mode of possession has not fit easily into the Western legal concepts of private property rights to land.[10] These circumstances often distinguish the situation of indigenous peoples from that of other cultural and ethnic minorities.

However, there are some important and apparent questions that need to be addressed in order to use the theories of Locke and Nozick to justify minority rights. The first question is linked to the fact that both these theorists were staunch individualists and therefore the whole purpose of their theories was to justify *private, individual* property rights. Indigenous peoples, on the other

---

10 When discussing 'special rights' for indigenous peoples it should be remembered, though, that when it comes to land rights it is often not a demand for special treatment but for an end to discrimination and for equal treatment square and simple. This is certainly the case in Norway where long de facto land use has been well established as a legal basis for the acknowledgment of formal *ownership* rights regarding ethnic Norwegian sheep and cattle farmers, but not until very recently when it came to Sami reindeer herders.

hand, typically have perceived their land as something they owned or used in common. Still, there are not necessarily any principal or logical problems at this point. A group of people should be able to collectively acquire possession rights that exclude other groups, just as individuals are able to acquire such rights that exclude other individuals.

The second question concerns the problem that John Locke more or less explicitly argued that the type of land use characteristic of indigenous peoples does *not* qualify for the appropriation of property rights (cf. Oskal 2000). When the Indians travelled across the prairie hunting their pray, this gave them the property right to the animals they could kill[11] but not to the land they were hunting on. Only when the farmer ploughed the land could he claim the ground as properly his[12] (Locke 1924:131–132). But the arguments Locke uses to establish this distinction are dubious. If one chooses to relax on Locke's strict ethos of work as the ultimate form of human self-realisation, one will probably end up with the conclusion that it is not the *type* of utilisation of land that is the salient point in this case, but rather, whether or not historically there has been an (more or less) exclusive utilisation of the land by a group of people for their livelihood.

The third question is whether this line of argument can be used to justify political self-determination rights or only land property rights. Kymlicka (1995:220), among others, points out that justified property claims does not by itself justify self-government claims. At one level this is certainly true. But seen in another context it is clear that the connection between a national group's control over their land and their political autonomy is often tight (cf. Castellino and Gilbert 2003:176). The political organisation of the Middle Ages was in most part based on land rights and much of the same principles are also central to the modern conceptions of the state. A further common characteristic of the situation of indigenous peoples is that they are victims of what is often called an *internal colonisation* by other nations (Tully 2000). This situation in most cases has both a property and a political aspect, with indigenous peoples at the same time being deprived of the land used for their livelihoods and of their status as free peoples. One might say that in the same way Locke and Nozick viewed it as an entitlement for individuals to possess land and other goods, it must be viewed as an entitlement for a group of people recognised as a nation to have the sufficient political autonomy to be able to set the terms for their coexistence and utilisation of their land and other resources. This can be understood as particularly important in the case of indigenous peoples, firstly because of their

---

11 "Thus this law of reason makes the deer that Indian's who hath killed it; it is allowed to be his goods who hath bestowed his labour upon it, though, before, it was the common right of every one." (Locke 1924:131)

12 "As much land as a man tills, plants, improves, cultivates, and can use the product of, so much is his property." (Locke 1924:132)

close connection to and dependency on their lands, and secondly because of the vast differences that often exist between their cultural and societal characteristics and those of the larger society which surrounds them.

The fourth question is whether it is a fair interpretation to put *desert* as a criterion of justice in the same category as the type of entitlement theory put forward by Locke and Nozick. As Olsaretti (2003b:2) points out, Nozick explicitly rejects desert as a criterion for justice in distribution (as does Rawls).[13] His argument is that desert is a "patterned principle," based on the presumption that the distribution of certain goods should reflect who have made themselves more or less deserved of those goods. He interprets this to be in opposition to his own entitlement theory, where the question is not whether you *deserve* something, but rather, whether you are *entitled* to it (Nozick 1974:217). However, the principle of original acquisition becomes morally blurred if one does not at the same time presuppose a principle of desert. Why should the fact that we pick up a piece of wood and make a tool out of it give us the right to own it if not because our effort have made us deserving of it? This connection is much clearer in Locke's theory of property.

Conclusion

After this discussion of justice arguments based on benevolence and on entitlement it can be concluded that arguments based on benevolence–that is equality and need–very often can be used to underpin demands for indigenous rights. However, perhaps even more often, it is arguments based on desert or entitlement that captures the unique in the situation of indigenous peoples, which separates them from other small and vulnerable groups. But again, this calls for specifications, because the debate over indigenous rights concerns different kinds of demands.

Primarily, the argument based on entitlement resulting from long-lasting factual possession and utilisation is well suited to support the claims made by indigenous peoples for rights to their traditional lands and waters. The same type of argument can justify general demands for indigenous autonomy, for example, demands for political self-determination. Norwegian authorities have to some extent acknowledged this. In 1997 HM King Harald in a speech to the Sami Parliament said that the Norwegian state was built on the territories of two peoples, the Norwegians and the Sami (Ministry of Local Government and Regional Development 2000–2001, Chapter 2.1). This is an open expression of some sort of symmetry between the two peoples based on historical possession of territories and clearly puts the Sami in another category than other national minorities. This in turn must be viewed as an important legitimating factor for

---

13 One libertarian who accepts desert as a criterion alongside entitlement is J. Narveson (Olsaretti 2003b:2).

an institution like the Sami Parliament. However, the possibility of legitimating various forms of political autonomy is not necessarily uniquely limited to indigenous peoples–although I believe this to be the situation in Norway. Many examples can be found around the world where other types of national minorities also have long-lasting historical connections to specific parts of a state's territory, which may very well give them a justifiable claim for political autonomy. In particular, this seems relevant for stateless nations. The specific case indigenous peoples can make is the unique claim for recognition of land rights *in combination with* a claim for political self-determination.

A third type of indigenous rights demands is for cultural rights, e.g., the rights to be able to use and receive education in their own language and various other measures aimed at preserving different aspects of a group's cultural traditions. These types of demands can best be justified with arguments based on equal treatment and needs. However, in this area there may not be any grounds for specific and exclusive *indigenous* rights. In this respect, the interests of indigenous peoples have to be evaluated on an equal footing with those of other national minorities and, at least in some cases, with those of ethnic groups (in the way Kymlicka uses these terms).[14]

In total, the special situation of indigenous peoples seems to be that their rights can be justified both from a position of weakness and a position of strength. On the one hand their culture is vulnerable and therefore often will have a stronger need for extra protection than the cultures of most other groups. On the other hand, their historical connection to their territories gives them a strong basis for claims for control over these territories, rooted in legal principles already accepted as valid for other peoples. It is in the combination of these two argumentative strategies that the best justification for the special status of indigenous peoples in international law is to be found.

---

14 Cf. Castellino and Gilbert (2003) who from a jurisprudence angle reach a similar conclusion: "In terms of the *International Covenant on Civil and Political Rights*, a hierarchy of entitlements would develop whereby territorially based indigenous peoples would have the rights akin to colonial peoples and would thus enjoy the full benefits of Article 1 including sub-paragraph 1(1). Indigenous peoples who do not inhabit distinct territories would have the right of self-determination as given by Article 1(2). By contrast, minorities would have the rights guaranteed by Article 27. [...] Furthermore, minorities located in contiguous territory might still entertain claims to 'internal' self-determination." (Castellino and Gilbert 2003:175) (Article 1(1) gives 'all peoples' the right to self-determination, Article 1(2) gives 'all peoples' the right to dispose of their natural wealth and resources, while Article 27 provides minorities with a right to have, express and practise their own culture, language and religion.)

References

Anaya, S. James. 1996. *Indigenous Peoples in International Law*. Oxford: Oxford University Press.

Aristotle. 1957. *The Politics*. Harmondsworth: Penguin.

Aristotle. 1976. *Ethics: The Nicomachean Ethics*. London/Harmondsworth: Penguin.

Barry, Brian. 1989. *Theories of Justice*. Berkeley: University of California Press.

Barry, Brian. 1995. *Justice as Impartiality*. Oxford: Oxford University Press.

Castellino, Joshua and Jérémie Gilbert. 2003. "Self-Determination, Indigenous Peoples and Minorities." *Macquarie Law Journal* 3:155–178.

Daes, Erica-Irene A. 2000. "Protection of the World's Indigenous Peoples and Human Rights", in Janusz Symonides (ed.): *Human Rights: Concept and Standards*. Aldershot: Ashgate/UNESCO.

Dworkin, Ronald. 1977. *Taking Rights Seriously*. London: Duckworth.

Dworkin, Ronald. 1985. *A Matter of Principle*. Cambridge, Mass.: Harvard University Press.

Freeman, Michael. 2002. *Human Rights. An Interdisciplinary Approach*. Cambridge: Polity Press.

Hannum, Hurst. 2000. "The Rights of Persons Belonging to Minorities", in Janusz Symonides (ed.): *Human Rights: Concept and Standards*. Aldershot: Ashgate/UNESCO.

Heywood, Andrew. 2004. *Political Theory. An Introduction,* Third Edition. Basingstoke: Palgrave Macmillan.

ILO. 1989. "ILO Convention 169: Indigenous and Tribal Peoples Convention." International Labour Organisation. http://www.ilo.org/ilolex/english/convdisp1.htm

Kymlicka, Will. 1989. *Liberalism, Community and Cultural*. Oxford: Clarendon Press.

Kymlicka, Will. 1995. *Multicultural Citizenship. A Liberal Theory of Minority Rights*. Oxford: Clarendon Press.

Kymlicka, Will. 2001. "Theorizing Indigenous Rights", in *Politics in the Vernacular*. Oxford: Oxford University Press.

Locke, John. 1924. *Two Treatises of Government*. London: Dent.

Marx, Karl. 2001. "Critique of the Gotha Programme." The Electric Book Company. http://site.ebrary.com/lib/tromsoub/Doc?id=2001644

Miller, David. 1999. *Principles of Social Justice*. Cambridge, Mass.: Harvard University Press.

Ministry of Foreign Affairs, Norway. 1999–2000. "Report No. 21 to the Storting: Focus on Human Dignity – A Plan for Action for Human Rights." http://odin.dep.no/ud/engelsk/publ/p10001859/032001-040007/hov004-bn.html

Ministry of Local Government and Regional Development, Norway. 2000–2001. "Report No. 55 to the Storting: On the Sami Policy." http://odin.dep.no/krd/norsk/dok/ regpubl/stmeld/016091-040002/hov002-bn.html#hov2.2.1

Nozick, Robert. 1974. *Anarchy, State, and Utopia*. Oxford: Blackwell.

Olsaretti, Serena (ed.). 2003a. *Desert and Justice*. Oxford: Clarendon Press.

Olsaretti, Serena. 2003b. "Introduction: Debating Desert and Justice", in Serena Olsaretti (ed.): *Desert and Justice*. Oxford: Clarendon Press.

Oskal, Nils. 2000. "Det moralske grunnlaget for diskvalifiseringen av urfolks eiendomsrett til land og politisk suverenitet." *Norsk Filosofisk Tidsskrift* 35:167–182.

Rawls, John. 1971. *A Theory of Justice*. Oxford: Oxford University Press.

Rawls, John. 1993. *Political Liberalism*. New York: Columbia University Press.

Scherrer, Christian P. 2003. *Ethnicity, Nationalism and Violence. Conflict Management, Human Rights, and Multilateral Regimes*. Aldershot: Ashgate.

Swift, Adam. 2006. *Political Philosophy. A Beginners' Guide for Students and Politicians,* Second Edition. Cambridge: Polity Press.

Tully, James. 2000. "The Struggles of Indigenous Peoples for and of Freedom", in Duncan Ivison, Paul Patton, and Will Sanders (eds): *Political Theory and the Rights of Indigenous Peoples*. Cambridge: Cambridge University Press.

CHAPTER 9

Marine Resource Management and Social Justice from the Perspective of Indigenous Peoples

SVEIN JENTOFT

Introduction

For many indigenous peoples, the rights of access to fisheries and coastal re-sources are crucial for the sustenance of their livelihoods and distinct cultures. In a country like Norway, for example, marine resources and ecosystems are a pillar for the indigenous people, the Sámi (Jentoft 1998). The same is the case for coastal indigenous peoples in many other parts of the world, including Nicaragua, where I have worked and done a considerable amount of research (Jentoft 2005).[1] As in Norway, for the coastal indigenous communities in Ni-caragua it is becoming increasingly more difficult to access marine and coastal resources as property rights and other management mechanisms are either in-adequately developed or poorly enforced–as a whole they do not incorporate indigenous rights and concerns.

This raises serious questions regarding ecosystem health, sustainable liveli-hoods and food security, and also about social justice and equity. Indigenous peoples more often than not find themselves on the losing side when resources are getting more scarce, competition more fierce and when governments be-gin to regulate. Their situation is perhaps not all that unique as they seem to share a similar fate with non-indigenous, small-scale fishing peoples in many parts of the world's coastal regions. Regardless of ethnic background, the poor, marginalized, excluded and disempowered tend to lose-out in the end. Poverty becomes chronic and embedded in social institutions and structures, and "re-quires a stronger and more thoroughgoing challenge than a technocratic focus on 'poverty reduction' can offer" (Hicks & Bracking 2005: 862).

In this chapter I will address three interrelated topics. First I will discuss poverty and sustainable livelihoods which is a legitimate issue among small-scale fishers and coastal indigenous and non-indigenous peoples. I will also evaluate resource (property) rights and tenure–a key issue in the indigenous rights movement–which has relevance for both the land and the sea. Finally, I will address a fairly recent management approach called ecosystem-based management. Depending on how it is designed and implemented, this approach may have positive implications for indigenous coastal communities because it is more space-based and thus might help reinforce territorial claims of sea tenure and indigenous ecological knowledge.

---

1   http://www.sami.uit.no/uraccan/ (accessed on 5 August 2007)

193

Property and Social Justice

A WorldFish Centre and FAO report (2005) estimates that there are about 150 million people living in households that depend primarily on small-scale fisheries. In addition, assuming that the incidence of poverty among fisheries-dependent people is only as high as the average in their respective countries, there would be some 23 million fisheries-dependent people living on less than the equivalent of one US dollar per day. Indigenous fishing peoples are not specifically mentioned in the FAO report, but there is every reason to assume that they figure at the lower end of that scale. They are not only struggling to sustain their distinct cultural identity in the face of globalization, but also–due to the current rate of resource exploitation globally–indigenous fishers and coastal people must also cope with poverty due to *inter alia* ecological crisis and resource degradation. Thus, they must be included in efforts to alleviate poverty among small-scale fishers. The WorldFish Centre/FAO report should be taken at face value, but these organizations should be mindful that indigenous peoples also have particular problems and therefore should receive special focus, for example, regarding the issue of property rights and culture.

Secure property rights are an essential part of a solution to end poverty in indigenous and non-indigenous fishing peoples, in addition to a number of other institutional support mechanisms (Jentoft 2003). However, property rights may easily become part of the problem if they are defined and enforced in ways that ignore their potential social justice implications; the risk is not only realistic, but materializing. The property rights systems that are currently being introduced in fisheries and coastal management are largely negligent of the social justice issues involved so the people who have to live with their distributional consequences often experience them as violations of their basic interests and rights.

Few would challenge the view that eco-system health is basic to sustainable livelihoods: without it people would starve. Economic efficiency pursued reasonably is itself a worthy goal so as not to waste natural resources by either overuse or under-use. Social justice is another basic concern of fisheries and coastal management (Kooiman et al. 2005). Obviously, fisheries and coastal management that attain eco-system health and economic efficiency may produce outcomes that benefit some groups while marginalizing others. Social justice should be seen as a value in itself; it is an essential part of good governance and it demonstrates respect for the human rights of indigenous peoples.

It is for these reasons that fisheries and coastal resource rights are among the issues that figure into the *UN Draft Declaration on the Rights of Indigenous Peoples,* although perhaps not as prominently as coastal indigenous peoples desired as it mainly addresses land rights and terrestrial resources. Social justice is a basic value in fisheries and coastal management in and of itself, but it also has functional merit. It affects the legitimacy of management systems and decisions, and therefore, the degree of users' compliance to rules and regulations. Fishers might be more inclined to accept strict harvesting restrictions if they were defined, implemented, and enforced in such a way that fishers perceived as just and fair.

Social justice is among the conditions that are basic to the effectiveness of management; otherwise management systems would rely on coercion and repression because people tend to resist and rebel through "voice" but most likely through "exit" (Hirschman 1970). In that case, management is unlikely to be effective with people who are coping with poverty and hunger. Fisheries and coastal management rarely commence with a deliberation on what constitutes social justice, what principles should be central, what is negotiable and non-negotiable, and what are the social and cultural thresholds. Consequently, current management systems are often as unjust as they are ineffective. Managers of such systems tend to get justice claims straight in their face after implementation as people protest–sometimes violently–to what they see as unfair treatment and a violation of their natural rights as fishers, communities, and peoples.

Scientists are partly to blame for the lack of attention paid to social justice issues and principles in management as they are more inclined to focus on the techniques of management and rarely reflect on the extensive academic discourse on justice. Scholars such as John Rawls, Will Kymlicka, Tom Campell, Jon Elster, David Miller and Amartya Sen–to name a few who have addressed the social justice issue philosophically–do not appear on the list of references in scholarly papers concerning fisheries and coastal management.[2] This is an unfortunate omission as social justice scholars have much to reveal about issues relevant to resource management (Hernes, Jentoft and Mikalsen 2005). Social justice concerns tend to be omitted when fisheries and coastal management are only defined in technical and functional terms.

What is needed is a broader *governance* approach as proposed by Kooiman et al. (2005) where issues of environmental and social ethics and morality are emphasized. Marginalized indigenous and non-indigenous coastal peoples would benefit from this shift in focus, although there is always a risk of "throwing the baby out with the bath water." The tools, techniques, and instrumental rationality of fisheries and coastal management are still important as long as they have been filtered for their ethical and moral considerations and for their implications for poverty and social justice. For indigenous peoples, rights to property, land, water, space, and resources are a human rights issue and thus a social justice and legal issue. Property rights are a useful instrument because they encourage environmental stewardship.

In the resource management literature following Garrett Hardin's seminal article on the "Tragedy of the Commons," property is perceived in instrumental terms and not as a human rights issue (1968). He postulated that it is in the

---

2   Coward et al. (2000) is an exception.

absence of clearly defined property rights that the tragedy unfolds. Thus, when resource management theorists and practitioners talk about getting "property rights right," they are thinking about their functional merits and the incentives they entail. From a governance perspective it is argued that both the *value rational* and *instrumental rational* aspects of property are both relevant to natural resource management and that the two aspects should merge. (Weber 1978) As separate discourses, the human rights and functional aspects of property rarely overlap but they are equally relevant to all marginalized peoples–indigenous and non-indigenous alike–even if the latter do not enjoy the same legal support for their justice claims as the former (Smith 1990).

Property Rights and Management

Once the legal issues concerning indigenous rights to fisheries and coastal resources are resolved (and for most peoples there is still a long way to go) all the other elements of a workable and socially-just management system need to be considered. What kind of property rights should be adopted within indigenous communities? Should fisheries and coastal management be based on effort control or quotas? How should rules and regulations be enforced?

The outcome of the UNCLOS (United Nations Convention on the Law of the Sea) process that led to the 200 miles zones in the late 1970s might be re-experienced if such questions are not considered in advance. During that period there was widespread belief that UNCLOS would resolve the problem of over fishing once and for all. If nation-states obtained control of their fishing territories, over fishing and resource degradation would become history. Thirty years later we understand that this belief was overly optimistic. In many cases, UNCLOS exacerbated the problem of over fishing and resource degradation rather than alleviating it. Governments and the fishing industry believed that if foreign fishing vessels were excluded from their zones they could justifiably expand domestic fishing capacity and effort. In Canada this belief and practice led to a resource crisis within the cod fishery from which they have not yet recovered (Alcock 2002).

Territorial rights are necessary to combat reckless harvesting practices, but they have proven to be far from sufficient in order to ensure sustainable resource use, development, and management. For indigenous people the history of the 200 mile zones where resource rights were not sufficient to guarantee sustainability could easily be repeated. Indigenous peoples who have control of their fisheries and coastal territories need to consider how to manage effectively, efficiently, and with social justice. Since property rights issues are inherently conflictive and tricky the difficult questions they pose should not be postponed in anticipation of a practical solution. Questions should be equally concerned with what comes after as well as before "the revolution". If not, there is a risk that natural resources will continue to diminish as traditional indigenous management systems are often vulnerable to both internal and external pressures. Sometimes indigenous fisheries use damaging fishing techniques and harvest threatened species and have the potential to exploit resources to extinction.

Marine property rights for indigenous communities or individuals do not automatically halt reckless harvesting practices. Property not only entails rights, but also risks and responsibilities. It is basically a social relationship encompassing permission to reserve for oneself and exclude from others a stream of benefits originating from a resource. Zygmunt Bauman says that as globalization unites it also divides (1998:2). The same can be said about property rights. They are divisive on any scale of measurement, whether individually or collectively. Securing natural rights to capital does not necessarily lead to social justice and equity, neither externally in relation to other groups, nor internally among group members. Individual and communal rights may consequently be as socially just as they are unjust. An example is the land demarcation process currently underway in Nicaragua. It will undoubtedly rectify previous injustices committed against indigenous communities but the issue that needs to be resolved is how the demarcation will affect the distribution of land and natural resources among indigenous local communities (Acosta 2003). Also, non-indigenous people living within Rama territory are also marginalised and poor, and some arrangement would have to be worked out for them.

Social justice does not only relate to distributive outcomes, but also to institutions and their governing principles and procedures. David Miller argues that justice "must include aspects of social relations that do not fall readily under the rubric of distribution" (1999:14-15). Procedural justice pertains to representation and decision-making. From a social justice perspective, management institutions and procedures must be subject to similar scrutiny as property rights and distributional outcomes. Who are the stakeholders? Are minority and indigenous stakeholders represented with recognition and are their voices heard? These are concerns that arise after property rights are secured and it would be wise to consider them sooner rather than later. It there is truth in what Schattscheider (1960) pointed out–that inevitably "organization is the mobilization of bias"–then the question is what constitutes a socially just bias?

Indigenous peoples are not exempted from this dilemma and a whole range of difficult decisions and institutional demands when it comes to natural resource management. They must consider how to balance ecological sustainability, economic efficiency, and social justice, while also ensuring that the rules and regulations are implemented and enforced. This is no less true when the challenge is to alleviate extreme poverty in indigenous communities (Barrett et al. 2004).

Fisheries and coastal management are largely driven by theoretical concepts, ideal-type models, and assumptions. Accordingly, if aggregate fishing efforts are too large, there is already a ready-made explanation and a pre-packaged solution. It is on such assumptions that management systems are built and implemented. Too often than not, fisheries managers have preconceived solutions where they look for problems to solve rather than investigating the problem and then devising a solution. For example, individual transferable quotas (ITQs) are being introduced all over the world, Norway included, and both indigenous and non-indigenous communities suffer the consequences. ITQs are built on the assumption that fishers are individuals whose sole ambition in life is to maximize their individual use of common fisheries resources for the sake of profits (St. Martin 2001).

The risks would be decreased if assumptions were made solely for analytical purposes and not for policy intervention. It is safer in the long run to make such assumptions into empirical questions rather than recipes for solutions in the real world. Questions that should be posed include "What are the small-scale fisheries out there?," Are they different in indigenous communities than in non-indigenous communities?," Is there really a Malthusian mechanism that Garrett Hardin envisaged in small scale fisheries? Small-scale fishers may be poor for a whole range of reasons, including the Tragedy of the Commons. Thus, when identifying solutions to poverty alleviation, the definition of what constitutes small-scale fisheries and fishers should not be generated from preconceived notions of problems but from a thorough empirical investigation into the actual situations and problems of small-scale fisheries.

The risk is similar with regard to social justice. Philosophical reflection can lead us deep and far but it can also lead us astray. It is necessary to understand the real life context within which management systems, including their indigenous property rights, are supposed to function. The deliberations on the intentions of social justice in fisheries and coastal management in general, and for indigenous peoples and their communities in particular, should not be removed from their empirical settings. They should be rooted in people's realities and lived experiences and should transpire in proximity to where problems are experienced. This does not mean that social justice standards are only local; there are also universal standards –like human rights – that fisheries and coastal management must also adhere. But justice principles and standards find their concretization expressed in concrete circumstances, such as fisheries as they occur in particular communities. In some situations they lead to confirmation of already existing principles and practices while in other situations to their reform or abolishment. Customary indigenous management practices are not always socially just, sometimes they can be cruel, discriminatory, and undemocratic (Jentoft 2004).

Ecosystem-based Management
Fisheries and coastal management are now moving away from the single-species stock assessment and sector approach towards an "ecosystem-based" mod-

el and an integrative and holistic approach (cf. Pikitch et al. 2004). The new methodology emphasizes the need to include humans in the equation, which is remarkable because the natural scientists are promoting it. This signals an interdisciplinary approach to fisheries and coastal management, thus breaking through the disciplinary boundaries that until now have been strictly upheld in this discussion. Humans are the most destructive users of marine and coastal resources and the institutions that we develop to protect resources from depletion are human-made. Social scientists, whose main focus has always been institutions, are now moving away from the state-centred, top-down approach to fisheries management towards a more bottom-up and participatory management model where community should play a proactive role.

This is a positive development for indigenous peoples because they would need to employ similar approaches themselves if management responsibilities were to be devolved from state bureaucracies. A holistic ecosystem approach with governance structures that allow for grassroots input is in keeping with the approach indigenous peoples have historically used in the management of their marine and terrestrial resources. Consequently, a move towards ecosystem management would lead to more recognition of small-scale indigenous harvesting practices, indigenous ecological knowledge, traditional marine tenure systems, and other management practices.

However, if humans are to be perceived as a genetically more sophisticated species and as individual, rational, profit-maximizers there is a risk that the new ecosystems approach to fisheries and coastal management may not be holistic. The users of marine and coastal resources, both indigenous and non-indigenous, come with social and cultural commitments and dispositions, and their resource use and management systems are embedded in social networks and institutions at multiple levels–family, community and nation. A holistic, multi- or interdisciplinary fisheries and coastal management model should therefore work beyond the perspective that resource users are no more than "predators" driven by narrow economic calculus. As people pursue economic utility they also seek meaning, identity, direction, and security, as well as justice in their lives. When small-scale indigenous fishing people need to adapt to change, cope with ecological crisis, and strive to survive in the face of poverty, it is a collective effort; they take action as households, groups, communities, and nations. In this way, small-scale fishers and their dependents are not only mobilizing natural and financial capital but also social and cultural capital. A primary focus of fisheries and coastal research should pertain to how these different forms of capital are built and activated among poor, indigenous small-scale fishing people when coping with poverty and adapting to ecological crisis.

Consequently, an ecosystem and social system approach to fisheries and coastal management is necessary–a combined approach recognizes that social systems are as diverse and dynamic as natural systems. Under globalization these systems are becoming increasingly complex, diverse, and dynamic, and they impose greater risks on indigenous fishers and coastal people. Such changes require a better understanding of the multiple interests and power mechanisms that drive the processes of marginalization of indigenous small-scale fisheries. It is particularly important to stress this in natural scientific circles where ecosystem management with a human emphasis is gaining in popularity. In addition, managers are increasingly turning their attention away from social scientists and towards natural scientists and economists.

If the new ecosystem approach to fisheries management is to embrace both natural and human dimensions, it is also important to consider that natural and social systems are fundamentally different. As far as humans can tell fish are scarcely concerned with social justice. Clearly, indigenous fishers care deeply about social justice because they so often find themselves among the poorest of the poor, like for example in Nicaragua (Gonzalez et al 2006). When people find injustice disturbing and demand rectification, it is part of their coping strategy and also because injustice is a violation of their social values and principles. Social justice has to be among the prime concerns of holistic fisheries and coastal management, and it cannot be postponed or compromised by ecological sustainability or economic efficiency. The rights, interests, considerations, and aspirations of indigenous peoples must be included.

Of all the main concerns in current management systems, social justice is usually the last consideration. Justice is often willingly sacrificed by many academics and managers in order to realize other concerns which they view as more pressing. The first concern is that resources must be sustained; second is the resource rent – that is the economics of it all; and finally social justice and community health. This line of thinking typically does not lead to property and secured rights of access to marine and coastal resources but at best to some form of compensation in the form of subsidies and welfare schemes. In many instances, however, the closing of the commons and restricted access means that people are forced to leave the fishery or are denied entry and then they are forced to fend for themselves to the best of their ability. If there is no labour market that can absorb them, then poverty increases. This is the vicious circle of poverty (Jentoft 2005).

If you do not fish then you starve, but if you fish you ruin the stock and then you starve. This is but one of the reasons why small-scale fisheries "rhymes with poverty" (Béné 2003). As Béné argues, poverty among small-scale fishers is not only caused by overuse of fish resources but also to the socio-institutional mechanisms that regulate access to marine and coastal resources and the relations of power that determines how wealth is accumulated and distributed. Thus, there is reason to fear that FAO, national governments and others who worry about resource degradation can create more rather than less poverty which may well lead to an even greater pressure on natural resources. When people get hungry enough they fish. They fish with whatever technological means are available to them regardless of the state of the fish stocks and regardless of whatever limitation government authorities impose on them. This is also why indigenous marine harvesters need secured property rights and a management system that works to their benefit.

References

Acosta, M.L.: "Encroaching Upon Indigenous Land: Nicaragua and the 'Dry Canal'." In S. Jentoft, H. Minde and R. Nilsen (eds.): *Indigenous Peoples: Resource Management and Global Rights.* Delft. Eburon Academic Publishing, 2003.

Alcock, F. 2002: "Bargaining, Uncertainty, and Property Rights in Fisheries." *World Politics,* Vol. 54: 437-61.

Barrett, C.B., D.R. Lee and J.G. McPeak: "Institutional Arrangements for Rural Poverty Reduction and Resource Conservation." *World Development,* Vol. 33, No. 2, pp. 193-197.

Bauman, Z: *Globalization. The Human Consequences*: London: Polity Press, 1998.

Béné, C.: "When Fishery Rhymes with Poverty: A First Step Beyond the Old Paradigm on Poverty in Small-Scale Fisheries." *World Development*, Vol. 31, No. 6, pp 949-975, 2003.

Coward, H., R. Ommer and T. Pitcher (eds.): *Just Fish: Ethics and Canadian Marine Fisheries.* St. John's, Newfoundland: ISER Press, 2000.

Hardin, G.: "The Tragedy of the Commons." *Science*, Vol. 162, pp. 1243-1248, 1968.

Hernes, H-K, S. Jentoft and K. H. Mikalsen: "Fisheries Governance, Social Justice and Participatory Decision-making." In T. S. Gray (ed.): *Participation in Fisheries Governance.* Dordrecht: Springer Publishing, 2005.

Hick, S. and S. Bracking: "Exploring the Politics of Chronic Poverty: From Representation to a Politics of Justice?" *World Development,* Vol. 33, No. 6, pp 851-865, 2005.

Hirschman, A.O.: *Exit, Voice and Loyalty.* Princeton, N.J.: Princeton University Press, 1970.

Jentoft, S.: "The Poverty Trap: Defending Indigenous Peoples' Resource Rights in Nicaragua." Centre for Sami Studies, University of Tromsø, 2005.

Jentoft. S.: "The Community in Fisheries Management: Challenges, Opportunities and Risks." In B. Hersoug, S. Jentoft and P. Degnbol: *Fisheries Development: The Institutional Challenge.* Delft: Eburon, 2004.

Jentoft, S. (ed.): *Commons in Cold Climate: Coastal Fisheries and Reindeer Pastoralism in North Norway.* London: Parthenon Publishers, 1998.

Kooiman, J., M. Bavinck, S. Jentoft and R. Pullin (eds.): *Fish for Life: Interactive Governance for Fisheries.* University of Amsterdam Press, 2005.

Gonzalez, M., S. Jentoft, A. Koskinen, and D. Lopez (eds): *The Rama People: Struggling for Land and Culture.* Managua: URACCAN University, 2006.

Miller, D.: *Principles of Social Justice.* Cambridge: Harvard University Press, 1999.

Pikitch, E.K., C. Santora et al.: "Ecosystem-based Fishery Management," *Science*, Vol. 305, 2004; pp. 346-347.

Schattschneider E.E.: *The Semi-Sovereign People.* New York: Holt, Rinehard and Winston, 1960.

Smith, C.: "Om samenes rett til naturressurser – særlig ved fiskerireguleringer." *Lov og rett.* Pp. 50-534, 1990.

Weber, Max: Economy and Society: An Outline of Interpretive Sociology, Vol. I and II New York, Bedminster Press, 1978.

WorldFish Centre and FAO Collaborative Programme: *Towards and Interdisciplinary Approach to the Assessment of Small-Scale Fisheries and its Role in Food Security and Poverty Alleviation and Sustainable Resource Use.* Rome 2005.

CHAPTER 10

Distribution, Recognition, and Poverty Experiences from Guatemala and Norway.

GEORGES MIDRÉ

Introduction

Our notions of social justice are intertwined with our ideas about equality and difference. However, there are diverging ideas about when and to what extent equality is justified. For instance, most of us would agree that some of the differences that result from higher competence are legitimate. Higher education, specialized knowledge, performing hard, dirty, or dangerous work should be rewarded. In this case the notion of justice is linked to an idea of merit.

In this chapter I will limit my focus to two conceptions of equality, and emphasise how these ideas are the basis for the functioning of public institutions and national elites in relation to ethnic categories in a population. The concepts of equality in question are *equality of opportunity* and *distributive equality*. There is a tension, however, between these concepts, and in terms of their application in public institutions and in citizenship. How are we able to reconcile recognition of differences in values and lifestyles with our requirements for accessing material and other goods? These tensions are particularly visible in countries were ethnic minorities confront majority populations. I will discuss these concepts in drawing on examples from two countries, Norway and Guatemala.

Equality of Distribution

In Norway, equality has been a main political goal for a long time and has been supported by most of the population and institutionalized in the form of a Welfare State. Its main merits have been to reduce social differences in wealth, morbidity and for improving the possibility of obtaining an education. Compared to most other countries, the poverty level is very low in Norway.

As part of the construction of the Welfare State after the end of WWII, acceptable minimum level living standards were set up in key areas like income, health, nutrition, education, and housing. A growing bureaucracy with a number of public employees was given the responsibility to assure that these standards were met.

In hindsight we see that the enthusiasm and the laudable intentions of the reformers of the Norwegian Welfare State had concealed the fact that the functioning of such an equalitarian system also had a dark side. It may be that the Welfare State in Norway not only tried to create justice by implementing a number of equalizing institutions, but that it also required equality in terms of lifestyles and values as a precondition for being fully accepted as a member of that same welfare society (Thuen 1995). The distinction between deplorable living conditions due to poverty and illness, and lifestyles that were found within cultural minorities became blurred. This is clearly evident in the treatment of national minorities like the Finnish speaking *Kven* in Northern Norway, and particularly the *Romani* people in the south. In the case of the latter, their children were forcibly taken from their parents and implanted into families with what was perceived as more correct lifestyles, or they were put into boarding schools in order to supposedly protect them from the obnoxious influence of their parents (Hvinden 2000). This history has recently been fully documented, and the Norwegian government has to some extent acknowledged its mistakes.

The Norwegian government's treatment of the Sami people has many similarities. The Samis are the only ethnic minority in the country that has gained the status of an indigenous people, which means that the State has accepted a special responsibility for protecting their culture, and for stimulating the development of that culture on the premises of what the Sami themselves intend (Minde 2003). The inclusion of the Sami into the Welfare State has been accompanied by gaining access to a number of social entitlements. But until the 1970s and 80s, these entitlements were linked to requirements in the form of giving up essential cultural markers (Eidheim, Henriksen et al. 1985). To put it bluntly: their identity as Sami was exchanged for the gift of being included in the institutions of the beneficent Welfare State. The welfare state reformers viewed poverty, underdevelopment and Saminess, as one conglomerate, and the way to prosperity entailed a willingness to leave these entirely behind. And many Sami seem to have believed the reformers views and have left Saminess behind.

According to Eidheim et al (1985), since the Sami were regareded as citizens of the Norwegian state they were not recognized as Sami, but as Norwegian, and they were punished when they emphasised and expressed their Sami identity. In order for the Sami to benefit from the entitlements of the Welfare State, education, health care and social security, as well as an increased participation in the formal labour market, they had to suppress Sami and develop Norwegian knowledge and skills. Eidheim and others argued that such demands were transformed into general ideals of what were acceptable lifestyles, and about how they could be acquired. Ideas about what constituted welfare, and the ways leading to a higher quality of life, were Norwegian and not Sami. The cultural expressions of Sami lifestyles were viewed by the majority population as irrelevant and could be perceived as backwards and outdated. For these reasons, many Sami were ambivalent in relation to their ethnic identity.

These processes led to strong pressures in the direction of embracing a Norwegian lifestyle. The Sami culture was oppressed and they might have felt subdued in the sense that they were despised for their background. We can witness a paradox: the more successful and efficient the Welfare state, the stronger were the negative effects for the ethnic self-esteem of an increasing number of the Sami people. In fact, the Welfare state was to a certain extent a general threat for the Sami culture, in spite of the material and other improvements that the Sami gained as Norwegian citizens (Eidheim, Henriksen et al. 1985).

Some of the harmful effects of the public policies on the lives of the Sami people were related to the concepts of equality on which the Norwegian welfare policies are based. One dominant concern is connected to a concept of equality of distribution, and the end result of the distributional processes regarding wealth and other characteristics of welfare. The public programmes aim was to secure a minimum of welfare for all of the population, regardless of cultural and social background. There was, however, a lack of attention paid to the right to be different, to choose alternative lifestyles and priorities. In particular, the Norwegian approach at that time did not tackle the difficult issue of defining the limits of the Welfare State in relation to the minority cultures within its borders. The enthusiasm and pride of the reformers when proposing to build a Welfare State, was not coupled with sufficient restraint when dealing with the Sami. The concept of equality of distribution in combination with the conviction that the reforms were aiming at offering an undisputable good (welfare) and fighting against evil (poverty), in many cases produced suffering and pain instead of making them disappear.

Equality of Opportunity

When studying countries outside of Scandinavia we find that an alternative idea of equality seems to be more common. This is the liberal notion of *equality of opportunity* and relates to the access of all citizens to basic institutions like the political system, education and the market (Verba, Kelman et al. 1987). In contrast to the concept of equality of distribution, there is less concern about the actual outcome of the distributional processes in a society, as long as all are believed to have had the same opportunities. The resulting unequal distribution in terms of welfare and poverty seem to be justified–or at least tolerated–if people have had the possibility to influence the distributional processes, for example by increasing their social capital, by working harder or being smarter. Put simply, according to this line of thought people tend to merit what they get.

It is well known that poverty is widespread in Guatemala, and particularly so among the indigenous population. In the case of the latter about 75% are classified as poor. For the indigenous population, the need for public, life-sustaining support is without a doubt more accentuated. In 2001 I participated in a study which looked at how a sample of Guatemalan Ladino elites, politicians, civil servants and health workers, perceived the situation of the country's poor (Midré and Flores 2002). We were also interested in their views on how poverty could be alleviated and were particularly interested in the informants' ideas about what basis public policies in the health and housing areas could be justified.

When we analysed the interviews we found that the ideas of equality of opportunity were dominant. According to the informants, *ethnicity* was neither a relevant nor a legitimate criterion for selecting a target population in the distributional processes. As a matter of fact, claims that related to ethnic divisions regarding social and health policy programmes were largely missing in our sample. The informants regarded targeting the indigenous poor as implying a form of discrimination, understood as ethnic discrimination against the non-indigenous population—the Ladinos. As grounds for distributional policies this was viewed as both constitutionally illegal and illegitimate since all Guatemalans were considered to be equal. The ideology supporting this argument is informed by the value of equality, but in the meaning of equality of opportunity.

At least within the areas of health and housing, the informants simply did not acknowledge *ethnicity* as a relevant criterion for public policy measures. This position can be demonstrated with a statement from one of the informants, with responsibilities within the housing area, who said:

> I speak of socio-economic stratification, not an ethnic one. The Indigenous enters into the class of the dispossessed. They are treated within that category, with direct, targeted subsidies.

Our informants, then, explicitly dismiss *ethnicity* as a legitimate basis for why there are social problems. Judging by our sample, the state and its administration do not frame social problems in ethnic terms—but, rather as relating to social class divisions.

We also noted, however, that in some cases informants employed a concept of inequality of condition: there was a preoccupation with the situation of the poor, homeless, and the sick. In other words, we encountered a type of idea regarding equality of distribution. The informants seemed to be concerned about strata in the population that were disadvantaged and they supported policies that would provide relief to the poor. And this was not understood as discrimination. Consequently, the indigenous population could not enter the programmes as *indigenous;* but as *destitute, homeless, sick* or *poor.* Since a large part of the indigenous population will fall into one or several of these categories, they are, at least in theory, eligible for services and benefits from the programmes. On the other hand, the concept of equality of opportunity was viewed as more relevant when considering ethnic differences.

The presumption encountered in the elites' discourses, that all citizens in the country have the same rights and opportunities, contributes to perpetuating the unequal distribution of benefits and services. In spite of constitutional guarantees, it is obvious that not everyone in the population has equal rights. As Anatole France puts it in a famous and ironical manner:

> For the poor, citizenship consists of supporting and sustaining the power and idleness of the rich. They must work for those goals before the majestic equality of the laws, which forbids rich and poor alike to sleep under bridges, to beg in the streets and to steal bread.

But even if we were to assume that all ethnic categories in Guatemala have equal, formal rights, the actual opportunities to improve their social situations are unevenly distributed. The consequence of basing social policy programmes on a principle of equality of opportunity may likely ossify and increase social inequalities. It may also contribute to upholding the patterns of ethnic domination/subordination in the country. Furthermore, basing social justice on a principle of equality of opportunity deflects attention from the discriminatory processes in Guatemalan society. It prevents an interpretation of poverty that is a result of systematic marginalisation of the indigenous peoples by the *Ladino* elites. Testimonies of these processes are not absent in the interviews with the elites. But the overall impression is that the ideology of the elite, based as it is on equality of opportunity, will fail to address the problem of ethnic marginalisation and poverty.

Poverty and Possibilities

The legitimacy of employing the concept of equality of opportunity rests on the presumption that people have a choice between different options, and that the distributional outcomes based on the choices made will reflect the priorities of the people in question. By definition, however, the poor have a limited set of options or alternatives; this may be the central characteristic of a life in poverty. If one is extremely poor, in Guatemala and elsewhere, it means that what little resources one might have is immediately used for basic life sustenance–all resources available are used to that end. In order to reach any level of improvement, one has to be able to set some resources aside for alternative use and to find some resources to address future goals. In a situation characterized by extreme need, one cannot divert resources away from the most basic and vital needs that have to be satisfied. They cannot be suspended or forgotten (Bourdieu 1979). In order to have some surplus that could be invested in a future improvement requires some *room for manoeuvre* (Clay and Schaffer 1984). A concept of equality that is based on the premise that people have room for manoeuvre– that they have several alternatives from which to choose or that they can set aside some of their resources to be used in the future–does not take into account what it means to be poor.

On the other hand, there is a danger in assuming that the poor are without *any* possibilities and choices, that they are completely tied up in their poverty, and that they are victims forced to remain immobile and passive in relation to their oppression. Webster and Engberg-Pedersen have developed the concept of room for manoeuvre as *political space*. Their objective is to avoid the tendency to view the poor only as passive victims. They hold that /.../ *the poor are constantly seeking to manoeuvre within given conditions and to generate room for profitable activities* (Webster and Engberg-Pedersen 2002:255). Even if room for manoeuvre in the poor is strongly limited, they will always have some possibilities to act. Programmes that are initiated to fight against poverty have to take into account the concepts of the people themselves, their rationalities, strategies for survival, and how they obtain and use their resources.

The concept of *political space* as proposed by Webster and Engberg-Pedersen contains three dimensions. The first has to do with the access to institutional channels in a society. Democratization and de-centralization can, for instance, be important for increasing the political space of the people. The second dimension relates to a competition between alternative discourses about poverty and the poor. Spokespeople of the poor will attempt to present discourses that will benefit their interests and strengthen their political position, but so will their adversaries. The political space of the poor is partly dependent on how they are being presented and represented. The third dimension is about organized action. It can be the relation between the State and different kinds of intermediate organization and social movements.

All of these dimensions seem to be relevant and important when trying to understand the nature of the political processes and the discussion about poverty in Guatemala.

The formation of discursive practices is evidently important. In the previously discussed investigation of the ladino elites, we found that in the view of our informants, the explanations as to why poverty was widespread in the country had to do with the habits, customs and ways of life that characterize the indigenous population. According to these views the indigenous culture was an important, if not the main, reason for why improvements were so difficult to achieve. These discursive models imply that social development requires that parts of the indigenous culture be replaced by modern, westernized lifestyles and patterns of thought. Based on the interviews, we concluded that the ladino elites do not consider the indigenous cultures in the country to have a legitimate and valuable place in a modern project for developing the country. In this point, the similarities between the Guatemalan elites and the Norwegian welfare reformers are striking. In both cases, the dominant ideas are preventing a policy for reducing poverty that is based on recognition of the identities of the indigenous populations. And in both cases the improvements in the lives of the peoples involved are dependent on their willingness to abandon their ways of life.

The concept of political space and particularly the earlier concept of room for manoeuvre focus on the necessary conditions in order to gain and execute political power. This is clearly important when trying to influence the distribution of economic and other resources in a society. Any realistic development project should take into account the functioning of the political system, and additionally the concept of political space refers to different strategies and discursive preconditions needed to increase the chances of the poor population to improve their position in life.

At the same time I believe that a life in poverty signifies that the room for manoeuvre is limited in a more fundamental sense than what is implied when discussing political space, even when it is defined as broadly as in the definition of Westberg and Engberg-Pedersen. Extreme poverty leads to an extremely limited space for manoeuvre due to the external constraints for taking action; among them are the political and discursive. But their concept of room for manoeuvre does not contain all the relevant dimensions that should be taken into consideration.

Amartya Sen and Martha Nussbaum are concerned with the existential room of human beings.[1] They developed concepts that compare qualities of life, not by primarily asking about the command of resources or levels of satisfaction, but about what people actually are *able to do* or *to be* (Nussbaum 2000). They emphasize human life and human dignity as ends in themselves. They are also concerned with what the requirements are for living a good life, independent of varying preferences and cultural differences. Sen argues that development is a process where peoples' real freedoms are enhanced.

The idea of *capability* concerns the possibilities that people have to realize the goals they have set up for themselves. According to Nussbaum central capabilities *are held to have value in themselves, in making life that includes them fully human* (Nussbaum 2000:74). The goals individuals strive for, for example, having decent living conditions, are called *functionings*. While Sen consequently refuses to construct a list of the kinds of capabilities, and the minimum values that must be obtained on these capabilities in order to have a decent, human life, Nussbaum chooses to do so. She has elaborated on a list of criteria that in any case, regardless of cultural differences, must be met in order to have a fully human life (Nussbaum 2000:78 ff). Nussbaum has met some opposition on this point, and many have argued that any general inventory of

---

1   They both refer to Rawls' concepts of primary social goods, *powers* and *opportunities* (Rawls 1971).

goods, of functionings and capabilities, can lead to a lack of sensitivity to cultural differences (Lash and Featherstone 2002:11).

Both Sen and Nussbaum say that poverty is a deprivation of basic capabilities (Sen 2000). Having a minimum of control over ones political and material environment is of central importance. The resources that an individual can control, and consequently the freedom of the people, depends on how the economic and socio-political institutions operate. It is at this particular point that the thinking of Sen and Nussbaum, and that of Westberg and Engberg-Pedersen converge. Their thinking is also similar in their insistence on viewing development as a reduction of constraints, as broadening freedoms. All of them are concerned with people's resources and the liberty to construct ones own life projects. Poverty, on the other hand, is the lack of freedom in this regard.

Self-Respect and Self-Hate.

The scholars to whom I have referred in the previous sections explain poverty by focusing on oppressive forces in societies, mainly due to the marginalized position of the poor in relation to distribution of material resources. But freedoms and the limitations are also connected to mechanisms and institutions that are neither political nor material. The narrow spaces have a mental dimension. The psychology of the people is impacted by: extreme want, deplorable external and material conditions, experiences of disappointments and oppression, and the eternal labour required to get the sufficient means of survival. Oppression can induce energy resulting in resistance and rebellion, but it can also lead to feelings of hopelessness, apathy and low self-esteem. The state of mind and such feelings may be understood as consequences of limited existential spaces for manoeuvre.

The oppression is also maintained by an efficient ideological system where ignorance is a key element. These kinds of mechanisms were clearly exposed in an investigation concerning how indigenous leaders in Guatemala perceived poverty (Midré 2005). In the interviews, the indigenous leaders often talked about how a life in extreme want had a psychological impact on the people. They talked about how ignorance was linked to poverty, ignorance understood simply as lack of knowledge acquired at school, but more importantly, as a lack of a critical perspective concerning the existential position in which a person finds him or herself. Education and knowledge were viewed as prerequisites for obtaining a realistic idea of what the mechanisms are that cause poverty. According to these views, a crucial basis for resistance is that the oppressed have the possibility to obtain critical consciousness.

Living under domination has often induced a negative self-image or a *stigma* in people (Goffman 1968).[2] Taylor explains these mechanisms accurately when he writes:

---

2   Eidheim has analyzed these processes in relation to the Sami people (Eidheim 1971).

Our identity is partly shaped by recognition or its absence, often by the misrecognition of others, and so a person or group of people can suffer real damage, real distortion, if the people or society around them mirror back to them a confining or demeaning or contemptible picture of themselves (Taylor 1994:25).

In my own investigation among indigenous leaders I found the same processes at work. Indigenousness and poverty are frequently conceptually united, among the Ladinos, but also among the Indigenous. One of the informants talked about the indigenous poor as being in a situation where they were forced to *drink their own condemnation.* He also underlined that a decisive element in fighting against poverty and an oppressive society was to establish a more positive view of oneself, as a valuable human being. These issues are particularly important in Guatemala, where the subordination of the Mayas and racism is still widespread (Arenas Bianchi, Hale et al. 1999). A number of the indigenous leaders talked about the importance of self-respect and of valuing oneself–*valorar a si mismo.* Others talked about how semi-feudal working conditions destroy a person's self-esteem over time.

Distribution and Recognition.

In these accounts despising one-self is described as an outcome of the operation not only of economic and social, but also ideological systems of repression. On the individual level they may result in apathy and submissiveness, and on the societal level that poverty is sustained. Some of the important dimensions that emerged from the analysis of the accounts of the indigenous leaders were the quest for recognition and dignity and their opposites: lack of recognition and marginalization. They are also central issues in the contemporary debates in philosophy and the social sciences. A number of scholars address these questions when writing about poverty and the possibility of people obtaining individual skills, as well as collective power to fight against it. Many of these scholars are referencing a shift in the scholarly debate, from questions related to distribution, to a discussion about the importance of recognition.

Nancy Fraser writes about these changes and outlines a move from a social-political concern– where one addresses the issue of justice in terms of there being more equal distribution of material and other goods–to a cultural-political debate where respect for differences is more accentuated. In her opinion, these perspectives are not mutually exclusive. On the contrary, they can and should be combined, as these processes are tightly linked, both theoretically and empirically. Cultural misrecognition will often be accompanied by material deprivation, and vice versa. The lack of recognition can therefore be viewed as a kind of injustice that is strongly related to the injustices that are caused by an unequal distribution of wealth in a society. According to this view, the objective must be to develop a critical policy of recognition that acknowledges the right to be different, but at the same time guarantees a social policy of distributive equality (Fraser 1995; Fraser and Honneth 2003). The challenge consists of defending *an approach of a politics of recognition that synergizes with the politics of egalitarian distribution and avoids essentializing group differences* (Dahl, Stoltz et al. 2004:376). In many multi-ethnic societies belonging to an ethnic category often implies that one's living conditions are influenced by bi-dimensional social cleavages, both in terms of unequal distributions and a lack of recognition. Therefore, the marginalizing mechanisms are both socioeconomic as well as cultural.

In keeping with this point, one can note an important difference between the Norwegian state and its relationship with the Sami, as compared to the Guatemalan state and the indigenous populations. In the first case, the cultural misrecognition was evident and led to more or less an explicit requirement that one had to renounce Sami identity in exchange for obtaining social citizenship in the Welfare State. In this case, distributional equality is connected to cultural misrecognition.

By contrast, when studying the situation of the indigenous peoples in Guatemala, it becomes clear that the social positions in which they find themselves, as well as the kinds of injustices they confront, originate in both of the areas discussed by Fraser; both in the economy and in the culture. As Fraser (2003a) suggested, even if the bases for the injustices are different, the relation between them should be understood as dialectical.

Fraser and Honneth's attempt to combine recognition and distribution are interesting when discussing poverty and ethnicity in Guatemala. Although poverty is widespread among all ethnic categories, without a doubt it is most common among the indigenous population. When one is indigenous, it often means that one is confined to a certain strata in the economy, in positions that generate and reinforce poverty. Access to alternative and more promising positions may be restricted from people who have an indigenous background. When addressing these kinds of injustices it is necessary to change the mechanisms that relate to economic distribution, agricultural structure, the labour market, as well as those found in the cultural area.

Social Movements and Political Participation

In Guatemala, without a doubt the lack of recognition and the low self-esteem that concerned many of the indigenous leaders are tightly linked to the material deprivation a majority of the indigenous population experiences. A significant improvement regarding the recognition of the indigenous population as well as their position in relation to the distributional processes depends on their representation in the country's political-economical arenas. Indigenous organizations have been demanding this for a long time. According to Fraser, the possibility for participation as peers is crucial. Even when the political sys-

212

tem is accessible to all of its citizens in theory, as in Guatemala, the lack of recognition influences the extent to which the marginalized population can exercise their constitutional rights. Lack of recognition tends to exclude people from political and other relevant arenas and it makes them invisible (Fraser and Honneth 2003:29). Injustices in material distribution are the result of the lack of institutionalized possibilities for *participatory parity*. These views are concurrent with those of Webster and Engberg-Pedersen's discussion of the importance of opening the political space for marginalized populations (Webster and Engberg-Pedersen 2002).

Inspired by the theories of Fredrik Barth, anthropologists' analysis of the ethno-political situation in Northern Norway showed that until the 1960s there was a social stigma attached to the category "Sami." This stigma could only be erased if the role and the identity of the Sami could be positively evaluated by the Norwegian majority: *self-awareness and dignity can only be achieved when they are positively and permanently confirmed in relations with relevant alter identities* (Eidheim 1971:73).

In the Norwegian case the argument of these scholars was that it would be a mistake to reduce the visibility of ethnic differences. It should be acceptable that differences are articulated, and it is not acceptable to obtain distributional equality while implying that there is an obligation to denounce Sami identity. Equity should be based on a recognition and respect for differences, not on the premise of hiding them or making them disappear. As long as blurred ethnic categories are the consequences of *misrecognition*, resulting in a low level of self-esteem, it seemed to be important to define ethnic boundaries more clearly. The question of distributional justice and recognition are connected to the possibility of participation in the political system, and being able to present demands and make oneself heard. As discussed in other chapters in this collection, the political struggles of the Sami were in many respects successful. The Sami people enjoy the same universal social entitlements as Norwegian citizens, as well as specific collective rights. One of the reasons for this has been that they obtained respect and recognition by becoming visible. Their political participation was institutionalized by the establishment of a Sami Parliament, and by reforming the educational and health systems in Sami areas. The Sami relation to the Norwegian political system is not without tensions, but it could be argued that the new institutions as well as reforms in the previous institutions, demonstrate a higher level of recognition that has increased the political space of the Sami people within the Norwegian nation state.

What are the possibilities of the indigenous population to be able to participate as the peers of the Ladino in Guatemala? The overall impression is that their political space is increasing. We witnessed a strong political movement to revitalize the Mayan culture (Cayzac 2001; Montejo 2002; Esquit 2003). There are large numbers of Mayan organizations presenting demands that concern material improvements, as well as recognition of Mayan culture and values. There is also a space for divergent indigenous voices, in Guatemala as well as elsewhere in Latin-America (Warren and Jackson 2002). The Mayan movement is both tactically and strategically divided in devising a basis for collective action. One of the contested issues concerns whether or not the Mayas should unite with marginalized Ladinos–that is to transcend the ethnic boundaries in order to collaborate on the basis of common class interests. Another current of ideas underlines the importance of a specific indigenous cultural basis for putting forth political demands. There have been several attempts to bridge these differences; the most prominent example is probably the COPMAGUA[3] (Warren 1998). However, internal tensions in combination with external pressures led to its demise at the end of the 1990s.[4]

At the same time, indigenous communities are being transformed by a process of *ladinización,* where the individuals and groups acquire westernized lifestyles. Particularly in the eastern areas of the country, many of the traditional cultural markers are disappearing. This development could be explained by the lasting misrecognition of indigenous status. Ethnic hybridization could be understood as a result of ethnic oppression, as discussed by Demetrio Cojtí in this volume. But one might also interpret ethnic hybridization in the case of the Mayas as an attempt to ease daily pressures, as a wish to improve in living standards and position in society.

However, *ladinización* is not necessarily accompanied by material and social improvements for indigenous peoples. A considerable part of the rural ladino communities are extremely poor, as well as the ladinised indigenous communities. In the previously mentioned study concerning indigenous leaders and poverty, some of the indigenous leaders argued that indigenous cultural practices, ways of thinking and values could assist people in their life situation, and to cope with or endure a life in poverty (Midré 2005). According to the leaders, these kinds of coping mechanisms can disappear in the person who no longer identifies as indigenous. Furthermore, while ethnic revindication may be regarded as a basis for strengthening the possibility of collective forms of action, the process of ladinisation may lead to fragmentation and thereby a reduction in the strength of coordinated actions when indigenous peoples are entering the political space in order try to gain a higher degree of distributional justice.

A similar set of processes appeared in Norway. According to the censuses a significant part of the Sami population in certain geographical areas "disappeared" under the pressure of *fornorskning* (Bjørklund 1985).[5] In the 1960's

3 Coordinación de Organizaciones del Pueblo Maya de Guatemala.
4 One of the reasons, perhaps the most important, for the loss of momentum was the set-back for the Mayan movement following the referendum on constitutional reforms in 1999. The proposals were rejected by a majority. See (Warren 2002) for an account of the process that led to that result.
5 The expression could be translated to *norwegianization*.

and 1970's the organizational capacity of the Sami increased. This was both a precondition for and a result of recognition of their rights by the Norwegian society. These processes were strengthened by the international trends that the Sami were able to exploit in their national struggle, as discussed by Minde (Minde 2003). The emerging political strength was institutionalized and it secured a combination of distributional and recognitional justice.

The position of the Mayas is different. In spite of significant improvements in their situation in Guatemala, the process for obtaining recognition from the Ladinos has been slow and has been met with significant obstacles and setbacks. There is a deficit in justice relating to both distribution and recognition. This situation can probably only be changed by a combination of strategies that have been represented by the Popular and Mayanist organisations.[6] According to Esquit (2003), the differences between different Mayan organizations regarding these strategies have become less pronounced and significant. If the Sami experience has relevance for the Mayas, one could argue that the recognition of Mayan culture and identities should be combined with a policy that improves the living conditions for all of the country's poor, whether or not they are Mayas. In the field of distributional justice, the poor Indigenous and poor Ladinos have overlapping interests.

This approach would probably be in keeping with the ideas put forth by Fraser. Since hybrid cultural forms and identities also have the right to be recognized and respected she is skeptical of essentializing ethnic or other group differences and combining redistribution policies with those of recognition. When Fraser discusses the real possibilities different categories of the population have regarding participation in society, she is closer to the position of Nussbaum and particularly to that of Sen.[7] In my opinion the concepts of *room for manoeuvre* and *capability* seem to be closely related and are both suitable for describing some of the key features of a life in poverty. The *room for manoeuvre* of the poor is extremely limited. One could equally say that their *capabilities* are limited; they lack the possibilities to reach the goals they have set for themselves. Not participating in social life as other people do, is both a cause and a consequence of their lack of *room for manoeuvre*.

In the interviews with Indigenous leaders they also underlined poverty's mental dimension. They talked about the role of critical consciousness for unveiling the social processes that was causing their poverty and for what kept them in that situation. Poverty subdues consciousness and makes it more dif-

---

6   The Popular Mayan strategy focused on social rights, opening up the possibility for alliances with Ladinos, while the Mayanist gave priority to a cultural strategy and indigenous identity formation.

7   Fraser criticizes Sen and Nussbaum. She holds that their approach is concerned with distributive justice, a perspective that excludes recognition (Fraser 1995). Ingrid Robeyns, on the other hand asks if not Fraser's concept of *participatory parity* is identical with Sen's version the concept of *Capability* (Robeyns 2003).

ficult to confront the mechanisms that produce poverty in the first place (Midré 2005). Seen from this perspective, the concept of critical consciousness is related to Sen and Nussbaum's idea of capabilities. It is implied that if the poor gain critical consciousness they have increased their capabilities.

Conclusion

In this chapter I began with a brief discussion of two concepts of equality, equality of opportunity and equality of distribution with respect to indigenous peoples and the nation states. The discussion was informed by examples from Norway and Guatemala. Despite the fact that the dominating concepts of equality in the two countries seemed to be different, the consequences for the two indigenous minorities had important similarities. In both cases, the resulting policy vis-à-vis the indigenous population implicated that their culture and identities were irrelevant or harmful to the countries' socio-economic development. The idea of equality of condition, which is often found in the discourses of the Guatemalan elites, is particularly unsuitable to address the situation of the poor.

Policies towards the indigenous peoples of Norway and Guatemala had similar characteristics despite the differences between these countries and the different ideas about equality upon which policies were based; in both countries the policies were not based on recognition of the particular culture of the indigenous peoples.

The lack of recognition has a number of problematic effects on the people including low self-esteem and lack of self-confidence. It also affects the organizational capacity because the elites discourage them from participating. Their absence from strategically important social and political arenas will eventually influence their place in the distributional process, and contribute to them remaining poor.

I then discussed the concept of equality of opportunity in relation to different concepts of *room for manoeuvre*, as well as to Sen/Nussbaum's discussions on *capabilities* and *functionings*. The concept of capabilities bears some similarities with the idea of room for manoeuvre. They both relate to opportunities and limitations when people try to realize their goals, be it day-to-day survival or more distant and ambitious aspirations when trying to escape from poverty.

In both countries there have been significant and positive changes. In the case of the Sami, the situation has changed beginning in the 1980s, partly due to their increased organizational capacity and the political strength of Sami organizations, but also because they were linked to international developments that served to strengthen the Sami position in the national arena.

In the case of Guatemala, changes came later, and so far the results are not very impressive. However, after the signing of the Peace Accords in 1996, there have been several attempts to institutionalize the Accords into state policies.[8] Representatives of the Mayas are much more visible in the political arena; difficult issues like racism and discrimination against Mayas are frequently debated in the media. Despite the enduring tendencies of organizational fragmentation and competition, it is likely that the strength of the Mayan movement will increase. A greater number of indigenous professionals graduate from the universities. Consequently, their room for manoeuvre appears to be increasing. However, to what extent and when these processes will improve the living standards of the majority of the indigenous population is yet to be seen.

References

Arenas Bianchi, C., C. R. Hale and G. P. Murga. Eds. (1999). *¿Racismo en Guatemala? Abriendo el Debate sobre un tema tabú.* Guatemala, Asociación para el Avance de las Ciencias Sociales en Guatemala (AVANCSO).

Bjørklund, I. (1985). *Fjordfolket i Kvænangen. Fra samisk samfunn til norsk utkant 1550-1980.* Tromsø, Universitetsforlaget.

Bourdieu, P. (1979). "The disenchantment of the world." *Algeria 1960.* Cambridge, Cambridge University Press.

Cayzac, H. (2001). *Guatemala, proyecto inconcluso. La multiculturalidad, un paso hacia la democracia.* Guatemala, Facultad Latinoamericana de Ciencias Sociales (FLACSO).

Clay, E. J. and B. B. Schaffer. (1984). "Conclusion: Self Awareness in Policy Practice." *Room for manouevre. An exploration of Public Policy in Agriculture and Rural Development.* E. J. Clay and B. B. Schaffer. London., Heinemann.

Dahl, H. M., P. Stoltz and R. Willig. (2004). "Recognition, Redistribution and Representation in Capitalist Global Society: An interview with Nancy Fraser." *Acta Sociologica* 47(4): 374-382.

Eidheim, H. (1971). "When Ethnic Identity is a Social Stigma." *Aspects of the Lappish Minority Situation.* H. Eidheim. Oslo, Universitetsforlaget.

Eidheim, H., G. Henriksen, P. Mathiesen and T. Thuen. (1985). "Samenes rettsstilling. Likeverd, velferd og rettferdighet." *Nytt norsk tidsskrift* 2(2): 67-85.

Esquit, E. (2003). "Caminando hacia la utopía: La lucha política de las organizaciones mayas y el Estado en Guatemala." *Reflexiones.* Guatemala, Instituto de Estudios Interétnicos USAC.

Fraser, N. (1995). "From Redistribution to Recognition? Dilemmas of Justice in a "Post-Socialist" Age." *New Left Review* 212: 68-93.

Fraser, N. and A. Honneth (2003). *Redistribution or Recognition? A Political-Philosophical Exchange.* London, Verso.

Goffman, E. (1968). *Stigma. Notes on the Managment of Spoiled Identity.* Harmondsworth, Pemguin Books.

Hvinden, B., Ed. (2000). *Romanifolket og det norske samfunnet.* Bergen, Fagbokforlaget.

Lash, S. and M. Featherstone (2002). "Recognition and Difference: Politics, Identity, Multiculture." *Recognition and Difference: Politics, Identity, Multiculture.* S. Lash and M. Featherstone. London, Sage.

---

8 Recently a law proposal was passed to this effect. Decreto Número 52-2005, Ley Marco de los acuerdos de paz. Augusto 3, 2005.

Midré, G. (2005). *Opresión, espacio para actuar y conciencia crítica. Líderes indígenas y percepción de la pobreza en Guatemala.* Guatemala, Instituto de Estudios Interétnicos, Universidad de San Carlos de Guatemala.

Midré, G. and S. A. Flores (2002). *Élite ladina, políticas públicas y pobreza indígena.* Guatemala, Instituto de Estudios Interétnicos, Universidad de San Carlos de Guatemala.

Minde, H. (2003). "Assimilation of the Sami-Implementation and Consequences." *Acta Borealia* 9(2): 121-146.

Montejo, V. (2002). "The Multiplicity of Mayan Voices: Mayan Leadership and the Politics of Self-Representation." *Indigenous Movements, Self-Representation and the State in Latin-America.* K. B. Warren and J. E. Jackson. Austin, University of Texas Press.

Nussbaum, M. C. (2000). *Women and Human Development. The Capabilities Approach.* Cambridge, Cambridge University Press.

Rawls, J. (1971). *A Theory of Justice.* Harvard, Harvard University Press.

Robeyns, I. (2003). "Is Nancy Fraser's Critique of Theories of Distributive Justice Justified?" *Constellations* 10(4): 538-553.

Sen, A. (2000). *Development as Freedom.* New York, Anchor Books.

Taylor, C. (1994). *Multiculturalism and the Politics of Recognition.* Princeton, Princeton University Press.

Thuen, T. (1995). *Quest for Equiety. Norway and the Saami Challenge.* St. John's, Institute of Social and Economic Research, Memorial University of New Foundland.

Verba, S., S. Kelman, G. R.Orren, I. Miyake, J. Watanuki, I. Kabashima and G. D. Ferree jr., (1987). *Elites and the Idea of equality. A Comparison of Japan, Sweden, and the United States.* Cambridge, Mass., Harvard University Press.

Warren, K. B. (1998). *Indigenous movements and their critics. Pan-Maya activism in Guatemala.* Princeton, Princeton University Press.

Warren, K. B. (2002). "Voting against Indigenous Rights in Guatemala: Lessons from the 1999 referendum." *Indigenous Movements, Self-Representation and the State in Latin America.* K. B. Warren and J. E. Jackson. Austin, University of Texas Press.

Warren, K. B. and J. E. Jackson, Eds. (2002). *Indigenous Movements, Self-Representation and the State in Latin-America. Austin,* University of Texas Press.

Webster, N. and L. Engberg-Pedersen, Eds. (2002). *In the Name of the Poor. Contesting Political Space for Poverty Reduction.* London, ZED Books.

CHAPTER 11

Sami Identity as a Discursive Formation: Essentialism and Ambivalence

LINA GASKI

Introduction

Currently, the Sami Parliament and its politicians are an important force in the process of building a Sami nation and in the development of self-determination. The Sami political elite[1] are continuously creating and developing the Sami nation in a process where the masses are invited into history, and to a certain extent, the people constitute the raw material.

The process of developing self-determination is dependent on legitimacy and support, thus the people from northern Norway who meet certain criteria are invited to choose to define themselves as Sami, to assert Sami values and claims publicly, to participate in Sami politics, and to vote in the elections for the Sami Parliament. However, many of the potentially new Sami voters are hesitant. They live outside the so-called Sami core areas where the ethnic border between Sami and Norwegian is blurred; many of them can not speak the Sami language and they do not bare visible cultural traits or possess knowledge that is traditionally connected to "Saminess." For this group, imagining the Sami nation is not very obvious, which represents a challenge for developing and expressing Sami nationhood. The empirical question pursued in this chapter is how Sami identity is constructed in such an ambiguous context. Do Sami politicians, through public political discourses, manage to embrace this marginal Sami population in a Sami national narrative? Who are included, and conversely who are constituted as "the others" in such a context?

To explore these questions, one particular area of policy is considered, namely, land claims and resource control which are of high importance to the Sami people. The focus will be on the construction of Sami nationhood and identity through Sami politicians' narrative spatial practices concerning this policy area; how dominant political actors, by using certain interpretative repertoires in public discourses, construct versions of reality; and further, how these discursive practices produce certain categories and identities. The issue at stake represents a persistent dilemma that occurs in the Sami endeavour to create Sami nationhood and to demarcate a political community: How do the

---

1   By elite I mean people who exert substantial power over the public and influence political outcomes, where power is based on the possession of various resources, including political support, control of organizations, symbolic means and personal resources.

Sami construct nationhood in such a fragile context without compromising the underlying popular assumption about what constitutes nationhood or the culture of an ethnic group?

The Sami People: Ethnic Revival and Nation-building

The official ambition in Norway until around WW II was to assimilate the Sami, and the state's efforts to make the Sami change their national identity have been "extensive, long lasting and determined" (Minde 2003a:133). This process resulted in a radical decline in the number of people who identified themselves as Sami, and together with poverty, political powerlessness and lack of knowledge about their own history, many Sami experienced feelings of inferiority. Being a Sami was regarded as a hindrance, and many Sami did not teach their children the Sami language.

The first attempt to organize Sami interests was in the early 1900s, but the efforts were unsuccessful because of the overwhelming opposition they faced from the state and government. The breakthrough for organizing Sami interests came in the 1950s when the Sami movement created an alternative basis for expressing Sami identity. Their goal was to forge a new Sami self-image, a new relationship between Sami and Norwegian society, and to create a self-concept of the Sami as being a distinct people who had lived in the area before the present states came into existence and drew their national borders. The basis for the Sami movement was political, but the process of ethnic revitalization was also expressed through music, art, education, research and popular culture. In the 1970s and 80s the process began to take on the characteristics of nation-building and the movement created different symbols that represented a nation–a Sami map and flag–and they transformed the negative stigma associated with Saminess to more positive markers of Sami identity (Stordahl 1996, 2000). The Sami elite also made contact with other indigenous populations and were active in the World Council of Indigenous Peoples so in this period there was an increasing aboriginalization of Sami ethno-politics. (Eidheim 1992, Minde 1996, 2003b).

At the end of 1970s, one particular event marked the turning point in the relationship between the Sami and the Norwegian state: the decision to build a power dam across the Alta River in the Sami core areas. The political discourse that followed this conflict revealed the unresolved problems of governance concerning the relationship between the State and the Sami (Minde 2003b), and the prolonged conflict over the dam forced the government to reappraise its policies. One result of the Alta case was the establishment of the Sami Parliament in 1989 as a directly elected assembly. Even though the Sami Parliament mainly has advisory powers, it has become the foremost supplier of the conditions for formulating and developing Sami politics and the Sami future in Norway. It has the right to take its own initiatives, and has been granted authority over

220

some areas. An important constitutional step forward was taken in 2005 when the Norwegian government and the Sami Parliament agreed upon procedures for consultations in matters of interest to the Sami people.

The changes in Sami society over the past fifty years have been dramatic. From being a poor, stigmatized and politically unorganized population, the contemporary Sami constitute a much more self-confident society. The Sami Parliament's most important goal is to work towards the Sami achieving self-determination, based on their rights as a people and as an indigenous people as stated in the Consecutive Plan for the Sami Parliament 2002-2005.[2] The process of developing self-determination is dependent upon several factors including obtaining legitimacy and support from the potential electorate as well as furthering acknowledgement from the Norwegian central authorities.[3] In order to be entitled to vote in the elections and to be eligible to be elected to the Sami Parliament, one must register in the Sami electoral register. The criteria for registration are to have a self- ascription as Sami and that oneself, a parent, a grandparent or great-grandparent speaks or has spoken Sami. Presently, about 12,500 out of an estimated 40,000 people who fulfil the linguistic criteria have registered.[4] Based on these estimates, many people who fulfil the linguistic criteria have refrained from registering and participating in Sami politics.[5] The potential electorate might therefore be twice the size it is today. To increase their legitimacy and to win popular support for developing self-determination, Sami politicians need people in northern Norway who meet the requirements to choose to define themselves as Sami and identify with the politics of the Sami Parliament.

If politics are seen as maximizing of interests and competition, the Sami Parliament is only a medium for groups' and individuals' strategic actions. But politics may also be responsible for creating identities and for answering the question of who "we" are as a people. The Sami political processes are not an

---

2   It is not clear what this claim implies in a Sami context. The Sami aspirations for self-determination is not linked to achieving independent statehood, but to a combination of political autonomy in some matters and to the right to negotiate with the state in other matters that affect the Sami people. See Broderstad (2001) and Semb (2005) for interpretations on how the concept can be understood in a Sami context.

3   This depends on where the legitimacy of the claim for self-determination stems from; if the legitimacy exists in international law or if it is a "top-down" claim from the political elite, the claim is less dependent on popular support. But even if this may partly be the case in the Sami context, the Sami parliament need to strengthen its legitimacy in the Sami civil society (Bjerkli and Selle 2003).

4   It is not possible to get an accurate estimate of the Sami population, due to (1) the policy of assimilation, (2) contested views regarding who is Sami and (3) an overall registration of the Sami population does not exist (www.sami-statistics.info). This estimate is from Statistics Norway and includes children (www.ssb.no/english/subjects/00/00/10/samer_en/).

5   One reason is the politics of assimilation and another possible reason is that the status of the Sami Parliament is still contested among the Sami.

exception; they might be significant for creating meaning and identity (Broderstad 1994). However, the group that constitutes the Sami potential is heterogeneous and the Sami politicians want them to be included in the Sami nation and to identify with their particular politics. There are several ethnic groups where the Sami have historically lived and where most currently live in northern Norway. Besides the Sami population, there are descendants of the Finnish-speaking minority of Norway (*Kven*), ethnic Norwegians, and a considerable amount of people who are of mixed origin. Norwegianization and modernization have resulted in the disappearance of cultural idioms and contemporary Sami society hence displays a wide range of cultural articulations, varying conditions of economic adaptations, settlement histories, population movements, and diverse encounters with the majority. This accounts for the Sami society being characterized as a hardly recognizable "cultural entity" (Thuen 1995:38)[6]. The Sami movement's creation of a symbolic elaboration of positive and shared emblems of cultural distinctiveness was therefore essential in creating what Eidheim (1992) termed "a new master paradigm" for Sami self-understanding.

Even if this movement was both emancipatory and unifying, these processes did not produce a coherent system of cognitive identification for the Sami people as a whole. The new self-image was conventionalized by many groups, but a lot of Sami were not comfortable with the clear ethnic dichotomization implicit in the metaphoric kinship the new emblems symbolized. Some Sami disagreed with the demands coming from the Sami movement by setting up a Sami union who "should base their work on the principles of the Norwegian Constitution, show respect for the King and his Government, the Norwegian Parliament, and other state authorities in a democratic manner."[7] Others see themselves as marginal in relation to the political centre of the modern Sami nation, and at the same time as a result of assimilation many consider Saminess to be part of the distant past and of no relevance to their present identification (Gaski 2000). Many people consider themselves to be "mixed" and often describe themselves in what could be considered ethnically neutral terms in some situations. Some even call themselves "bastards" and thereby challenge what could be considered the demand for purity in the discourse of ethnicity (Kramvig 1999, 2005).

These are the new potential Sami voters; many of them are not able to speak the Sami language, do not bare visible cultural traits, nor posses knowledge traditionally connected to Saminess. As described, the ethnic border between Sami and Norwegians is blurred, and for these people imagining a Sami nation is not very obvious. Trying to create a "we" in this context, where identity is both contested and ambiguous, is therefore a challenge.

---

6   Here the concept of culture is used in a more essentialist way, to describe a sum of shared emblems on which there is a common agreement as to its character of cultural distinctiveness (Thuen 1995:38).

7   The aims of the Sami organisation, SLF, established in 1979.

Framework for Empirical Research

How is Sami identity created and expressed through public political discourses concerning territory and place? The theoretical point of departure for this investigation is inspired by constructivist approaches to the concept of identity, where national identity is given meaning through discourse and where discourses produce particular representations of identities. In such an approach, identity is not an essence or a fixed category, it is "made, not given" (Henderson and McEven 2005:173). From the perspective of discourse theory, identity is assigned, accepted, or resisted in discursive negotiations and identification is seen as a never-ending, continuous construction. In keeping with Stuart Hall's (1996) guidance, the focus will be on identification rather than on identities. Further, identity discourses depend crucially on contrasting. They operate through a division between us and them, and to examine discourses that give the concept "national identity" a particular meaning, is to "examine who a community systematically includes and excludes, as well as who is made visible and invisible" (Verdery 1996). Naturally, the challenge is to identify the processes which constitute categories and to make these explicit. The aim is not to classify people or groups, but to explore the "politics of categories" (Brubaker 2004) by revealing the discursive practices through which categories are constructed and legitimated. This means focusing less on "what the group *is*, but more on what the political leaders of such groups *demand* in the public sphere" (Benhabib 2002:16).

The analysis for this investigation is influenced by the discourse theory of Wetherell and Potter whose approach is concerned with analyzing the role of talk and texts in social practices. The central focus of their approach is how participants in a discourse use commonly shared *interpretative repertoires*; how utterances have something in common and might be manifestations of a shared pattern of talking. Shared interpretative repertoires are "broadly discernible clusters of terms, descriptions and figures of speech often assembled around metaphors or vivid images" (Wetherell and Potter 1992:90). They are some of the resources used for making evaluations, constructing factual versions of reality and performing particular actions– and they express what is taken for granted and what counts as a good argument. To identify the interpretative resources in a political discourse becomes a way of understanding the content of discourse and how that content is organized, what is achieved by the language used and the nature of the interpretative resources that allow that achievement (ibid). The interpretative repertoires simultaneously provide a particular set of subject positions, which are certain points of identifications which are constructed and offered to the public through political discourses, part of this analyses will therefore be to identify the subject positions the Sami politicians offer.

The data for analysing the public political discourse consists of statements where the Sami politicians have given an opinion on "the right to land and water" issue or other issues related to use of the territory. The statements are mainly from two different newspapers; *Finnmarken* (Norwegian regional newspaper covering the eastern part of Finnmark) and *Sagat* (Sami newspaper in Norwegian) from December 2004 until April 2005, but also from Sami TV news and a plenary session at the Sami parliament in August 2004.[8]

Creating Nationhood through Narrative Spatial Practices

The idea of a Sami territory is strongly associated with Sami ways of living and a distinct Sami culture. Also, for the Sami politicians the relationship between the Sami people and the land is considered to be profound, and to protect and preserve the land and the natural resources are viewed as absolute conditions if the Sami culture is to be maintained and developed. The link between the Sami population, culture, and territory is essential for constructing nationhood. Part of imagining the nation[9] relies on continuously making this relationship explicit and to create and recreate the connection to landscape and resources as one of the solutions to what has been considered a loss of culture and significant loss of identity. The Sami Parliament's politicians are naturalizing the connection between territory and identity in several ways. Using the term *Sápmi* is one. The term exists in all Sami dialects and denotes what is conceived of as Sami lands and water, as well as the Sami people and culture. Also in political speeches and documents the assertion about the relationship to nature is put forth in several ways, and described in what could be perceived as an unspoken, common Sami habitus. For example in the following expressions in the Plan of the Sami Parliament for the period 2002-2005: "The Sami culture is closely related to nature, both spiritually and practically" (2002:3) and "Still large parts of the Sami value foundations are attached to a life close to nature" (2002: 4). The Sami Parliament itself is a material expression of this relationship to nature; part of the building is formed like a traditional Sami tent, and is built in a natural and uncultivated landscape surrounded by heather and moss.

The debate about the rights to territory and the resources in this vast area has been a hotly debated Sami political issue for decades. Finally in the spring of 2005, after many years of uncertainty surrounding legal relationships in Finnmark, there was a solution when the Finnmark Act was adopted by the *Storting*.[10] (The Norwegian Parliament) Paralleling the overall debate about Sami

---

8   All the quotes from these sources are this author's translations.
9   Imagined here does not mean unreal; places and geography undoubtedly have a material reality, but are only made meaningful by the qualities assigned to them.
10 Until 2006, 96% of the land in Finnmark was owned by *Statsskog SF*, a state owned enterprise. On the basis of the rights of the Sami people, the land was in July 2006 transferred to the people of Finnmark, who will own the land jointly through the so-called "Finnmark Estate." The purpose of the Finnmark act is to facilitate the management of the land and natural resources. The manage-

rights preceding the Finnmark Act, there were innumerable smaller and more local discourses including: managing king crab in the Barents Sea, driving of off-road motorized vehicles on the tundra, building turf huts, seal hunting, nature conservation, and tourism to name a few. The following sections will identify the discursive patterns which politicians mobilized in public discourses concerning the relationship between people and territory.

Norwegianization and Struggle

Sami politicians often present debates over land use as equated with and linked to certain historical events or periods in Sami history. This comparison with certain historical events often has as its foundation a metaphor of struggle, which makes the territorial issues appear as a continuation of a prolonged historical conflict. The representation of history as a struggle between us and them is an element implicit in many of the political debates related to utilization of natural resources in northern Norway. A typical example is the ongoing debate about marine resources. Many of the fishermen in the smaller fjords are not allowed to fish as an occupation because they harvest too few fish to formally make the quota. In plenary debates in the Sami Parliament references to the "old times" are often used when the politicians argue for a change in management regime. It is argued that the Sami themselves managed the resources in an ecologically sound way but that it was destroyed by capitalism and outsiders; building on ecological principles it is argued that if the Sami–not "the others"–are allowed to be in charge of managing the resources the ecological practices of the past will be restored. [11] Similar arguments are frequently repeated in the discourses about rights to land and water, where the self-governing Sami communities from the past are represented as peaceful, self-sustaining, and ecologically sound. This nostalgic act of remembering a lost Golden Age is common and likely to emerge in both ethnic groups and nations, as an act of resistance (Smith 1986).

Another typical example of how the struggle metaphor is used to frame the narratives on territory can be read in this extract from a letter to the editor from two Sami politicians who wrote in support of two chairmen (one is also a Sami MP) from two different municipalities in inner Finnmark. The chairmen had publicly expressed their opposition to the County Council which wanted to restrict the use of off-road motorized vehicles in Finnmark.

> About the Kautokeino "revolt" and the contribution from our top politicians in Inner-Finnmark, we agree with the chairman in Karasjok: We must not give in to the (Norwegian) government, rather we must give in to the population; we are elected by the people. We are not elected to represent the Norwegian state, but the users in

ment shall be carried out for the benefits of the residents in the county, and particularly ensure that Sami interests are secured.

11 Plenary session, Sami Parliament 21-23.08.04

local communities. And neither will we support the statements from the (local) top politicians who work for the government.[12]

The Sami politicians denote the chairmen's action as the Kautokeino "revolt." Historically the Kautokeino Revolt is a very significant event in Sami history, where in 1852 Sami people from the village of Kautokeino revolted against the Norwegian authorities and several of the Norwegians where killed (Zorgdrager 1997). This is one of the most dramatic events in Sami history, and the only time that the Sami violently rioted against the Norwegians during the long lasting period of the norwegianization policy. Several Sami were convicted for this revolt, and two of them were beheaded by the Norwegian authorities. To use the Kautokeino revolt as a metaphor for the relationship between us and them–with its indisputable negative connotations–is a way to construct and maintain the relationship between the Sami population and the Norwegian government as asymmetrical and repressive, and to frame the local conflicts about land use as ethnic conflicts.

It is not uncommon for Sami politicians to draw from history and the politics of assimilation when expressing their point of view. For instance when *Statsskog*, the state entity that owned the land in Finnmark until 2006, wanted to evaluate the use of cabins for sustenance in Finnmark's inland tundra areas. They were interested in finding out if they were used for this purpose or for recreation. The outspoken leader of a Sami organisation uttered that "Statsskog is continuing the norwegianization by their crusade against turf huts and cabins in Finnmark."[13] The metaphor of crusade is explicit here, and everyone knows the meaning of it; it might be the military expeditions by the Christian rulers in Europe during the Middle Ages to recover the Holy Land from the Muslims–or it might mean a struggle against something believed to be negative. Here the metaphor is used to structure how people are supposed to think about the matter; the crusader is *Statsskog*, which until recently has governed and owned the land in Finnmark, and the holy land they are claiming are the cabins and turf huts which belong to the Sami population. To use crusade as a metaphor and norwegianization as an interpretative resource is to place this conflict in a continuing historical context of assimilation where the Sami people have been victims of the Norwegian government's policy. Norwegianization is a concept that only has negative connotations, and it functions as a metaphor for structuring how people should think about these conflicts.

---

12 *Sagat* 15.01.05
13 *Sagat* 28.12.04

Indigenous Rights Discourse

The public discourse about the Sami territory is also related to global discourses on indigeneity. Since the 1970s, the Sami movement has had contact with the international indigenous peoples' movement and the international discourse concerning indigenous peoples' legal rights; through this contact they have found inspiration and a fighting spirit which has played an important role since the Alta affair (Minde 2003b). The indigenous rights discourse has not only been used as an interpretative repertoire in the overall debate preceding the Finnmark Act, but also in smaller and local discourses. The ILO Convention No. 169 is the convention most frequently referred to in the media. One typical example is this letter to the editor from a Sami member of parliament concerning who is exempted from the laws regulating the use of motorized vehicles in the pastures around Karasjok. The politician argues using the ILO convention that local trappers should be allowed to drive their snowmobiles in these areas. This is simultaneously an example of how Sami political interests, both on the national and local levels, are increasingly formulated as legal claims in Sami politics.[14]

> I remind you that Norway was the first country to ratify this convention, and they have a particular responsibility to carry it out. Use §6/../refer to ILO-169/../and read this loud and clear to any county governor trying to suspend these exemptions given by a local body elected by the people.[15]

The trans-national indigenous discourse is also used as an interpretative repertoire by employing its rhetoric demonstrating the relationship between the Sami and other indigenous groups. For example, how this Sami politician argued against establishing a nature reserve: "Norwegian laws are norwegianization, an unreasonable intervention from the "big white Father in the south." It is not surprising that the debate surrounding the rights to land and water are frequently framed and referred to as an indigenous people's matter. As Minde (2003b) demonstrated, once the Alta affair was defined as an indigenous people's matter, the Sami political claims seemed to be asserting a higher priority when seeking a solution precisely because indigenous political claims are regarded as being of a higher moral order. Framing an issue not only as a Sami issue, but also as an indigenous issue gives the arguments normative connotations where the concept "indigenous" implies the existence of a particular relationship to the landscape. By applying the concept frequently to themselves in the discourse about territorial issues, an implicit, normative statement is given about the Sami relationship to nature; indigenous people are considered more "rooted in their natural soil" (Malkki 1992), and therefore their relationship to territory is con-

---

14 Mellingen (2004) points to how this increasingly characterizes Sami politics.
15 *Sagat* 01.03.05.

227

sidered more natural and sacred. Simultaneously, the concept "indigenous" also tends to be ontologically saturated with essentialist and primordialist conceptions of culture (Sylvain 2002). As a consequence, referring to a matter as an indigenous peoples matter and connecting it to legal claims often entails being trapped in an essentialist discourse because the requirements in legal discourse often have an essentialist tendency. This was exemplified when the Minister of Fishing visited the Sami Parliament's plenary session and required that the Sami people should not be entitled to special rights to the marine resources because their way of fishing is not as traditional as that of other indigenous peoples.[16]

Culture and Tradition

In statements from the same Sami politician regarding land use there are two concepts frequently employed–which also appear in almost every utterance about Sami politics–the related concepts of *culture* and *tradition*. There are numerous examples of the use of these concepts in interviews, speeches, and letters to the editor. A typical example of the use is in the recurring debate about how much and where people should be allowed to use motorized vehicles out on the tundra. In the media, Sami politicians argue that current regulations are too strict, and thereby violating what they consider to be traditional use of Sami land. They refer to the use of motorized vehicles using expressions such as "culture-based harvesting" or "traditional harvesting" or "nature-based harvesting," all of which have originated in this discourse and are now frequently used in the newspapers and on the radio and TV. The concepts are employed by politicians to denote something the Sami people do when they go fishing, hunting, or berry picking in areas they have traditionally used, with or without a four-wheeler. The expressions are used as symbols to frame and legitimate their use; the term "culture-based harvesting" indicates far more than for instance "fishing"; it is not only fishing but simultaneously "practicing culture." To drive with a four-wheeler along an old track is presented as culture and tradition, and expressions like "they are hindering us from practicing culture" are common when someone is not granted exemption from the motorized vehicle law or when they are not allowed to build or restore a turf hut in a certain spot. The Norwegian laws require that you are registered as receiving a certain amount of income from natural resources in order to be exempted from some of the restrictions. In the media, Sami politicians reject this approach to restrictions and exemptions and denote every Sami person utilizing natural resources as someone engaging in "culture-based harvesting." Certain actions thereby become culture.

---

16 The Minister of Fishing, giving a talk addressing the plenary session of The Sami Parliament 23.09.04. Bjerkli (1996) is pointing out exactly this dilemma, and has recommended more critical thinking about the concept of traditions when it comes to indigenous groups and land rights.

In contrast, the county council categorizes driving on the tundra as either *unnecessary* or *necessary* driving. In response to the county council a Sami politician uttered that *"there is nothing called recreational driving for us Sami people, this concept doesn't exist. We have harvested from nature since time immemorial and wish to continue doing this/.../the only way to translate the Sami four-wheel driving to Norwegians is to say that it is a part of Sami culture."[17]* Similar conflicts have been addressed several times in the media in Finnmark.

In presenting their own use of nature as something else–and something more–than simply utilizing resources, the Sami culture's close and strong relationship to nature is confirmed.

The connection to "tradition" and "culture" in this context are positive and the connotations imply certain knowledge about how to use the landscape. This is also explicitly expressed by politicians in the media in utterances like "we have the skills necessary to take care of nature"– in contrast to the others who do not have these skills–"they know nothing about nature-based harvesting." By referring to the others as having no knowledge about this, they confirm an image of the Sami people as having intimate knowledge of nature. Even if "we" in these matters are often meant to be the Sami people, the people carrying out these traditions and culture are frequently also referred to as "the locals," which includes everyone living in a village or a municipality.

Statements like "we have harvested from nature throughout history, and want to continue this" also display a people's belonging and that they have a history of their own. Tradition thereby becomes something solid and lasting, which represents continuity and should not be disturbed but should be left to develop naturally; it is doing "what we always have done," without interference. Both *culture* and *tradition* are metaphors in this context that are used to structure the discourse by emphasizing some aspects of culture – while hiding others. Simultaneously, these concepts are reiterations functioning to frame and constitute certain matters as Sami matters and politics. To denote something as "practicing culture" or "tradition" is a strategy to legitimize and have a case be heard. In contrast, to prevent practicing anything which has been categorized as culture would be to obstruct tradition and destroy culture.

The Centre-Periphery Discourse

In both the process leading up to the resolution of the Finnmark Act, and in many of the smaller and more localized debates about land use, Sami politicians are increasingly integrating a stronger emphasis on the mutual interests of the Norwegian and the Sami populations in the north. This is done in several ways. First, terms like "Sami," "indigenous," "local," and *"Finnmarking"* are used interchangeably in political statements, interviews and so on. In state-

---

17 *Finnmarken* 11.12.04

ments regarding the management of marine resources this has become particularly obvious, where categories like "fjord fisher," "coastal Sami," and "people in coastal Sami areas" are used interchangeably. The mixed use of categories presents a polyphonic message, addressing exactly the heterogeneous group of people that live in Finnmark. In this way "we" becomes synonymous with both the *Finnmarking*, a term which might be considered ethnically neutral inasmuch as it is neither specifically Sami nor specifically Norwegian (Kramvig 1999), and the Sami. For example in this heading on the Sami vice-president's letter to the editor arguing in support of accepting the Finnmark Act: "The *Finnmarkings* – they are able to govern themselves….we want the people in Finnmark to manage the resources."

In keeping with this line of thought, the politicians have emphasized several times that "we are all in the same boat," and that "we don't want more politicians from Oslo telling us how to behave."[18] In this way, the politicians appealed to the large number of people with mixed descent, who represent the greatest potential as voters, by establishing the others as a certain category; namely the southerners and the strangers. The relationship between us and them is also framed in the centre-periphery discourse as a conflict, but not in ethnic terms. The conflict is between north and south, between ordinary people and the authorities and between strangers and old acquaintances. In particular, a distinction is drawn between two types of people: the ordinary man and woman and the authorities. The first category–we–is often denoted as the laypeople and presented as victims. "The others" are "depriving the coastal population of the right to fish,"[19] "stealing the Sami's livelihood,"[20] or they might be "assaulters."[21] "The others" might be Norwegian bureaucrats or authorities, and are often categorized as someone who does not know anything about local conditions or how to use natural resources.

Simultaneously, the politicians act like entrepreneurs by combining the centre-periphery discourse with other interpretative repertoires. In this way, different existing discourses are combined to form a new interdiscursive mix. This extract from a letter to the editor in *Sagat* is a typical example:

We have always said that the population in Finnmark should be able to harvest from our rich resources and at the same time take care of the environment, like we have done for generations, without the interference of central authorities. Every municipality in Finnmark has the competence to take care of their areas, if they only dare to make a protest against the big white Father in the south. I call for contributions from other (Sami) political parties, or are they norwegianized?[22]

18 *Finnmarken* 29.03.05
19 *Finnmarken* 27.01.05
20 *Sagat* 01.02.05
21 *Sagat* 02.04.05
22 *Finnmarken* 18.01.05

This politician is employing several interpretative repertoires at the same time; we see the references to the centre-periphery discourse in the way he is referring to the "population in Finnmark" being opposed to the "central authorities." At the same time the "big white Father" is unquestionably a reference to the international indigenous discourse, and simultaneously the author is also using history as a resource by referring to the "norwegianized."

Legitimizing Their Case by Constructing Illegitimacy

To create and make explicit a nation's relation to landscape through discourses has an aspect of power because the narratives presented may present an effect of realism and become a part of people's self-understanding. The interpretative repertoires identified above structure the discourse by emphasizing some–and thereby hiding other–aspects of this relation, and they make a particular reality appear solid and factual. This particular construction of reality has gained a hegemonic position in the media discourse about the Sami people's relation to territory. This construction makes reality appear to be solid due to the way competing versions of reality are undermined and presented as distorted. The hegemonic narrative–most often represented by male politicians who repeatedly make their appearance in Sami newspapers and on Sami radio and TV–has seldom been challenged until recently; few Sami politicians have raised objections to these representations of reality.

There are some oppositional voices–such as a Sami chairwoman who publicly opposed the view that the Sami should be allowed to build turf huts wherever they choose. She was introduced on *Oddasat*[23] as a "Sami chairwoman who herself had been living in a turf hut when she was a small girl." In this way she was granted legitimacy and "the right to speak." She said "nobody is saying this, /.../ but we can't accept that someone takes the law into their own hands. Does Sami society really want to accept this?" In the newspapers this chairwoman has been described by her rivals as an individual who works "for the state government" and as someone who is still suffering from the consequences of norwegianization. Another female Sami politician was humiliated in the Sami Parliament's plenary when she opposed statements about four-wheel driving; she was accused of not possessing sufficient knowledge to be entitled to give her opinion.[24] Also, on several other occasions, Sami people who challenge this hegemonic narrative have been accused of being norwegianized; of acting as alibis of the Norwegian authorities; to be in the company of the Norwegian Society for the Conservation of Nature[25]; as possessing insufficient knowledge

---

23 Sami TV news , 21.01.05
24 Plenary session 20-24.09.04
25 This organization is presented by the politicians as relating to nature in a very different way than the Sami; as interested in watching birds, animals and pristine nature, while the Sami are presented more like using and taking advantage of nature; harvesting wood, fish, and berries for the winter, and hunting, and having a pragmatic view of the use of motorized vehicles.

about Sami culture; or as simply having lived too long in the city to be able to understand. By attacking people with a different opinion, they close off the debate by saying that "you" are not one of "us" and therefore you are disqualified from having an opinion.

Creating Subject Positions

The interpretative repertoires that the political elite deploy when framing the Sami relation to territory have been presented; the discourses of history and struggle, indigenous rights, culture and tradition, and centre and periphery. In addition to identifying interpretative repertoires, it is important to also examine discursive constructions of difference and to reveal how the discourses produce conceptions of who "we" and "the others" are and the kinds of subject positions that are constructed and offered through these interpretative repertoires. Who is being spoken to when the politicians are using these interpretative repertoires, and who is left out?

The discourses produce several subject positions which are discursively constructed according to context. First, as demonstrated in the history-discourse the politicians commonly draw on accounts of both concrete historical events and more abstract historical interpretations to perform particular sorts of identity work. Through certain historical narratives they engage in a process of identity construction where contemporary characteristics are linked to certain historical events and more general experiences–framing territorial issues as part of a prolonged struggle. In this way, they create the relation between us and them as one of struggle, where we, the Sami people, are the victims and the others are the assaulters. Second, in the indigenous rights discourse, the categories not surprisingly constitute a clear-cut dichotomy; indigenous–non-indigenous, often with essentialist and primordialist connotations. Third, as shown in the culture discourse, "we" are the ones who posses and practice traditions and culture. The Sami relation to nature becomes expressed as a reified notion of "having a culture."[26] The identity categories created in this discourse are ambiguous, but always distinguished by their close relation to nature. Culture is viewed as something that is possessed, which the Sami people/the locals are practicing on special occasions. Fourth, in the centre-periphery discourse, the group-making efforts are directed towards all of the people from the North and the categories used to make sense of the world create insiders and outsiders but they are not based on ethnicity. On the one hand, they embrace both the indigenous and the non-indigenous while on the other hand they construct the counterpart; the authorities, the bureaucracy, and the strangers.

This organization and their sympathizers are thereby often presented as if threatening to limit the "traditional use" of land.

26 At the same moment as the social sciences experienced a loss of faith in the culture concept, the concept was "loose on the streets" (Eriksen 1997); in everyday-speech, culture is commonly expressed as clearly bounded and having unchanging entities.

In order to validate their claims, the politicians are constructing essentialized discourses in certain ways. At the same time the discourses are producing distinct dichotomies: *victims –oppressors, ecology– environmental degradation, indigenous– non indigenous, closeness –alienation* and at last *tradition/ culture/authenticity–modern.* Ethnicity is relevant in these dichotomies in the way that the first elements in these dichotomies are referring to something considered to be a marker of the Sami relation to territory. The opposing element is not always referred to explicitly as Norwegian–it might be a foreign mining company, tourism, or people from the South–but often they are represented as representing some kind of Norwegianess. But as demonstrated, not all of these subject positions are connected to a clear ethnic dichotomy. Both the culture/ tradition and the centre/periphery discourses are constructing ambiguous subject positions in one and the same discourse. Especially in the centre-periphery discourse where the narrative created is polyphonic, embracing all the locals or the people from the North, the ethnic dimension is often unspoken.

Conclusion

Sami politicians employ certain discursive resources to tell certain stories. As shown, there are several parallel discourses about making place, constructing different categories, and thereby offering different types of subject positions. Elements in the discourses have the distinct qualities of a nationalistic discourse, as they help construct Sami identity by creating Sami-Norwegian dichotomies. Other parts of public discourses are also creating dichotomies, but then it is between "locals" and "non-locals," or northerners and southerners, somewhat independent of ethnicity. These representations clearly show how geography might become political, and how subject positions created are dependent on context. A common denominator is that the interpretative repertoires are founded on normative, explicitly pronounced assumptions about ones own group's close and sound relationship to and knowledge about nature and the landscape, in contrast to the other's alienation to the same landscape.

Concerning this particular area of policy, land rights and resource control–which has been the Sami political issue most often presented in media the last years–the most visible politicians utter views which are often both essentialist and stereotypic. Even if the centre-periphery discourse seems to be an increasingly important interpretative repertoire, constructing identity still seems to be done within a frame where culture is regarded as a separate and distinct entity. It is not uncommon for the cultural rights claims of indigenous groups to result in assertions of cultural authenticity that resonate with earlier anthropological conceptions of culture, and that making such claims sometimes requires that they are framed in terms of an essentialized, homogenous, and traditional culture. Reification is a social process which is central to the practice of politicized ethnicity, and it would therefore be a mistake to criticize Sami politicians

for reifying. The practice of reifying is precisely what the role of ethnopolitical entrepreneurs demand (Brubaker 2004). Their task is arguably to provide
historical, cultural, political, and economic arguments to both sustain the distinctive character of the Sami nation and to legitimize its demands for further
autonomy. [27]

The essentializing and primordializing tendencies evident in Sami public
discourse on identity and nationhood are also an outcome of external political
factors based on the need to conform to the Norwegian state's identity expectations. To secure certain rights to protect culture, the Sami, like other indigenous groups, are expected to promote claims within a dichotomous interpretive
frame. An illustration of this was when the former president of the Sami Parliament met with the Minister of Culture to discuss financial support for Sami
sport and the Minister of Culture stated that the Sami could not have support
for ordinary skiing, only for skiing with a lasso.[28] In such a context, claiming
essentialist differences might be seen more as a strategic utterance than an ontological position; this clearly demonstrates that a determining factor in how a
group constructs identity is dependent on what kind of opposition it confronts.

The Sami elite to some extent seem to have failed at creating an identity from
which to mobilize because the narratives presented by the politicians through
public discourses constrain the way the future may be imagined, thereby dismissing people from identifying with Sami politics. Despite insistence from the
politicians– in many other contexts–that the Sami population is heterogeneous
and the Sami society modern, they continue to focus on the idea of "a traditional and genuine common culture." The subject positions created through
this discourse force people to have to choose between being excluded from
the public discourse or to place themselves in an essentialist and dichotomized
vocabulary.

The constant recurring antagonism afflicting the Sami nation-builders is
how to create nationhood and demarcate a Sami political community without
essentializing. Is it possible to create Sami nationhood without dichotomizing
and without alluding to the ever-present underlying assumption about traditionalism and purity? The territorializing discourse is not a special case, but
represents an immanent antagonism in the Sami nation-building project, both
in terms of everyday politics and also in defining goals and planning for further
development. For Sami politicians, this represents a considerable challenge;
how to preserve distinctiveness without being essentialist and without dichotomizing. If they want to "invite the population in to the nation," dichotomies are
excluding many potential members and are misrepresenting peoples' complex
identities. To do the contrary– to try to include all of the people from the North
into what is claimed as one of the most significant markers of Sami culture

---

27 As Guibernau(2000) describes the role of the intellectuals in 'nations without states.'
28 A lasso is used to roundup reindeer by Sami reindeer herders.

and way of life–could jeopardize one of the most primordial, hegemonic, and enduring ideas of "Saminess." There is always the question about how spacious and generous a "we" may remain, before the borders are all gone.

References

Benhabib, Seyla. 2002. *The claims of culture. Equality and diversity in the Global Era.* Princeton N. J.: Princeton University press.

Bjerkli, Bjørn. 1996. "Land Use, Traditionalism and Rights", *Acta Borealia.* 13: 3-21

Bjerkli, Bjørn og Selle, Per. 2003. "Sametinget - kjerneinstitusjonen innenfor den nye samiske offentligheten", *Samer, makt og demokrati.* Bjerkli, Bjørn og Selle, Per (eds). Oslo: Gyldendal Norsk Forlag. .

Broderstad, Else Grete. 1994. Samepolitikk – interessemaksimering eller identitesskaping? Master, ISV, Universitetet i Tromsø.

Broderstad, Else Grete. 2001. "Political Autonomy and Integration of Authority: The understanding of Saami Self-Determination", *International Journal on Minority and Group Rights .* 8: 151-175.

Brubaker, Rogers. 2004. *Ethnicity without groups.* Massachusetts: Harvard University Press.

Eidheim, Harald. 1992. "Stages in the Development of Sami Selfhood", *Workingpaper no.7.* Department of Social Anthropology, University of Oslo.

Eriksen, Thomas Hylland. 1997. "The nation as a human being – a metaphor in a mid-life crises?", Hastrup, Kirsten and Olwig, Karen (eds) *Siting Culture.* London: Routledge.

Gaski, Lina. 2000. "Hundre prosent lapp?" Lokale diskurser om etnisitet i markebygdene i Evenes og Skånland, Rapport II Skoddebergprosjektet. *Diedut* nr. 5. 2000. Guovdageaidnu: Sámi Instituhtta.

Guibernau, Montserrat. 2000. "Nationalism and Intellectuals in Nations without States: the Catalan Case", *Political studies.* 48: 989-1005.

Hall, Stuart. 1996. "Introduction. Who Needs 'Identity'", Hall, Stuart and du Gay, Paul (eds) *Questions of cultural identity,* London: Sage.

Henderson, Alisa and McEwen, Nicola. 2005. "Do shared values underpin National Identity? Examining the Role of Values in National Identity in Canada and the United Kingdom", *National Identities.* 7:173-191.

Kramvig, Britt. 1999. "I kategorienes vold", Eidheim, Harald (ed) *Samer og nordmenn.* Oslo: Cappelen Akademiske Forlag.

Kramvig, Britt.2005: "The silent language of ethnicity", *European Journal of Cultural studies.* 8:45-64.

Malkki, Lisa.1992. "National Geographic: The Rooting of Peoples and the Territorialization of National Identity among Scholars and Refugees", *Cultural Anthropology* 7: 24-44.

Mellingen, Hedda Kristine. 2004: *Rett og politikk. En studie av NSR og Ap på Sametinget 1998-2004.* Hovedoppgave Institutt for Sammenliknende politikk. Universitetet i Bergen.

Minde, Henry.1996. "The making of an International Movement of Indigenous Peoples", *Scandinavian Journal of History.* 21:.221-246.

Minde, Henry. 2003a. "Assimilation of the Sami: Implementation and Consequences", *Acta Borealia* 20:121-146.

Minde, Henry. 2003b. "The Challenge of Indigenism: The struggle for Sami Land Rights and Self-Government in Norway 1960-1990", in Jentoft, Minde, Nilsen (eds): *Indigenous peoples. Resource Management and Global Rights.* Delft: Eburon Academic Publishers.

Sametingsplanen [The Plan of the Sami Parliament] 2002-2005. Kárásjohka: Sametinget.

Semb, Anne Julie. 2005. "Sami self-determination in the making?", *Nations and Nationalism*. 11:531-549

Smith, Anhony D. 1986. *The ethnic origins of nations*. Oxford:Blackwell.

Stordahl, Vigdis. 1996. *Same i den moderne verden*. Kárásjohka: Davvi Girji.

Stordahl, Vigdis. 2000. "Et samisk alternativ", *Ottar*.232: 9-16.

Sylvain, Renée. 2002. "Land, Water and Truth": San Identity and Global Indigenism", *American Anthropologist* 104:1074-1086.

Thuen, Trond.1995. *A quest for Equity. Norway and the Sami Challenge*. Newfoundland: Social and Economic Studies No. 55. Institute of Social and Economic Research. Memorial University of Newfoundland..

Verdery, Katherine. 1996. "Wither ´nation´and ´nationalism", Balakrishnan G. (ed), *Mapping the Nation*. London: Verso.

Wetherell, Margaret and Potter, Jonathan. 1992. *Mapping the language of racism: Discourse and the Legitimation of Exploitation*. Hemel Hempstead: Harvester Wheatsheaf.

Zorgdrager, Nellejet. 1997. *De rettferdiges strid. Kautokeino 1882*. Nesbru: Norsk Folkemuseum og Vett og Viten AS

CHAPTER 12

Addressing the Trade Consequences
of Injustice with Indigenous Peoples[1]

RUSSEL LAWRENCE BARSH

We Have Not Adequately Addressed the Real Economic Situation.

I want to begin by telling why I left the UN after twenty years of work on indigenous peoples' issues in Geneva and New York. It was because of what I saw when I was on a UN field mission to the Philippines in 1997.

I was sent to the Philippines by the International Labor Organization to evaluate a new development aid programme for the indigenous peoples in that country. One night, after visiting with indigenous leaders on one of the islands in the Philippines to tell them about the UN aid that was being sent to strengthen their communities and promote their rights, I went to a café for some dinner. At the next table was a group of Canadian and European mining engineers, talking happily about how they were going to dig up all of the territory of the same indigenous people. It struck me as very strange: There we were, a bunch of foreigners, Europeans and North Americans, sitting at two adjacent tables in a café in the Philippines, and I was there to promote human rights projects and they were there to take everybody's land. We came from the same countries, yet our missions were completely contradictory. The same countries that were providing the humanitarian aid were sending mining engineers to plunder the land. The international community must address this contradiction, and I would like to make a small suggestion about the way to do it.

I agree that the UN's work on human rights–and particularly on the rights of indigenous peoples–has strengthened the confidence of indigenous peoples in asserting their rights, and strengthened the visibility of indigenous peoples' struggles around the world. That has certainly been a good thing. However, there is very little evidence of much change in the actual material conditions of indigenous peoples in most countries. We have not adequately addressed the real economic situation. We have not addressed the economic motivations that continue to displace and marginalize indigenous peoples. So we have strengthened global awareness of what is right and what is wrong, but we continue to do wrong on a global scale.

---

1   This chapter is a revised version of a lecture given at the Conference arranged by Forum for Development Cooperation with Indigenous Peoples held at the University of Tromsø in October 10, 2005.

International leaders have begun a search for better mechanisms to defend indigenous peoples, better than the human rights machinery of the UN. One of them is targeted development assistance, which is to say getting resources to indigenous communities, rather than simply talking about how unjust it is that they are being oppressed (UNDP 2004). I think targeted assistance is much more important now than words. But even so, the amount of money that is available globally to assist indigenous peoples is very small, compared to the amount of money that is made by oppressing indigenous peoples, and we must deal with that contradiction. I believe that we need to go beyond talking about ways of increasing development assistance. I think we must also directly address the economic incentives that continue to accelerate displacement of indigenous peoples, and the destruction of the territories in which indigenous peoples live.

Unjust Global Trade, and Unjust Enrichment

Globalization has been criticized at many conferences as an evil force that has exposed indigenous peoples (indeed, all peoples) to greater economic exploitation. At the same time, globalization means that when an indigenous people is exploited–when it loses its land, its minerals, its water, its timber, or its livelihood–that people everywhere else in the world profit to some extent from that loss. Since we have globalized the problem, we have also globalized responsibility. We can no longer blame any single country for what happens within its borders, and pretend that no one else in the world is profiting from events in that country. By globalizing the economy, everyone profits, everyone loses; we all participate in the economic process that is destroying the indigenous communities that the UN keeps telling us that we should protect and defend with respect and honor.

Land is the clearest example of what I am talking about. Suppose that an indigenous people is displaced for a copper mine. The copper will end up everywhere in the world, and the money that was made from mining and selling the copper will also certainly end up in many different countries (see, e.g., UNO 1991; UNO 1992; UNO 1994). If the mining company makes money, it will encourage others to do more mining on indigenous peoples' lands. Now let me take this argument a step further. Many governments protect and invest in their favorite national industries and entrepreneurs by giving them free access to indigenous peoples' land and resources. Giving away land that is not yours is a very cheap way of helping your friends. Once the land is gone, moreover, indigenous peoples become workers in industries where they are not protected and their labor comes cheap. Indigenous peoples' land and labor becomes a "hand-shake," a gift or subsidy to particular national industries and corporations (Barsh 2001).

238

This is not a new insight. The International Labor Organization made the same point fifty years ago in the specific context of the indigenous peoples of Latin America (ILO 1955). And yet we have not acted to eliminate this kind of subsidy for land thieves. In the context of world trade (which governments seem to take more seriously than human rights or social justice), the continuing violation of indigenous peoples' land rights has global economic effects in the form of subsidizing industries in the countries where indigenous peoples live. Taking indigenous peoples' lands, exploiting their labor, or stealing their knowledge is not only unjust to the indigenous peoples concerned, but involves what I would like to call *unjust enrichment*, and *unjust trade*. Indigenous peoples lose, but somebody else also profits (Barsh 2002).

At the UN we spend a great deal of time talking about how terrible the loss of land is, but we have avoided dealing squarely with who profits (*e.g.* UNO 2001). We have accepted a division of the problem by international institutions into a "rights" debate and a "trade and development" debate, which are kept hermetically sealed and separated from one another. We continue to use UN human rights bodies to address the situation of indigenous peoples around the world, when the actual machinery of destruction of indigenous peoples is more properly discussed at the World Trade Organization, where the questions of who profits from trade and what kind of world economy we want are the main issues. The UN is in one room talking about how badly indigenous peoples are mistreated, while governments are in another room talking about managing the world economy, as if these are two separate discussions. But they are not really separate. Globalization means that they have to be the same discussion. The UN has tried to get into the economic debate, but the governments have agreed to leave most social and humanitarian issues outside the doors of the World Trade Organization. Should indigenous peoples stay outside the door of the WTO (*e.g.* CEACISA 1999), or are we missing the point that a powerful new international institution is being built that needs to take account of indigenous peoples interests, rights and demands?

Perhaps we gave up too quickly on the WTO because its purpose seemed too obvious about promoting profit rather than promoting rights. Perhaps we have become part of the problem by staying outside the doors of the WTO. I would like to argue for a moment here that the legal framework of the World Trade Organization *requires* it to deal with indigenous peoples' rights and with other peoples' rights. I am going to argue, moreover, that protecting indigenous peoples' rights will help the WTO achieve its core mission of building an open global economy. Most of the world's people do not benefit from a trade system that is blind to theft and oppression. Social justice groups continue to condemn the WTO from outside the door, however, because it is easier (and they may believe it is more "principled") than serious efforts to catch the WTO in its own contradictions and make it to deal with the *trade consequences of injustice*.

Recognition of Social Justice Programmes by WTO

I would like to talk for a moment about one part of the WTO legal framework called 'The Subsidies and Countervailing Measures Agreement.' It defines what kinds of subsidies governments can lawfully give to industries or regions within their country. It is basically an agreement *not* to subsidize industries except in a few special cases. Interestingly, the agreement was written very carefully to protect subsidies that are part of social justice programmes. Governments, however, must still explain exactly how a particular subsidy promotes social justice. Giving government money to a northern city such as Tromsø is a social justice subsidy if it is aimed at ensuring healthy living conditions in a region where costs are so much higher than other regions in the country, for example. It can be part of a social justice programme, not simply a way that politicians in Oslo help their friends make more profit. Providing economic advantages to the poorer regions of Europe through the European Community framework, similarly, is not regarded by the WTO as a subsidy if the real aim and effect is achieving greater equality of employment, education and well-being. A legitimate re-distribution of wealth to achieve social justice is considered lawful by the WTO, whereas giving money, property, or any other special treatment to any region or company in a way that affects trade and is *not* legitimately aimed at achieving social justice, is unlawful and can be grounds for a trade dispute.

This gets very interesting in the case of land rights. I will give you an example with a real case in mind. Consider the construction of a hydroelectric dam with government financial assistance. If the intention and the actual effect are improving the lives of the people who live in that region, the government concerned can argue that subsidizing the building of the dam is a lawful social investment—even if the dam also sells electrical power to other countries and makes a profit, and even if by generating cheap electricity, the dam makes manufacturing so much cheaper in that county that all of its exports are cheaper and more competitive as well. But if the dam takes land and displaces people, and its only actual economic benefits go to a big national aluminum manufacturing company, there is a trade problem and probably a violation of international trade law. If there is a "trade effect"–for example, the aluminum company gains a larger share of the world aluminum market because it benefits from cheap, government-subsidized electricity–the country that built the dam may be subject to WTO-supervised trade sanctions. An injustice combined with profit (from a competitive trade advantage) is unfair trade.

Most governments have already eagerly agreed to play by the rules of the WTO. Within that legal framework, it is clear that seizing the land of indigenous peoples, displacing them, and doing it all with the effect of helping one of the country's key industries make more money from its exports, is unlawful. Any other country that does not like it because it affects *their* trade can launch a trade dispute.

At WTO policy meetings, some trade unions and environmental NGOs have already argued that international trade law must be harmonized with all of the human rights conventions and environmental treaties that governments have already ratified. This would include, for example, the ILO Convention on the Rights of Workers, which assures workers some form of social security or old-age pension. It would include the Convention on Biological Diversity, which has been almost universally ratified. Where governments have signed treaties promising to protect workers and protect the environment, the WTO should be able to criticize or punish them for not doing those things, even if they have some effects on trade. It is logical and consistent with the international legal framework that a government is free to do anything that it is required to do by international law. Likewise, governments should not be able to profit from breaking their promises. If a government violates the Convention on Biological Diversity in order to enrich its friends in business, it seems to me that this is not only a violation of the CBD, but it is also a violation of the trade agreements administered by the WTO if it has trade effects.

A Test Case: Canadian Lumber Exports to the United States

This is not pure theory. I have been involved in testing this as a proposition at the WTO. I worked with Canadian indigenous peoples on the recent dispute between Canada and the US over Canadian lumber exports to the United States. Canada is a major producer and exporter of lumber. So is the US. The US government complained that Canadian lumber exports were artificially cheap because the Canadian government was charging Canadian companies very low fees for the use of public lands. The very low fees, the US argued, comprised subsidies that gave the Canadian lumber corporations a trade advantage.

Canadian indigenous people tried to intervene in that case when it was being considered by the WTO. They argued that the real reason Canadian lumber was cheap was because the land had been stolen. Canada had violated international law by giving away the land and trees of indigenous peoples without their consent and without paying them for it, and this theft had a specific trade effect: it gave Canadian lumber producers a trade advantage – an unfair trade advantage, arising from a violation of international environmental laws and human rights laws (WTO 2001; Barsh 2002).

We then had two interesting surprises. The first surprise was that the US government agreed with us. They suddenly realized that this could help them win their case, and once the US government made indigenous peoples' rights an issue, indigenous people in the US got interested, and began to ask why the US was not doing more to protect *their* trees. Indigenous peoples in both the US and Canada began paying more attention to the fact that, in a global marketplace, they are both the victims and potential beneficiaries of land theft and unfair trade practices. Canada was at fault in this particular case, but it was easy to think of examples where the US was at fault.

Our second surprise was that the WTO "dispute resolution panel" agreed to consider our arguments, despite the fact that we were not representing a member of the WTO–that is, a government. The WTO had begun accepting legal briefs from NGOs in other cases, and we were simply the first to submit a brief on behalf of indigenous peoples. WTO lawyers have taken the position that NGOs (and indigenous peoples) are a reliable source of *facts*. Thus, while an NGO cannot bring a trade dispute against a government, an NGO can offer its expertise to the WTO in a particular case in the role of *amicus curiae*, or "friend of the judges." Suppose that two countries are arguing about copper exports. An NGO located in the country concerned knows a great deal about where the copper came from, and perhaps it also knows which indigenous people was displaced in order to get the copper. Those are considered matters of fact that a WTO panel can and should consider, because it will help them understand the dispute and decide which country should win the trade dispute.

I would describe this as an "open window" that allows indigenous peoples to bring their side of land and labor conflicts to WTO trade panels. Bringing indigenous peoples' concerns into specific WTO cases reunites the economic aspects and rights aspects of the global economy in a forum that has power. And it focuses on what is the core question in my way of thinking: Who profits? Have they profited unjustly?

The lands and resources of indigenous peoples are already very clearly protected against theft or damage by international conventions, including not only the ILO Convention on Indigenous and Tribal Peoples, 1989 (No. 169); but also the UN Convention on the Elimination of All Forms of Racial Discrimination; and the UN Convention on Biological Diversity (reviewed in Barsh 2006). The eventual adoption of the UN Declaration on the Rights of Indigenous Peoples will largely synthesize and reiterate a body of existing law. It is therefore fair to say that unjust enrichment at the expense of indigenous peoples is a violation of international human rights and environmental laws and, when it affects prices in world markets (as it almost always does), it is an unfair trade practice and a violation of international trade law.

There are few things to consider carefully as potential drawbacks of pursuing indigenous peoples' interests through the WTO. Most governments have done harm to indigenous peoples to a greater or lesser extent, and none of the governments involved in a particular trade dispute may come with "clean hands," as English-speaking lawyers say, at least insofar as their treatment of indigenous peoples if not human rights and social justice broadly. So while one government in a trade dispute may be stealing indigenous peoples' timber, the other government is stealing some other indigenous peoples' minerals. For the WTO, these are two separate trade disputes because they involve different industries and different exports, and probably different kinds of subsidies. When a trade panel considers the timber case, it is only looking at the timber industry in the country that stands accused of unfair trade practices. The panel is not authorized to consider the mining industry in the country that brought the complaint unless there is some direct connection with timber.

When we used a lumber dispute to challenge Canada's failure to protect indigenous land rights, the focus was timber; but for indigenous peoples in the US, the big issue would be *water*. That would be a different dispute. In that case the US would be vulnerable because it has not provided full protection for the water used by the indigenous peoples in the US. I do not view this as a problem. If all governments have something to hide, there are more opportunities to raise indigenous peoples' issues in different trade disputes. Indeed almost every trade dispute potentially raises important issues of human rights and social justice. Think in terms of trade in commodities such as copper or rice. Think of any commodity, and there is a strong probability that somewhere in the world there is a government that is profiting by stealing that commodity, or the land on which it is produced, or the labor that produces it from people that live within its borders.

So that is why I say that this is an evolutionary process. It is a programme of repeatedly drawing global political attention to the economic basis for the destruction of indigenous peoples' communities and territories. It must be persistent background music as the WTO struggles to harmonize the world trading system and ensure that no country gets away with unfair competitive advantages. I think this is true even though we are unlikely to "win" many trade disputes, in the sense of punishing governments so severely with trade sanctions that they feel obliged to provide full compensation or restitution to indigenous peoples for stolen lands or resources.

Beyond Free Trade, to Fair Trade – Consumers and WTO
The great majority of the world's people have an interest in seeing that we not only have more trade, but also in making trade that is fair and is consistent with governments' other treaty obligations, including their human rights commitments. This brings me to the other side of this story: the side that has to do with everyone whether or not they consider themselves indigenous people.

I personally believe that bringing indigenous peoples' interests into the realm of trade and trade policy is important in order to make sure that everyone in the world who benefits from the exploitation of indigenous peoples and other peoples is fully aware of this fact. The dispossession of indigenous peoples results in profits and–we must face this frankly –cheaper goods. Hence consumers profit, too, from stolen land. And all of us must face the fact that all of us are consumers of goods provided by international trade.

Once we accept the fact that we are all consumers, we know where the real responsibility ultimately lies: with investors, with stockholders and with consumers in *every* country. It is a responsibility not to buy stolen goods, and not to invest in companies that steal. There is a lot of potential power in convincing people to take personal responsibility for what they consume and how they invest (Barsh 1998; Barsh & Khattak 2002).

There have been efforts to harness consumer power by organizing consumer boycotts; by setting up "fair trade" organizations to purchase goods directly from people in the Third World so that they can earn a better livelihood; and through social investment projects, especially popular in the US and UK, which advise investors about companies' social and environmental records, and urge investors to shift their money from socially irresponsible companies to more responsible ones. These are all private mechanisms that have tended to emerge recently in First World countries. They are good. I have actually seen them do a lot more good than many of the international debates at the UN. One of the only success stories in terms of real recognition of indigenous knowledge involved the threat of disinvestment by a number of major investors in the Pfizer Corporation located in New York: "If you try to make money from indigenous peoples' traditional medicine, we will pull our money out of your company." The company listened because a lot of money was at stake. What mattered was not their conscience, but their money.

But private schemes are not enough. Just as I suggested that development assistance is not enough, I think it is not enough simply to promote more social investing and more fair trade cooperatives. Boycotts are not enough to put pressure on those who profit from or benefit from the destruction of other peoples' lives. It seems to me that we take it directly to where the strongest rules are made today, which is the World Trade Organization. We tie the WTO up in the contradictions inherent in its own legal framework, which aims to promote trade and wealth, but also says that governments must not violate international law in order to help some of their friends make a profit. We go beyond *free* trade, to *fair* trade. It is basically trying to fix the rules of the game. All of our governments are trying to fix the game in their own favor all of the time, but we must make it clearly part of the rules that governments do not steal from each other or steal from their people just in order to make more trade. Let us hold them to it! Let us follow the money! Let us take the profit out of violating anyone's rights rather than simply reminding ourselves over and over again that people have rights, which we should already know.

These ideas have been on my mind since I left the UN, and I share them with you in the hope that it will begin a discussion about making fair trade a worldwide project for both human rights advocates and indigenous peoples, working in our respective countries. I think we have no choice in the matter: we are each part of the world trading system, and we must each take responsibility for fair play.

References

Barsh, Russel L. 2006. "Indigenous Peoples". In Jutta Brunnée, Daniel Bodansky, and Ellen Hey, eds., *Handbook of International Environmental Law* (Oxford: Oxford University Press).

Barsh, Russel L. 2002. "A Social Theory of Fair Trade, with Special Reference to Indigenous Peoples". *Proceedings of the 96th Annual Meeting of the American Society of International Law*, 279-290.

Barsh, Russel L. 2001. "Is the Expropriation of Indigenous Peoples' Land". GATT-able? *Review of European Community and International Environmental Law* 10(1): 13-26.

Barsh, Russel L. 1998. "Changing Forces and Non-State Actors in the Struggle for Human Rights". In Yael Danieli, Clarence Dias and Elsa Stamatopolou, eds., *The Universal Declaration of Human Rights Fifty Years Later* (New York: Baywood Publishing), 403-410.

Barsh, Russel L., and Nadia Khattak. 2002. "Non-Governmental Organizations in Global Governance: Great Expectations, Inconclusive Results". In Gudmundur Alfredsson and Maria Stavropoulou, eds., *Justice Pending: Indigenous Peoples and Other Good Causes; Essays in Honour of Erica-Irene A. Daes* (The Hague: Martinus Nijhoff 2002), 5-31.

Comite Exterior de Apoyo al Consejo Indio de Sud America (CEACISA). 1999. "Declaración de Seattle de los pueblos indígenas". Currently available on-line at http://www.puebloindio.org/Seattle_dec/99.htm (last visited 5 October 2006).

International Labour Organisation (ILO). 1955. International Labour Conference, 39th Session, Report No. VIII (1), *Living and Working Conditions of Indigenous Populations in Independent Countries*. ILO: Geneva.

United Nations Development Programme (UNDP). 2004. UNDP Statement on item 4(a) economic and social development, Third Session of the Permanent Forum on Indigenous Issues, 18 May 2004. Currently available on-line at http://www.undp.org/cso/documents/PFII3_devstatement (last visited 5 October 2006).

United Nations Organization (UNO). 2001. *Indigenous Peoples and Their Relationship to Land; Final Working Paper Prepared by the Special Rapporteur, Mrs. Erica-Irene a. Daes*, UN Doc. E/CN.4/Sub.2/2001/21.

United Nations Organization (UNO).1994. *Transnational Investments and Operations on the Lands of Indigenous Peoples; Report of the Centre on Transnational Corporations*, UN Doc. E/CN.4/Sub.2/1994/40.

United Nations Organization (UNO).1992. *Transnational Investments and Operations on the Lands of Indigenous Peoples; Report of the United Nations Transnational Corporations and Management Division*, UN Doc. E/CN.4/Sub.2/1992/54.

United Nations Organization (UNO).1991. *Transnational Investments and Operations on the Lands of Indigenous Peoples; Report of the United Nations Centre on Transnational Corporations*, UN Doc. E/CN.4/Sub.2/1991/49.

World Trade Organization (WTO). 2001. *United States – Provisional Anti-Dumping Measure on Imports of Certain Softwood Lumber from Canada* (Case DS247), Brief of Natural Resources Defense Council, Defenders of Wildlife, Northwest Ecosystem Alliance, Grand Council of the Cree (Eeyou Istchee), and Interior Alliance (10 May 2001).

Part III

Politics of Knowledge

CHAPTER 13

Nation Building Through Knowledge Building
The Discourse of Sami Higher Education
and Research in Norway[1]

VIGDIS STORDAHL

Introduction

All over the world indigenous cultures have been described and their history written by people other than the indigenous peoples themselves; moreover, they have been excluded from the curriculum of the institutions where they have had to receive their education. A high priority for indigenous peoples has been to get into positions where they can produce knowledge about themselves, for knowledge is a source of power. Thus, the capacity to produce knowledge has been viewed as a cultural asset, as cultural capital, and has been commonly considered a means by which to safeguard a group's right to preserve their heritage, language, and identity.

One way of producing knowledge that has proven to be increasingly important is through higher education and research. Thus, higher education and research are not merely understood to be an individual privilege that each member of an indigenous group possesses as citizens of a particular state, but also an integral element of self-determination and nation- building. From such a perspective, higher education and research are activities aimed at self-understanding and self-esteem–at the collective as well as the individual level.

A tendency that is not specific for indigenous peoples is that research and education are part and parcel to the nation-building process. There are, as will be demonstrated in this chapter, some distinctions to be made between majority and indigenous peoples in this context.

Compared to other indigenous peoples, even within the Nordic countries, the case of the Sami in Norway appears to be a story of success. In this chapter we will take a closer look at how the Sami in Norway, over a few decades, have gone from being objects of study to having a fair number of academics as well as their own University College and research institution.

---

1   I am grateful for collegial comments on earlier versions of this article from Terje Brantenberg, Ivar Bjørklund, Henry Minde (all at the University of Tromsø), Liv Østmo (Sami University College in Guovdageaidnu-Kautokeino) and Robert Paine (Memorial University of Newfoundland)

The struggle of the Sami to get into the position to be able to produce knowledge about themselves has aroused controversies, even in academia. From time to time the debates surrounding this controversy have created an unpleasant atmosphere. Non-indigenous scholars report that they have been asked by indigenous scholars not to conduct research in Sami society. In confidential settings and as "off-the-record" remarks, Sami scholars have reported that they have felt that their research has not been accepted as representing a Sami perspective by the Sami scholars in the Sami research institutions. The meta-communication in operation is that they are not participating in Sami knowledge building. The consequence is that individual scholars find themselves as being almost *persona non grata* and trapped in a classic double-bind situation; whatever you do or say is wrong. One reason for this feeling might be that the arguments have not always been easy to conceptualise in the sense that it has been difficult to discern when the topic being discussed is knowledge, research paradigms, and methodologies and when the topic being discussed is the politics of Sami knowledge, for instance, the right to knowledge production and institutions.

It is important not to avoid these debates because they are an inherent part of academic practice that deals with indigenous issues, particularly when knowledge building is strongly perceived as being a tool in nation building, which has been the case for the Sami in Norway. But in order for the debates to be understood as more than personal strains or to be perceived as political rhetoric and thus of no significant importance for academia, it is necessary to conceptualise them and view them as an inherent part of academic practice that deals with indigenous issues. By conceptualising, the different lines of argument become visible and thus easier to comment on.

Analysing the debates that have been witnessed over the decades on Sami higher education and research calls for applying a frame of interpretation that reflects the specific characteristics relevant to indigenous peoples and the field of knowledge. Thus, the chapter begins with a presentation of such a frame followed by an outline of the processes that have generated the development in Norway in order to give the reader a context for the debates, which will then be revisited and analyzed as two related, but different discourses.

Indigenous Peoples, Knowledge, Power: Political Characteristics ofKnowledge

Indigenous peoples do not possess the instruments of self-determination inherent in an institution such as the nation-state. In fact, such is the case by the very definition of the concept "indigenous people"[2], i.e., they can harbour no hope of taking charge of their own living conditions on the basis of normal, pluralistic, democratic principles. Thus, they are totally dependent on official policies be-

---

2   Cf. the ILO convention 169, Article 1.

ing directed towards them, and their struggle for some form of self-government is waged against a state, the very state that is supposed to safeguard the rights that indigenous people feel are threatened (Eriksen 1992). Noel Dyck (1985) draws attention to three characteristics of western, liberal, democratic states:

- The state has always played a leading role in facilitating the exploitation of lands and resources held by indigenous peoples. The state's subsequent involvement in governing minority indigenous peoples who have been largely or entirely dispossessed of their lands and resources has been historically governed by complex social and ideological considerations, as well as by economic factors.
- The modern state is not a monolithic structure, but consists of an assemblage of agencies, institutions and processes that are hypothetically capable of being–but that are often not–centrally coordinated and controlled. The result is that the actions of one government ministry are often offset by those of another ministry, level, or body of government.
- The last characteristic is one that indigenous peoples refer to as the "state's double-dealing." In other words, the state operates in various guises.

The last point is something Eidheim (1985) discusses when he argues that the Norwegian state operates alternately as *host*, *patron* and *guardian*:(1) as *host* the state grants the Sami the right to inhabit and make use of its territory; (2) as *patron* it sees to it that material and immaterial needs are covered for Sami individuals, according to its own assessment, and it formally guarantees equal rights for individual citizens and; (3) as *guardian*, it makes decisions, on the basis of its own judgement, like a virtual custodian of Sami interests and Sami welfare–thereby disregarding and dismissing their right to manage what is essentially their own interests and their future as a people–consequently, the Sami have been assigned the role of ward.

Not only does the state operate in several guises, as Nils Oskal (1999) has pointed out, it is by no means a neutral party:

> In its very essence it promotes adherence to the majority culture, since opportunities to exploit one's own cultural resources in political participation are ethnically differentiated. (p.162)

The political approach that indigenous peoples in western, liberal democracies have chosen is to appeal to the humanist set of values: human rights, anti-racism, and self-determination of peoples (Dyck 1985, Paine 1985). By referring to these fundamental values in a global society, they have been practicing what Dyck (1985:16) calls "politics of embarrassment." Since western, liberal, dem-

251

ocratic states are not monolithic structures, politicians representing indigenous peoples have been able to penetrate the state apparatus by advocating for their interests in terms of humanist appeals which are also used as a basis for entering into dialogue at political, as well as, organisational and professional levels.

As for research and education, this political approach, or strategy, has yielded a number of concessions on the part of the state as well as within the academic world. In the academic field we have witnessed the emergence of new solutions, such as

- Establishment of indigenous controlled institutions
- Establishment of Native Studies programmes or centres
- Integration of indigenous themes in research and education in the curriculum at national universities
- Indigenous research programmes within national research councils
- Quotas for indigenous students in specific studies
- Public reports on indigenous issues, which has served as a basis for state government to outline policies for indigenous research and education

The concessions made will vary from one state to another which leads to another aspect of structural conditions that should be kept in mind; namely national peculiarities. In order to have a better understanding of why one indigenous people seem to be more successful in establishing their own educational and research institution than another, it is important to describe and analyze the processes that have generated the situation.

From Objects of Missionary and Assimilation Policy to Masters of Their Own Knowledge Institutions

The field of knowledge has always been an important issue on the political agenda of the Sami. This is due to the fact that the issue has been of great interest to missionaries, governments, and researchers and thus insolubly attached to both political and ideological ideas throughout the centuries. A constant controversial issue throughout history has been the question of whether to use the Sami or Norwegian language in missionary and educational work. The first educational initiative towards Sami society was established in Trondheim in 1717, the so-called *Seminarum Scholasticum*, which aimed to teach educators, clergymen, and missionaries the Sami language and to prepare them for missionary work among the Sami. Sami boys that were considered gifted were also given education in Norwegian and scripture. The advocate for this college, the missionary Thomas von Westen, also called the Apostle of the Sami, was influenced by the Reformation and Luther's emphasis on the importance of one's mother tongue for understanding Christianity. Thomas von Westen was supported by the Danish-Norwegian government represented by King Frederik

IV (1699 – 1730). The Danish-Norwegian king directly supported and secured missionary work because it also had a political aspect, the tension between Denmark-Norway on the one side and Sweden on the other.[3]

The last half of the 1800s marked the transition to a new direction, the assimilation or Norwegianization policy. In 1862, the so-called Language instruction[4] was created which confirmed a new language policy towards the Sami. The Sami language could now be used as a support language in certain municipalities in Finnmark and there was no longer translation of schoolbooks into Sami. Teachers who could demonstrate good results in teaching Norwegian among their Sami pupils were awarded with extra pay (the so called *Finnefondtillegget*). Finally, the government began establishing boarding schools and Sami children were interned. When Norway became a sovereign nation in 1905, the assimilation policy was intensified (Dahl 1957b, Eriksen and Niemi, 1981).

The change in Norway's assimilation policy towards the Sami came after the Second World War (Eidheim 1971, 1997). There was no longer favourable conditions for the ideologies of the former minority policy; namely, of Social Darwinism and nationalism. The commitment that Norway made to the United Nation's work with The Declaration of Human Rights was another nail in the coffin of assimilationist ideologies. A democratic and humanistic nation which had committed herself to the idea of equal rights in the Declaration of Human Rights, could not risk being perceived as not fulfilling these ideas within her own borders. There were, however, some years to come before these new ideas would become politically binding vis-à-vis the Sami in Norway. First the areas burned by the German army's scorched earth policy in the autumn of 1944, had to be rebuilt. The Norwegian government decided that the reconstruction was not only to be a restoration of the old settlements and infrastructure but that the region was also to be brought to the same level of social and economic standards as the rest of the country. North Norway was no longer to only be a strategic, albeit important, outpost; it was to fully become part of the new Norwegian nation state–the welfare state. Thus, over a few decades, the northernmost region was developed from burned ruins into modern towns and townships and the welfare state reached the smallest out-of-the-way-places.

The rebuilding was in many respects impressive. However, the flip side of the coin soon became evident; the Sami lacked the skills to take advantage of the many new opportunities available to them in terms of employment, education, healthcare, etc. (Eidheim 1958). Civil servants, intellectuals, and representatives of the newly re-established Sami associations[5] began to demand

---

3　Norway was part of Denmark-Norway from 1380 to 1814, then in union with Sweden. The union lasted until 1905 when Norway became a sovereign nation.

4　This was followed by instructions in 1880 and 1898

5　The first Sami Association in Norway was established in Oslo in 1947. In 1968, together with local associations in the north, it formed the National Association of Norwegian Sami. The Nordic Sami Council was established in 1956. However, the first Sami association to be

a more principal role, as well as a clearer goal and instructions for the work pertaining to Sami issues; a new minority policy was needed.

In 1956, a committee was appointed with the mandate of considering the main questions of the situation of the Sami in Norway and to propose specific economic and cultural actions in order to make the Sami able to fully participate in Norwegian society. The so-called Sami Committee released its report in 1959. They stressed that besides assuring the Sami the same standard of living as the Norwegians, there had to be the establishment of an institutional basis for group existence. In order to ensure this, their proposal was to establish a Sami homeland in the interior of the county of Finnmark, where the Sami were in the majority, in order to secure "a Sami administration among the Sami." In this homeland–the Sami Core Area as the Committee called it–the Sami language was to be given equal status to Norwegian; law and justice was to be practiced in accordance with a Sami sense of justice and there was to be restrictions on land use in order to protect reindeer pastures. The Committee also proposed that the right to land and resources be defined in order to safeguard the economic foundation of the Sami.

According to Norwegian practice, the Committee's report was circulated for comments to appropriate bodies. The proposals for giving the Sami special status by creating a Sami Homeland and granting the Sami language equal status created much debate and negative comments, even among the Sami. The idea of a Homeland was compared with the apartheid policy in South Africa. Granting Sami language equal status to Norwegian was "…a fatal step backwards and would reverse the development and create a lot of difficulties for our youth and their future existence."[6]

In May 1963, Parliament discussed the report and all the MPs agreed that previous policies of assimilation now belonged to the past. The Sami were to become equal members of the State. However, a salient point is that this equality was not based on acceptance of the Sami being an ethnic group or a people equal to Norwegians, as the Sami Committee had proposed, but an equality based on the Sami as individual members of the nation state: "Sami speaking Norwegians" as the term went. The responsibility of the State was to ensure that the Sami had access to education, health-and social services, housing and economic development. The responsibility to keep the culture and language alive was up to every individual Sami. However, since the Sami had "special problems" due to their specific language and cultural background, the right to choose Sami language in schools was to be introduced.[7]

---

established in Norway and Sweden was as early as the beginning of the 1900.

6   Citation from a resolution from a mass meeting in Karasjok in the Easter of 1960. The citation can be found in *St.meld* 21 (1963-64), p. 50 (This author's translation)

7   In 1969 the right to education in Sami was introduced, and a new area in education was introduced.

The Sami organization was not satisfied with being granted equality based on individual Norwegian citizenship. Their goal was to gain acceptance as an ethnic minority group. During the late seventies, the claim became the right to be accepted as an indigenous people.

The watershed in the relationship between the Sami and the Norwegian state came two decades later with the opposition to a planned damming of the Alta–Kautokeino river system (see Minde and Lina Gaski in this volume). The Alta River ended up being dammed, but a new dimension appeared on the national political agenda: the Sami were to be considered an indigenous people. The constitutional position of the Sami in the Norwegian society needed clarification, and a commission to that end was established. The first results of its work was an amendment to the Constitution in 1988 which stated that it is the responsibility of the State to enable the Sami people to preserve and develop their language, culture, and way of life, and in 1989, the establishment of a separate Sami Parliament elected by popular vote of qualifying Sami.

Thus, the processes of change that are witnessed after WW II are on the one hand, a planned integration of the Sami society into the nation state; and on the other hand, there was a political revival and mobilization on ethnic grounds, leading to the integration into Sami nationhood and a new self-understanding. These two processes are running parallel to one another, and the one presupposes the other. So, even though there were three decades between the Sami Commission and the Sami Rights Commission, Sami society was not characterised by stagnation. The Sami organizations, as well as local Sami politicians, used the arguments of the welfare state for what it was worth. The result being that Sami communities not only kept on track with the general social and economic development of the state, but also managed to build an infrastructure of Sami institutions like museums, a radio and TV station, health care institutions, secondary high schools, a research institution and eventually a University College. The catchword in remote areas was "job creation" in order to prevent the population from moving. One of the most important incitements for this development was the decision to start developing the new primary educational system in the northernmost county of Finnmark which resulted in the Sami municipalities being among the first in Norway to get nine years of compulsory schooling. Importantly, many Sami parents did not turn their back on the schools as generations had done before them, despite the fact that education at that time represented a one-way ticket to the south of Norway up until the 1970s when Sami institution building increased. The outcome of this is that the Sami of Norway are among one of the highest educated indigenous peoples and, contrary to many other indigenous institutions around the world, the Sami institutions are mainly staffed by Sami people.

The institution building in the Sami society occurred parallel to institution building in North Norway in general due to the policy of integrating the north into the welfare state. On March 28, 1968 the Norwegian Parliament decided to establish a fourth national university, in the town of Tromsø located in the far north on the 70th parallel. The argument for the establishment of the university in the north was first and foremost an urgent need for an academically trained workforce. The idea was that if the region's own students were trained in the north they would more likely occupy employment positions there. Consequently, the University in Tromsø was a political project which also came to characterize both the way the university was organized as well as the focus of the teaching and research. The university was to be of relevance to its region, not least in educating medical doctors. The social sciences were also viewed to be important tools in understanding and solving the problems the region was facing, among them what the Sami were facing as a marginalized and stigmatised minority. One of the so-called research groups[8] established was Sami Studies at the Faculty of Social Sciences. It was said that this research group was to become an active and well-qualified milieu for Sami studies. Also a Sami language department was established in the Faculty of Humanities.

The scene at the beginning of the 1970s was that coinciding with the efforts of the Sami to establish their own academic institutions the new university of the north also had Sami knowledge building on its agenda. Therefore, from the very beginning, the university found itself in the position of being viewed as a competitor to the young Sami academics who were arguing for a Sami-controlled academic institution. Throughout the decades, Sami politicians and academic institutions have repeated this argument. Thus, despite its initial goal of being an active partner in Sami knowledge building, the University of Tromsø never gained a status other than being "an other."

Two Related, but Different Discourses

The first Sami scholar to address the prevailing asymmetry in research between the Sami and the Nordic societies was the philosopher Alf Isak Keskitalo at the newly established Nordic Sami Institute in Kautokeino. At the Nordic Ethnographic Conference in Tromsø in 1974, he presented a paper called "Research as an Inter-Ethnic Relation" (Keskitalo 1976 or 1994) where he focused on two main issues. One was what he called the "Asymmetry of Ethno-Science in Practical Research" where he focused on the asymmetry that prevailed in minority research; be it the relation between minority–majority institutions and scholars or between the researcher and the researched in the field. Ludger Müller-Wille wrote in the preface to the republication of Keskitalo's article in 1994 that: "As a scientist at the recently founded *Sámi Instituhta* [Nordic Sami Institute] he clearly faced the challenges and threats of the imbalance in minority–majority relations that were pervasive at the time."

---

8   The faculty of Social Sciences was organized in inter-disciplinary research groups focusing on issues that were seen as important at that time, namely Sami Studies, Community Studies, School Research and Social Politics.

However, Keskitalo did not only argue for the need of the Sami as a minority to be given institutional and economic opportunities to conduct research themselves; that is, given "a right to an academic form of activity" (p.22) in order for this asymmetric relationship to be developed into a cooperative relationship. The other issue he addressed he called "Dynamics of Knowledge and Understanding." In his opinion, the Sami had to do research themselves because "…there certainly are phenomena which per se can be significantly studied and described only by members of the group themselves" (1994: 24). It is this argument that has been interpreted as Keskitalo arguing not only for a separate Sami research paradigm built on a Sami theory of knowledge, a Sami epistemology so to speak, but defining Sami research as a culture-bound phenomenon.[9]

Müller-Wille recalls that there was "a bristling atmosphere" when Keskitalo completed his presentation and a heated and intensive discussion among the participants at the conference. In Müller-Wille's view, Keskitalo's paper did not receive the attention in the social sciences it fully deserved. One reason may be evidenced in the experiences and subsequent reflections of Karen Larson, an American anthropologist of Scandinavian descent, who found herself unwelcomed in the Nordic Sami Institute to do fieldwork in Sami society. She was told "by various majority culture researchers" namely "that in northern Norway no one has dared to take up the debate of what properly constitutes Saami research or distinguish it from non-Saami research and the topic is perhaps best left unbroached." (p. 14) Larson, however, wanted to comment on the matter in order for her "to make what otherwise might have ended as a frustrating and disgruntling professional experience into constructive commentary on the position I found myself, and on the general problematic of the relation between ethnopolitics, cultural boundaries and research" (p. 5-6). If Sami research is to be defined as a culture-bound phenomenon, Larson argues, the "Saami-based standards of disciplinary tenability will have to be specified, given the otherwise non-Saami origin of standards of disciplinary tenability and the historical assumptions of research neutrality in those traditions." Further, she asks: "With researcher identity itself as a cornerstone of methodology on ethnopolitical grounds, what framework for cultural translation will apply?"(p.13)

Larson is the only scholar to my knowledge that has thoroughly discussed Keskitalo's argument of the superiority of the native to non-native researcher in order to be able to fully understand the Sami culture and society. The Norwegian anthropologist, Trond Thuen, however, two decades later in the preface to

---

9   The Sami philosopher Nils Oskal is of the opinion that such an interpretation of Keskitalo does not serve him justice because Keskitalo, as the ethnographers he was addressing, was inspired by the new anti-positivist research paradigm of the time. In my opinion, that does not change the fact that there were scholars that interpreted Keskitalo as they did. (Oskal's comment was presented at the seminar The Discourse of "Indigenisme," October 2-4, 2005 at the University of Tromsø), see also Oskal's chapter in this volume

his book *Quest for Equity*, with the subtitle, *Norway and the Saami challenge* (Thuen 1994), takes up the gauntlet in order to, as he puts it, "avoid the dead-lock position which at times permeates the debate" (p.xii). In his opinion, "it would be wise to distinguish between two related, yet different types of arguments for enlarging indigenous control with research" (p. xi):

- The concern with exercising of control as part of general ethnopolitical emancipation; this includes the establishment of Sami research institutions.
- That a deep understanding of Sami culture and ethnic experience can only be achieved by the Sami, and consequently, that an understanding from the outside is unavoidably biased.

As to his first line of arguments, he as well as most other scholars in this field, is fully aware of the fact is that the Sami–for a very long time–have been the objects of research without having much say in how this object has been constituted. He also understands that Sami institutions and researchers, who see themselves as being in competition with non-Sami institutions, may find that they are not given a proper position as advisers when research programs focusing on Sami issues are formulated by non-Sami. He further argues that there is also much to the contention that the process of doing research and of mediating its results is in itself a forceful way of engendering cultural awareness and pride.

As to the second line of argument, that a deep understanding of Sami culture and ethnic experience can only be achieved by the Sami and consequently that an understanding from the outside is unavoidably biased, he is fully aware "that the challenge of interpretation is never completely and unimpeachably approached, and that there is always a gap, narrow or large, between the outsider and the insider position." But, he argues, "there is also a distance between the investigator and the investigated which the indigenous researcher has to cope with. While the indigenous understanding may have, sui generis, another quality – and by indigenous standards a superior one – to that of the outsider, there is still a problem of interpretation inasmuch as a culture is differently represented in the minds of those who reckon themselves to be its bearers" (p xii). Thus, "the 'insider perspective' may at times oversimplify the complexity and pluralism of ethnic experiences in making its claim of authenticity and representatively."

As he sees it, Keskitalo is arguing for an "indigenous monopoly" and that is detrimental to the ideals of a scientific community of intellectual freedom. Thuen elaborates on this by stating that this argument, of course, works both ways in the sense that "…the minority should be given better opportunities to research their own society according to their own priorities" and he also agrees that there are limits to transcultural understanding and specific limits to understanding by way of a "scientific," "Western," or "majority language." However, he further argues: "These difficulties also confront members of the cultures in question when they engage in communicating their realities to the outside world, and even when communicating between themselves. There are many realities, many experiences."

In line with Thuen (op.cit) it is useful to analyze the debates as two related, but different discourses. One is what can be referred to as the discourse of the right of the Sami to their own knowledge building, including higher education and research. It is here were the question was posed "Who owns Sami research?" and featured in a national newspaper (Bjørklund 1989, Mathisen 1989, Minde 1989, Jernsletten, Kalstad and Minde 1989). Other themes that can be discerned in this discourse are the need for institutions where the Sami language is the language of instruction and where the study programs are not necessarily copies of national programs, and the need for scholarly journals and books in the Sami language in order to develop the Sami language as a scholarly language (Gaski 1991). The debate concerning the role of the University of Tromsø as to Sami knowledge building belongs to this discourse (Bjørklund 1990, Hansen 1989, Magga 1990, Magga 2002, Thuen 2002, Aarbakke 2002).

The fact that the University of Tromsø has particularly been targeted for critique by Sami academic institutions, like the Nordic Sami Institute and the Sami University College, is because this university could serve as a symbol for "the other" since it has had its own Sami knowledge building project and thus could be seen as being in competition for the same resources as well as undermining the knowledge building project of the Sami themselves. Such a critique is by no means unique for the Sami-Norwegian context, but a discourse we find worldwide among indigenous peoples (Deloria 1997, Friedman 1993, Trask 1999). Not least of which, anthropology has been targeted for critique (Herbert 1999). This critique, Geertz (1988) argues, altered the moral context of anthropological research entirely, resulting in what is known as the self-reflexive era in anthropology.

The other discourse concerns research paradigms, methodologies, epistemologies and perspectives (Fossbakk and Stordahl 1989, Hovland 1996, Stordahl 1996, Thuen 1989, Thuen 1996). The discussion on Keskitalo's position that there are phenomena in the Sami society that only can be understood by a Sami, i.e., that Sami research has to be defined as a culture-bound phenomenon, arguably belongs to this discourse. Likewise, the question as to what constitutes Sami research (Lasko 1992).

Perspective vs. Paradigm

Neither Keskitalo nor other Sami academics of his generation at the Sami academic institutions have to my knowledge, commented on the non-Sami academics' reactions; nor have they elaborated on the arguments that there are phenomena that can only be understood by an insider. What is left is the argument that it is a necessity for research and researchers to have a "Sami perspective," "first hand knowledge," "closeness to," or "familiarity with" Sami culture and society (Pedersen 1990). Given the new era of self-reflexivity in anthropology, where the insider-outsider discussion was important, one might have expected that Sami scholars at the Sami research institutions would use this opportunity for scholarly dialogue. In line with Keskitalo's argument, the reason might have been that it is impossible, because non-Sami scholars by definition would not understand.[10]

In recent years, a new generation of Sami scholars, inspired by the debate among indigenous scholars worldwide (Meyer, nd, Smith, L., 1999, Smith, G., 2003), have picked up the debate on methodologies and research paradigms (Kuokkanen in this volume, Porsanger 2004, 2006). Porsanger (2006) is of the opinion that indigenous knowledge is a scientific knowledge equal to traditional (i.e. western) science. The difference between indigenous scientific knowledge and traditional scientific knowledge is that they are founded on different epistemologies. The indigenous epistemologies, therefore, need to be studied, and also in order to enrich the scientific world as such.

Despite the fact that for decades now Sami academic institutions have been arguing that Sami research has as its knowledge base and an epistemology other than mainstream research, an elaboration of this is unfortunately lacking. As far as can be determined, most of the research being done by Sami scholars, being it at Sami or Norwegian institutions, is well within mainstream research paradigms of their time. Likewise, with Sami research that has been conducted by Norwegian academics. To the extent that there has been a debate on research paradigms, it has been observed that there is a paradigmatic shift on ethnicity in the social sciences since the late 1960s.

One of Keskitalo's colleagues, Ole Henrik Magga (currently Professor of Sami language at the Sami University College), in his capacity as both a leading Sami politician and scholar, has commented in several newspaper chronicles and speeches on the Sami knowledge building project at the University of Tromsø. Scholars have mainly interpreted his arguments–which at times have been highly rhetorical in nature–as arguments for the right of the Sami to their own knowledge building. Thus, Magga has mainly been interpreted as a Sami nation builder. On the other hand, if we read Magga in his capacity as a scholar, then his critique over the decades of research in the social sciences conducted in the Sami society might as well be read as comments on the new research para-

---

10 Keskitalo, in a postscript to the reprint of his article, says something that can be interpreted as an opening for a future dialogue: "Since I think, oppositely to what often seems en vogue, that scholarly and scientific research begins with theory, then in any case, some sort of equal change of ideas is possible." (p. 31)

digm on ethnicity that the social sciences witnessed by the analyses of Fredrik Barth in *Ethnic Groups and Boundaries* (Barth 1969) and Harald Eidheim in *Aspect of the Lappish Minority Situation* (Eidheim 1971). In these texts, ethnicity is seen as an analytical perspective on the way that people socially organize themselves according to mutual understanding of the differences between them and others, and that the groups involved use cultural signs to mark these differences. However, the important shift is that these signs are not objective cultural signs, but signs that are seen as such and thus can function as markers of ethnic groups and ethnic borders. Thus, there were no signs that could be said to be more authentic than others. One implication of this is that culture and ethnicity were separated; and the same ethnicity could be expressed in different ways. Another implication of this new way of perceiving ethnicity and culture was that ethnic identity is not something an individual is born with but acquires.

This paradigm separated itself dramatically from descriptive ethnography which up until then had been prevalent in research on Sami culture and society. When viewed from the perspective of the new paradigm, this research tradition[11] was to a large extent essentializing cultures when it understood the Sami and the Sami society as radically different from their neighbouring societies. Magga can be read as taking a different view when he argues for a descriptive research paradigm in the social sciences.[12] According to him, this is a tradition that has proven closeness to its objects contrary to the new research tradition that represents "theories that are out of touch with real life," as he somewhat ironically puts it (Magga 1990). This closeness was due to the fact that the researcher in this tradition learned as well as documented Sami language and culture; they acquired Sami cultural competence, so to speak. Whether he is also arguing that the descriptive ethnographic tradition did have an insider perspective because of this acquired cultural competence is not clear. Since this research paradigm, according to his view, seems to be synonymous with the research tradition of "*lappologi*[13] many social scientists have a problem seeing how this tradition could be understood as having an insider perspective since it is a research tradition of non-Sami researchers, and further the concept of "insider perspective" was not in the vocabulary or a relevant perspective of the researchers of that time.

---

11 A classical work here is for instance Vorren and Manker, 1958

12 Magga is not the only Sami scholar that represents this research paradigm. Odd Mathis Hætta, an associate professor of Sami cultural studies at the College of Finnmark, I have found to be another one (see for instance Hætta 2006).

13 Lappologi is the term used to describe the research tradition on the Sami culture and society in the latter half of the 1800's. It bore traces of the Romantic view of 'primitive peoples' as well as the ideas of the evolution of the races prevailing at that time. While research on European cultures and societies at that time were a field comprising many disciplines, it was only ethnography and philology that made up Lappologi (Hansen and Olsen 2004).

Those of us that represent the new research paradigm might explain to ourselves and our students alike that we are fully aware of the fact that the new research paradigm of deconstructing the concepts of culture and ethnicity can be perceived by those that are the objects of study to be both destroying their own understanding of what it means to be a Sami for example, while the other research paradigm is confirming their existence as a unique and separate cultural group. Such consequences, however, are of another order than the analytical clarification belonging to a paradigmatic discourse. Hopefully, the new generation of Sami scholars, for instance Kuokkanen and Porsanger (op.cit), will address the challenge of elaborating on the Sami epistemology and will present a new research paradigm for Sami research in order for the scholarly discussion to move forward.

What can be said to have been the force of Sami research so far? Where has it succeeded, so to speak? In my opinion, the force of Sami research so far–be it at the University in Tromsø or at the two Sami academic institutions, the Nordic Sami Institute and the Sami University College–has been that it has generated a new perspective. This is a perspective that chooses to look at the relation between the Sami and Norwegian societies from the minority position. It has been a perspective that has challenged the existing body of knowledge within academia as well as among the Norwegian authorities and general public and, importantly, empowered the Sami society in general.

Concluding Remarks

As argued in the introduction, discourses like the one we have witnessed in Norway must be understood as an inherent part of academic practice dealing with indigenous issues, and must be interpreted in a framework that reflects the specific characteristics of an indigenous people and its field of knowledge. There is undoubtedly another claim owed to indigenous peoples, namely, that they be given the right to and the resources for knowledge building, such as when Keskitalo approached the scholars at the Nordic ethnographic meeting in 1974. At the same time, the Norwegian experience reveals that when knowledge building is perceived as an important tool in nation building there is the risk of running into a deadlock position and from time to time also into an essentializing discourse that may constrain the scholarly dialogue that all parties recognize and need to address. It is therefore important that researchers, regardless of their ethnicity, analyze their own as well as their colleagues' research in order to discover what perspectives and interests they represent (Eriksen and Höem 1999, Gullestad 1998).

Knowledge building will undoubtedly always be an important part of nation building processes. Sami research is undoubtedly marked by being an advocate for changing the position of the Sami people within the Norwegian nation state.

The Norwegian experiences reveal that such a perspective has empowered the Sami. However, if research and the knowledge building that accompany it are only perceived as part of a political project, one possible consequence could be then that the only legitimacy Sami research and higher education institutions are granted is political, and not scholarly. As argued in this chapter, that is not enough.

References

Barth, Fredrik.1969. *Ethnic Groups and Boundaries*. Universitetsforlaget.

Bjørklund, Ivar.1989. "Hva er samestudier?" *Dagbladet* May 31st.

Bjørklund, Ivar.1990. "Magga og samfunnsfagene". *Ukebulletin* Uke 21, Universitetet i Tromsø.

Dahl, Helge.1957 *Språkpolitikk og skolestell I Finnmark 1814 – 1905*. Oslo: Universitetsforlaget.

Deloria, Jr., Vine. 1997. *Red Earth, White Lies. Native Americans and the Myth of Scientific Facts*. Golden Colorado: Fulcrum Publishing.

Dyck, Noel. 1985. "Aboriginal Peoples and Nation – States: An Introduction to the Analytical Issues", in Noel Dyck (ed): *Indigenous Peoples and the Nation-States*. ISER, Memorial University of Newfoundland.

Eidheim, Harald.1958. *Erverv og kulturkontakt i Polmak*. Oslo: Samisk Samlinger Vol IV.

Eidheim, Harald.1971. *Aspects of the Lappish Minority Situation*. Universitetsforlaget.

Eidheim, Harald.1985. "Indigenous Peoples and the State", in Jens Brødsted et. al.: *Native Power*. Oslo:Universitesforlaget.

Eidheim, Harald.1997. "Ethnopolitical Development among the Sami after World War II: The Invention of Selfhood", in: Harald Gaski (ed): *Sami Culture in a New Era. The Norwegian Sami Experince*. Karasjok: Davvi Girji.

Eriksen, Knut Einar and Niemi, Einar.1981. *Den finske fare*. Oslo/Bergen/Tromsø: Universitetsforlaget.

Eriksen, Thomas Hylland and Ingjerd Höem.1999. "Norske diskurser om kulturell annerledeshet". *Norsk antropologisk tidsskrift*, 10(2), 125 – 149

Fossbakk, Beate and Stordahl, Vigdis.1989. "Tromsø-antropologiens postkulturell krise (Samene er forsvunnet – Hva gjør vi nu?)". *Antropolognytt*, 4.

Friedman, Johnathan.1993. "Will the Real Hawaiian Please Stand: Anthropologists and Natives in the Global Struggle for Identity", in T. van Meijl & P.van der Grijp (ed): *Bijtragen tot de taal-, land-en volkenkunde; Politics, tradition and change in the Pacific*. Leiden, The Netherlands 149(4), 737-767.

Gaski, Harald.1991. "Krise for samisk", *Dagbladet* March 19th.

Geertz, Clifford.1988. *Works and Lives*. Polity Press.

Gullestad, Marianne.1998. "Kulturforskningens normative og politiske aspekter", in Hodne (ed): *Kulturstudier*. Program for kulturstudier, Norges Forskningsråd.

Hansen, Lars Ivar.1989. "Samisk kulturhistorie og kulturfagene ved Universitetet i Tromsø". Chronicles in *Nordlys*, February 6 and 7.

Hansen, Lars Ivar and Olsen, Bjørnar. 2004. *Samens historie fram til 1750*. Oslo: Cappelen Akademiske Forlag

Hovland, Arild. 1996. "Fellesdiskurs og tveegget sverd". *Norsk antropologisk tidsskrift* 7(1): 44 – 63.

Hætta, Odd Mathis. 2006. *Samiske tradisjoner og skikker*. Karasjok: Davvi Girji.

Jernsletten, Nils, Kalstad, Johan Albert, and Minde, Henry.1989. "Hvem eier sameforskningen?" *Dagbladet* June 23.

Keskitalo, Alf .Isak. 1994. "Research as an Inter-Ethnic Relation", *Diedut* no 7, 1994.

Lasko, Lars Nila. 1992. "Definitioner av samisk forskning". *Diedut,* No 5.

Larson, Karen.1988. "Ethnopolitics and Research Ethics for the non-native Researcher". *Acta Borealia* 1/ 2.

Lewis, Herbert S.1999. "Misrepresentation of Anthropology and Its Consequenses", *American Anthropologist* 100(3):716-731

Magga, Ole Henrik. 1990. "Universitetet i samepolitikken". Paper presented at the *Vårkonferansen* at the University of Tromsø.

Magga, Ole Henrik. 1999. "Etnisitet – menneskets dypstruktur". Chronicle in *Aftenposten*. October 17.

Magga, Ole Henrik. 2002. "UiTø og samisk kulturutvikling", Chronicle in *Nordlys* 2nd of November.

Mathisen, Per.1989. "Sameforskning består", *Dagbladet* May 11.

Minde, Henry.1989. "Dødsdom over samestudier", *Dagbladet* April 27.

Meyer, Manulani Aluli. nd. Remembering our Future: Higher Education Quality Assurance and Indigenous Epistemology. (Unpublished paper?)

Oskal, Nils. 1999. "Kultur og rettigheter". Eidheim (ed): *Samer og nordmenn*. Oslo: Cappelen Akademisk Forlag.

Paine, Robert.1985. "The Claim of the Fourth World",. Brødsted et al: *Native Power*. Oslo: Universitesforlaget.

Pedersen, Steinar.1990. "Samisk historieforskning – hvorfor?", *Diedut* nr 3, 49-57.

Porsanger, Jelena.2004. "An Essay about Indigenous Methodology", *Nordlit* (Special Issue on Northern Minorities), No 15, 105 – 120, Faculty of Humanities, University of Tromsø.

Porsanger, Jelena. 2006. "Forskning og kompetansebehov for urfolk i nordområdene. Innlegg på Norges forskninsråd nordområdekonferanse", accessed on April 2 2007 at: http://www. samiskhs.no/nor/dutkan/aktuelt/urbefolkningenes_tradisjonskunns.htm

Smith, Graham Hingangaroa. 2003. Indigenous Struggle for the Transformation of Education and Schooling. Keynote Address to the Alaskan Federation of Natives (AFN) Convention, Anchorage, Alaska, U.S.

Smith, Linda Tuhiwai.1999. *Decolonizing Methodologies: Research and Indigenous Peoples*. London: Zed Books.

Stordahl, Vigdis.1996 "Antropologi i den fjerde verden", *Norsk antropologisk tidskrift* 7 (3), 175 – 186.

Thuen, Trond.1989. "Samiske studier og antropologi – 'The never ending story'?", *Antropolognytt* 3.

Thuen, Trond.1996. "Kommentar" [to Vigdis Stordahl]. *Norsk antropologisk tidskrift* 7:3, 186 – 192.

Thuen, Trond.2002. "Antropologene og samene", *Nordlys*, November 6th

Thuen, Trond.2003. "Samiske studier." in: Rugkåsa and Thorsen (ed): *Nære steder, nye rom*. Oslo: Gyldendal Akademisk.

Trask, Haunani-Kay. 1999. *From a Native Daughter. Colonialism and Sovereignty in Hawai'i*. Honolulu: University of Hawai'i Press.

Vorren, Ørnulf and Manker, Ernst. 1958. *Samekulturen: en oversikt*. Tromsø – Bergen – Oslo: Universitetsforlaget.

Aarbakke, Jarle. 2002. "Samisk kulturutvikling og UiTø". Chronicle in *Nordlys*, November 7th.

265

CHAPTER 14

Sami Higher Education and Research Toward Building a Vision for Future

RAUNA KUOKKANEN

Introduction

In the past few decades, the presence of indigenous people in academia and the emergence of their scholarship have presented new questions and radical challenges for conventional academic scholarship and practice. Indigenous academics have contested the ways in which indigenous peoples and their cultures and societies have been studied in the past and constructed as an object of knowledge to serve colonial interests and needs. Indigenous peoples' scholarship unsettles dominant assumptions and modes of knowledge that have been assumed to be "natural" or "proper" in mainstream academic and intellectual conventions. What is distinctive about indigenous scholarship, however, is that it not only criticizes epistemological assumptions rooted in modernity, it also presents a radically different way of perceiving knowledge and also more generally, the world and our position and relationships in it. New research methods and academic practices by indigenous scholars stem from and are grounded in specific cultural, social and epistemic traditions and values that better reflect the needs and concerns of indigenous communities.[1]

In this chapter I consider issues of Indigenous higher education and research in the context of contemporary Sami society and scholarship. The approach in this chapter is comparative; drawing parallels from and contrasting the current situation of Sami Studies and research to recent processes and endeavours of other indigenous peoples. As a Sami scholar who has lived and studied the past several years in Canada and therefore, viewed and analyzed Sami society from a distance, my perspective has its advantages but also limitations.[2] The advantages include the comparative perspective that allows conspicuous recognition of some general trends in Sami society. The limitations are related to my lack of daily contact with Sami research and higher education, although my analysis also draws upon my observations of and conversations with several Sami

---

1   This is of course true with dominant paradigms as well; they have attempted to obscure their rootedness in specific geographic, societal and cultural contexts and conventions that are also gendered and class-constructed.
2   This article was written while I was working at McMaster University, Hamilton, Canada.

scholars during my visits in Sápmi while I was living abroad. A particular focus is on establishment of a new program called the Studies in Sami Culture at the Giellagas Institute at the University of Oulu, Finland, the leading program in Sami Studies in Finland and the Sami Studies program.[3] First, however, I will outline the main objectives of Indigenous higher education in Turtle Island/ North America and Aotearoa/New Zealand and then I will address the preceding discussion on Sami higher education and research.

Indigenous Higher Education: Rebuilding and Restoring Our Communities

For many indigenous peoples, higher education is considered a path to self-sufficient societies that both empower and are empowered by its own people (e.g., Barnhardt 1991). It is not surprising, then, that one of the statements most frequently heard among indigenous students and scholars is that we are not only educating ourselves and doing research for our own careers or personal advancement, but rather, for our entire communities; that is, the well-being and future of our people. As Linda Smith maintains, the work of an indigenous scholar is never limited solely to the academic world (Smith 1992). Verna Kirkness and Ray Barnhardt also argue that the aspirations of many indigenous students are often connected "with much broader collective/tribal considerations, such as exercising self-government, or bringing First Nations perspectives to bear in professional and policy-making arenas" (Kirkness and Barnhardt 1991: 5; see also Medicine with Sue-Ellen Jacobs 2001; Garrod and Larimore 1997).

Moreover, after centuries of being studied, measured, categorized and represented to serve various colonial interests and purposes, many indigenous peoples now require that research dealing with indigenous issues has to emanate from the needs and concerns of indigenous communities, rather than those of an individual researcher or the dominant society. A central principle of indigenous philosophies that of 'giving back' forms the backbone of current research conducted by many indigenous scholars and students. It expresses a strong commitment and desire to ensure that academic knowledge, practices and research are no longer used as tools of colonization and ways of exploiting indigenous peoples by taking their knowledge without ever giving anything back in return. Instead, indigenous research ethics expect academics to 'give back,' to conduct research that has a positive outcome and that has relevance for indigenous peoples themselves (e.g., Deloria 1992; Smith 1999; Battiste 2000; 2001).

---

3   Previously the Program of Sami Language and Culture at the University of Oulu, the Giellagas Institute was established in 2001. The mandate of the Institute reads as follows: The Giellagas Institute "was given the national responsibility in the Saami language and culture. This means that the institute must give and promote teaching at the MA and Ph.D. levels and carry out the highest research in these fields. The institute receives its funding directly from the Ministry of Education" (Accessed on April 2 2007 at: http://www.oulu.fi/giellagas/englindex.htm).

Since the 1960s, critical discourses of various disciplines have seriously undermined the modernist, positivist fallacies of neutrality that derive from specific values and perceptions of the world and serve certain interests in society. It is not possible to include here a detailed discussion on the various theories and arguments which have undermined and dismantled the superiority of western and Eurocentric intellectual and epistemological canons, conventions, and legacies that were once declared universal and neutral. Only some generalizing outlines are possible. Emerging under the rubric of poststructuralism in the late 1960s—concurrent with and related to the student uprisings in both Europe and North America—the new wave of criticism signified the beginning of a crucial paradigm shift in western discourse. This led to a period of profound transition in the human and social sciences of the 1980s (see e.g., Clifford and Marcus 1986; Marcus and Fisher 1986). Numerous trends in postcolonial and feminist theories and analyses, including various considerations of race and ethnicity have greatly contributed to questioning the validity of colonial, patriarchal, and capitalist 'Master Narratives' that have long excluded, marginalized, and oppressed vast sections of the world. Many of these theories and critiques have offered countless invaluable insights and the opening of new spaces for understanding that have also assisted indigenous issues in gaining entrance to the academic arena.

Moreover, various theories and practices in the field of critical, anti-racist pedagogy and critical race theory have, in particular, contributed to the development of indigenous scholarship, a great portion of which focuses on reclaiming and creating space for indigenous people as well as further elaborating indigenous pedagogies and educational practices. These paradigms and discourses that are critical of conventional Eurocentric epistemic and methodological conventions and canons, however, have not gained much attention in Sami scholarship and higher education at large.[4] Why does it seem that quite a few Sami scholars, junior and senior, are more skeptical of indigenous research paradigms and epistemologies than those of the West?[5] Could it reflect the level of internalization of the colonial understanding and perspectives of

---

4 This does not imply that there are no Sami scholars who are engaging with critical theory in their work, especially literary scholars such as Gaski (2000), Lehtola (1997), Hirvonen (1999) and myself (Kuokkanen 1996; 1997; 2001; 2007a; 2007b) have employed critical theory approaches, mainly postcolonial and feminist theories.

5 Epistemology is commonly defined as a study of knowledge or (philosophical) theories, definitions and identifications of knowledge. Further, it is often used to denote a system of knowledge or a way of knowing which may or may not include value systems, ontologies and understanding of the universe – none of which can really be separated from knowing (Fay and Tiblier 1967). There is a difference, for instance, between the ways in which western philosophical discourses and indigenous discourses employ the concept of epistemology. In the former, epistemology is usually applied to denote a (theoretical) study of knowledge, while in the latter, the application is much wider; it is commonly used as a synonym for system of knowledge, way of thinking, worldview, traditional philosophy etc.

knowledge? There are no immediate answers to these questions but perhaps if there is an interest in finding them, this would make an important research topic on epistemological positions of Sami discourse. It is clear that there is a visible lack of recognition that the production of knowledge is always political and situated in time and place. The almost impermeable faith in 'objectivity' is so conspicuous and ever-present that it can be overwhelming for those who have any awareness of the degree of criticism the assumption of 'neutral, objective and value-free research' has garnered in the past three decades. As Sandra Harding and Kathryn Norberg note, value-free research is not only an unachievable ideal but it is also an undesirable one (Harding and Norberg 2005: 2010). Likewise, there is a common desire and demand to present 'all sides,' which is a comment and criticism often heard in Sami research contexts; But one must also ask the necessary question of 'why'? Has mainstream research cared about this kind of objectivity? As Robin May Schott argues: "objectivity is not jeopardized but strengthened by the contextualization of the practices of knowledge and its norms of justification" (Schott 2003: 56).

Previous Considerations on Sami Research and Higher Education

Some of the concerns raised almost thirty years ago by Sami researchers such as Alf-Isak Keskitalo (1976) continue to be valid and timely today (for non-Sami engagements in challenges posed by Keskitalo, see Larson 1988; Müller-Wille 1991). Keskitalo addresses the various asymmetries (including linguistic, power, financial) in what he calls "inter-ethnic" research, that is, Nordic (non-Sami) "ethno-scientists" (ethnographers and anthropologists in particular) conducting research in Sami communities. He is also critical of the tendency of these scholars to often focus on archaic aspects of Sami society "and thus underestimate its complexity and differentiation" (Keskitalo 1994: 12). In his postscript to the 1994 printing of his article, he notes: "Whether small ethnic minority groups can, in fact, develop a system of scientific institutionalization, at least to some degree, remains to be seen" (Keskitalo 1994: 31). This is a striking remark for two reasons. First, it is surprising that Keskitalo should refer to the Sami as a "small ethnic minority group" rather than an indigenous people (on the topic, see, e.g., Henriksen 1999; Sami Council 2002). Second, the idea of developing "a system of scientific institutionalization" for Sami research (Keskitalo does not elaborate on this) gives the impression of a desire to model Sami research after mainstream structures and notions of knowledge and knowledge production. Considering how the problems of "scientific institutionalization"' of indigenous systems of knowledge have been discussed by numerous indigenous scholars in the past three decades, it is clearly an issue that needs to be addressed by contemporary Sami scholarship as well.

The debate on the roles and objectives of Sami research and higher education remains fairly limited. Thus far, the focus has mainly been on definitions of Sami research and the relations of Sami scholars to their own society as well as to that of dominant, mainstream societies. In the following, I consider some of the contributions by Sami scholars. Siv Kvernmo and Vigdis Stordahl discuss what it means to be a Sami academic in their aptly titled article "From Sami to an Academic = From Participant to an Observer?" (Kvernmo and Stordahl 1991). The sentiments considered by Kvernmo and Stordahl, that Sami academics are often viewed as suspect in their society and even in the Sami movement, are widely shared by other indigenous academics worldwide (see, e.g., Mihesuah 1998; Smith 1999) and continue to be timely today. According to their article, Sami academics can and must simultaneously be both participants and observers, especially in the sense of being able to critically examine cultural assumptions one takes for granted. In discussing their own field, Sami health services, they emphasize the role of culture but also point out cultural blind spots of Sami people themselves, not least of which is due to heterogeneity within the Sami society.

Harald Gaski (1991) considers the expectations placed on academics as "the conscience of society" and the failures of Sami scholars to fulfill these roles. In his view, one of the main reasons for Sami academics' lack of participation in public debates in Sami society is their own involvement in advocacy, politics, and shaping policies. If they were to critically engage in debates on current issues, they would be, in many cases, "barking at themselves" (Gaski 1991). Gaski introduces Bourdieu's adaptation of the concept of doxa–"the unsaid in the field of cultural possibilities, making it seem as if there are not multiple, but only a single possibility" (Bourdieu 1977: 164)–and urges Sami academics to reconsider their positions in relation to it: Who are the defenders of the 'doxa' and who are ruled by it (without realizing it themselves) in Sami society?[6]

Stordahl (1996) has also analyzed the tensions between Sami society and anthropologists, particularly concerning the production of knowledge, the translation of cultures and the purpose of Sami studies. She maintains that the tensions and the debates that follow are a good example of the challenges that the Fourth World brings to the academy and that they need to be taken into account in order to be able to move forward in ways that are also productive for Sami society and its aspirations (Stordahl 1996). Further, Stordahl addresses

---

6   In his otherwise illuminating article, Gaski, however, offers a reductionist interpretation of postmodernism's central tenets. Even if done in a tongue-in-cheek fashion, I find his remarks problematic considering how little Sami scholarly circles have engaged with (and assumedly, knows about) postmodern criticism. According to Pauline Rosenau, "there are various interpretations and manifestations of what is meant by 'postmodernism' but what is relevant here is the way the discourse has rejected universalist claims of objective truth and knowledge and regarded them more as products of Western, ethnocentric ideologies" (Rosenau 1992: 78). According to North American Native scholars Yvonne Dion-Buffalo and John Mohawk, postmodernism "should be seen as a consequence of the halt of five hundred years of European expansion" (Dion-Buffalo and Mohawk 1992: 17)

the role of education as a central means to encounter the contemporary challenges of Sami society, such as the crisis in the reindeer herding industry in
Northern Norway. She suggests: "education is the key to the 'good life,' be it in
the Norwegian or the Sami society" (Stordahl 1997: 152). Education provides
economic security, social status, and for the Sami in particular, it is a way of
reclaiming their history, culture, and language.

However, it seems problematic that, for instance, the "problem of overgraz-
ing" is not examined in a more critical light in her article. Questions such as
what the factors are that have created this 'problem' are not raised and the fact
that whatever the reasons are (development projects, failed policies, the interference of the government, the non-recognition of Sami land title, the modernization of reindeer herding, etc.), by establishing and discussing the issue
in terms of it being a 'problem' not only dispossesses younger Sami people
of their traditional livelihoods (and thus, severing their cultural ties) but also
fails to acknowledge that the trend encouraging them to turn away from their
livelihoods violates the very rights of the Sami as recognized by the Constitution of Norway to their culture, in which reindeer herding is a central part (both
economically and culturally).

Also related to the question of reindeer herding, the article does not critically analyze the gender question raised briefly at the end of the article. Stordahl
notes how the large majority of the students at the Sami high school in Kárásjohka and teacher trainees at the Sami University College in Guovdageaidnu
are women. She suggests that "modernization" in Sami society has resulted in
Sami girls having greater confidence to acquire competence and skills outside
the traditional livelihoods (Stordahl 1997). What is not mentioned, again, is the
way in which the processes of modernization, such as the restructuring of Sami
livelihoods, have made it difficult, if not impossible, for Sami women to earn
their living in traditional livelihoods (Joks 2001; Sárá 2003; Vuolab 1994). As a
result, seeking higher education remains the only viable option for many Sami
women.

Vuokko Hirvonen has addressed the invisibility of Sami women, especially
in the earlier research on Sami people. Until very recently, ethnographers have
limited their representations of Sami culture to the activities of men, which
have been generalized to apply to all Sami people.[7] Hirvonen calls for advancing Sami women's studies with goals "to gather, visualize and mediate
knowledge about Sami women's lives, history and visions and try to influence
the development of the Sami region" (Hirvonen 1996: 10). What is needed in
this regard is new approaches and perspectives in understanding and addressing power relations in society as they related to the multiple realities of women
(Kuokkanen 2007a).

---

7   This, of course, has been a common concern for most "othered" cultures studied by ethnog-
    raphers and anthropologists. Trinh T. Minh-ha calls this "the scientific conversation of man
    with man" (Trinh 1989).

Jan Henry Keskitalo is one of the few Sami academics thus far to consider Sami higher education and its challenges. He points out how mainstream educational programs and vocational training do not prepare students for working in Sami society, resulting in a situation where the education of Sami students does not necessarily increase the number of Sami professionals in Sami society but often only benefits individual careers. Keskitalo also considers some of the objectives and future goals of Sami education established by some Sami institutions (Keskitalo 1997). The Sami Parliament in Norway, for example, maintains that "post-secondary education and research on Sami matters are central instruments in the maintenance and improvement of a Sami society based on Sami premises" (cited in Keskitalo 1997: 161). One of the places where this is carried out the furthest is the Sami University College that was established in 1989 to train Sami teachers. It has since broadened its focus to also facilitate Sami capacity building in the fields of journalism, indigenous knowledge, multiculturalism, economic development, traditional Sami crafts, indigenous art history, and other fields.

In Keskitalo's view, some of the primary needs of Sami higher education and research include the establishment of a Sami research policy-making body to guarantee that the Sami themselves have a central role in defining and conducting Sami research. Second, Sami research must be based on a more formal collaboration between various Sami institutions as well as indigenous research institutions elsewhere. In this way, he argues, it is possible to ensure that research serves the needs of the Sami people.

Cultural Studies or Indigenous Scholarship?

In the fall of 2004, the Giellagas Institute at the University of Oulu launched Studies on Sami Culture as a new major in addition to the existing curriculum that focuses on linguistics.[8] Unlike many other Indigenous Studies programs worldwide, however, the proposed Sami culture curriculum did not emphasize the needs of contemporary Sami society or Sami community advancement by means of research and higher education. Instead, the mission statement is limited to increasing knowledge and understanding about Sami culture and contemporary realities at large.[9]

---

8   The mandate for the Sami Language Program reads as follows: "It is our aim to educate competent professionals for various needs of Saami society. This is done by offering the students many-sided teaching based on competent research. The students will be introduced to do research in many interesting fields of linguistics. Our institute is renowned especially in educating the students to be concerned for the purity of the Saami language" (http://www.oulu.fi/giellagas/language.htm, Accessed in 25 May 2005).

9   The goal of the newly established Sami culture is to offer " teaching in Saami knowledge and culture, but in a wider northern and indigenous context. This is because the language and culture of the Saami is tightly connected to the history, society and legal conditions of the Nordic countries. It is our aim to offer many-sided general information about the Saami traditions and various sides of Saami society, and in doing this to add interest in these matters. On the

If the proposed curriculum places an emphasis on training individuals for "intercultural communication", one may ask whether we are allowing the concerns and agendas deriving from the interests of dominant societies to dictate and govern our intentions and plans? One of the responses for appeals to learn from and model the new curriculum according to the examples of successful Indigenous Studies programs was that Sami Studies cannot rely too heavily on indigenous discourse and that instead, we need to ground ourselves in disciplines such as contemporary Cultural Studies.[10] Whether this reflects a lack of knowledge and understanding of indigenous scholarship and higher education, including the emphases, objectives, long-term visions of Indigenous Studies programs in other countries or something else, we need to consider the idea of employing Cultural Studies as the foundation for studies in Sami culture more closely. In their introduction to *Native American Studies in Higher Education, Models for Collaboration between Universities and Indigenous Nations*, Duane Champagne and Jay Stauss argue for the increasing need to "distinguish Indigenous studies from race, ethnic, cultural and multicultural studies. None of the latter approaches fully appreciates or emphasizes Indigenous rights of self-government, land, and negotiated relations to state governments" (Champagne and Stauss 2002: 12).[11]

Cultural Studies is an interdisciplinary field of study that draws upon sociology, literary theory and cultural anthropology to study cultural phenomena, particularly in industrial societies. Cultural Studies considers the way in which a phenomenon relates to matters of power, ideology, race, social class, and/or gender. In its non-anthropological tradition, it examines issues related to the politics of identity and difference but also to mass media and popular culture. Considering its focus and approaches, it is apparent that Cultural Studies neither promotes nor includes understandings of culture, history, and society that are grounded in perceptions of the world that are not necessarily compatible with the liberalism and individualism prevalent in western, mainstream societies.

Cultural Studies does not address the specific concerns of indigenous peoples that emerge from being encroached on by those very same western, industrial (and colonial) societies and their specific ideologies and interests. It does not have the analytical or conceptual tools to make sense of the specific contexts of indigenous peoples where they attempt to assert their rights, maintain their

---

other hand we try to equip the future teachers, civil servants, media workers and researchers with good practical facilities in cultural questions" (Accessed April 2 2007 at: http://www. oulu.fi/giellagas/culture.htm).

10 Interestingly, the opposite seems to be the case with Native studies in North America: "Unable to bring academic knowledge to its proper unity, more and more students are supplementing the shortcoming of Western thought by placing it in the context of their own tribal traditions" (Deloria 1999> 152).

11 See also Guerrero who discusses why multiculturalism is an inadequate approach to indigenous peoples and to the establishment of Indigenous Studies Programs (Guerrero 1996).

cultural integrity and status as distinct peoples and address the contemporary, cumulative effects of colonization. What is more, Cultural Studies tends to focus on culture and identity to the exclusion of economics and thus, overlooking contemporary forms of exploitation. As Gayatri Spivak contends, "'a culturalism' that disavows the economic in its global operations cannot get a grip on the concomitant production of barbarism" (Spivak 1987: 168).

This does not mean that Cultural Studies, or many other analytical/theoretical approaches, for that matter, could not play an important role in bringing much needed critical and self-reflective analysis to previous ethnographic approaches of studying cultures and supplementing and fostering indigenous studies discourses and scholarship. As Yvonne Dion-Buffalo and John C. Mohawk contend, "Cultural studies might be seen as the discourse about what must be conceived or constructed to replace and accelerate the demystification of the dominant ideologies" (Dion-Buffalo and Mohawk 1992: 17).[12] Further, whereas "identity politics can distract from structural problems and resource constraints" (Brysk 2000: 287), they do not have to always be mutually exclusive (see Eschle 2005). But in order to be productive, an analysis must go beyond merely creating spaces to express ourselves; it also needs to pay attention to both internal and external hierarchies and various forms of domination and privilege (Bannerji 1991; Razack 1998).

However, the foundation of any Sami studies program must be rooted in and reflect the goals, interests, premises and institutions of Sami communities. Like other Indigenous Studies Programs, there is no need for Sami Studies Programs to try to fit into the intellectual specializations and categories of mainstream academia and scholarship. Champagne and Stauss suggest:

> Applying the Western intellectual experience and categories of discourse and analysis to the study of Indigenous Nations puts the prospective scholars or Indian life at an initial disadvantage. ... The focus of Native American studies must move out of efforts to mimic mainstream disciplines and find its own organization and purpose through analysis, research, policymaking, and participation in Indian communities. Just as Western civilization is the focus and center of most mainstream academic work, American Indian communities, traditions, and values must be the focus of Native American/Indian studies and the center of its scholarship, teaching, and community outreach (Champagne and Stauss 2002: 8).

In the academy, indigenous people and indigenous scholarship are confined within limiting, often oppressive structures and dominant western or Eurocen-

---

12 The writers note, however, that Cultural Studies is not alone in this process of demystification but there are other important discourses such as critical theory (Dion-Buffalo and Mohawk 1992: 21). See also a discussion of the convergence of postmodern thought and indigenous worldviews by Wilmer (Wilmer 1996).

tric canons, standards and notions of knowledge and research which serve certain values and interests and marginalize and exclude others (Hampton 2000). Many indigenous scholars also argue that the intellectual and epistemological basis of the academy is profoundly saturated by colonial, patriarchal and racist assumptions and practices which define and characterize the conditions of academic and intellectual endeavours (Battiste 1986; Graveline 1995; 2002; Green 2002; Monture-OKanee 1995; Irwin 1988; LaRocque 1996a).

Further, indigenous scholars criticize the Eurocentric bias which results in questioning and undervaluing the validity of indigenous research by other departments and colleagues. Research by indigenous scholars is often deemed irrelevant or "revisionist" because, in many cases, it either falls outside "mainstream" research or focuses on personal experiences as a member of a "minority group" (Stein 1994; Smith 1992; Black-Connor Cleary 2002; Mihesuah 1996). Indigenous research conducted on their own communities and issues may also be assumed to be subjective and biased and consequently dismissed as self-serving (Deloria 1987; Dorris 1987; LaRocque 1996b). The great irony, of course, is that it does not occur to us to similarly criticize mainstream academics who conduct research on their own cultures – including Cultural Studies' focus on industrial societies.

These and other examples of systemic and institutional discrimination demonstrate the continued colonial mentality present in academic institutions. As first pointed out by Frantz Fanon and Albert Memmi, colonialism does not only signify the occupation of territories but also a certain type of relationship between the colonizer and the colonized in which the latter is considered inherently inferior (variously called 'uncivilized,' 'savage,' or 'primitive'). Although the categorical dichotomy between the colonizer and the colonized has been challenged, the fact nevertheless is that the legacy of that relationship remains.

Largely focused on linguistics[13] and descriptive considerations of history, culture and society (aspects that could be considered 'non-threatening' from the perspective of mainstream societies?), Sami scholarship, by and large, tends to lack a critical analysis of the more subtle forms of colonization such as what Spivak calls 'epistemic violence'; the imposition and internalization of a foreign set of codes and values (e.g., Spivak 1990). This type of subtle violence has gone mostly unnoticed in contemporary Sami society and also in Sami research, which further contributes to its unconscious reproduction. However, in order to put an end to various forms of reproduction of epistemic violence

---

13 Here one could point out the critique of Western language sciences that at least used to be the foundation and starting point of studies in Sami language at the Sami Studies at the University of Oulu from the early to mid- 1990s. Born out of the nominalist philosophical tradition, general linguistics tends to treat language as an arbitrary system of signs with little or no relation to the "real world." As Jeffrey Wollock notes, such a view is a threat to biodiversity because it does not take into account that "language is the main guide to action" (Wollock 2001: 255).

or internalized colonialism, it is necessary to become more aware of the subtle forms of colonization which have become internalized during the hundreds of years of colonization and which today affect much of our basic (and often unconscious) assumptions and thinking. Lacking a critique of discursive practices of colonialism in particular, the dominant Sami discourse has thus far not paid adequate attention to the gradual displacement and erasure of the Sami episteme–the deeper structures of Sami values, worldviews, and their underlying assumptions and principles.[14]

Sami scholars need to critically engage in examining the cumulative effects of colonial processes on us and in our communities in order to have a shared, common vision for our future society. We need to 'study up' – research that examines "the powerful, their institutions, policies, and practices instead of focusing only on those whom the powerful govern" (Harding and Norberg 2005: 2011). We also need 'socially engaged research'– "research that holds itself ethically and politically accountable for its social consequences" (Harding and Norberg 2005: 2010) and research that advances social transformation and assists us in finding new ways and models of being in relation to existing racist, sexist, neoliberal, neocolonial constructions of privilege. We need to elaborate methodologies and modes of research based on and drawing upon Sami cultural, social and intellectual conventions and not merely follow Western practices. Sami scholarship needs to resist the definitions of the world that derive from western scholarly tradition and instead, name it according to Sami systems of thought as well as integrate cultural structures which emphasize the 'collective' rather than the 'individual' (Smith 2000a).

This does not imply a wholesale rejection of all 'outside' theories, thinking and research methodologies. Instead, it implies an active engagement and negotiation between mainstream and indigenous intellectual traditions and heedful application and adoption of mainstream academic knowledge and methodologies into our thinking and academic practices. Indigenous methodologies are not a prescription to essentialism, but rather a way of grounding our research on who we are (Weber-Pillwax 2001).[15] This implies the adoption of what is commonly referred to as an indigenous perspective in research. Simply put, an indigenous perspective is an internal perspective, a perspective that places

---

14 Vine Deloria, Jr. points out: "No one is suggesting that Indians 'revert' to the old days or old ways. Rather we must be able to understand what those old days and ways really were and model our present actions and beliefs within that tradition" (Deloria 1992: 16). He particularly recognizes the responsibility of scholars in this process of renegotiation.

15 It is clear that indigenous epistemologies, methodologies or theories do no imply what Gayatri Spivak calls the "impossible ahistorical quest for purist positions" but instead, it is a process of constant negotiation with the structures of cultural imperialism (Spivak 1990: 150). Recognizing the tension and need for negotiation in the intersection of western and indigenous 'domains,' Australian Aboriginal scholar Martin Nakata calls this space a 'cultural interface' and acknowledging how the boundaries between the two domains are never clear-cut or definite (Nakata 2002).

indigenous peoples (in this case, the Sami) and their research questions, methodologies, priorities and protocols at the center of the inquiry. It is an attempt to consider, interpret and understand processes and phenomena from a perspective of indigenous people and in this way validate and make indigenous knowledge and values more visible.

Gaining awareness of the subtle forms of assimilation also requires putting an end to what Graham Smith calls 'the politics of distraction'[16] imposed by liberal ideologies of mainstream societies or the various demands of being native informants (Spivak 1999; Razack 2001) and starting to prioritize our own societal needs and community development. The Sami academics who remain fearful of potential charges of discrimination if they focus on their own people and their own concerns need to be reminded that it is exactly what mainstream societies have always done–even at the expense of indigenous peoples and others.

Moreover, and contrary to what some have suggested,[17] we are not upsetting democracy if we become more proactive in advancing our own concerns and by attending to needs that will be not addressed by others. Instead, we need to remain critical of liberal notions of democracy that "tend to reproduce the interests of dominant groups" (Smith 2000b: 212). As Jacques Derrida pointed out, western liberal democracies have been "secured through colonial exploitation and capitalist expansion in other parts of the world" (cited in Morton 2003: 29). 'Democratic' processes, therefore, do not necessarily recognize or support indigenous peoples' issues and rights – not to mention how the concept has been corrupted in recent world politics.

Abandoning our participation in the politics of distraction implies centering our concerns in a way that attends to structural concerns rather than settling for mere surface, decorative or cosmetic changes, what Graham Smith calls the "bag of tricks" approach (Smith 2000a). Surface changes will not address the more foundational epistemic and ontological questions that are at issue with the production of knowledge, research, and higher education. Building critical consciousness in Sami scholarship also means asking ourselves some important questions: As Sami people, what is the future that we envision? Do we choose to accept and comply with the current status quo and its covert mechanisms of assimilation (such as cooptation into mainstream ideology, allowing Western

16 The "politics of distraction" refers to concerns of secondary significance to indigenous people stemming from the interests of the mainstream academy and society (Smith 2000b). Engaging in the politics of distraction implies that we allow issues that are of lesser importance and relevance to us to control our agendas. In that way, we get distracted from the larger picture of long-term objectives and more urgent and real concerns that would need our firsthand attention. Smith notes how, in recent years, Maori have transgressed the politics of distraction fostered by dominant white interests and "stopped feeling guilty about serving our own interests first" (Smith 2000b: 211).

17 A suggestion that was recently posed to me by a Sami scholar from Norway.

modes of understanding to occupy our research, and not recognizing how 'incorporation' is a subtle means of assimilation)? Do we conform to liberal ideas and ideals of equality of individuals and 'responsible citizenship' at the cost of limiting our collective rights as the Sami people?[18] In short, the first step that is needed is to engage in a broad and open discussion of the needs, perspectives and visions of the Sami people and society.

One of the concepts in Sami discourse and research that requires reconsideration and scrutiny is 'nation-building.' Too often it is understood narrowly to refer only to those conventional political processes that we see in the politics and structures of the dominant (Nordic) societies. We tend to understand 'nation' and 'nation-building' only in mainstream, hegemonic political terms and thus not consider them as multifaceted, complex, social, economic, cultural, intellectual and legal processes. In the context of indigenous research and higher education, discussing 'nation-building' is not to submit to the interests and agendas of indigenous political organizations and leadership but rather, to engage in intellectual self-determination (Warrior 1995; Forbes 1998). As Andrea Smith argues, we need to conceptualize alternative models of nation that are not based on domination and hegemonic nation-state models (Smith 2005).

A Vision for Sami Scholarship: Initial Considerations

A shared, collective vision for the advancement of Sami society and epistemological foundation would not only guide Sami academics in their work and enhance the intellectual, theoretical and disciplinary diversity in Sami research, it would also encourage and enable educated Sami people to return to their communities to not only work as experts on language and culture, but also as educators, lawyers, counselors, engineers, architects, physicians, biologists, political scientists, economists, experts on environmental and policy issues, geographers, historians, administrators, business managers, among other professions.

Below, I will propose some thoughts that I consider timely and important when considering the future of Sami scholarship. They emerge from discussions with other Sami academics and students and observations of the accomplishments and aspirations of other indigenous people in places like Turtle Island/North America and Aotearoa/New Zealand. The ideas and suggestions that I present here are by no means a prescription for a fixed, single model. Rather than providing ready answers, my intention is to outline some issues that I consider central, to give some examples of concrete goals for further consideration and ultimately, to inspire others to envision the future of Sami scholarship and society. Obviously, a shared, collective vision and philosophy necessitates a comprehensive and far-reaching debate within Sami scholarship by all interested parties; academics, educators, students and others.

---

18 See Cathryn McConaghy on how the notion of citizenship has been applied to "civilize" Aboriginals in Australia (McConaghy 2000).

As far as I am concerned, the main objective of Sami higher education and research has to be creating conditions for a meaningful and appropriate Sami self-determination. This goal is advanced by an approach that critically looks to both the past and the future in order to assist us and our work in the present. The approach consists of the following aspects:

Looking to the past. (1) A critical understanding of doing research in Sami communities. We need to carefully examine the earlier research practices: what are they, how have they impacted the Sami people and our lives, what are their strengths and shortcomings, as well as how and what we can learn from them in our current scholarship? (2) An in-depth analysis of colonial discourses and processes that continue to affect the Sami people, society and scholarship. Questions that require consideration include: How has a colonial mentality been internalized and what are its contemporary consequences? What are the subtle mechanisms of assimilation and integration that continue to play a role in Sami communities? This analysis is essential in the Sami aspirations to move forward–without an understanding of these discourses and mechanisms we will not be able to establish strategies that would counter the problems and assist our current endeavours. (3) A systematic process of reclaiming our worldviews, philosophies and values upon which Sami research principles and methodologies can be established. Once we have a solid foundation reflecting who we are, we can start supplementing it according to our respective needs, disciplines and interests while staying aware of the "colonizing" potential of theories that may distort our realities and epistemologies.

Looking to the future. (1) A strong commitment to conduct research and analysis on contemporary Sami realities and conditions. There is a need to recognize the leadership role of Sami academics in order to enable the changes that are imperative along the path of creating a self-sufficient, viable Sami society. (2) A determined and proactive stance to issues and concerns of contemporary Sami society which will remain unaddressed without our attention. With the privilege that formal higher education accords academics, Sami scholars must take initiative and espouse our collective responsibility toward contributing to the well-being of our people. We cannot look to the future as privatized academics but as scholars whose work is related and has relevance to our communities. We also must ensure that the knowledge we have and generate is shared with other members of Sami society who may not have access to it otherwise. (3) An active engagement with new fields of research, including questions related to theory and methodology. What, for example, is the role of Sami knowledge and values in politics, legal processes and health care and also, how to strengthen that role in the future?

Besides the overall principles and vision for Sami scholarship, we also need concrete goals. Conversations with Sami researchers and educators at both the Sami College and Sami Institute as well as at Sami Studies programs at the Universities of Oulu and Tromsø demonstrate that there is a clear need and desire for a center of Sami higher learning and research located in the heart of the Sami region. The idea of a Sami University is not new–it is a prospect that has been addressed time to time by Sami academic and political leaders at various meetings and conferences for decades.[19]

In February 2005, the Sami University College made the groundbreaking decision to gradually start developing the College into a University and called for the responsibility and input of the governments of Norway, Sweden, Finland and Russia to ensure the implementation of this initiative. Besides this pro-active first step, there are other factors that most likely will contribute to the realization of the long-term dream, such as moving the Sami University College and Sami Institute in the near future to Diehtosiida, a new building that will house also other Sami institutions in Guovdageaidnu.[20]

After the significant decision to begin the transformation of Sami higher education and research to a Sami University, it is crucial that we as Sami scholars and academics are able to put our personal preferences and disagreements aside and commit ourselves to working together to strengthen our intellectual self-determination and transformation of Sami society. Now is the time to be more concerned about our collective academic and intellectual development rather than the possible changes in our individual positions and academic security.

The Sami University has a central role, both as a part of Sami advancement and as a means to it. Rather than getting distracted by the challenges and potential obstacles, we have to engage in a constructive and creative dialogue about the underlying philosophy and foundation as well as actual structures, funding, staffing, questions concerning disciplines and faculties and other practical matters related to establishing an academic institution. There is a need to form a working group of dedicated individuals to draft a blueprint based on existing Sami institutions and resources. Several invaluable lessons could also be drawn, for example, from Vuokko Hirvonen's detailed evaluation of the Sami Curriculum for comprehensive schools in Norway which were first introduced in 1997 (Hirvonen 2003).

In her analysis which was based on interviews with Sami teachers, Hirvonen points out the difficulties of implementing the Sami Curriculum as experienced

---

19 For example, the Sami Conference that convenes every fourth year and represents many Sami organizations from all four countries where the Sami currently live has issued twice in the past few years (in 1989 and 2004) a statement on transforming the Sami College into a Sami University.

20 The Sami Institute has recently been reorganized into "an independent Nordic institution" in connection with the Sami College. The new shared facilities, that will also accommodate the Sami Archives and others, are expected to be complete in 2009 (http://www.nsi.no/).

by teachers themselves in their everyday practice. The needs and challenges that the teachers referred to should form one of the starting points when considering the priorities of the Sami University. As Hirvonen notes, the Sami Curriculum is not just about switching from one plan to another, but about a much more profound societal and political transformation, particularly as it relates to multicultural encounters. In short, the future Sami University must not become "a mainstream university translated into Sami" as is currently the case with many so-called Sami schools (Hirvonen 2003). We cannot lose sight of today's Sami students who are our future leaders and it is our collective responsibility to give them the necessary tools and understanding to foster the development of Sami society.[21]

In short, making the vision of the Sami University a reality requires educating a critical mass of indigenous intellectuals who have a consciousness about their heritage and responsibilities (cf. Smith 2003). To paraphrase Champagne and Stauss, we need to teach Sami students analytical skills, Nordic-Sami history and policy, and an appreciation and understanding of Sami self-governance models and culture to enable them to become critical, informed, and active participants in Sami community life as well as in Sami issues at the regional and national levels. Sami Studies programs must be in a good position to assist Sami communities with issues of law, policy, the environment, repatriation, recognition, state-Sami relations, and other concerns. The advantage of direct engagement with Sami communities is that the separation of academic and community life is broken down, and students and scholars learn firsthand about a Sami community and its important issues and have an opportunity to work directly within the community (cf. Champagne and Stauss 2002: 9).

There is no doubt that we can do this and much more if we together commit ourselves to envisioning and building Sami higher education and research for the benefit of future Sami generations. It is also important that Sami academics participate in the broader, global process of indigenous transformation and decolonization. The principle of sharing and learning from others is one of the central aspects of many indigenous epistemologies, including that of the Sami. We can and must put it into practice in our scholarship and teaching.

---

21 As Hirvonen indicates, one of the obstacles in reaching the goals of the Sami Curriculum is the very education of the Sami teachers themselves (of whom only 15 % have been trained at the Sami College) which has imposed the powerful ideology of assimilation on several Sami generations. Due to this ideology, it is difficult to depart from the official interpretations of the nation (Hirvonen 2003).

References

Bannerji, Himani (1991). But Who Speaks for Us? Experience and Agency in Conventional Feminist Paradigms. *Unsettling Relations: University as a Site of Feminist Struggle*. H. Bannerji, L. Carty, K. Dehli, S. Heald and K. McKenna. Toronto, Women's Press: 67-107.

Barnhardt, Ray (1991). "Higher Education in the Fourth World: Indigenous People Take Control." *Canadian Journal of Native Education* 18(2): 199-232.

Battiste, Marie (1986). Micmac Literacy and Cognitive Imperialism. *Indian Education in Canada: The Legacy*. J. Barman, Y. Hebert and D. McCaskill. Vancouver, UBC Press. 1: 23-44.

Battiste, Marie, Ed. (2000). *Reclaiming indigenous voice and vision*. Vancouver, UBC Press.

Battiste, Marie (2001). Decolonizing the University: Ethical Guidelines for Research Involving Indigenous Populations. *Pursuing Academic Freedom: "Free and Fearless"?* L. M. Findlay and P. M. Bidwell. Saskatoon, Purich: 190-203.

Black-Connor Cleary, Delores (2002). Contradictions in the Classroom: Reflections of an Okanogan-Colville Professor. *Women Faculty of Color in the White Classroom*. L. Vargas. New York, Peter Lang: 183-99.

Bourdieu, Pierre (1977). *Outline of a Theory of Practice*. Cambridge, Cambridge University Press.

Brysk, Alison (2000). *From tribal village to global village. Indian rights and international relations in Latin America*, Stanford University Press.

Champagne, Duane and Jay Stauss, Eds. (2002). *Native American Studies in Higher Education. Models for Collaboration between Universities and Indigenous Nations*. Walnut Creek, CA, Altamira Press.

Clifford, James and George E. Marcus, Eds. (1986). *Writing Culture: The Poetics and Politics of Ethnography*. Berkeley, University of California Press.

Deloria, Vine, Jr. (1987). Revision and Reversion. *The American Indian and the Problem of History*. C. Martin. New York & Oxford, Oxford University Press: 84-90.

Deloria, Vine, Jr. (1992). Commentary: Research, Redskins, and Reality. *The First Ones: Readings in Indian/Native Studies*. D. R. Miller, C. Beal, J. Dempsey and R. W. Heber. Regina, Sask., Saskatchewan Indian Federated College Press: 15-19.

Deloria, Vine Jr. (1999). Higher Education and Self-Determination. *Spirit & Reason. The Vine Deloria, Jr., Reader*. B. Deloria, K. Foehner and S. Scinta. Golden, CO, Fulcrum: 144-153.

Dion-Buffalo, Yvonne and John C. Mohawk (1992). "Thoughts from an Autochthonous Center. Postmodernism and Cultural Studies." *Akwe:kon Journal* Winter: 16-21.

Dorris, Michael (1987). Indians on the Shelf. *The American Indian and the Problem of History*. C. Martin. New York & Oxford, Oxford University Press: 98-105.

Eschle, Catherine (2005). ""Skeleton Women": Feminism and the Antiglobalization Movement." *Signs* 30(3): 1741-1771.

Fay, Cornelius Ryan and Henry F. Tiblier (1967). *Epistemology*. Milwaukee, Bruce.

Forbes, Jack D. (1998). "Intellectual Self-Determination and Sovereignty: Implications for Native Studies and for Native Intellectuals." *Wicazo Sa Review* 13(1): 11-23.

Garrod, Andrew and Colleen Larimore, Eds. (1997). *First Person, First Peoples. Native American College Graduates Tell Their Life Stories*. Ithaca, Cornell University Press.

Gaski, Harald (1991). "Dutki, servodat ja kritihkka", *cafe Boddu* (Ed. H.Gaski), Davvi Girji, Kárášjohka. (pp. 131-141).

Gaski, Harald (2000). The Secretive Text. Yoik Lyric as Literature and Tradition. *Sami Folkloristics*. J. Pentikäinen. Turku, Nordic Network of Folklore: 191-214.

Graveline, Fyre Jean (1995). "Lived Experiences of an Aboriginal Feminist Transforming the Curriculum." *Canadian Woman Studies* 14(2): 52-5.

Graveline, Fyre Jean (2002). Everyday Discrimination: We Know How and When, but Never Why. *Women in the Canadian Academic Tundra. Challenging the Chill.* E. Hannah, L. Paul and S. Vethamay-Globus. Montreal, McGill-Queen's University Press: 72-84.

Green, Joyce (2002). Transforming at the Margins of the Academy. *Women in the Canadian Academic Tundra: Challenging the Chill.* E. Hannah, L. Paul and S. Vethamany-Globus. Toronto, McGill-Queen's University Press: 85-91.

Guerrero, M. Annette Jaimes (1996). Academic Apartheid. American Indian Studies and 'Multiculturalism'. *Mapping Multiculturalism.* A. F. Gordon and C. Newfield. Minneapolis, University of Minnesota Press: 49-63.

Hampton, Eber (2000). First Nations-Controlled University Education in Canada. *Aboriginal Education: Fulfilling the Promise.* L. D. a. L. L. Marlene Brant Castellano. Vancouver, University of British Columbia Press: 208-223.

Harding, Sandra and Kathryn Norberg (2005). "New feminist approaches to social science methodologies: An introduction." *Signs* 30(4): 2009-2015.

Henriksen, John B. (1999). *Saami parliamentary co-operation: an analysis.* Guovdageaidnu, Nordic Sámi Institute.

Hirvonen, Vuokko (1996). Research Ethics and Sami People - From the Woman's Point of View. *Awakened Voice. Sami Knowledge.* E. Helander. Guovdageaidnu, Nordic Sami Institute: 7-12.

Hirvonen, Vuokko (1999). *Sámeeatnama jienat. Sápmelaš nissona bálggis girječállin.* Guovdageaidnu, Dat.

Hirvonen, Vuokko (2003). Mo sámáidahttit skuvlla? Reforpma 97 evalueren. Kárášjohka, Čalliid Lagadus.

Irwin, Kathy (1988). "Maori, Feminist, Academic." *Sites* 17((Summer)): 30-8.

Joks, Solveig (2001). *Boazosámi nissonolbmot – guovddážis báike- ja siidadoalus, muhto vajálduvvon almmolaččat.* Guovdageaidnu, Sámi Instituhtta.

Keskitalo, Alf-Isak (1994). *Research as an Inter-Ethnic Relation.* Rovaniemi, Arctic Centre, University of Lapland.

Keskitalo, Jan Henry (1997). Sami Post-Secondary Education – Ideals and Realities. *Sami Culture in a New Era. The Norwegian Sami Experience.* H. Gaski. Kárášjohka, Davvi Girji: 155-71.

Kirkness, Verna J. and Ray Barnhardt (1991). "First Nations and Higher Education: The Four R's - Respect, Relevance, Reciprocity, Responsibility." *Journal of American Indian Education* 30(3): 1-15.

Kuokkanen, Rauna (1996). From the Jungle Back to the *Duottar. Awakened Voice. Sami Traditional Knowledge.* E. Helander. Guovdageaidnu, Sami Institute: 54-63.

Kuokkanen, Rauna (1997). Etnostreassas sápmelašvuođa ođđasis huksemii. Sápmelašvuođa govven dálá sápmelaš girjjálašvuođas. sámegiela lágadus, Oulu universitehta. Pro grad.

Kuokkanen, Rauna (2001). Let's Vote Who is Most Authentic! Politics of Identity in Contemporary Sami Literature. *(Ad)dressing Our Words. Aboriginal Perspectives on Aboriginal Literatures.* A. G. Ruffo. Penticton, Theytus: 79-100.

Kuokkanen, Rauna (2007a). Myths and Realities of Sami Women: A Postcolonial Feminist Analysis for the Decolonization and Transformation of Sami Society. *Making space for Aboriginal feminism.* J. Green. Halifax, N.S., Fernwood Books.

Kuokkanen, Rauna (2007b). Saamelaiset ja jälkikoloniaali analyysi: Kolonialismin vaikutukset nykypäivänä. *Kolonialismin jäljet: Perifeerisyys ja Suomi*. J. Kuortti, M. Lehtinen and O. Löytty. Helsinki, Gaudeamus.

Kvernmo, Siv and Vigdis Stordahl (1991). Fra Same til akademiker = Fra deltaker til observatør? *Samesymposium*. M. Aikio and K. Korpijaakko. Rovaniemi, Lapin yliopisto: 71-85.

LaRocque, Emma (1996a). The Colonization of a Native Woman Scholar. *Women of the First Nations. Power, Wisdom, and Strength*. C. Miller, P. Chuchryk, M. S. Marule, B. Manyfingers and C. Deering. Winnipeg, University of Manitoba Press: 11-18.

LaRocque, Emma (1996b). When the Other Is Me: Native Writers Confronting Canadian Literature. *Issues in the North*. J. Oakes and R. Riewe. Edmonton, Canadian Circumpolar Institute. 1: 115-23.

Larson, Karen (1988). "Ethnopolitics and Research Ethics for the non-native Researcher." *Acta Borealia* 1/2.

Lehtola, Veli-Pekka (1997). *Rajamaan identiteetti: lappilaisuuden rakentuminen 1920- ja 1930-luvun kirjallisuudessa*. Helsinki, SKS.

Marcus, George E. and M. Fisher, Eds. (1986). *Anthropology as Cultural Critique: An Experimental Moment in Human Sciences*. Chicago, University of Chicago Press.

McConaghy, Cathryn (2000). *Rethinking Indigenous Education: Culturalism, Colonalism, and the Politics of Knowing*. Flaxton, Qld, PostPressed.

Medicine, Beatrice with Sue-Ellen Jacobs (2001). *Learning to Be an Anthropologist & Remaining "Native." Selected Writings*. Urbana & Chicago, University of Illinois Press.

Mihesuah, Devon (1996). "Epilogue: Voices, Interpretations, and the 'New Indian History': Comment on the *American Indian Quarterly*'s Special Issue on Writing About American Indians." *American Indian Quarterly* 20(1): 91-108.

Mihesuah, Devon A., Ed. (1998). *Natives and Academics. Researching and Writing about American Indians*. Lincoln & London, University of Nebraska Press.

Monture-OKanee, Patricia (1995). Introduction: Surviving the Contradictions. *Breaking Anonymity: The Chilly Climate for Women Faculty*. T. C. Collective. Waterloo, Ont, Wilfred Laurie University Press: 11-28.

Morton, Stephen (2003). *Gayatri Chakravorty Spivak*. London; New York, Routledge.

Müller-Wille, Ludger (1991). Indigenous Nations and Social Sciences: Minority-Majority Relations in Sápmi, Finland. *Samesymposium*. M. Aikio and K. Korpijaakko. Rovaniemi, University of Lapland: 151-70.

Nakata, Martin (2002). Indigenous Knowledge and the Cultural Interface: Underlying Issues at the Intersection of Knowledge and Information Systems. *68th IFLA Council and General Conference*.

Razack, Sherene H. (1998). *Looking White People in the Eye. Gender, Race, and Culture in Courtrooms and Classrooms*. Toronto, University of Toronto Press.

LaRocque, Emma (2001). Racialized Immigrant Women as Native Informants in the Academy. *Seen But Not Heard: Aboriginal Women and Women of Colour in the Academy*. R. Luther, E. Whitmore and B. Moreau. Ottawa, Canadian Research Institute for the Advancement of Women: 51-60.

Rosenau, Pauline Marie (1992). *Post-modernism and the social sciences: insights, inroads, and intrusions*. Princeton, N.J., Princeton University Press.

Sami Council (2002). The difference between minorities and indigenous peoples under international law, Statement to the Council of Europe, 10 January.

Sárá, Máret, Ed. (2003). *Boazodoalloealáhusa nissonpolitihkalaš seminára. Seminar om kvinnepolitikk i rendriftsnæringen.* Raporta/Rapport. 10 Dec. 2002 Romsa/Tromsø. Alta, Boazodoallohálddahus.

Schott, Robin May (2003). *Discovering feminist philosophy. Knowledge, ethics, politics.* Lanham, Rowman & Littlefield.

Smith, Andrea (2005). "Native American Feminism, Sovereignty, and Social Change." *Feminist Studies* 31(1): 116-132.

Smith, Graham Hingangaroa (1990). *The post-colonial critic: interviews, strategies, dialogues.* New York, Routledge.

Smith, Graham Hingangaroa (1997). Sami Generations. *Sami Culture in a New Era. The Norwegian Sami Experience.* H. Gaski. Kárášjohka, Davvi Girji: 143-54.

Smith, Graham Hingangaroa (1999). *A critique of postcolonial reason: Toward a history of the vanishing present.* Cambridge, Mass., Harvard University Press.

Smith, Graham Hingangaroa (2000a). "Maori Education: Revolution and Transformative Action." *Canadian Journal of Native Education* 24(1): 57-72.

Smith, Graham Hingangaroa (2000b). Protecting and Respecting Indigenous Knowledge. *Reclaiming Indigenous Voice and Vision.* M. Battiste. Vancouver, University of British Columbia Press: 209-24.

Smith, Graham Hingangaroa (2003). Indigenous Struggle for the Transformation of Education and Schooling. *Alaskan Federation of Natives (AFN) Convention.* Anchorage, Alaska.

Smith, Linda Tuhiwai (1992). Ko Taku Ta Te Maori: The Dilemma of a Maori Academic. *NZARE/AARE Conference.* Deakin University, Geelong, Victoria, Australia.

Smith, Graham Hingangaroa (1999). *Decolonizing Methodologies. Research and Indigenous Peoples.* London, Zed Books.

Spivak, Gayatri Chakravorty (1987). *In other worlds: essays in cultural politics.* New York, Methuen.

Stein, Wayne J (1994). "The survival of American Indian faculty." *Thought and Action* 10(1): 101-113.

Stordahl, Vigdis (1996). "Antropologi i den fjerde verden." *Norsk Antropologisk tidsskrift* 3.

Trinh, Minh-ha T. (1989). The Language of Nativism: Antropology as a Scientific Conversation of Man with Man. *Woman, Native, Other: Writing, Post-coloniality and Feminism.* Bloomington, University of Indiana Press: 47-76.

Vuolab, Kerttu (1994). *Čeppari Čáráhus.* Davvi Girji.

Warrior, Robert Allen (1995). *Tribal Secrets. Recovering American Indian Intellectual Traditions.* Minneapolis, U of Minnesota Press.

Weber-Pillwax, C. (2001). "What is Indigenous Research?" *Canadian Journal of Native Education* 24: 166-74.

Wilmer, Franke (1996). "Narratives of Resistance: Postmodernism and Indigenous World Views." *Race, Gender & Class* 3(2): 35-58.

Wollock, Jeffrey (2001). Linguistic diversity and biodiversity: Some implications for the language sciences. *On biocultural diversity. Linking language, knowledge, and the environment.* Washington, Smithsonian Institution Press: 248-264.

CHAPTER 15

The "Battlefields": Identity, Authenticity and Aboriginal¹ Knowledges in Australia

VICKI GRIEVES

(Aboriginal) traditions embody a unique and profound view of reality that may even now be developed by Aboriginal scholars to enrich the mainstream of human thought...What might happen if some of the really great Aboriginal minds, retaining their own awareness of nature, become literate scholars in the western tradition as well, is surely worth the contemplation of our educators. (Charles Rowley *The Destruction of Aboriginal Society,* 1970)

The impetus for this article arose out of the experience of international Indigenous scholars at the conference of the International Committee of Historical Sciences, *Comite Internationale des Sciences Historiques*, (CISH) conference in Sydney, July 2005. Sami scholar Professor Henry Minde and others were interested to observe that the panel developed around Australian Aboriginal history did not include Indigenous historians and they were also intrigued by the idea that Aboriginal history is seen to be the "battlefield" of Australian history, contested by scholars from the "right" and "left" of Australian politics (Haebich 2005).

The "history wars" in Australia have developed out of a conservative reaction to the upsurge of new scholarship by increasing numbers of academics across Australia that, within the past three decades, has provided a very different view of colonial history. The old explanations for Aboriginal disadvantage that relied on racist assumptions of Aboriginal inability to rise to the challenge of modernity, rather than victimization from brutal colonial dispossession, have been sorely tested by a new wave of historians following on from the work of Henry Reynolds' trailblazing publication *The Other Side of the Frontier* originally published in 1981 (Reynolds 2006). This revisionist history that has been labelled as "leftist", has irrevocably altered the national debate about Australia's identity: what Australia was, is, and how it and ought to be

---

1   The term "Aboriginal" is used as a blanket term to cover the plethora of Indigenous groups in Australia. Local and regional groups prefer to refer to themselves by terms from their own languages such as: "Koori", NSW and Victoria; "Murri" northern NSW and Queensland; "Nyoongar" SW Western Australia (WA); "Nungah" South Australia (SA); "Yammatgee" north of Perth and south of Broome WA; "Wongi" the Goldfields area of WA; "Anungu" Pitjanjatjara lands in South Australia; "Yolngu" from Arnhem Land, Yirrkala, Northern Territory.

into the future. This new wave of Aboriginal history, rather than histories, is the key to legitimising a different consciousness, morality and understanding of Indigenous issues that opens the way for Australia to pursue a different path. The conservative and reactionary response to this has been spearheaded by Keith Windschuttle (2002: 2001) and others, who seek to characterise the revisionist histories as weak scholarship, ideologically based, and therefore unfounded, in order to neutralise or nullify Indigenous claims for rights. The history wars have become an overriding concern for Australian historians because issues in Aboriginal history have become central to questions of national identity, and the mainstream debate rages over how to interpret history and its meaning for the moral, social, economic and political issues of today and into the future (Manne 2003:12; Hall 1998).

Indigenous scholars and intellectuals retain a more nuanced view of the history wars. Marcia Langton, refers to the history wars as part of a constellation of events such as the rise of Hansonism (the racist right) as "eliminat(ing) Indigenous people from the category of Australians worth considering as real people" (Langton 2006). The Koorie historian and writer Tony Birch who, when in a national radio debate on the history wars remarked that he did not want an ongoing involvement in commentating the history wars as he had what he considered to be more serious and engaging things to do with his time (Adams 2003). Birch has recently parodied "the travelling 'History Wars' circus, which has done more to stifle the voices of Aboriginal people in recent times than a boatload of imperial warlords armed with gunpowder and a compass" (Birch 2007: 32). Essentially in agreement, I recognise that there are other, more silent, contested domains within Australian scholarship and education policy that impact on the development of Indigenous knowledges and reduce opportunities for Indigenous power in the academy – that is, the "battlefields" of Indigenous knowledges development. The prominence of the history wars in Australian scholarship and the marginalised Indigenous intellectual and academic engagement with this debate are both symptomatic of the lack of status and poor resourcing of Indigenous knowledges in Australia.

This chapter aims to critique the history wars of the "left" and "right" in Australian colonial settler society and extend the battlefields metaphor beyond, to deeper associated issues arising from the hegemony of western sites of knowledge production. This hegemony extends to making issues of Indigenous identity and authenticity more complex by taking them out of Aboriginal community control, influencing the nature of Indigenous knowledge production. Questions are raised about the current nature and direction of Indigenous knowledge development within the shifting paradigms and new norms for Indigenous identity. Since Indigenous Australians have had to recently fight for their identity, against the widely held settler colonial conviction that all Aboriginal people had "died out" and at any rate the culture had been "lost", this is a contentious and conflicted issue within Australia. As Birch says, "white Australia's history of the occupation of Indigenous land and country had been reliant on particular forms of violence designed to dispossess Indigenous people of both land and identity" (Birch 2004:19). Thus, the massacres and wars have been replaced by attacks on the identity, culture and rights of Indigenous Australians as part of an ongoing colonial project, an overwhelmingly "white" preoccupation, that has drawn its support historically from both the "left" and the "right" of politics. While there are attacks on Aboriginality *per se* there are also many examples of individual claims to Aboriginal identity being viewed as fraudulent within Aboriginal communities themselves. These issues also arise in other settler colonial societies causing confusion and conflict: Native American scholar, Eva Marie Garroutte's theory of "radical Indigenism", developed in response to questions about who are the "real Indians" within Native American contexts (Garroutte 2003), is salient to issues impacting on Indigenous knowledges development in Australia and will be discussed later in this chapter.

Indigenous Knowledges and the "History Wars"

The read and write mob the one bin doing all the killing. -(Peggy Patrick (2003) talking about the massacre at Mistake Creek, which occurred in 1915)

Indigenous Australians, without a just and proper settlement over the wrongs of colonial takeover, are without an economic base and thus socially, politically and economically hamstrung from being able to record, develop and promote their knowledges in anything like an adequate and ongoing way. The potential that inspired Rowley (referred to in the quote at the beginning), is not yet realised and the situation is arguably becoming more urgent. The powerlessness of Indigenous Australians over Indigenous knowledge production has led to the locus of control of Aboriginal knowledges, identity and authenticity shifting out of Aboriginal domains and firmly into the control of white institutions such as governments and universities. The prominence of the "battlefields" in Aboriginal history is symptomatic of this in that it is essentially a preoccupation of white Australian intellectuals.

Moreover, the "history wars" is a battleground dominated by the opposing factions of the "right" and the "left" in the politics of the Australian settler colonial state where Aboriginal people are marginalised. Our importance lies in being the political football and the handy representatives of the "race card" often played by politicians before elections to garner more of the overwhelmingly white vote. And, in Australian intellectual life, defences from academics of the "left" meet attacks on us from the "right". While these defences are currently important and necessary, it is crucial that an Indigenous dimension enters the "battlefield", with its potential to change the nature of the conflict, or indeed be the catalyst for different approaches, even peace and accommodation.

An example of this potential is contained in the documentary *Dhakiyarr vs the King* which was developed in close association with *yolngu* people in order to deal with an important issue they needed to resolve. Yolngu historians Dhukal and Wuyal Wirrpanda trace the past of their elder Dhakiyarr Wirrpanda who was found guilty in the Darwin Supreme Court of the murder of a white policeman and jailed in Fannie Bay in the early 1930s. Later when the guilty verdict was subsequently overturned and he was released from jail he never made it back to his community but disappeared, believed to be murdered, in revenge for the death of the policeman. Through *yolngu* ceremony, in this case deliberately made public, the old man could be laid to rest and his descendents made peace with the relatives of the policemen and the court in Darwin (Murray and Collins 2003). This is a very powerful rendition of the power of Aboriginal culture, not only in the preservation of the land and sea country of which we are rightful custodians but in the potential of Aboriginal philosophies to contribute to the resolutions of conflict in this country.

Tantalising understandings of foundations of the philosophical base from which contemporary conflicts resolution can come are found in the contribution of Peggy Patrick of the Gidga people to the "battlefields" debate. She revealed the story of the Mistake Creek massacre in 1915 from her mother's eyewitness account:

> I bin born la bush. I never bin go school. We got own language, Gija, Miriwoong, Worla. We talk blackfella English not this gardiya (white people's) high English.
> Early day gardiya bin really cruel la blackfella. My mother bin little girl when her mum, her mum sister, her father bin get killed right in front of her. The read and write mob the one bin doing all the killing. They never write down what they did. We don't read and write but we hear about what bin happen before from our mother and father and we still got it in our mind. We never talk to gardiya about this cruel thing because people bin still frightened. If they say anything they might get killed themself (Patrick 2003: 260).

Peggy Patrick's oral testimony has been challenged the "right". Windschuttle, author of *The Fabrication of Aboriginal History Vol.1; Van Dieman's Land 1803-1847* argued that violence against the Aboriginal people of Tasmania had been vastly exaggerated by "leftist" historians with ideological agendas (Windschuttle 2002). In line with his critique of "fabricated" histories, he also challenged Patrick's reporting of the massacre at Mistake Creek (Windschuttle 2001). In response to this Patrick said:

> Then people tell me that one gardiya call Windschuttle never listen to my word proper. He never come up here and talk to me face to face in my own country. He write bad way about me because he cant listen to my word proper way. He make

fun of me. He reckon I bin say 'my mum' when I bin really talk 'ganggayi' or 'my mum mum' not my 'mum'….

He keep going pretending that I got high English and try to make me look stupid. Bad enough his terrible thing bin happen before. That Windschuttle hurt my family feeing and it make us feel bad for all the relation bin get killed at Mistake Creek…..

He keep going saying that I really say my own mother bin get killed when I never say that. I bin talking for my ganggayi, my mum mum and her family…..

…….We know people bin get killed all over the country. Now people like this Windschuttle try to say nobody bin get killed because gardiya never write 'em down what they bin do…..

He reckon he good one telling true story proper way. He say other people should make sure they got true story. He cant take notice when people tell him he make mistake himself. Some of people say 'gardiya never believe blackfella'……

We bin bring out hard story what bin happen to blackfella. We talk about bad story so black and white can be friend when we look at true thing together. Look like nothing change. Gardiya killed blackfella with gun and poison now look like he killing our life making fun of my word. Not worth (Patrick 2003: 260-1).

Peggy Patrick's testimony is a powerful statement of the nihilism implicit in a situation where the colonising culture does not understand or accept the philosophical base of the "other". The notion of the sanctity of one's "word" has a very different meaning in Aboriginal contexts where the culture has been orally transmitted and formalities around telling the *true story* exist. This is evident in Peggy Patrick's use of the English words "proper way", "hard story", the idea of talking about such things "face to face" and in ones "own country". In the Aboriginal languages in which she is fluent, these words have more weight. To be careless with the truth in Indigenous law and protocol is to make bad business for the future, even for the country, least of all never to be trusted again by your own people.

Indigenous knowledges spring from an entirely different social and cultural base; they are not just fanciful, exotic or pre-modern variations on a theme within western epistemologies and pedagogies. These knowledges have either been appropriated and adapted or too easily dismissed by many western scholars and certainly by Australian society generally, as out of date, unreliable, antithetical to modernity or primitive and dangerous.

Indigenous Knowledges and Australian Politics of the "Right' and the "Left"

The prominence of the political alignments of the right and left in the "battle-fields" of Aboriginal history contributes to the reduction of Aboriginal peoples' involvement merely to the use of their testimony within historical, theoretical and conceptual frameworks of non-Indigenous scholars work. The overwhelming dominance of these debates detracts from the possibility of Indigenous people of high degree setting up their own research agendas. This illustrates how profoundly Indigenous scholarship in Australia is hampered by being located within western institutional sites of knowledge production. In Australia there is yet another layer of complexity adding to the current situation. Since Aboriginal people have been seen as the "missing link" and the most primitive of humans, we have endured acute scrutiny from the academy over more than 150 years (Hiatt 1996). Scholarship has been traditionally about Indigenous people rather than by them (Bourke and Bourke 2002). While custodians of traditional knowledges have been interviewed and reported by white academics, and many have developed autobiographies, they have had scant opportunity to be involved in the building of knowledge power bases within Australian society.

To place the "battlefields" of Aboriginal history in the context of Indigenous knowledge development, it is essentially a white preoccupation, a battle between the political alignments of the "right' and the "left" within the polity of the Australian settler colonial state. Important yes, but in many ways not central to the preoccupations of Indigenous people. We have a deep understanding from our own people and family experiences that the battles began as massacres, that the takeover of lands was contested, that many people lost their lives, that the subsequent polices of segregation have hardly blown over, and that the colonialist project has not yet ended in Australia.

The Australian political view of the "battlefields" is expressed in the following cartoon:

Nicholson, The Australian *27 September 2003*

This "white" view of the debate has included the irony of a white academic rushing in to help the mortally wounded Indigenous man. Arguably, white Australia's perception of what it means to be Aboriginal in this country does not yet include recognising our intellectual potential or that we are able to save ourselves, it is white people (academics) who can save us, or perhaps think they can? Birch has recently revealed the bitter irony of access and ownership of Indigenous testimony and history by the "Professional Historian or ...'The Sophisticated One':

> It will be easy to identify him. He will be him, and will wear a suit and an old school tie, and carry the walk of unquestionable authority and self assurance. It will be the duty of the Professional Historian to wage a war, a 'History War', in defence of the defenceless – the Aborigine – who knows nothing of 'history' beyond myths and legends. When the 'Sophisticated One' cometh, praise him. And do not ask questions (or request a key to the door) (Birch 2007: 32).

Importantly too, while leading Indigenous intellectuals seem to have aligned themselves with the left, many remain essentially non-aligned. It is not clear that the left has a monopoly over the granting of Indigenous rights or that either of the major Australian political parties is currently prepared develop an adequate bipartisan Indigenous rights agenda publicly on their political platforms. Prominent Aboriginal scholar Marcia Langton has argued that the "left" were almost out of character in their support of the land rights movement of the 1970s, having been "almost completely silent" on the erosion of Aboriginal rights in the post World War Two period (Langton 2002:7). She hopes for the possibility of halting the "racialist political football that has been Aboriginal affairs for three decades" and for "a genuine bipartisan agreement that Aboriginal poverty is not the political property of any party but an historical legacy that brings no honour to those who suffer it nor to those who play politics with it" (Langton 2002:17). And witness for example, the Australian Labor Party, the major political party most likely to be "leftist", has signalled its intent to support the government's proposed legal challenge to the granting of Native Title over the city of Perth in Western Australia to the *Nyoongah* people (Message Stick 2006).

This is not to say that individual non-Indigenous scholars are not aware of the power imbalance in western knowledge production. For example, Stephen Muecke clearly understands and respects the intellectual worth of the Nyigina elder Paddy Roe and claims to be the first white academic to share the ownership of the book produced (Muecke and Roe 1984) as intellectual property, including royalties (Muecke 1999). However, Paddy Roe, Peggy Patrick and their peers have no opportunity for status in the academy and no opportunity to generate the collection and preservation of their knowledges in directions that they might choose. There is no opportunity for such Indigenous intellectuals/informants to be resourced in order for them to generate further research, publication, teaching and intellectual mentoring within higher education in accordance with their cultural imperatives and community needs. And, as it happens, there is no opportunity for important Indigenous intellectuals, historians and philosophers of that ilk, to present their work at a conference such as the CISH. As Moreton-Robinson has asserted: "The question that needs to be asked is: Who benefits the most from the research?" (Moreton-Robinson 2003)

Border Thinking: Beyond "Right" and "Left"

Walter Mignolo has importantly articulated similar ideas to those that many Indigenous scholars know to be true: that Indigenous philosophies have the capacity make people think "beyond the legacy of Western epistemology", to consider the ethics and politics of teaching and research within westernised institutions and to have western academics realise they have a real investment in the perpetuation of colonial differences and social injustices (Mignolo 2000). Mignolo's concept of an epistemic metaphor of the "border" and thus "border thinking", that moves along the diversity of the historical process itself, from the perspective of the colonised allows:

> ...an effort toward thinking beyond the hegemonic Western conceptualization (of everything), for the right and for the left, which went together with Western capitalistic and colonial expansion. Why? Because you have, on the one hand, a hegemonic "right" discourse (modified and adapted to local histories, whether those histories are U.S., Indonesia or Bolivia) dictating the discourse of the market, of the law and or society. And you have, on the other hand, also a hegemonic "left" discourse (modified and adapted to local histories, whether those local histories are of the U.S., Indonesia or Bolivia). Shall the world continue to think and speak from the hegemonic models of thinking, from the right and from the left that emerged in Europe under capitalism? (Delgado and Romero 2000:4)

In contrast, border thinking can arise from a diversity of colonial experiences and it allows the possibility of imagining different, highly innovative, scenarios in human futures:

> That is to say, of engaging the colonialism of Western epistemology (from the left and from the right) from the perspective of epistemic forces that had been turned into subaltern (traditional, folkloric, religious, emotional, etc.) forms of knowledge.....
> making it possible to 'think other wise', from the interior exteriority of the border. That is, to engage in border thinking is to move beyond the categories created and imposed by Western epistemology (Delgado and Romero 2000:5).

294

The perspective of the "border" can assist in developing new approaches to the complexity of Indigenous scholarship, and scholarship around Indigenous issues, outside of western constructions of knowledges.

The Persistence of Colonialism in Indigenous Education Contexts

Indigenous knowledge production within Australian universities is very new, located in a modern hybrid space, and plagued by the questions: Who is Indigenous? Who has the right to speak and be heard? What is the truth? And perhaps even more salient, the question of who is to have control over what is to be researched and studied: how is this control to be exercised? There is contestation around these questions that arise again and again: the complex layers of issues and disagreements that revolve around modern political ideological differences on the one hand and the hegemonic control of the Australian settler colonial state over Indigenous identity and education on the other, are in need of research scrutiny and analysis, including new perspectives such as Mignolo's "border thinking". The development of Aboriginal political and educational initiatives has been entirely within the domain of the hegemonic white political nation state where Indigenous Australians have been defined as another special category within welfare initiatives, as *empty vessels* to be filled with western knowledges, rather than people with a real contribution to make to the intellectual life of the nation. We are captives within the hegemonic colonialism of western epistemology. In the current situation Indigenous intellectuals are still *battling* to have their voices heard. And the voices that are yet to be heard, the intellectual life yet to be showcased, has the potential to be truly different to anything that can currently be imagined in contemporary Australian scholarship.

Why are we viewed as empty vessels to be filled with western epistemology and pedagogy? The persistence of colonial attitudes about the inherent inferiority and lack of humanity of Indigenous people, most starkly evident in Australian popular culture, reiterated by Australian intellectuals such as Windschuttle (Grieves 2003:12) also informs education policy and program development, however much this is masked. Associated with this is a devaluing of Indigenous cultural philosophies such that Indigenous religious philosophy, known as the "Dreaming" is understood to be little more than children's stories. More recently the concept has been inappropriately appropriated in for titles of texts that essentially attack Aboriginal culture such as *Waking up to Dreamtime* (Johns 2001) and *Bad Dreaming* (Nowra 2007). While Aboriginal culture, famously represented by Indigenous art, has its value measured overwhelmingly in economic terms, the relationship of the artist to land depicted only of curiosity, even anachronistic, value (Rothwell 2007). In modern Australian settler society, Indigenous philosophy and culture is only valuable when it is entertaining and of economic value; the important areas of governance and social order, management of landscapes, marine environments and diverse ecological systems, rural-regional sustainability and appropriate technologies and importantly the education of Indigenous people, are overwhelmingly the preserve of the oppositional nation state.

The mirror image is the western romanticisation of Aboriginal religious philosophy through "alternate" or "new age", social movements over the last four decades that has simplified this philosophy to such an extent that it is in some instances almost unrecognisable. This phenomenon has a range of people who subscribe to alternative ways of life to the western, adopting what they imagine to be Aboriginal ways of being and doing and imagining Aboriginality. Perhaps the most outrageous of the new age appropriations of Aboriginal culture was published as a "true story", *Mutant Message from Downunder* (Morgan 1995), that led to an Aboriginal delegation the US to express their opposition to the work. Meanwhile, the less newsworthy but constant appropriation of Aboriginal culture into modern educational, political and social contexts has meant a diminution of the power of elders, custodians of Indigenous knowledges, over time and associated confusion about the nature of "traditional" culture that weakens Aboriginal autonomy and the strength of Indigenous knowledges.

Authentic Indigenous knowledge formation is hampered by the fact that even within the existing higher education system, governments tend to privilege the academic endeavours of "white" researchers. For example, the recent development of a Research Quality Framework (RQF) in Commonwealth education initiatives for universities threatens to undermine the value of the contribution of Indigenous researchers and Indigenous research. Its concentration on research outputs rather than research process is antithetical to Indigenous philosophy and pedagogy. The National Tertiary Education Union (NTEU), in its response to the issues paper on this proposal, has estimated the total number of Indigenous staff at universities to be about 260 and even fewer in senior academic or administrative positions. Indigenous staff need to undertake more than their fair share of administrative and governance duties (and arguably a greater level of student support), so the proposed individual assessment of staff members on research performance would be inequitable. And, importantly in relation to Indigenous research, the NTEU recognises that:

> Given that issues surrounding ownership, control and substantiation of Indigenous research are yet to be adequately addressed within current university practices and structures, the issue of how Indigenous research impact and quality will be measured, and by who, needs to be given serious consideration.
>
> It is not only the assessment mechanisms but also the framework in which this assessment is carried out that need to be culturally relevant and appropriate. If the RQF alienates Indigenous staff, there is a very real danger that it will also marginalize the research activities in which they are engaged. For example, for many Indig-

enous Australians it is not the cultural norm to engage in the type of self-promotion or 'big noting' that an RQF would encourage. Collaborative research practices may also mean that individual staff are not captured by a particular mechanism. Furthermore, while not all Indigenous staff are directly involved in 'Indigenous research', the involvement of Indigenous researchers in contributing to research on or about Indigenous people is an important ethical consideration. An RQF that discriminates against Indigenous researchers therefore, may have further implications regarding Indigenous research more broadly (NTEU 2005: 6).

Australian governments' control of Indigenous education initiatives has been hegemonic and, in comparison to other policy arenas, such as in natural resource management (Grieves 2006: 28-31), totally disregarding of Indigenous cultural heritage factors and wellbeing (ibid: 58). In fact it is essentially the main colonial assimilation project, which subscribes to saving the Aboriginal people (children) through white epistemology and the agency of white pedagogy. Australian education policy from schooling to higher education has in fact mitigated against the development of Indigenous knowledges by producing an impetus to assimilation amongst Indigenous students who are overwhelmingly taught by white teachers in white education contexts. Nakata has identified in the last three decades "the field of Indigenous education refers instead to cultural appropriateness, cultural content, cultural learning styles, culturally responsive pedagogy, Indigenous perspectives - issues but not knowledge" amounting to "(an Indigenous) cultural framework largely interpreted by Western people in the education system and filtered back to Indigenous students who learn or are allowed to express the acceptable little bits and pieces of their culture that are integrated into educational practice" (Nakata 2002:6).

If Indigenous higher education students choose to continue into research and publication they must develop critiques of the white epistemology and pedagogy that have produced them. This is a truism amongst Indigenous academics. Glenn Woods from the Gnibi College of Indigenous Australian Peoples, Southern Cross University NSW, has identified how existing government education policies:

(Have) managed to deflect almost entirely any consideration of the importance of Indigenous philosophy, ideology and values as a measure of group and individual identity. Rather the coloniser has reconstructed 'indigeneity' into a serious of racialised, homogenised and generally static icons that can be easily engaged and 'serviced'. This is subsequently 'taught' to both Indigenous and non-Indigenous children as evidence of the move towards equity in educational participation and outcomes. Any failure on behalf of Indigenous children to capitalise on this positive change is typically attributed to uncontrollable and external factors (lack of family support or social support services) rather than lack of meaningful and successful process within schools themselves.

Further, he asserts that, in relation to Australian Indigenous education policy:

> The refusal to engage or even credit Indigenous identity by (Indigenous philosophy) seems to confirm both the continuation of cultural genocide in Australia and a failure on behalf of Australia as a nation to develop ways of doing and being much beyond the crude systems of process inherited from it's earliest and deeply traumatised colonial beginnings (Woods 2005).

This adds up to a situation whereby Indigenous identity formation in Australia is currently chaotic and corrupted by colonialist constructions of Indigenous identity and authenticity. This has the potential for diabolical outcomes for Indigenous knowledge formation.

Indigenous Identity and Authenticity in Australia

> Who am I? Who are my people? Aboriginal lives have been smashed against Australia's whiteness for over 200 years. Yet we've reached out, trying to find a way to live together and share this land. My people's lives need to be treated with tenderness, but concern for the future means throwing off sentiment for clear-eyed analysis. In my search for my own truth, I'm inspired by the words of another great black writer, Toni Morrison: "My work requires me to think about how free I can be as an African-American woman writer in my genderised, sexualized, wholly racialised world" (Grant 2002).

What then is the construction of Indigenous identity that draws from an Indigenous philosophical basis and opposes the colonial constructions? What is important about the epistemology and pedagogy of the people so identified? The United Nations Working group on Indigenous populations definition is important in this:

> Indigenous communities, peoples and nations are those which, having a historical continuity with pre-invasion and pre-colonial societies ..., consider themselves distinct from other sectors of the societies now prevailing in those territories ... They form at present non-dominant sectors of society and are determined to *preserve, develop and transmit to future generations their ancestral territories, and their ethnic identity, as the basis of their continued existence as peoples, in accordance with their own cultural patterns, social institutions and legal systems* (my emphasis) (ECOSOC).

This internationally recognised definition referring as it does to historical continuity, the impetus to transmit to future generations knowledge of territories

298

and identities, identifies material and non-material cultural heritage as the major preoccupations of Indigenous peoples. This is in fact what it means to be Indigenous: thus the preservation, development and transmission of cultural heritage, including history, is the central project of Indigenous knowledges development and central to Indigenous wellbeing. Wellbeing is one of the intangible social values that have been associated with Aboriginal cultural heritage (English 2002).

The International Labour Organisation (ILO) Convention no. 169 of the UNHCR remains the only multilateral treaty to recognise the collective right of Indigenous peoples to preserve and develop their cultural identity. It states recognition of:

> The aspirations of these peoples to exercise control over their own institutions, ways of life and economic development and to maintain and develop their identities, languages and religions, within the framework of the States in which they live (Vrdoljak 2005:10).

The capacity to "maintain and develop.... identities, languages, religions" is in effect the power to transmit our own intangible cultural heritage, or way of life, to the succeeding generations, to ensure their wellbeing. It is also the right to transmit Indigenous identity.

Government definitions of Aboriginal identity were largely race-based until the Commonwealth developed self-determination policies in the 1970's. NSW Aboriginal elder Mr Les Ridgeway, chairperson of the Worimi Elders Group, and an activist for Aboriginal rights, was a recruit to the newly formed Department of Aboriginal Affairs in 1973 when the Commonwealth definition of an Aboriginal person was developed. The Commonwealth definition states that to be considered an Aboriginal a person must: (1) be of Aboriginal descent, (2) identify as Aboriginal and (3) be accepted as Aboriginal by the community in which they live. Ridgeway has recently expressed deep concern that the three principals that were laid down at that time have been disregarded or improperly administered in a range of contexts including within universities and Indigenous policy and program development areas of governments. He says that these principles relate to Aboriginal kinship and that this has been subsequently disregarded in the administration of the definition of Aboriginality (Ridgeway 2006). Indeed this concern has led him to attempt the development of a nationwide network of Aboriginal elders to develop approaches to this issue, amongst others. It is widely understood that this definition was specifically developed to circumvent existing race-based qualifications for Aboriginality, there being no such thing as an Aboriginal race (Anderson 2003:243) and so rely on the "more meaningful divisions of humankind... suggested by region, culture, religion and kinship" (Gardiner-Garden 2000).

A recent debate in the *Koori Mail* newspaper has seen Mrs Noeleen Briggs-Smith, Aboriginal family historian who heads the Indigenous Unit at the Northern Regional Library in Moree, NSW call for a change to the current definition. She is alarmed at the influx of people seeking a confirmation of Aboriginality status from a position of dubious Aboriginality. To deal with this she suggests that the requirements need to be changed to read:

- You must be of Aboriginal descent through immediate Aboriginal genealogy bloodline;
- Name your ancestors who have identified, lived and were known and accepted in their Aboriginal community;
- Name yourself and immediate family members who currently identify, live are known and accepted as being of Aboriginal descent; and
- You must currently live as an Aboriginal community-oriented person, and be known and accepted by the Aboriginal community where you live and work (Koori Mail 2006).

This suggestion comes from her experience that people who are not in fact Aboriginal "are taking Aboriginal designated employment, housing, pre-school placements, university bursaries and education opportunities" (Koori Mail 2006). Such people are in universities and in government departments.

While Aboriginal people who share the view that there needs to be a firm line drawn around Aboriginal identity could be accused of essentialism, it is important to note that they are not advocating intrinsically different and characteristic natures or dispositions for an amorphous mass of people called "Aboriginal". Rather they are couching these concerns from the continuing dynamic of cultural traditions that is outside of western understandings of Aboriginality. This includes the knowledge that there is not an amorphous mass of Aboriginal people: at the core of Aboriginal society, are people cognisant of the complexity of their differences from one another. These differences represent the expression of Aboriginal cultural values within Aboriginal society, in accordance with geographic location in relation to land, (whether theirs for whom they are custodians, or whether someone else's in which they are a visitor or a migrant) and within the orbit of kin affiliations, usually expressed as family names. Macdonald (1997) has identified these cultural continuities within Wiradjuri in southeast Australia, and also the regular and predictable conflicts that occur around these understandings of difference. She recognises that "access to resources since the early 1970s has been dependent upon conformity to an idealised notion of the cohesive and harmonious community – "one people' or 'one mob'"(Macdonald 197:65). The changed paradigms and fluidity in Aboriginal identity that this has created is now causing huge tensions and debates around identity within Aboriginal groups.

Another continuing cultural tradition that challenges any charges of essentialism is the primacy of kin relations, including relationship to land, over all other social, political and economic considerations. An important example is Fold's reporting of the persistence of cultural values amongst the Pintupi, who adhere to their own culturally based interpretations of the world around them including government policy and programs, through adherence to the primacy of walytja. This means total support of kin above all else, including demand sharing, nothing like western cultural values around family (Fold 2001). Macdonald has documented the continuation of demand sharing amongst the Wiradjuri in SE Australia where there has been a long held assumption that Aboriginal people are bereft of cultural traditions (Macdonald 1998: 2000). The research findings from a Redfern focus group on Indigenous wellbeing show that this representative group of urban Aboriginal people are driven by core values that are very different, even antithetical to the values of the modern western society in which they are located, even submerged or embedded, as a minority group. And their identity is at least in part shaped in opposition to what they see as the lesser western values of not being able to share, for example (Grieves 2006: 43-61). These intangible cultural values, not racism or essentialism, inform Aboriginal people about who is Aboriginal and who is not.

Indigenous Identity, Wellbeing and Education

While there are important Indigenous scholars from universities making a formidable and important contribution, it can be argued that this is a recent and long overdue development. And this development occurs out of institutions that are based on a largely uninterrogated assumption of the profundity of relationships between whiteness and knowledge, often creating recognisable stress for Indigenous scholars on many levels in such environments (Williams, Thorpe and Chapman 2003: 68-91). For example, there are significant tensions that can exist from the competing demands of community and family obligations, the educational needs of Indigenous students and negotiating the already existing imperatives of the university workplace for Indigenous staff.

A recent analysis of the take-up of the concept of Indigenous wellbeing in Australian government Indigenous policy has revealed that, while wellbeing occurs often in health and natural resource management policies, albeit poorly if ever defined, the concept is entirely missing from Commonwealth education policy development (Grieves 2006:20). This is important since the factors that contribute to Indigenous wellbeing are those intangible cultural heritage factors that identify what it means to be Indigenous.

As part of the project *Indigenous Wellbeing: a framework for Governments' Aboriginal Cultural Heritage Activities* an Aboriginal focus group based in Redfern, an area of a comparatively large Aboriginal population close to the CBD in Sydney, was asked to report the factors that contributed to their wellbeing. This group were based around the Eora College of Technical and Further Education (TAFE) that has post schooling programs in literacy and numeracy, the performing arts, Aboriginal studies. Members of this group were clearly Aboriginal, well versed in Aboriginal cultural ways and there were no newly identifying Aboriginal people (Grieves 2006:32-33). The factors that this group ranked in affecting their wellbeing were overwhelmingly intangible cultural heritage factors: spirituality; the ability to give to family and friends and the ability to share; knowing about my peoples' history and culture; knowing about and exercising my rights as an Indigenous person; knowing family history. Also registering as important to wellbeing was a better level of education. A summary of the respondent's views on what this means to them shows their need for Indigenous ways of being and doing, intangible cultural heritage factors, to have primacy within the education process and their recognition of a lack of this in their own experiences. It is as follows, with my emphasis:

> A better level of education increases wellbeing by allowing *fulfilment*, by being able to understand what is going on around you and being able to operate well within society, including getting employment. There is recognition of *different method-ologies in teaching in "white" and Aboriginal cultures and also an indication that people within the group feel inadequate to deal with and succeed in the former*. A better level of education is achieved through *the building on of life experiences and through a shared learning experience with teachers/elders* and others around you, working together with an open communication. A better level of education *includes those aspects of knowledge that are important in Aboriginal culture including values and morals and that this occurs outside of formal education contexts. There is a sense of the importance of lifelong learning* (Grieves 2006: 50).

This view of what constitutes a better education may hold some clues to the reported failures in Indigenous education initiatives. Considering the Commonwealth has been funding initiatives in Indigenous student support and teaching programs within schools and universities for three decades, the indicators for Aboriginal success in the current education system are low, reportedly falling, and the development of Indigenous knowledge programs has been inordinately slow. It is important to note that the higher education sector has been held as the success story in Indigenous education. While there is widespread reporting of the systemic failure of the education of Indigenous students: attendance, retention, literacy and numeracy rates are far below the national averages, there has been a marked increase in the participation of Indigenous students in higher education (Neill 2002:244). In 1972 there were less than 100 Indigenous students in higher education programs by 1992 there were 4,000 (Neill 2002: 16) and in 2006 some 7,539, representing 0.9% of the Australian higher education student body as a whole (DEST 2007) when the Aboriginal population of Australia is 2.1% of the total (ABS 2006). Most recently, from 1997 the Commonwealth government funded six Centres of Excellence in Indigenous Research within universities, designed to be the catalyst for broader and deeper developments in Indigenous research. With guaranteed funding for six years, they were expected to develop their own economic base from research grants and consultancy (Grieves 2002:3; CIRC; Umilliko). While some of these survive today, others have disappeared.

The situation in universities is made even more complex by contemporary developments in scholarship and in government Indigenous policy in which the establishment of Indigenous identity is problematic. For example, under current government guidelines for funding, universities do not have a uniform policy or Aboriginal community based system for identifying Indigenous people amongst prospective students and staff, including academic staff. Some universities ask for no proof at all, others ask for a certificate of Aboriginality that is prepared by a range of policies and processes (in New South Wales by Aboriginal Land Councils), some are satisfied with self-identification, sometimes by way of statutory declaration. The policy of accepting people who claim only Aboriginal *descent*, (excluding the other requirements of the Commonwealth definition), as university undergraduate and even as staff within Aboriginal programs, often without any proof such as genealogical evidence can lead to tension, frustration and conflict amongst the student and staff body. A Sydney-based Aboriginal university student from the Moree Aboriginal community, has remarked that she would like a dollar for every time a so-called "Aboriginal" student has said that they don't know their family history or any Aboriginal relations and thus their real connection to Aboriginal culture. And at the university she attends, scholarships for Indigenous students have had the criteria changed to exclude community based qualifications (Personal communication 2006).

Problematically, it is from university based Indigenous programs and government bureaucracies that do not of necessity have any accountability to Aboriginal elders, that the basis of Indigenous identity is now being forged, not from within Indigenous communities and clan-based structures. Indigenous experts in their own cultural heritage and histories, from outside of the academy, sometimes versed in their own languages and often speaking Aboriginal variations of the English language, perhaps not literate in English or academic English, remain as the objects of study, not the owners and strategic managers of that knowledge. The capacity of this situation to distort and confuse Indigenous identities needs to be recognised; where once identities were sourced from largely regional Aboriginal communities with a cultural continuum, Indigenous identity is increasingly emerging from urban-based universities out of white epistemologies. Where the constructions of Indigenous knowledges are based in white privileged institutions such as universities, government bureaucracies and the media, there exists the capacity for even Indigenous people to believe the "truths" constructed about them (Nakata 2001).

This introduces another layer of complexity in the development of Indigenous identity and knowledges. Some Indigenous academics with many years experience in university programs are noticing a phenomenon amongst "newly" identifying Aboriginal students and increasingly staff. An Academic and Cultural Advisor based at a university in Sydney, has observed that some students, who do not come from a strong Aboriginal cultural heritage and family base are interested to demonstrate their Aboriginality, and they rely for this on the stereotypes of Aboriginal people from the media and popular culture, tending to act these out. Such stereotypes include the idea that in Aboriginal society there are "no rules", including personal accountability, there is excessive alcohol and substance use, promiscuity, loudness and rudeness to others, especially "whites" and they can also promulgate "new age" unresearched and insubstantial ways of being and doing they imagine to be Indigenous (Personal communication 2006).

Debates about the inappropriate involvement of non-Indigenous academics in researching Aboriginal issues and the appropriation of Indigenous knowledges (Moreton-Robinson 2003) are clouded by the seemingly dubious credentials of some recently identifying Indigenous people. This is now compounded by the influx of people who have been brought up "white", that is without knowledge or reference to "Aboriginality", without suffering the social, political and economic injustices that are felt by Aboriginal people, and without the opportunity for the transmission of cultural heritage, ways of being and doing, tangible and intangible, from their families. On the basis of finding descent from an Aboriginal person generations ago such people can now claim Aboriginal status, sometimes providing evidence of Indigenous descent and without cognisance of the other two criteria for Aboriginality that lock in kinship. Increasingly there are more and more Australians who are standing up to be counted in terms of their Aboriginal ancestry and the problem is that they are accepted as Aboriginal in many education contexts without due regard for Aboriginal community processes of acceptance. And, Aboriginal status gives them the right to be an Aboriginal student, the right to be an Indigenous academic and eventually, the right to speak on behalf of what is assumed to be an amorphous mass of Indigenous Australians when in reality the diversity of Indigenous people is centred on vast regional and local differences. There have been instances where young graduates from backgrounds such as I have just described, have been touted as "the new leadership" in Aboriginal affairs.

It is notable in this too that these are people who are not necessarily affected by the Stolen Generations, though many people assume they are, and some allow these assumptions to continue. Some come from families that have kept their Aboriginal descent a secret, clinging to the assimilationist idea that the Aboriginal aspects of a person are "bred out" (Anderson 2003:219-220) over time and that this can only be a good thing. People able to pass as "white" often shed their black relations and do not suffer the same social opprobrium as Aboriginal people come to expect. While contemporary people of Aboriginal descent cannot be held accountable for the deeds of their forebears and are usually treated kindly by Aboriginal people, the unfortunate truth is that they have scant claim to intangible cultural heritage that, transmitted within families and from generation to generation, produces "Aboriginality".

While it is difficult to assess without research, it is estimable that the majority of the Stolen Generations, those people who were taken by government authorities to be raised away from their families, have found their way back. Theirs is a different story, often including the painful recognition that they have to work hard at developing a sense of being Aboriginal, to grow up again within the Aboriginal cultural milieu of their natural family (Read 1998). It is problematic then, that when people see Aboriginal descent as desirable (whether they in fact have it or not) and take on this identity, all of the accepted characteristics of Aboriginality accrue to them. They become *de facto* victims of colonialism, of broken families with Stolen Children, they acquire a history of dispossession, of survival against the odds, a special relationship with the natural world and land, and a notion of inherent wisdom of the ancient Aboriginal world. They are seen to be people who know what it is like to be Aboriginal.

The Aboriginal journalist and intellectual Stan Grant tackles the issue of identity for the urbanised, middle-class, university graduate, and professional. While his words are for other Aboriginal people they allude to the current complexity of identity:

I stand at a crucial moment in Aboriginal history. Our challenge is no longer solely from without, but equally from within. Aboriginal identity today is fractured, lacerated by class, gender and geography is ways that we have never before seen. Our identity as Aborigines is as problematic as personal choice, and the bonds of injustice and poverty no longer apply. It's a mockery to talk of black unity, as it is to reject white people. Whiteness abounds in ways that we can't even – or maybe don't want to – see. We deny the obvious to maintain our often dubious, identities.

Expressing our blackness exposes our hypocrisy. Australia has us trapped in its pervasive whiteness. We embrace our success, enjoy its trappings with a feigned contempt, while taking for granted the comfort of a full stomach and a warm bed. We haven't yet learned to identify ourselves beyond the prism of poverty. We have a perverse longing, a lingering attachment to the injustice and oppression that we imagine nourish our identity. Shamelessly we compete for victim status and turn pain and loss into virtues.

White Australia, our perceived enemy has become our greatest ally. It engages what sociologists call an 'imperialist nostalgia', the lament for the loss of a culture it helped destroy. Australia is recreating Aboriginal society as it imagines it should be; it's a blackness seen through white eyes and offers blacks something to believe in, or even cash in on. But it offers no freedom, simply subservience. We have moved beyond the fact of race and arrived at race as a concept. We are chained to the predictability of Aboriginal identity by a laziness that fails to grapple with our inconsistencies and fraudulence; we remain perplexed by our very existence.

The old definitions of Aboriginality no longer adequately serve the range of contending groups that lay claim to a black identity in Australia. No-one can be denied an identity; each person is entitled to express their self-image. Similarly the construction of that identity cannot go unexamined (Grant 2002: 4 - 6).

In the activist phase of the sixties the number of Aboriginal people involved were so small as to allow a general knowledge of who was Aboriginal and who was not. In retrospect, Aboriginal activists of this period who experienced first hand the racist constrictions of Australian society and who railed against the stigma of Aboriginal descent were laying the foundations for the contemporary period when claims to Aboriginality have become more than acceptable, a badge of honour, particularly within the urban elite. Since then the Aboriginal rights movement generally has been plagued by questions of authenticity of Indigenous voices.

Recent developments in Australian universities have left the issues surrounding Sally Morgan's identity far behind and her culturally based Aboriginal identity without question, as more and more "white" Australians choose to identify as "black". It is an incredible irony, but deserving of deep consideration, that it is conceivable that the white race privilege that has allowed them the benefit of western education, has also allowed the later claim to the privilege of being an Aboriginal academic.

Radical Indigenism

What is the solution to all of this? The discussion so far has raised more questions than it has answered and it is clear that the solutions, like the issues, are not going to be uncomplicated. Issues of Indigenous identity are similarly problematic in other settler colonial societies, where the Indigenous people are a minority and the rates of intermarriage are high. Eva Marie Garroutte in Real Indians importantly documents the problems of Native identity in the USA: *Identity and the survival of Native America* (2003). This book examines competing definitions for Native identity and every chapter of this book has its Aboriginal Australian equivalent. *The Chief who never was*, a story of deception, masquerade and constructions of "nativeness" to suit the white entertainment industry, has equivalents here that are well known by Aboriginal people.

306

What is perhaps the ultimate appropriation of Indigenous cultural heritage, the take-up of an Indigenous identity has its famous examples. Garroutte's chapters about the problems of definitions through legal processes, biology, descent and ideas about what it means to be a "cultured" native echo the issues and debates in Australia and the chapter on self – identification, *If you are Indian and you know it (but others don't)*, which outlines "self-identification" is instructive for the situation in Australian universities that I have described above. Native American associations that control scholarships, academic professional associations and advise on Native education nationally have all "registered official warnings about university students who dishonestly assert an Indian identity in the hopes of gaining access to minority education funding" and tribes are re-thinking the requirements they have for tribal citizenship (Garroutte 2003:6).

Garroutte has moved forward from postcolonial theory, building on the work of Mignolo for example, and found a way for native Americans to move from intense conflicts over identity and to "bring together the project of Indian people to live together in communities in a good way *with* the project of the academy to cultivate knowledge". Her approach requires the development of a new intellectual perspective, dramatically different, with new ideas about the very nature of scholarship that she calls "radical Indigenism". This has no connection to Marxist theory, not is it meant to be confronting, but:

> Radical Indigenism illuminates differences in assumptions about knowledge that are at the root of the dominant culture's misunderstanding and subordination of indigenous knowledge. It argues for the reassertion and rebuilding of indigenous knowledge from its roots, its fundamental principles (Garroutte 2003:102).

Further she argues:

> Radical Indigenism suggests resistance to the pressure put on Indigenous scholars to participate in academic discourses that strip Native intellectual traditions of their spiritual and sacred elements. It takes this stand on grounds that sacred elements are absolutely central to the coherence of our knowledge traditions and that if we surrender them, there is little left of our philosophies that make any sense (Garroutte 2003:104).

What are the implications of radical Indigenism for identity questions? Radical Indigenism holds the promise of dealing with the debates and conflicts over Indigenous identity by developing a whole new approach to what it means to be an Indigenous intellectual. Garroutte's approach requires that Indigenous academics be prepared to not only study Indigenous philosophies but also enter into Indigenous relations, respecting and practising the "*methods* and the *goals of enquiry* toward which Indigenous philosophical assumptions direct us".

Trusting, practising and living within kinship obligations, protocols and ceremonial life, viewing the world through the lens of Indigenous ways of knowing, rather than reading about and thinking about them, from the position of observer. Garroutte argues that the scholar must be prepared to accept a lower level of authority than they may be accustomed to. "Radical Indigenism is not a disguised mechanism by which scholars can impose their own conclusions upon tribal communities or become their own, self-appointed mouthpieces" and the Indigenous scholar needs to be bound by community decisions about what is discussed publicly (Garroutte 2003:108-9). This means a recasting of the Indigenous intellectual into one not informed by western epistemology and pedagogy but consciously learning about and adopting Indigenous ways of being and doing as they apply to intellectual enquiry – what is researched, how the research is to be carried out, what will be reported on and to whom, accepting the true custodians of Indigenous knowledge.

Current developments around Indigenous identity in Australia, having shifted from a centre in Indigenous communities into universities and government departments over time can be characterised as anarchic. The real issues for Indigenous Australians threaten to be obscured by important but tangential debates such as the "battlefields" of Aboriginal history. The fact of the enduring "battlefields" teach us that the Australian settler colonial society is far from accepting Indigenous evidence and versions of our history. The "battlefields" exist as part of a debate over whether or not governments will give us rights, both human rights and Indigenous rights through public policy development including education initiatives. More importantly there is scant acceptance of the viability of our philosophy and traditions for informing and enriching Australian society and charting new, post-colonial ways of living together in this country. However, the real gains are to be made when Indigenous identity and knowledge development are once again centred within Indigenous communities rather than centres of white knowledge production, including options for partnerships and other innovative ways of working together. The implications of radical Indigenism for Australian Indigenous identity, authenticity and scholarship deserve close examination and consideration by Indigenous Australian scholars and intellectuals.

References

ABS (2006) Australian Bureau of Statistics 2034.0 - *Census of Population and Housing: Aboriginal and Torres Strait Islander People*, Australia, 1996. Accessed on 20 January at: http://www.abs.gov.au/ausstats/abs@.nsf/productsbytitle/C159FA62A2E98D2FCA2568A9001393E4?OpenDocument

Adams, P (2003) "The History Wars": part 1 and 2, ABC Radio National, 3 and 4 September. Accessed on 20 January 2007 at: http://www.abc.net.au/rn/talks/lnl/s937459.htm

Anderson, W (2002) *The Cultivation of Whiteness. Science, Health and Racial Destiny in Australia. Melbourne*, Melbourne University Press.

Atkinson J, J Graham, G Pettit and L Lewis (2002) "Broadening the focus of research into the health of Indigenous Australians", *Medical Journal of Australia* 177 (6), pp 286-287.

Awaye: ABC Radio National. Accessed on 20 January 2007 at: http://abc.net.au/rn/awaye/stories/2001/331201.htm#

Birch, T (2004) "Who gives a fuck about white society anymore?: a response to the Redfern riot", Overland 175, Winter, Brookvale NSW: Tower Books.

Birch, T (2007) "Testimony", *Aboriginal History Journal* Vol 30, Canberra ACT: Australian National University.

Bourke, C and E Bourke (2002) "Indigenous Studies: New Pathways to Development" in S. Marginson (ed.) Investing in Social Capital, *Journal of Australian Studies*, Issue 74, Perth WA: Australia Research Institute at Curtin University of Technology.

Briggs-Smith, N (2006) *Koori Mail*. 27 September, 2006

CIRC (Curtin Indigenous Research Centre), accessed on 20 January 2007 at: http://gunada.curtin.edu.au/research/index.cfm

Delgado, E L and R J Romero (2000) "Local Histories and Global Designs: an interview with Walter Mignolo", *Discourse: Journal for Theoretical Studies in Media and Culture* 22.5, Fall, Detroit, Michigan USA: Wayne State University Press.

Department of Education, Science and Training (DEST) (2007) *Students 2006: selected higher education statistics.* Accessed on1 April 2007 at: www.dest.gov.au/sectors/higher_education/publications_resources/profiles/students_2006_first_half_year_selected_higher _education.htm

ECOSOC: United Nations Economic and Social Council Sub-Commission on the Prevention of Discrimination and Protection of Minorities, Working Group on Indigenous Populations. UN document: E/CN.4/Sub.2/1983/21/Add.8, para. 369/

English, A (2002) *The Sea and the Rock Gives Us a Feed: Mapping and Managing Gumbaingirr Wild Resource Use Places.* Sydney: NSW National Parks and Wildlife Service Accessed on 20 January at: http://www.nationalparks.nsw.gov.au/npws.nsf/Content/sea_and_rock

Folds R (2001) *Crossed Purposes: the Pintupi and Australia's Indigenous policy.* Sydney: University of NSW Press.

Gardiner-Garden, J (2000) "The Definition of Aboriginality", Research Note 18, 2000-01,Parliamentary library. Accessed on 20 January 2007 at http://www.aph.gov.au/LIBRARY/pubs/rn/2000-01/01RN18.htm

Garroutte, E M (2003) *Real Indians: Identity and the Survival of Native America.* Berkeley: University of California Press.

Grant, S (2002) The tears of strangers: a memoir. Australia: Harper Collins.

Grieves, V (ed.) (2002) *Wollotuka staff responses to Minister Brendan Nelson's report Achieving Equitable and Appropriate Outcomes: Indigenous Australians in Higher Education of August 2002.* September 2002. Accessed on 20 January 2007 at: http://www.backingaustraliasfuture.gov.au/submissions/issues_sub/issues3.htm

Grieves, V (2003) "Windschuttle's fabrication of history: a view from the 'other' side", *Labour History Journal*, November accessed on 20 January 2007 at: http://www.historycooperative.org/journals/lab/85/grieves.html

Grieves, V (2006) *Indigenous Wellbeing: a framework for Governments' Cultural Heritage activities.* A report prepared for the NSW Department of Environment and Conservation, Policy and Knowledge Branch, Cultural Heritage Division. Accessed on 20 January at: http://www.nationalparks.nsw.gov.au/npws.nsf/Content/Indigenous+wellbeing+framework

Haebich, A (2005) "The battlefields of Aboriginal history", in M Lyons, and P Russell, P (eds) *Australia's History: themes and debates.* Sydney: University of NSW Press.

Hall, R (1998) *Black armband days: truth from the dark side of Australia's Past*. Sydney: Random House.

Hiatt, L (1996) *Arguments about Aborigines*. Cambridge: Cambridge University Press.

Johns, G (ed) (2001)*Waking up to Dreamtime: the illusion of Aboriginal self-determination*. Singapore: Media Masters.

Langton, M (2002) " A New Deal? Indigenous development and the politics of recovery" Dr Charles Perkins AO Memorial Oration, University of Sydney. Accessed on 20 January at: www.koori.usyd.edu.au/news/langton.pdf

Langton, M (2006) "Why isn't multiculturalism a core value in Australian life?" *Forum on Multiculturalism*. SBS Radio transcript accessed on 20 January at: http://www.radio.sbs.com.au/index.php?page=wv&newsID=131890

Macdonald, G (1997) " 'Recognition and justice': the traditional/historical contradiction in New South Wales ", in D E Smith and J Finlayson *Fighting Over Country: Anthropological Perspectives*. Canberra ACT: CAEPR Research Monograph no 123, Australian National University.

Macdonald, G (1998) "Continuities in Wiradjuri traditions", in W E Edwards (ed.), *Traditional Aboriginal Societies*. Melbourne Vic: Macmillan.

Macdonald, G (2000) "Economies and Personhood: demand sharing among the Wiradjuri", in G Wenzel, G. Hovelsgurd-Brute and N Kishigami, *The social economy of sharing: resource allocation and modern hunter-gatherers*. Japan: National Museum of Ethnology.

Manne, R (ed) (2003) *Whitewash: on Keith Windschuttle's fabrication of Aboriginal history*, Melbourne: Black Inc. Agenda.

Message Stick: Aboriginal and Torres Strait Islander Online (2006), Australian Broadcasting Commission (ABC), "Beazley backs possible Nyoongar ruling challenge", Accessed on 20 January at: http://abc.net.au/message/news/stories/ms_news_1745527.htm

Mignolo, W (2000) *Local Histories/Global Designs: Coloniality, Subaltern Knowledges, and Border Thinking*, New Jersey: Princeton University Press.

Moreton-Robinson, A (2003) "Tiddas talkin' up to the white woman: when Huggins et al took on Bell", in Anderson I, Grossman M, Langton M, Moreton-Robinson A (eds) *Blacklines: contemporary critical writing by Indigenous Australians*, Melbourne: Melbourne University Press.

Morgan, M (1995) Mutant Message Downunder. NY: Harper Collins.

Muecke, S (n.d.) "Challenges to perform: history, passion and the imagination" text of a National Library of Australia event. Accessed on 20 January 2007 at: http://www.nla.gov.au/events/history/papers/Stephen_Muecke.html

Muecke, S and P Roe (eds) (1984) *Reading the Country*, Fremantle Arts Centre Press.

Muecke, S (1999) "Visiting Aboriginal Australia", *Postcolonial Studies* Vol 2, Issue 1, Melbourne Vic.: Institute of Postcolonial Studies.

Murray, T and Collins, A Dhakiyarr vs the King, Film Australia, Sydney NSW. Accessed on 20 January 2007 at: http://www.filmaust.com.au/showcase/8478/default.asp?content=prodstory_dhakiyarr

Nakata, M (2001) "Another window on 'reality'" in B Osborne B (ed) *Ethnicity, Social Justice and Education: A research basis for action*, Melbourne, Vic: Common Ground Press.

Nakata, M (2002) "Indigenous Knowledge and the Cultural Interface: underlying issues at the intersection of knowledge and information systems" *IFLA Journal* Vol. 28, No. 5/6, Netherlands: International Federation of Library Associations.

National Tertiary Education Union (NTEU) (2005) *Research Quality Framework: Response to the Issues Paper*, March.

Neill, R (2002) *White Out: how politics is killing black Australia*. Crows Nest NSW: Allen and Unwin.

Nicholson (2003) (Cartoon) of *The Australian*, Accessed on 20 January 2007 at: http://www.nicholsoncartoons.com.au/cartoon_1620.html

Nowra, L (2007) *Bad Dreaming: Aboriginal men's violence against women and children*. Melbourne Vic: Pluto Press.

Patrick, P (2003) "Statement of Peggy Patrick", in R. Manne, R (ed) *Whitewash: on Keith Windschuttle's fabrication of Aboriginal history*, Melbourne, Vic: Black Inc. Agenda.

Read, P (1998) "The return of the stolen generations" *Journal of Australian Studies* Perth WA: Australia Research Institute at Curtin University of Technology.

Reynolds, H (2006) *The Other Side of the Frontier.* Sydney: UNSW Press (First published 1981 by James Cook University of North Queensland).

Ridgeway, L A (2006) Personal correspondence, 27 September 2006.

Rowley, C (1970) *The Destruction of Aboriginal Society*. Canberra ACT: Australian National University Press.

Umilliko Indigenous Higher Education Research Centre. Accessed on 20 January 2007 at: http://www.newcastle.edu.au/research/centre/umilliko.html

Vrdoljak, A F (2005) "Minorities, Cultural Rights and the Protection of Intangible Cultural Heritage", paper delivered at the ESIL Research Forum on International Law: Contemporary Issues, Geneva 2005. Accessed on 20 January 2007 at: http://www.esil-sedi.org/english/past.html

Williams, C, B Thorpe and C Chapman (2003) *Aboriginal Workers: history, emotional and community labour and occupational health and safety in South Australia*. Henley Beach, South Australia: Seaview press.

Windschuttle, K (2001) "Doctored evidence and invented incidents in Aboriginal historiography" paper given at the conference on Frontier Conflict, national Museum of Australia, Canberra, ACT, December 13-14. Accessed on 20 January 2007 at: http://www.sydneyline.com/National%20Museum%20Frontier%20Conflict.htm

Windschuttle, K (2002) *The Fabrication of Aboriginal History*. Volume One: *Van Dieman's Land 1803–1847*, Paddington, NSW: Macleay Press.

Woods, G (2005) "Killing me softly" unpublished paper presented at the World Indigenous Peoples Conference on Education (WIPC:E) 2005 Aoteroa New Zealand. Accessed on 20 January 2007 at: http://www.wipce2005.com/#

CHAPTER 16

Higher Education and the Mayan Movement in Guatemala

DEMETRIO COJTÍ CUXIL

Introduction

Guatemala is a "sovereign" Republic which gained independence from Spain in 1821. It is made up of four ethnic groups: the Criollo-Ladino people born of European or mixed European and Indigenous parents, the Mayan people, the Xinca people, and the Garífuna people of Afro-Caribbean descent. Collectively, the indigenous peoples represent 60% of Guatemala's 12 million inhabitants. The Mayan people are the largest indigenous group with twenty-two different linguistic communities or "ethnic groups."

The historic and current ethnic structure in Guatemala is based on an internal colonialism where legitimate authority is granted to the Criollo and Ladino people who rule over the three indigenous peoples. The indigenous peoples do not have the basic right to represent nor to govern themselves, which should correspond to their status as distinct peoples. They are objects of public policies that promote assimilation and integration towards "the national culture." Regardless of the political system of the moment- authoritarianism, feudalism or democracy- the colonial Criollo and Ladino state seeks to build a mono-lingual, mono-ethnic, and mono-cultural nation.

Estimates prepared by Torres Rivas (2005) on social stratification reveal that the majority of the indigenous people in Guatemala live in conditions of poverty or extreme poverty:

- 70.9% of the total number who live in extreme poverty are indigenous
- 48.5% of the total number of poor are indigenous
- 20.5% of the lower-middle class are indigenous.
- 6.8% of the middle class are indigenous
- 2.7% of the upper class are indigenous

This chapter will examine the relationship between higher education and the Mayan Movement. It will begin by addressing some of the weaknesses and barriers in the current higher educational system for the country's indigenous peoples based mostly on data collected from research conducted by this author (Cuxil 1995; 1997; 2004), (IESALC – UNESCO 1996; 2003; 2004); (UNDP 2005).

Public Policy, Higher Education, and Indigenous Peoples

The leading authority for higher education in Guatemala is San Carlos University – USAC, the state university, which has been granted the responsibility to represent the four peoples of the country. Regarding universities, the Guatemalan Constitution in article 82, establishes that San Carlos University (USAC) is an autonomous institution and has the status of being *"the one and only state university."* Its function is to direct, organise, and develop higher and professional education in the interest of national development and to help solve national problems. The direct effect of this constitutional disposition on indigenous peoples is that it grants a monopoly for higher public education to USAC, making the creation of a Mayan University as established by the Peace Accords impossible.

The Constitution also establishes in article 87 that only the degrees, titles, and diplomas conferred by universities duly authorised to function in the country will be recognised; it also states that San Carlos University is the only university entitled to accredit professionals who graduated from foreign institutions. Diplomas granted or endorsed by foreign universities or institutions as a form of support granted to people from the indigenous population may or may not be acknowledged, in which case indigenous graduates of foreign universities may not be entitled to work within their profession at institutions where it is necessary to have such accreditation.

According to article 86 the function of the Private Education Board is to authorise the creation of new universities. The board is composed of a representative from San Carlos University, two representatives from private universities, and a representative elected by the presidents of the associations of professionals. The indigenous peoples have neither representation nor participation on the board, so the universities tend to assume an assimilating orientation and lack opposition thereof.

In order to study towards a university degree, indigenous students are required to use the mechanisms provided for all citizens: either the state university or the private universities. The Constitution in article 66 certainly recognises the existence of the indigenous peoples and communities in the country as well as the responsibility of the State to acknowledge and promote their cultures; however, defining the mechanisms to fulfil those responsibilities are still pending. Legislation that favours indigenous people is generally not implemented; therefore, the universities do not make any distinction between the ladino and the indigenous citizens by recognising the cultural differences or the social disparities among the respective groups. What is implied in the policy is that indigenous students are treated as if they were ladino students and the private universities tend to assume that they come from the middle or upper classes.

Despite their autonomy and their ambitions towards becoming centres for critical thinking, the universities reflect and reproduce a ladino-centred approach to education and they have not been able to move beyond the mono-cultural and mono-lingual national project. They also reflect and reproduce liberal ideology which recognises the existence of individuals but not the existence of distinct peoples. The 'ladinising' universities in the provinces and indigenous areas demonstrate a failure on the part of the State to adapt to the cultural diversity in the different regions of Guatemala accordingly.

Higher education in Guatemala lacks affirmative action or equity programmes designed for the benefit of the indigenous peoples.[1] The state university has a scholarship programme but there is no specific quota assigned in favour of indigenous students or university professionals to compensate for their numerical and social disadvantage.

Indigenous students enrolled in higher education tend to become invisible as a result of the mono-ethnic and ladino-centrist vision and practice. The universities do not keep specific statistics on the enrolment of indigenous students, apparently in order to prevent them from feeling as though they are being "discriminated against." It is not possible to establish the total number of indigenous students registered in each school or degree programme or the total number registered in all of the universities. The few studies conducted in that respect have been based on the students' surnames which are of limited value due to mixing of ethnic groups, not all the indigenous students have Mayan surnames.

Another consequence of this practice is that in most universities, schools, and programmes, studies relevant to indigenous peoples and to indigenous issues are omitted. For example, in architecture school, Mayan architecture is not taught; in medical school Mayan medicine is not taught. In general subject matter areas, the ethnic diversity of the country is scarcely covered. In some courses, programmes, and schools, when the topic of indigenous peoples is addressed, the Mayan civilisation of the classical period is exalted but the contemporary indigenous culture is undervalued or ignored. The tendency to ignore or contest the reality that Guatemala is a multicultural country remains; graduates leave the university without fully understanding the cultural diversity of the country and they often practise certain grades of discrimination against indigenous peoples by promoting assimilation and integration.

However, an extraordinary development has occurred as a result of the Peace Accords: an increase in temporary and permanent programmes for higher studies related to indigenous topics including certificate programmes, technical programmes, bachelors and even masters' degrees. Before the Peace Accords, few universities had degree programmes associated with indigenous culture such as

---

1   Affirmative action and/or equity programmes for indigenous people recognise their history of exclusion from the social, economic, and political systems and create policies that seek to eliminate these historical barriers so that indigenous ethnic groups can have access to higher education.

Mayan linguistics. After the signing of the Peace Accords, more universities and schools have created programmes in different fields relevant to Mayan culture. Even at the state university there are some certificate programmes of relevance to the indigenous population, for example a programme in Indigenous Law.

Even though these changes are positive, they might be viewed as "insertions" into the universities curricula because they are temporary or dependent on external pressure; they do not reflect a general policy that the universities follow. These programmes have not necessarily illuminated the university milieu nor have they generated multiculturalisation in their respective schools and universities. Some of these programmes exist just because there is a demand for indigenous professionals in state institutions and cooperating agencies that require a particular type of education.

Favourable Changes

Even though it has not been possible to create an indigenous oriented university and that indigenous students cannot be supported by policies such as affirmative action it does not mean that they cannot be provided such an education. There is a de facto incipient favourable policy. Various schemes for supporting higher education for indigenous peoples have been generated within the existing legal framework by making use of the autonomy and margins of operation that can often characterise national and foreign universities, non-governmental organisations (NGOs), cooperating agencies, and bilateral and multilateral organisations. Through the implementation of certain types of affirmative action in favour of indigenous students, they have introduced or stimulated programmes of total or partial scholarships and have generated programmes with indigenous approaches.

Some of these programmes have conciliated with the legislation that does not recognise the diplomas conferred by foreign universities by means of certifying such studies at other Central American universities. Other programmes have ignored this prohibition by allowing students to take the risk of not being hired by some legalistic employers. Only certain types of employers require diplomas certified and recognised in the country; the majority of employers give preference to diplomas obtained abroad because they are of the impression that they offer greater quality and credibility than diplomas from national universities.

The following table (Table 1) demonstrates the types of support that indigenous students can access or receive. Interested or financing entities fund students directly, channel support or certify programmes from abroad.

Table 1. Types of support for indigenous students.

Interested or financing entity	Performing entity	Type of support or programmes supported	Beneficiaries
Public entities: Ministry of education, Ministry of Culture.	National none-state universities.	Certificate programmes for technicians and educators on indigenous topics.	Mainly indigenous people.
Non-Indigenous foreign universities: Mexico, Paris, Tromsø, etc.	Departments in foreign universities, indigenous and non-indigenous NGOs.	Masters' in: sustainable development, anthropology, indigenous studies or scholarships for higher education.	Mainly indigenous people.
Indigenous Foreign Universities: Saskatchewan, Uraccan, etc.	Indigenous and non-indigenous NGOs: PRODESSA, ESEDIR, TULAN. Chi-Pixa'b.	Secondary teaching degrees and bachelors degrees. Certification in: project management, community development from the Mayan culture, and on Mayan education.	Mainly indigenous people
Bilateral collaborators: USIS, AID, EU, NORAD, etc.	Grant service or support directly or channel through national academic units (URL) or indigenous NGOs (OKMA).	Scholarships for indigenous people to study in the USA, scholarships for indigenous people for specific careers within the country for bachelor or master degrees.	Mainly indigenous people
Multilateral organisations: UNESCO, UNDP	Indigenous NGOs, national universities (UVG).	Certificates in Multicultural Affairs, Technicians for Bilingual Education, Etc.	Indigenous and non-indigenous people.
Foreign private foundations: Ford, Fulbright .	Indigenous and non-indigenous NGOs.	Scholarships to complete studies on the bachelors level and obtain masters' or doctorates abroad.	Indigenous and non-indigenous people.
Foreign academics, Spain, France, Germany.	Direct service or support through national academic units.	Bachelors, masters and doctorate degrees in foreign universities.	Mainly indigenous people

The last sections of incipient support in the table could be considered marginal or embryonic because few Mayan students are enrolled. Most students are required to cover their own expenses either through employment or from financial support from their families. Also, there is a general lack of knowledge about the availability of scholarships to study abroad and Mayan students are hindered by their lack of fluency in English which most scholarships to study abroad require.

There seems to be exclusionary mechanisms built in to these incipient affirmative action programmes so they almost never exclusively favour indigenous students. There are three arguments used to evade programmes that address the unequal participation of indigenous students at the university level. The first argument is that Ladinos should not be excluded from such support in order to avoid the risk of falling into a so-called pattern of "reverse discrimination." It is also argued that the entire Guatemalan population has been excluded or denied higher education, thus, privileging indigenous students is not justified. The last argument is that the total indigenous population already enjoys equal conditions with the ladino population so indigenous specific programmes are unjustified. Due to non-indigenous pressure, programmes that were initially affirmative action in favour of indigenous students can end up favouring the non-indigenous students more. The revealing fact remains that out of 6 million indigenous people in Guatemala there are only six indigenous people with doctorate degrees, all of whom obtained their degrees abroad and with the support of foreign academics or universities.

Limited Access: Quantitative or Qualitative Aspects

The limited *quantitative* accessibility of the aforementioned incipient programmes for the provision of higher education to indigenous peoples can be characterized as belonging to one of two categories: financial support for accessing certain degree programmes and programmes related to indigenous subjects.

Most of the programmes belong to the first category in the form of scholarships designed to facilitate access to a specific number of pre-existing degrees available for everyone. The objective is to have the same access to degrees as any non-indigenous person with financial means. These particular programmes may not necessarily have been decolonised or have a multicultural approach, nor have they necessarily been accepted by indigenous cultures. As a result, some indigenous students yield to "the pressure" against them– the university environment, curriculum contents, discriminating expressions and attitudes– and end up abandoning not only their studies but their ethnic identity as well. In such cases, scholarships can be important for indigenous students to support them in their last semesters so they are able to complete their thesis and to help provide them with food and lodging. If indigenous students receive such support there will be more indigenous professionals in different fields, particularly in the social sciences.

Fewer of the programmes belong to the second category of support for degree programmes designed within indigenous topics to be applied within indigenous communities. These types of programmes seek to satisfy the needs of the professionals who work in specific areas of indigenous peoples lives: education, linguistics, law, translation and literacy. These programmes require a syllabus previously designed with a particular career in mind and the training of a new teaching staff. Regarding these programmes, the national universities are weak due to inadequately trained professors and unawareness of the necessary profile of the graduate as required by the market or occupation—namely because of unawareness of indigenous reality.

The main weakness of these two categories of support for higher education of indigenous students is their limited accessibility. Each of the programmes in the table above, with the exception of EDUMAYA, has been able to grant a limited number of scholarships and on average they graduate less than thirty indigenous students in each graduating class. Despite the forms of support available, there is still a considerable lack of indigenous professionals in all fields on all levels.

An investigation conducted in 1985 (UNICEF 1996) found that out of 57,432 total students registered in higher education including the private universities:

- 93.81 % (53, 881) were Ladino
- 6.19% (3,551) were indigenous (Maya, Garífuna or Xinca).

Another investigation (UNICEF 1996) about Mayan education and university admissions in Guatemala demonstrated that:

- Out of 100 Ladinos of university age a total of 8 where granted admission.
- Out of 1000 Mayas of university age only 1 was granted admission.

In a similar study conducted by UNESCO - IESALC (2004), it was estimated that out of 2,000 students who finished secondary school, only 40 students went on to study at a university, representing only 2% of the secondary school graduates, and of them very few were indigenous.

Regarding specific Mayan ethnic groups, the Kaqchikel and K´iche´ have the highest reported number of university graduates, due in part to their physical proximity to the Capital. When it comes to indigenous women, the study revealed a gender gap that begins in elementary school and widens at each consecutive educational level, inferring that most of the indigenous university graduates are men. The humanities, education and psychology, are the schools or departments that have the most Mayan professionals because of accessibility and future career or employment possibilities. One consequence of the quantitative lack of indigenous professionals is that most qualified professionals are hired by international NGOs and organisations, the private sector and some higher paying public entities. The majority of public institutions pay low or average salaries making it difficult to retain skilled indigenous professionals.

There are three categories of *qualitative* limitations evident in the aforementioned incipient programmes for the provision of higher education to indigenous peoples: educational quality, lack of compensatory indigenous studies, and hostile environments.

An informal evaluation of the competence of indigenous professionals reveals some relevant deficiencies in the quality of education that indigenous professionals receive, which are evident in their job performance. Some limitations are products of their own personality *or character*, while others are products of their social environment or from the education they receive. In addition, in most of the indigenous communities, there is a division between 'those who work and those who study'. When schools where introduced into indigenous communities there emerged a belief and practice that when one receives an education he is relieved of manual labour. This practice led to a perception that it would be unthinkable for those who have a higher education to engage in manual labour.

Deficiencies are evident in each university, school and program as they do not have universal requirements for excellence. There is no official governmental or educational body that controls or certifies the quality of higher education. Consequently, they transfer to their graduates the deficiencies of their syllabi, professors, approaches, and overall quality standards. They also transfer to their graduates their particular approaches to indigenous subjects in their programmes.

Different factors contribute to low standards and questionable approaches in higher education. One factor is the current system for hiring professors and designing their contracts. In some departments, the hours they are contracted to work do not allow them to study and update their knowledge or to make an analysis, criticism, or evaluation of and in the subjects they teach. Some of them have never published anything or have repeated the outdated content of their syllabi year after year. For others, the subject they teach is simply a means to meet their expenses. There is also a tendency to make few external demands of students; students imply to the professors that they have to work and have other time limitations so few homework assignments are given. Foreign professors who have taught in national universities have noted this tendency.

A second category of limitations is the lack of relevant topics or subjects in the programmes curricula. Due to their ethnic identity, such topics are necessary for students and indigenous graduates to meet the expectations of future employers. In the workplace, especially in public institutions, there is an expectation that indigenous professionals know how to solve issues related to Mayan mathematics and the use of the Mayan calendar. They are expected to understand or practice Mayan spirituality, speak and write a Mayan language, master indigenous approaches to public policy, and be able to demonstrate methods of resistance to discrimination and racism against indigenous people.

In institutions where there is a desire to recognise and concretise multiculturalism in the country, non indigenous people assign the burden of knowledge and remedial proposals to indigenous people and not to ladino people. They believe that if indigenous people are "interested" in changing the country to reflect its multiculturalism, they should be informed on the topic and present solutions to achieve such change. If they do not assume responsibility then the situation will remain the same because Ladinos do not feel any responsibility to affect such change. Sometimes indigenous professionals know little about their culture. They may have learned some from their parents or had experiences in their communities, and perhaps they have knowledge about the classical Mayan culture, but this is often viewed as if it has nothing to do with present-day Mayas. Amazingly, there are paradoxical cases, extensions of colonialism, where Mayan professionals have had to consult Ladino professionals about Mayan topics.

The indigenous professional might have developed survival mechanisms or has found individual solutions to his or her own experiences of racism. He may identify as indigenous but publicly he downplays or denies it; she may experience feelings of guilt for personally refraining from expressing her anger and rage after suffering discrimination. But he may not have worked on collective or national solutions for multiculturalisation. If indigenous professionals do not have this type of additional knowledge and skills they lack the "added value" that employers seek in a competitive employment market. What would make an employer hire an indigenous professional if they could hire a ladino professional with the same formal competence but with higher recommendations and more influence?

A third qualitative limitation in the insipient forms of support for education received by indigenous professionals is the lack of preparedness to interact in hostile social and academic milieus. It is known that in the country of Guatemala, there exists generally racist and discriminatory hostility towards indigenous people.

Consequently, it could be argued that some of the social sciences are in need of measures to decolonise their colonialist approaches. Indigenous professionals– as a result of interacting in milieus characterised by the social evil of racism and discrimination– tend to develop more critical and creative thinking and have developed intellectual perseverance and courage. The interpersonal and group relationships in terms of teaching and learning have been influenced by discrimination against indigenous students; students must learn to detect discrimination, denounce and invalidate it. The indigenous graduates still need to establish parameters and a methodology to "learn how to unlearn"; part of this objective is to learn how to decolonise the social sciences. Even though not all social sciences are necessarily colonialist, as part of a meaningful decolonisation process, all content and form within the educational milieu should be subjected to criticism and revision.

Psychological factors play an important role in learning to interact and survive in hostile environments. In his book *L'Homme Dominé*, Albert Memmi (1962) demonstrated that the objective colonial condition results in psychological and cultural destruction of the colonised, especially in urban, cultivated or academic environments. Due to the pervasive discrimination and racism in Guatemalan schools and other social institutions, indigenous students often finish their education with a depleted and damaged sense of self; colonised and subordinated peoples oftentimes internalise racism and lack of objectivity. In the case of Guatemala, the ideal is to prepare indigenous professionals who can interact with non-indigenous professionals on an equal level. The indigenous professional needs supplementary training in order to look forward to inner growth and self development and to gain psychological and intellectual independence. The ability to engage in social and intellectual criticism is a precondition for a collective decolonisation.

In the process of decolonisation and building a multicultural society that reflects the multi-ethnic composition of Guatemala, the current indigenous professional may not be very useful due to the limitations discussed. In order to transform the State and civil society and to eliminate the existing racism against the indigenous people, a competent professional is essential. Current indigenous professionals may be competent in other occupations, such as productive tasks to which all the population is compelled to subsist. They might stand out in the domain of universal knowledge, but they might not have the knowledge necessary to affect changes to the nation's ethnic policies, such as those recognised in the Constitution, the Peace Accords and international agreements on indigenous rights. Supplementary knowledge is crucial since until recently, the ladino factions in the government considered the burden of making proposals to reform current ethnic policies that of the indigenous peoples themselves.

Guatemala lacks indigenous professionals, both in terms of quantity and quality. Some who have graduated from institutions of higher learning have limitations competing in the market and satisfying the demands of employers or institutions since they have not been granted the supplementary or compensatory preparation needed for such demands. These limitations are due to living in a situation of subordination and working in discriminatory and adverse social environments. Regarding higher education and multiculturalisation in the country, the struggle against the archaic and homogenising vision has just begun.

The vision of assimilation and uniformity is still predominant but a pluralist, democratic, and heterogeneous vision is incipient. As a result, the universities, the national elites and the indigenous professionals have a tendency to allow the issues to remain unchallenged, or ignore them altogether.

Higher Education and the Indigenous Movement

The indigenous and Mayan movements could be considered synonymous because Mayas comprise the largest indigenous group in Guatemala and have demonstrated leadership in organisations that take action on and present proposals for the human rights of indigenous peoples. There have always been indigenous movements with traditional leadership at the local and regional levels, but it has been in the last thirty years that it has been widely recognised as a social movement by non-indigenous academia and public opinion. The 1970s can be understood as the decade that the Mayan movement had its inception (Cojtí 1997;6). Religious organisations played a role in the development of the Mayan Movement, but it was the prevailing racism and social injustice – including the continuous appropriation of indigenous lands by the non-indigenous people – that led the Mayas themselves to organise for change (LeBot 1987). Some of the reasons it has been popularly accepted is that it portrays a positive acknowledgement of cultural differences with a common Guatemalan ethnicity. Operating within the law it is directed towards the central government and appeals to the mass media using the Spanish language.

Indigenous civil and coordinating organisations are the core of the Mayan movement which could be characterised as a fan of specifications with a common stem. Organisations operate at different structural levels, ranging from the local rural levels, to regional, national and international levels. Some of the organisations have different principles, priorities, demands and organisational structures but they all ultimately share the same goals of promoting human rights of indigenous peoples within the existing political borders of the Guatemalan state. That is, none of the groups tend to promote the creation of a separate Mayan state, which is in keeping with the international indigenous movement. Most of the organisations have a main focus but may also participate in other aspects of the movement. For example, an organisation that primarily supports the protection of culture might participate or cooperate with an organisation that makes particular socioeconomic demands, or vice versa.

Leadership in the Mayan Movement and Higher Education

There are various styles and forms of leadership corresponding to the structural levels that organisations in the Mayan movement operate. One could argue that some leaders are born leaders, while others learn to lead. The necessary merits of a leader depend on the organisation and its focus and goals. Male leaders who work within the capital city on cultural-political and anti-colonial platforms tend to generate more popular recognition. This can be explained by the current centralisation of political power of the state on the city level, which makes the preservation or construction of regional or linguistic leadership more difficult. An existing "machismo" and patriarchal racism towards rural indigenous women provides an explanation for the preponderance of men in high profile positions of leadership.

On the local and rural levels, within indigenous communities, a leader may not necessarily need a formal education, but on the regional or central level exercising leadership demands a higher level of academic preparation. A leader may not necessarily have administrative authority, and the latter may not necessarily be perceived as a leader within indigenous communities. Leaders are often the soul of the organisation who have a strong sense of identity and inject dynamism, direction and prominence into the movement. Internal characteristics of leaders are successfully promoting indigenous rights, negotiating strong proposals and maturity in achievements obtained. External characteristics are respectful acknowledgement from non-indigenous entities such as the popular media, and a continued loyalty to the promotion and defence of indigenous rights, even if the leader changes their workplace.

Corresponding to leadership generally on the local level, indigenous women may not necessarily need a formal education to be leaders. There is a relationship between indigenous female leadership and education; leadership can be strengthened by a formal education and a formal education can lead to leadership. Female leaders often forged their leadership in high school or in their professions and Mayan spiritual leadership can accompany political leadership. Professional women who are *Ajq'ij* (spiritual guides) add moral authority to their leadership (Dary 2004;98). At the movement's inception, due to the general lack of female leaders in Guatemala, indigenous women stood out and were quickly accepted as political leaders.

In Mayan society and in the Mayan movement, leadership operates on a continuum, ranging from traditional to modern. Traditional leadership tends to operate internally in the rural, less literate areas; modern leadership tends to operate externally in the academic, urban and westernised domains and demands interaction with the dominant, non-indigenous people and non-indigenous state. Traditional leaders are informed by culturally specific practises and values, although modern leadership is less connected to the traditional Mayan culture, modern leaders defer to traditional leaders in matters concerning cultural authenticity and spirituality.

As previously discussed, Mayas have limited access to higher education and there are different codes and expectations depending on where one exercises leadership. Indigenous run public and private organisations often have poor performance and incompetence in fulfilling the objectives of the indigenous population. One of the reasons for this shortfall is the lack of knowledge and

324

training to understand and address the variables and proceedings in the western-ladino political culture. Leaders in the modern and national indigenous sectors are not always elected or promoted by indigenous peoples themselves; rather, they are informally promoted by non-indigenous entities like the mass media, research centres and cooperating agencies. This situation presents a conundrum; if the leader is trained by and meets the approval of non-indigenous people then non-indigenous people believe he merits support because of the existing racism against indigenous people. Then again, if he meets the approval of the non-indigenous population than his leadership is questioned and is considered illegitimate by the indigenous population, which is contrary to the local and rural leaders who are promoted and recognised within the indigenous population.

A university diploma is not an automatic ticket to indigenous political leadership. It is beneficial and improves the potential but does not necessarily guarantee qualified leadership. An indigenous university graduate can move with more ease into the political field than vice versa. Technically speaking, an indigenous university graduate tends to be more consistent in the political field than someone without an education. It is more challenging for someone in the political field to move into the academic field because the two fields have different codes and expectations. Academia requires impartiality, objectivity and accuracy and requires that one make conclusions based on empirical evidence. The political field deals more directly with strategies and tactics and articulating political analyses. Political assertions can be based on evidence, but not necessarily.

Not all indigenous graduates have a desire to be a part of the indigenous movement. As discussed earlier, some indigenous students surrender to the assimilating and racist pressures in academic and social institutions and end up denying their indigenous identity, thus withdrawing themselves from the indigenous rights movement. There is much hidden or lost indigenous talent due to the crisis of identity many indigenous students encounter. There are also varying degrees of commitment among indigenous professionals who have a strong sense of identity. Not all are involved with the movement with the same intensity or constancy. It is valid to want to earn a living and have a comfortable life. There are some who temporarily sacrifice their time at the Capital to fulfil specific commitments to their communities and others who are fulltime activists working for indigenous NGOs and at the same time volunteering weekends in their communities.

It is also important to consider that not all indigenous people need to necessarily fulfil leadership roles. The movement also requires the skills of organisers, ideologists, fundraisers and strategists to name a few. Indigenous intellectuals can work in specific areas of the indigenous movement; for example questioning national assumptions about the existing accepted ethnic and political order that the non-indigenous elites and intellectuals take for granted (Cuevas, 2000:11). The social mobility, whether real or imaginary that a university degree carries has particular implications for the kind of leadership one might exercise. For example, indigenous professionals are not always able to communicate with and live within the life conditions of indigenous peasants and they may not always have the recognition of the latter.

An analysis (Table 2) of the thirteen most high profile indigenous leaders reveals the following about leadership and educational levels: one has a doctorate degree obtained abroad, four have masters' degrees, four have bachelor's degrees, three have secondary diplomas, and one has primary education. [2]

Table 2. Male and Female Indigenous Leaders

Bal, Pedro	León, Juan.	Tiney, Juan.
Cajas ,Ricardo	Lux, Otilia.	Tuyuc, Rosalina
Caz, Raymundo	Menchú, Rigoberta	Vázquez, Juana.
Cojtí, Demetrio	Quemé, Rigoberto	
De Paz, Marco Antonio	Salazar, Manuel	

National and central leadership demands access to higher education, but there are also leaders who only have primary or secondary education. The widely known leader with a primary education, Rigoberta Menchú, has certainly demonstrated that indigenous leadership does not necessarily require a university degree; she has been bestowed more than ten honorary doctorates from different universities from around the world.

Western Universities and Indigenous Leadership in the Mayan Movement

There are various ways that western or non-indigenous universities can support or facilitate the higher education of indigenous Guatemalans, which can help strengthen potential indigenous leadership. The qualitative and quantitative limitations that indigenous students and future professionals encounter might be able to be addressed within western and or non-indigenous universities; namely by supporting the implementation of affirmative action in favour of indigenous people to have greater access to higher education.

---

2 In an investigation of indigenous organizations promoting ethnical-cultural issues, a register was made of the indigenous leaders that were mentioned in five studies. A total of 102 leaders were listed. 13 of these were mentioned in three of the studies indicating that these were considered the most prominent leaders (Cojtí 2006:35).

The lack of specific support for indigenous people puts them at a disadvantaged position in relation to the ladino people. There is a need to create programmes and centres specifically for the development of indigenous leadership (UNICEF, 1996: 65).

Students would benefit from a combination of theory and practice in such settings. An example might be having internships in indigenous students own communities, where they could apply what they are learning. Getting credit for such work would give them not only theoretical but also practical knowledge in their field.

In order to be successful in any type of leadership it is not enough to transfer and handle knowledge, it is also necessary to learn how to develop nets of relationships and to combine teaching and learning. Indigenous students need initiatives in the not so easy art of *learning to be*. This is the principle that human beings posses the condition of providing themselves with independent and critical thinking and using their own judgment to determine by themselves what to do in different life circumstances (UNESCO 1996:100). Indigenous students need resources to develop *treaties of the mind*: intellectual humility, courage, integrity, perseverance, and a sense of justice (ITESM 1998).

Indigenous students would benefit from learning the art of *learning to learn* understood as a means to understand the world around us and learning to enjoy having that knowledge (UNESCO 1996: 62). It also involves a sense of being efficient in self-learning and self-education (ITESM 1998: 28-31). It is equally important for indigenous students to *learn to unlearn*, understood as facilitating the decolonisation of knowledge about indigenous people. This involves a methodology to identify and eliminate flawed western or deliberately colonialist knowledge about indigenous people and topics, with the participation of indigenous peoples themselves.

Relationships between members of indigenous groups should be of solidarity and cooperation; it is difficult to work as a team and construct a collective future when people from subordinated groups have not learned appropriate political behaviour to create solidarity and avoid competition and selfishness. Learning the art of politics demands specific courses for indigenous students and potential political leaders that can empower them in negotiation and defining specific solutions to conflicts. Also, learning strategic planning, power and structural analysis, as well as learning how to conduct research about social and political movements would strengthen indigenous students in future leadership roles.

Conclusion

It could be argued that the relationship between indigenous higher education indigenous people and the Mayan movement is not mechanical; higher education does not necessarily entail leadership nor involvement in the indigenous rights movement. Education and leadership are not necessarily reciprocal for education and politics are almost two separate fields. However, there are relational incidences in that education can strengthen indigenous leaders, particularly on the national and international level. In some circumstances there is mutual causality because political involvement might demand education and indigenous professionals find themselves within the indigenous movement and often would have benefited from particular types of compensatory education and training in order to be effective in hostile environments imbued with racism.

It is for political reasons that indigenous topics at Guatemalan universities are given negligent treatment; but it is also for political reasons that such situations are amended. Among political advocates who have favoured strengthening indigenous peoples' access to higher education are indigenous male and female leaders, indigenous organisations, and indigenous movements from different countries. But on the other hand, universities produce and develop leaders in their respective countries and we find indigenous leaders among them. Indigenous graduates can be leaders in and of the indigenous movements in their country or they could even lead an entire country. We can say with certainty that a university education can provide technical skills necessary for indigenous people who want to become political leaders.

References

AMEU. (1998). *Las Universidades: La Situación de la Educación*

Superior en Guatemala en el Fin de Siglo, Asociación Maya de Estudiantes Universitario, Guatemala.

ASDI. (1996). (Swedish Internationalal Development Cooperation Agency).

International Cooperation and Guatemala's Indigenous Peoples, survey carried-out by Tracy Ulltveit-Moe,Guatemala.

ASDI. (Swedish Internationalal Development Cooperation Agency). (2003). *Estudio de Contexto del Movimiento Indígena de Guatemala y sus organizaciones.* Research carried-out by Boman, Peck and Velásquez Consulting, Guatemala.

Bastos, S. and M. Camus. (2003a). *Entre el Mecapal y el Cielo: Desarrollo del Movimiento Maya en Guatemala.* Guatemala: FLACSO-Guatemala and Cholsamaj Editorial.

Bastos, S. and M. Camus. (2003b). *El Movimiento Maya en Perspectiva: Texto para Reflexión y Debate.* Guatemala: FLACSO-Guatemala.

CCARC. (2002). *Organizaciones Indígenas y Negras en Centroamérica: Sus Luchas por reconocimiento y Recursos.* Research led by Gordon, Edmund and Charles R. Hale. Austin, Texas.

Cayzac, H. (2001). *Guatemala, Proyecto Inconcluso: La Multiculturalidad, un Paso Hacia la Democracia.* Guatemala: FLACSO-Guatemala.

Cayzac, H. (2004). "Aprendizaje de la Multiculturalidad en Guatemala." *Estudios Interétnicos*, Vol 11, No. 17, 7-57. Guatemala: IDEI-USAC.

CEDIM. (2004). "Resultados del Decenio Internacional de las "Poblaciones", *Indígenas del Mundo 1994-2004 – Caso Guatemala.* Guatemala: CEDIM.

Cojtí Cuxil, D. (1997). *Ri Maya' Moloj pa Iximulew*, Cholsamaj Editorial, Guatemala.

Cojti Cuxil, D. (1995). "Los Mayas en las Universidades Guatemaltecas Colonialistas." In *Ub'anik ri Una'oj Uchomab'al ri Maya'Tinamit*, Cholsamaj Editorial, Guatemala.

Cojti Cuxil, D. (2004). "El Estado Multiétnico: Concepto, Características y Soluciones." Paper at the International Seminar-Workshop: *La Educación Superior en un Estado Multiétnico: La Universidad Maya de Guatemala*. The Academy of Mayan Languages in Guatemala. April 15, 2004. Guatemala.

CEH. (1999). *Guatemala: Memoria del Silencio*, USAID, Guatemala.

Cuevas Molina, R. (2001). *Guatemala: El Movimiento Social Étnico Contemporáneo*. [http://www.koeyu.com/revista/83/guatemalamsec.html]. April, 2005.

Dary, C., et al. (2004). *Sembradoras de Esperanza: Situación de las Mujeres Mayas en Guatemala*. FLACSO, Guatemala.

Flores Alvarado, H. (1993). *Movimiento Indígena en Guatemala: Diagnóstico y Expresiones de Unidad*." INIAP and Friedrich Ebert Foundation, Guatemala.

Gálvez Borrell, V., C. D. Fuentes, E. Esquit Choy and I. Rodas. (1997). *¿Qué Clase de Sociedad Queremos?: Una Mirada desde el Movimiento y las Organizaciones Mayas*. FLACSO, Guatemala.

Garza, R. M. and S. Loventhal. (1998). "Aprender como Aprender", Universidad Virtual del Tecnológico de Monterrey - ITESM, Trillas Editorial, México.

IDEA. (1998). "Democracia en Guatemala: La Misión de un Pueblo Entero." *Report of the Mission Training,* Series 6, Institute for Democracy and Electoral Assistance, Tercer Mundo Editors, Colombia. .

Le Bot, I. (1987). "La Iglesia y el Movimiento Indígena en Guatemala." *Seminario de Integración Social Guatemalteca*. Notebook No. 31. José de Pineda Ibarra Editorial, Guatemala

López Fríaz, B.S. (1998). "Pensamientos Crítico y Creativo", Universidad Virtual del Tecnológico de Monterrey - ITESM, Trillas Editorial, México.

Llorca, J. C. (2005). "Cambios en el Mapa Político," *El Periódico*. January 30. Guatemala.

Memmi, A. (1962). *L'homme Dominé*. Petite Bibliotheque Payot, Gallimard, Paris.

MINUGUA. (2001) "Los Pueblos Indígenas de Guatemala: la Superación de la Discriminación en el Marco de los Acuerdos de Paz." Report. Guatemala. [www.minugua.guate.net]. September, 2003.

Monzón, A. S. (2004). "Mujeres Indígenas: Entre Normas y Derechos – una Aproximación," *Estudios Interétnicos*, Vol. 11, No. 17, 59 – 108. IDEI-USAC Publications, Guatemala.

PNUD. (2005). (D. Cojti) *Diversidad Etnico-Cultural y Ciudadanía: Organizaciones Indígenas pro Reivindicaciones Etnico-Culturales.*, Draft. PNUD, Guatemala.

Torres Rivas, E. (2005). "Guatemala: Estado, Heterogenidad Estructural y Ciudadanía, una Visión Etnocultural", paper, Guatemala.

UNESCO-IESALC. (2004). (E. Fabián et al.) *Educación Superior para los Pueblos Indígenas: Caso de Guatemala*. Instituto de Educación Superior de América Latina y el Caribe - IESALC, Guatemala.

UNESCO – IESALC. (2003). (D. Cojti) *Políticas Publicas para la Educación Superior de los Pueblos Indígenas: el Panorama en Guatemala*, Instituto de Educación Superior de América Latina y el Caribe – IESALC," Encré Diseños C.A., Caracas.

UNESCO. (1996) *La Educación Encierra un Tesoro*, Report of the Commission Jacques Delors to UNESCO, Alfaro Hermanos S.A., México.

UNICEF, GTZ (Deutsche Gesellschaft für Technische Zusammenarbeit) and the Ministry of Education of Guatemala. (1996) *Análisis de Situación de la Educación Maya en Guatemala*, Cholsamaj Editorial, Guatemala.

List of abbreviations

AMEU	Asociación Maya de Estudiantes Universitario.
ASDI	La Agencia Sueca de Desarrollo Internacional (Swedish International Development Cooperation Agency-SIDA)
CCARC	Caribbean and Central American Research Council
CEDIM	Centro de Documentación e Investigación Maya
CEH	Comisión de Esclarecimiento Histórico.
EDUMAYA	A programme for developing a Mayan university.
ESSEDIR	Escuela de Servicios de Desarrollo e Investigación Rural.
FLACSO	Facultad Latinoamericana de Ciencias Sociales.
IESALC	Instituto de Educación Superior de América Latina y el Caribe
IDEA	Institute for Democracy and Electoral Assistance
INIAP	Instituto de Investigación y Autoformación Política.
ITESM	Instituto Tecnológico de Educación Superior de Monterrey.
MINUGUA	Misión de Verificación de las Naciones Unidas en Guatemala.
NORAD	Norwegian Development Agency
OKMA	Oxlajuj Kiej Maya' Ajtz'i'b. An organization documenting and promoting Mayan languages.
PRODESSA	Proyecto de Desarrollo Santiago
UNDP	United Nations Development Programme
UNESCO	United Nations Education, Science and Cultural Organization
UNICEF	United Nation Children's Fund
URL	Universidad Rafael Landivar
USAC	Universidad de San Carlos de Guatemala
USAID	United States Agency for International Development
USIS	United States Information Service
UVG	Universidad del Valle de Guatemala.

CHAPTER 17

The Question of Methodology
in Indigenous Research
A Philosophical Exposition.[1]

Nils Oskal

Introduction

What is the place of indigenous research in indigenous communities and in surrounding societies and further in the international society? Like general discussions concerning the place of research in society, this approach to the question involves several different problems in terms of the politics of science and philosophy. In this chapter I investigate some cognitive theoretical and scientific theoretical questions that arise in connection with discussions concerning indigenous research. I stress the question as to whether, and in any case how, it is possible to establish a special and distinctive indigenous methodology, and if it is the case that it cannot be done what implications it might have for the validation of indigenous social research.

By way of introduction, I will begin by trying to sort out the different types of questions that are currently being debated around the issue of indigenous research. To this end, I seek to make distinctions between scientific-political and scientific-philosophical or scientific-theoretical approaches to the problem.

First of all, the theme concerns cultural, educational, and political questions. Research and higher education have a central role in creating and developing a national foundation with regard to culture, knowledge, and interdependence. The university and college sector has an important function as it is the motivating force for cultural reproduction and social integration in society, and therefore concerns to the highest degree cultural and minority policy questions. In this sense, research and higher education are central in nation building processes. Historically, the educational system was actively used in assimilation policies towards indigenous peoples. Nation building is not necessarily suspect in itself, unless it aims to destroy other nations or minorities, or if inevitably such a consequence is the result of concrete nation building. The question in the indigenous context is how research and higher education for indigenous peoples should contribute to transmitting and strengthening indigenous peoples'

---

1   This is a revised version of an article published earlier in Sámi in *Sámi dieđalaš áigečála*,
    1-2, 2007.

culture and social life, and thereby contribute to a more secure future for them. Such questions are the concern of some of the international discussions about indigenous research. (Smith 1999, Kuokkanen and, Stordahl in this volume, Mihesuah–Wilson 2004).

Secondly, there is the political question regarding universities and how the idea of a university can be institutionalized in society without curtailing its autonomy. On the one hand, the university must inevitably be anchored in the real-life world and must contribute to cultural transmission and renewal, cultural self-understanding and intellectual enlightenment. On the other hand, the university should be autonomous in relation to the surrounding society while at the same time it should contribute to cultural renewal. The core of the problem is how universities should be institutionalized in indigenous societies without their autonomy being threatened (Mihesuah–Wilson 2004).

Thirdly, there are questions regarding the politics of science. Like other groups of people, indigenous peoples also have research needs. Research based on the need for knowledge in the indigenous society, and indigenous peoples' own needs and goals are emphasized. But what are indigenous societies' research needs, and what is the relationship between them and the political prioritizing of research efforts and higher education? What research tasks should be prioritized and how should indigenous societies be assured influence in political control of such tasks and prioritizing? Is there reason to assume that indigenous peoples' influence over political priorities concerning research entails control across the scientific-internal obligation of seeking the truth in research (Bull 2002, Berg 2004)?

Fourth, regarding indigenous research, there are ethical questions that concern how indigenous societies that are studied should be involved in the research process, and which particular ethical considerations should be attended to in research about indigenous people as peoples, as minorities and as individuals.

I shall not pursue these political questions concerning education and research further, but limit myself to themes that concern scientific theoretical questions. I distinguish between these normative political questions and scientific theoretical questions concerning indigenous research and corresponding indigenous methodology.

Indigenous Peoples' Distinctive Epistemology, Ontology, and Ethics
In the literature that addresses the development of an "Indigenous Research Paradigm," the point of departure is preferably that indigenous people have a distinctive epistemology, ontology and ethical axiology (Kuokkanen 2000: Porsanger 2004: 2005: Wilson 2003).

Thomas S. Kuhn (1922-96) was the first to use the concept of a paradigm in a scientific theoretical discussion in connection to the natural sciences in the book *The Structure of Scientific Revolutions* (1962). His theory of paradigms has been the object of thorough investigations. On the basis of criticism, Kuhn consecutively tried to clarify and improve the theory (cf. Kuhn 1977). His main idea is that a scientific paradigm is neither a theory nor a hypothesis, but something that makes a theory and a hypothesis possible. A paradigm contains all the theoretical assumptions, explanatory principles, methodological norms/outlines/rules, observational norms and experimental techniques. The paradigm's content cannot be explained with clear or formal rules, and every paradigm has a quantity of "tacit knowledge." It is not possible to completely explain the paradigm's content, and in addition, there are different types of paradigms that are more or less incommensurable.

The paradigm idea is used widely in indigenous contexts; it captures aspects of the politics of science and the politics of culture, and is included in the indigenous movement's objectives of attaining autonomy and strengthening their own society. Here I stress scientific theoretical issues as the content emerges in the concept of an Indigenous Research Paradigm. As an example I use Shawn Wilson. She explains the paradigm idea's content in scientific contexts in this manner:

> Paradigms shape our view of the world around us and how we walk through that world. All research reflects the paradigm used by the researcher whether that researcher is conscious of the usage or not. Included in a research paradigm are our ontology and epistemology as well as our axiology and methodology (Wilson 2003: 161).

Indigenous researchers and theoreticians' ideas can be formulated as follows: indigenous people have their own way of thinking about what there is to know and what there is not to know. They also have their own way of thinking about how one can investigate whether different claims to knowledge are tenable or not. They have distinctive epistemologies, even if they are different from each other; they do not have a common epistemology. Indigenous peoples also have a special understanding of what the world is, and what life is, and, on the whole, what there *is*, and that which is. This is called ontology. Indigenous people have a distinctive ontology, even if it is not an ontology that is common for all indigenous peoples. Indigenous peoples also have a distinctive understanding of what is good and bad, what is right and wrong, beautiful and ugly, what is worth investigating and how it is ethically acceptable to investigate. They have a distinctive ethics, even if it does not mean a common ethics for all indigenous peoples.

The idea is not new, but the words used are new. The basic idea of cultural researchers has been that every people has a distinctive and complete culture. The same content is found in the Greek concepts as in the Latin. The advantage is that the Greek language concepts used in the discussion about indigenous methodology make it easier to relate that discussion to classical Greek philosophy.

Most cultures distinguish between knowing and believing, and that is also the case with the Sami, or in this connection, the North Sami. The most well known distinction between knowing and believing is the Greek concepts and the distinction between episteme and *doxa*, which is what Plato made known. From then on, there have been investigations written for over 2000 years of the relationship between episteme and *doxa*. The first to criticize Plato's way of distinguishing between what we believe and what we know was Plato's student Aristotle. To the word 'episteme' it was added the ending 'logy,' which means that the conversations about 'episteme' had gotten a distinctive 'logos,' or that the conversation had become a systematic conversation or teaching. Even if there is a clear continuity between these conversations, it is nevertheless very difficult to speak about the western world's epistemological tradition because it is varied and rich, nor is there just one tradition that one would be able to call the western world's philosophical tradition.

The scientific theoretical point seems to be that in order to consider indigenous peoples' epistemology, ontology and ethics when doing research that concerns indigenous peoples, and especially if one is going to do research from a culturally internal perspective, then a distinctive methodology is necessary. Methodology contains an understanding of how research is carried out or how it ought to be carried out. To carry out research in a culturally internal perspective one needs an indigenous peoples' methodology that in one sense or another respects indigenous peoples' epistemology, ontology and ethics. If one uses an indigenous peoples' methodology in research, it allows indigenous peoples the possibility of describing their own culture and history on the basis of their own epistemology, ethics and ontology (Porsanger 2005:268). The methodology should also aid in tidying up, structuring and limiting sources of knowledge, and investigating their dependability and trustworthiness.

The central question becomes how such an indigenous methodology should be justified? The question concerning justifications for methodologies generally is nothing new, and I will first investigate the Cartesian tradition that had as its fundamental idea the establishment of a reliable methodology from an epistemological basis. The goal is to examine whether it is possible to justify social research with a particular methodology that could provide epistemological certainty or assurance that research can produce tenable knowledge without reasonable doubt. I will not examine closely which method Descartes puts forward as the best method for assuring the tenability of the perception, and in the same way I will not investigate which methods are suggested in connection with indigenous methodology. The question is rather whether method can be established on epistemology and what that means, whether it be a Cartesian or another methodology that is used. I will not write anything about the content of a European or indigenous epistemology, but investigate what it means to have methodology founded on an epistemology. I put forward a general philosophical approach to the problem that there are traditions for discussing scientific theoretical contexts. The presentation does not claim to be original, and really belongs rather to basic academic knowledge or general knowledge, and therefore also lacks a scholarly apparatus. The goal is not to make it unnecessarily complicated or strive to give a complete picture of different philosophical traditions, but to put forth a longer train of thought.

After that discussion I will move from knowledge theory (epistemology) to the theory of science and investigate what kind of implications that objections to the epistemological tradition have for sociological research that seeks to understand society in a culturally internal perspective. After the hermeneutic turn, the interpretative aspect of sociological research was stressed, and the idea that one cannot assure understanding through methods (Rabinow & Sullivan 1979). The question in the last part of the chapter is: If the tenability of social research cannot be assured epistemologically through method, then is it even possible to distinguish sociological research from other propaganda and politically rhetorical activity?

Epistemology as a Foundational Enterprise?

Most famous in more recent times are Descartes' (1596-1650) thoughts on what we are capable of knowing. He is perhaps infamous because many scholars blame him for being the founder of the mechanistic worldview. The accusations against Descartes are famous even if those who accuse him can be more Cartesian than Descartes himself.

Earlier, epistemology was the most prominent discipline in philosophy, but today it is devalued and considered to be something one ought to exceed and overcome. Sixty years earlier, in the heyday of logical empiricism, epistemology was considered to be philosophy's basic discipline and flagship, and the theory of perception stood in focus. The division of labor was intended to be understood in the following way: scientific research created empirical knowledge, while philosophy was supposed to reflect on the basis of the claims to knowledge in empirical research.

This tradition was central only in the Anglo-American world. The objections to the epistemological tradition were prominent in continental Europe. Gradually, continental argumentations against this form of epistemology gained acceptance both in England and the USA.

Richard Rorty's well known book, *Philosophy and the Mirror of Nature*, definitively banished the epistemological tradition (Rorty 1980) in the English-speaking world. But it is unclear what it means to overcome the epistemological way of thinking, and leave it behind entirely. Rorty's basic idea seems to be that epistemology is not something that can be developed and improved, but something that ought to be annulled completely. The entire theoretical knowledge project appears to be a blind alley that should be abandoned.

The other famous book is Jean-Francois Lyotard's report, *The Postmodern Condition: A Report on Knowledge* published in 1984. His diagnosis of the times is that "the great narratives" (Grand Narratives) have definitely lost their reliability. The postmodern era has brought to an end all science that is based on any form of epistemological meta-narrative, such as "… the dialectics of Spirit, the hermeneutics of meaning, the emancipation of the rational or working subject, or the creation of wealth" (Lyotard 1984).

Therefore, it is interesting to discover that indigenous academics are trying to resume the epistemological tradition and restore the theoretical knowledge project that Europeans have attempted to discard. According to Richard Rorty (1980) the central function of epistemology is to establish and ultimately justify scientific research. It is supposed to provide a foundation for evaluating scientific tenability and the knowledge claims of research. The goal of epistemology is to give a final justification for the degree to which claims to knowledge can be fulfilled, and what makes the knowledge claims of research tenable.

Epistemology should not be dependent on empirical arguments or findings from empirical research, at the same time as epistemology should evaluate empirical research. Argumentation concerning empirical claims of knowledge should not be dependent on empirical conditions, and the validity of the arguments should not be bound to empirical observation.

Such an overcoming of epistemology would imply that the idea of the theory of knowledge (perception) as having a foundational function towards individual sciences should be rejected. Correspondingly, it would imply rejecting the idea that indigenous epistemology possesses a foundational justification for one form or another of indigenous science.

The Relationship between Epistemology and Methodology

If one follows Rorty in the understanding of epistemology, then rejecting or abandoning epistemology is the same as abandoning the idea that epistemology possesses a function as founder of empirical science.[2] In the empirical tradition there is a basic idea that epistemology should be "naturalized," or put in more modern terms, "contextualized,"[3] and that epistemology should be understood as an empirical science among other empirical sciences, and not as a discipline with a status independent of experience or *a priori* (Quine 1969). Even if it had been that epistemology was an empirical science, then the basic idea would

---

2   There is reason to point out that epistemology can be understood in an additional way than Rorty understands it. Correspondingly, getting past epistemology implies something other than rejecting the idea that epistemology has a founding function (Taylor 1995).

3   For a problematization of the idea of naturalized epistemology, see Putman (1982).

remain unshaken; knowing is to represent an independent reality. Knowledge then is understood as an inner depiction of an external reality.

This interpretation of what epistemology is has been influential. It has led to the formation of a background understanding both of what knowledge is and what it means to be a human being. And even if one were to abandon the idea that epistemology is a foundational discipline which epistemology itself is not dependent on empirical argumentation, it is nevertheless necessary to investigate assumptions of the other interpretation where epistemology is understood as an empirical science. In the latter interpretation, one of the assumptions for something to be learned knowledge is that it represents a certain connection between that which *is* outside, and the inner descriptions that the external world inflicts upon us.

The Cartesian Tradition

Descartes was the most significant critic of such a "mechanistic conception" of learning, or true knowledge. Science or true knowledge does not consist of a simple congruence between ideas in the researcher's consciousness and the external world. If my assertions accidentally agree with actual events in the world, then these do not necessarily represent a particular knowledge about the world. The congruence must come through using a correct method that provides a basis for trustworthiness. According to Descartes, science requires certainty (*évidence*), and this must be founded on an indubitable clarity, and one gets clarity by using correct methods.

Certainty is something the knowing subject must acquire himself through consciousness. The perceiving subject must himself investigate his opinions anew through his own reflection and reflexivity. Reflexivity is not a new idea; through reflection one is no longer supposed to do as Socrates and Plato did, namely to seek immutable ideas, or like Aristotle, to seek forms in a world changing steadily. What is new is that the perceiving subject, through his own effort, is supposed to turn against his own mind. She is supposed to turn her back to the outside world and instead direct attention to her own representations, presentations, thoughts or descriptions. A basic Cartesian idea is that certainty (*évidence*) is something the mind has to generate for itself in order for it to be obtained. This can occur by systematizing, structuring and explaining thoughts by means of a certain method. Descartes based the reflexive investigation on the understanding that the subject should limit and explain his thoughts without being concerned about to what these thoughts refer. Thoughts should be clarified; that can occur if one organizes the thoughts according to certain rules or methods. The stress is on the content of the thoughts, and not on the objects that the thoughts depict, refer, or represent.

Descartes did not only have thoughts about what epistemology, ontology and methodology are per se, he also had a clear understanding of how the relationship between these three concepts should be correctly understood. We cannot begin with the question of what the world is; because that presupposes that we know what it means to know. Therefore, we begin rather with the question of what it means to know. Only when we have answered the question of what it means to know, can we ask which method is most appropriate for getting reliable knowledge about the world. Thus, when we have clarified the method we can then begin to ask about what it means to live in the world.

In western philosophy there are well-established dissimilar traditions that direct criticism toward the Cartesian epistemological tradition. The Cartesian epistemological tradition developed an understanding of what it means to know, and what knowledge is, but it also accommodated an influential background understanding regarding questions about what a human being is, and how the relationship between individual and society should be understood. However, I shall address approaches to the problem that concerns the status of social science according to the so called hermeneutic turn, and what that means for the establishment of a distinctive indigenous methodology.

Hans-Georg Gadamer (1900-2002) assumed that understanding is part of living in the world, and that one cannot guarantee especially more through scientific methods than one can do with life itself (Gadamer 1960: 1971). Gadamer carried the criticism further against the Cartesian tradition: What implications does this criticism have for the scientific theories of humanistic social research?

Hermeneutics, Humanistic Research, and Society Research

The object of humanistic research and of sociological research is the human being, and the human being is understood as a self-interpreting creature. The themes are people's actions, practices, and the results of their actions. Sociological research is hermeneutic because sociological research is indissolubly bound to interpretations of one's own research object. To interpret is to explain, investigate and clarify the underlying meaning of something that at first glance appears to be unclear and fragmented. The meaning of the research object is always a particular subject's expression, or a particular expression of the subject. With comprehensible phenomena there is always something that brings forth meaning or someone who expresses himself. In subject-related phenomena, such as actions and feelings, the subject, of course, is an isolated human being to whom the actions or the feelings can be attributed. But because of the distinctive intersubjective quality of language, the society or the human community is ultimately the meaning-bearing subject that hermeneutic scholarship researches. Since sociological research is a hermeneutic science that means that sociological research uses different levels of meaning and interpretation.

On the one hand, researchers are themselves anchored in a life world and are themselves self-interpreting beings with a cultural understanding that cannot be set aside through methodological steps or in any other way. The construction of a concept apparatus in social science has a point of departure within its own cultural sphere or horizon, and social science theories and explanations exist as self-understanding within their own time and exist from pre-understandings that their own time offers and contains.

On the other hand, the researchers understanding of reality is the basis for their interpretations of a reality that already is constituted through the actor's, i.e. the research object's own interpretations. Through research, we meet concepts that belong to the sphere or horizon of research solidarity, concepts that belong to that reality which we are researching. We can say that the sociological researchers interpret a world that has already been interpreted before by the people who inhabit it, and in that respect, humanistic and sociological research are to a double degree hermeneutic sciences (Giddens 1976).

The meeting between different interpretive levels is also the meeting place for explanations on different levels. During preparation of social scientific explanations, the researchers meet actors who already have more or less clear and well-articulated answers to questions about what is happening and why it is happening. In addition, the actors themselves can understand and investigate interpretations that social science offers. What kind of methodological implications does this situation entail?

The hermeneutic aspects of humanistic and social scientific research have many methodological implications. I will only mention three of them that have relevance for methodological questions: Is it possible to improve and criticize the actors' understanding of reality and their self-understanding? Is it possible to base tenability on the explanations of sociological and social scientific research? What relationship should there be between the actors' self-understandings or self-explanations, and humanistic and social explanations?

The Actors' Self-Understanding and Scientific Explanations in Sociological Research

From the limitation of the object area of social science, it follows that social research must understand the actors' own self-understanding when one is supposed to identify what one is investigating, and in addition, what phenomena one seeks to explain sociologically. Social science–when it investigates phenomena that are endured by virtue of the concepts the actors themselves use and are the masters–is forced to appropriate the actor's understanding when it is supposed explain that understanding in social science language and terms.

Most other hermeneutics after Wilhelm Dilthey (1833-1911) reject the idea that understanding (*verstehen*) is the same as empathy (*einfühlung*). To understand other people means that we are able to use those concepts that constitute their world and that are constituted within their world. The social researcher must, in the least, be a possible participant in case he/she is not a real participant in the actors' activities. The researcher enters, in principle, into the same sort of processes of understanding as his own research objects who are also included with the people that the researcher attempts to understand. The difference from the understanding of daily life–which is usually not articulated verbally very explicitly and which precedes action, competence, and interaction with others– is that social science is a written discourse. Therefore, in order investigate the actors' self-understanding, it would entail that some of their tacit or "natural" knowledge is explained orally.

According to Charles Taylor, one should not confuse the claim of under- standing the actor's self-understanding with what he calls "the incorrigibility thesis" (Taylor 1995:123). The incorrigibility thesis encourages a methodologi- cal principle where social scientific explanations must build on the same expla- nations that the actors themselves make use of to explain themselves and their actions. The actors' self-understanding one should not to be falsely improved upon or criticized. Such an understanding, according to Taylor, would be an er- roneous interpretation of the nature of a hermeneutic science. Instead the proper place of the social sciences follows from the idea that people seldom truly understand themselves and their own actions with precise explanations, and further from it being erroneous to assume that people possess a complete and infallible self-understanding. But this is not an argument in favor of disregard- ing the actors' self-understanding. On the contrary, the assumption is that in order to be able investigate to what degree people's self-understanding is defi- cient, the researcher must understood their self-understanding. To understand the actors' self-understanding is unavoidable, even if the goal is to exceed it and offer a better understanding.

To understand the actors' self-understanding is more than just a starting point that can be abandoned when the researcher begins to make social scientific ex- planations and theories. The actors' self-understanding has implications for the explanations of the social scientist. The actors' concepts and self-understanding cannot be abandoned as if they were unimportant for how a social scientific explanation of them should be shaped. Taylor's point of departure is that every social scientific explanation should be able to be tied to the actors' self-under- standing. However, there are many ways social scientific explanations can be associated with the actors' self-understandings and self-explanations, and these different ways are connected to which underlying models for validation of so- cial scientific explanations one relies on.

In connection with Sami research, Alf Isak Keskitalo, has called attention to a problem concerning the connection between actor explanations and social scientific explanations. In the article "Research as an Inter-Ethnic Relation" (Keskitalo 1974) he explains the difference between two ways of connecting actors' and social scientific explanations:

There has, however, been an increase in research concerning the very management of minority policy, as well as attempts to describe the theory of the minority, and I suspect that ethno-scientists might try an extensional description of every form of minority action, including reflected academic activity in the minority on the phenomenon of this external description itself, an activity such as the presentation of this paper (Keskitalo 1976:37-38).

A plausible drawback of external policy description is that it tends to confuse extension and intentional phenomena, by 'extensional' I am here primarily thinking of an instrumental viewpoint, 'intentional' primarily as a communicative perspective. (…). A scientific description tends to be disproportionately extensional, thus for instance being able to refer to theoretically formulated statements merely as political or social phenomena, and thus suppress them from an intentional to an extensional level; in a sense rendering them ineffective as statements. To insist on the validity of extensional descriptions in the theory formulated by the minority, thus starting a theoretical war as to who is the best extensionalist … (Keskitalo 1976:39).

Keskitalo's main point is that if one explains the actors' intentional relationships and phenomena in extensional ways, then this invites a competition where one strives to be the most competent in explaining each other causally. When one explains in a causal manner, then one is not taking up the actors' own viewpoints and arguments, but rather looking for external causes that cause the actors to do or believe what they must do or believe. However, when one uses an intentional mode of explanation, then one is trying to understand people's thinking and motivations, and the way that their thinking is expressed in their society, institutions and social life. If one uses the extensional mode, the issue concerns trying to explain what causes people to think the way they do, what drives people to do what they do, etc. Their own thoughts turn into symptoms that they find underlying causes, and it is these causes that the social scientific researcher is supposed to look for and use as explanations. This is the keynote in the hermeneutics of suspicion (Ricoeur 1970:32).

Keskitalo does not explain more thoroughly whether these two levels of explanation can be linked, and how in that case, it can be done. The question of what it means to explain the actors' self-understanding intentionally remains to be answered together with the question of what relationship there should be between the actors' own explanations and social scientific explanations.

Vigdis Stordahl has pointed out a similar approach to the problem in the field of anthropology:

The tension between the anthropological knowledge about 'the others' and the others' own understanding remains just the same. Even if anthropologists argue (…) that this represents two knowledge systems, two modes of representation conventions that cannot be used to combat each other, we constantly see examples of them being understood as competing knowledge systems. In a situation where two different knowledge systems are interpreted– in reality or rhetorically– as competing with each other, the anthropological knowledge will then be placed face to face with a problem of educational political legitimacy (Stordahl 1996:177).

Stordahl draws our attention to the competitive situation with different explanations and problems related to scientific political legitimatization. In the same field, Arild Hovland has offered comparable remarks:

> The researcher and the researched enter into a common discourse where directly in discussions and indirectly in the course of life, reading, and engagement as students, cultural operators, or regular politicians, use and produce from within the same corpus of knowledge that the researcher works with (…) The texts and interpretations of the researcher and the researched can easily appear to be competing. This competitive aspect is an essential side of the common discourse (Hovland 1996:58).

Even if Stordahl underscores the research institution's responsibility for educating the students on the basis of their own experiences, and to teach them to distinguish between ordinary peoples' experiences and scientific explanations (Stordahl 1996:184), she nevertheless does not explain how one can connect the two levels of explanations.

Trond Thuen has commented on both Hovland's and Stordahl's articles. Thuen stresses the importance of distinguishing between *analytical concepts and empirical substance*, and between *the empirical level and the analytical level*. Thuen's solution is that these two levels of explanation should not be connected, and more precisely, one ought to make visible the difference if one is going to maintain a critical distance between these two levels of explanation (Thuen 1996:191).

For me the question remains whether common discourse and competition does not constitute a scientific theoretical problem, and not just a political problem. Hovland explains this common discourse and competitive situation:

> Common discourses are double-edged. They represent both a unique possibility and an increasing problem. Anthropologists can no longer protect themselves behind geographic and social distance in the common discourse. (…) We *are forced* to this [to reflect on dilemmas of anthropological practice, Nils Oskal] because 'we' and 'the others' share a communicative space. We ought to pursue it as part of an ongoing and necessary re-evaluation of the relationship between 'us' and 'them.' Reflections about knowledge policy and research policy point in that way in the same direction (Hovland 1996:60).

I agree with Hovland when he seems to assume a difference between scientific validation and the politics of science and research in argumentation. I also agree with Stordahl when she seems to claim that social research cannot avoid having to offer self-knowledge and self-understanding to those being researched.

Conclusion

Given that it is tenable that epistemology cannot justify a scientific methodology, and given that from this it follows that sociological research cannot maintain its own precedence with regard to the tenability of social scientific explanations in relation to the society that is being researched then this has certain implications.

According to the way of thinking in hermeneutic, humanistic and sociological research, there is an internal relationship between understanding and criticism. Sociological theories are validated according to this understanding in a different manner than models of empiricist and relativistic theories prescribe.

The way I understand it, the hermeneutic position contains three main assertions on the basis of Taylor (1985) and Fossland and Grimen (2001):

- Social scientific theory explains sociological phenomena and proposes and offers at the same time to the society the phenomena belong to a self-understanding.
- How we evaluate social scientific theories is (or ought to be) tied to how we evaluate the self-understanding the theory offers; the question of what is a good theory cannot be separated from the question of what is a good self-understanding.
- If concrete human and sociological research is tenable it must be answered and validated in a concrete argumentation between those whom the research concerns, that is, both in the joint research activity and those researched in the society, and also between these societies.

Because of the value neutral thesis, empiristic theorists have sought to direct criticism against sociological research for erroneously mixing values together with scientific research. The supporters of relativistic theories, in return, have sought to demonstrate that the value neutral thesis is nonsense, and that humanistic and sociological research is therefore nothing other than ordinary ideology that is validated in accordance with normal political rhetoric.

Differing from the first theories, hermeneutic human and sociological research stands firm on the idea that sociological models have a normative content independent of what the researcher desires. Differing from the other theories, is the claim that social scientific research is not empty rhetoric, but that sociology is differently obliged to another form of validation than that which the empiristic model offers.

343

This model of validation stands in contrast to the model where the actors are assumed to possess an infallible self-understanding, but it also stands in contrast to models that assume that social sciences possess a superior and privileged language that stands outside of all life values. The point of departure for this hermeneutic position is that social scientific models have an unavoidable philosophical anthropological content, but that this does not reduce social sciences to knowledge policy and research policy.[4] If anything, it obliges the social sciences to another validation model than the empiristic.

When it is difficult to distinguish between rational acceptance and ideological acceptance, persuasion, or cunning through serious argumentation on a methodological basis or a priori decisions, then such a validation must be carried out solely through concrete argumentation in the actual cases. There are no metaphysical guarantees that actual acceptance does not constitute an ideological acceptance built on power relations.

The discussion mentioned above on an 'Indigenous Research Paradigm' displays in my view the following results: it is not possible to justify a distinctive methodology that is supposed to guarantee an a priori tenability, and that it is independent of whether the methodology is based on epistemology or ontology, or by referring to "we" – "you" dichotomies or the researcher's sense of belonging. A hermeneutically enriched social science, rather, demands a scientific humility, openness and boldness, and not an establishment of new orthodoxies.

References

Berg, B.A. (2004). "Forestillingen om en samisk nasjon." In B.A. Berg and E. Niemi (eds.): *Fortidsforestillinger: bruk og misbruk av nordnorsk historie: rapport fra det 27. nordnorske historieseminar*, Hamarøy 27.–29.9.2002 , Skriftserie fra Institutt for historie, No 4: 103–115, Tromsø: Universitetet i Tromsø.

Bull, T. (2002). *Kunnskapspolitikk, forskningsetikk og det samiske samfunnet*, Samisk forskning og forskningsetikk, Forskningsetiske komiteer, 2: 6–21

Gadamer, H.-G. (1975). *Wahrheit und Metode. Grundzüge einer philosophischen Hermeneutik*, 4. Auflage, Tübingen: J.C.B. Mohr (Paul Siebeck).

Gadamer, H.-G. (1971). "Rethorik, Hermeneutik und Ideologikritik. Metakritische Erörterungen zu 'Wahrheit und Metode'." In Karl Otto Apel, Ed. *Hermeneutik und Ideologikritik*, Frankfurt am Main: Suhrkamp Verlag

Giddens, A. (1976). *New Rules of Sociological Method*, London: Hutchinson.

Fossland, J. and H. Grimen (2001). *Selvforståelse og frihet*, Oslo: Universitetesforlaget.

Hovland, A. (1996). "Fellesdiskurs og tveegget sverd. Antropologisk kunnskap og etnopolitikk i Sápmi." *Norsk antropologisk tidsskrift*, 1:44–63.

---

4 A knowledge-and scientific political debate is both necessary and important. It is also important that researchers participate in such debates as politically ascending citizens. An insistence on a difference of principle between political legitimation and scientific validation is not intended as an argument against political legitimation of scientific research. I hope that I have demonstrated that.

Keskitalo, A. I. (1976). *Research as an Inter-Ethnic Relation*, Acta Borealia, B. Humaniora 13: 15–42.

Kuhn, T. (1970). *The Structure of Scientific Revolutions*. 2. ed., Chicago: The University of Chicago Press.

Kuhn, T. (1977). *Second Thoughts of Paradigms, The Essential Tension*. Chicago: The University of Chicago Press.

Kuokkanen, R. (2000). "Towards an "Indigenous Paradigm" from a Sami Perspective." *The Canadian Journal of Native Studies*, 20 (2):411–436.

Kuokkanen, R. (2006). Sámi Higher Education and Research: Building the Future of Sami Society, Ms

Lyotard, J.-F. (1984). *The Postmodern Condition: A Report on Knowledge.* Minneapolis: University of Minnesota Press.

Miehesuah, D. and A. Wilson, Eds. (2004). *Indigenizing the Academy. Transforming Scholarship and Empowering Communities.* Lincoln: University of Nebraska Press.

Ricoeur, P. (1970). *Freud and Philosophy: An Essay on Interpretation.* New Haven: Yale University Press.

Porsanger, J. (2004). *An essay about indigenous methodology.* Nordlit, 15.

Porsanger, J. (2005). *"Bassejoga čáhci" Gáldut nuortasámiid eamioskkoldaga birra álgoálbmotmetodologiijaid olis*, Dr.art.-grada dutkamuš, Romssa universitehta humanisttalaš fakultehta.

Putman, H. (1982). "Why Reason can't be Naturalized." *Synthese*, 52:3–23.

Quine, W.V. (1969). *Epistemology Naturalized, Ontological Relativity and Other Essays.* New York: Columbia University Press.

Rabinow, P. and W. M. Sullivan, Eds. (1979) *Interpretive Social Science: A Reader.* Univ. of California, 1979.

Rorty, R. (1980). *Philosophy and the Mirror of Nature.* Oxford: Basil Blackwell.

Smith, L. T. 1999. *Decolonizing Methodologies. Research and Indigenous Peoples.* London: Zed Books Ltd,.

Stordahl, V. (1996). "Antropologi i den fjerde verden." *Norsk antropologisk tidsskrift*, 3:175–186.

Stordahl, V. (2006): Nation building through knowledge building: the discourse of Sami higher education and research in Norway, Ms, 2005.

Taylor, C. (1985). *Philosophy and Human Sciences*, vol. 2, Cambridge: Cambridge Univiversity Press.

Taylor, C. (1995). *Philosophical Arguments* London: Harvard University Press.

Thuen, T. (1996). (Comments) "Om forholdet mellom deltakelse, advocasy og forskning, og om dilemmaene som oppstår når de tre blandes sammen i undervisnings- og forskningssammenheng" *Norsk antropologisk tidsskrift*, 3:187–191.

Wilson, S. (2003). "Progressing Toward an Indigenous Research Paradigm in Canada and Australia." *Canadian Journal of Native Education*, 27, 2:161–178.

CHAPTER 18

Yoik – Sami Music in a Global World

HARALD GASKI

The cultural area that globalization has had the greatest impact on within indigenous cultures is without doubt popular music.[1] At the same time, it has been difficult for some music critics to figure out where to place new compositions that emanate from traditional music, the degree to which they represent new genres or whether they are just part of popular music. This approach to the problem has also been relevant for some world music, but there, however, the connections have been more clearly to the innovative use of folk music, jazz, and rock. However, in the case of Sami yoik, one can find examples among the Sami poet and multi-artist Nils-Aslak Valkeapää's[2] productions where it was rather a question of new compositions than versions of traditional folk music. This is the case especially with the two CDs, *Beaivi áhčážan* (1988) and *Eanan, eallima* eadni (1990). It is truer to an even greater degree for the prizewinning bird symphony *Goase dušše* (Prix Italia 1993), released on CD in 1994. Here yoik enters in only as part of nature's own symphony, which on the CD primarily consists of bird sounds.

It is natural that indigenous peoples have taken inspiration from each other. There have, after all, been a number of festivals and conferences since the end of the 1970s where groups have met and exchanged experiences and created a new political and cultural platform for the indigenous movement. Because the cultural dimension has always had a prominent position in indigenous politics, most political conferences have also functioned as cultural meeting places, with performances by musicians, dancers and poets. In that way, one can say that culture and politics to a large extent have gone hand in hand for indigenous groups in recent decades. A similar thing happened when small nations with newly gained freedom like Norway and Finland were engaged in nation-building in the first part of the twentieth century.

---

1   This chapter is to a large extent based on investigations and deliberations I did for the Sámi copyright organization, Sámekopiija, for an article in their publication on traditional Sámi rights and values. It also draws on two previous articles of mine written in Norwegian, but in all cases this new essay represents an update of the situation and a further exploration of the challenges presented to indigenous peoples regarding the problems associated with innovative use of traditional material in the new setting of globalization.
2   Read more about Valkeapää on the following web pages: http://www.utexas.edu/courses/ Sámi/diehtu/siida/reindeer/poem.htm or www.lassagammi.no

In this chapter I want to mainly focus on the traditional Sami musical genre, the yoik, and take a look at production conditions, evaluation methods and legal questions in connection with using traditional music in new settings. I have chosen to focus on one art form in one culture rather than comparing the situation among a number of peoples, mainly in order to be able to delve more deeply beneath the surface on one theme within one culture. However, by doing this I hope to touch on general approaches to the problems of other indigenous groups, and also, generally, to discuss the problems surrounding the innovative use of traditional cultural elements. Finally, I pose the question about what type of music will eventually evolve from the mutual influence and interaction between different indigenous peoples: Will the development go in the direction of a common indigenous sound or will consciousness about each group's own cultural heritage strengthen the desire to preserve the traditional sound?

Yoik is the original music of the Sami (Turi [1910: 91]/ 1997: 45). It has clear limits as to creation, function and performance. It belongs to a community and makes the person yoiked a part of that community. But, because the yoik is so collective in its essence, it also has a special ownership structure. It is not the one who creates the yoik who owns it but rather the person who is yoiked (Gaski 2000: 193). The creator, in a way, loses the right to his own creation and the recipient acquires the ownership right to it. An interesting consequence of this is that yoiks to animals, mountains and landscape consequently become their property, and as such are controlled by subjects that cannot give expression in a human sense to their own wishes. According to traditional Sami belief, however, nature has a soul, so with this background it is not a strange notion that a reindeer or a mountain can own a yoik.

As an example, in the case of what I have called Sámiland's alternative national song, namely Nils-Aslak Valkeapää's "Sámiid eatnan duoddariid,"[3] the relationship is entirely clear. It is the yoiked mountain plateaus of Samiland that are both subject and object: the yoik is both about them, and they *are* at the same time the yoik. This is so because the yoik is not a description of the mountain plateaus, but is understood as the plateaus' presentation of themselves through yoik. The concrete yoik is dedicated to the plateaus, which thereby also become the yoik's owners, just as Valkeapää himself wished. The yoik is an extolling of the relationship and dimension of closeness between the people and the land. It is therefore appropriate according to the traditional way of thinking that the land should get something back from those who use it, namely the Sami, and the nicest gift one can give to one's beloved is a beautiful yoik!

The yoik is tied to nature, and it describes humankind's nature. It has an immediacy about it that enables it to communicate the innermost thoughts and feelings between two nearly equal subjects, the yoiker and the one yoiked. Even

3   Available on the CD *Sápmi lottážan*, Reproduction 1992, AAD. DATCD-13/1.

though one yoiks about something, the object of the yoik is still not only the recipient; it affects and inspires the yoiker to make the yoik in a specific way according to the characteristics described in the melody. In other words, there is a reciprocal relationship between performer and receiver in a yoik. The point, however, is that a goal of the yoik is to create contact, either through memories or by a character sketch that takes hold of and describes what is distinctive about the person yoiked. But to be able to do this one has to be in a position to understand the nature of the person concerned. Therefore yoik as an art form is tied both to the surrounding nature–as in the case of Valkeapää's yoik to Sámi-land–and to human nature, the psychological dimension, as in yoik songs that are personal portraits.

Yoik belongs to the genre of oral literature, with clear parallels to storytell-ing and the use of adages, rhymes and jingles. At the same time there is a differ-ence in degree of precision in the rendering of a yoik compared to the telling of a story that one has heard. A yoik is always expected to be presented precisely in the same manner as far as the characterizing musical elements that describe the object are concerned, though there is more freedom as to where one begins and ends a yoik. Different yoikers can emphasize different aspects of the same person, something that will be heard in how one stresses certain passages of the yoik in front of other people. Nevertheless, it must be remembered that a yoik is a portrait, and that the portrait must be recognizable so as not to end up as a caricature or a libelous song.

On the other hand, as far as tales (stories) are concerned, the narrator has more liberty with regard to coloring the narrative and thereby demonstrating her or his own ability as a storyteller, but also as a gesture to and acknowledg-ment of the act of storytelling itself, the performance that is the contextual ar-rangement and adaptation of the story. A competent storyteller can embroider the story and give new digressions that help make it even more exciting or humorous to listen to. The story is more collective in its essence than the yoik, even if both are meant to be inclusive and identity-creating for those who enter into the community that both the yoik and the story establish.

The traditional role of art

The customary role of art in a culture where the collective aspect has been central is marked by the community keeping the culture alive. In such a soci-ety artists do not exist just for themselves, they are representatives of all the people; they are part of the division of labor within the tribe, and also at the same time, precisely through their creative activity, one of the tribe's faces to the outside world. Their traditional role can almost be interpreted as a parallel to having someone else dedicate a yoik to you. By receiving one's own yoik one becomes a distinct part of a collective, at the same time as one maintains, and even strengthens, one's identity and individuality as a person who stands out from the masses. The yoik dedication accentuates the person's distinctive value, but does this because the person has his or her position in the community precisely through getting his or her own yoik (Gaski 2000:204). The artists also have their status thrown into relief by belonging to a community that they have their origin in and are still connected to. Included as artists in this connection are competent handicraft workers, inventors, good yoikers and storytellers. The role of the artist in indigenous societies, however, has changed in step with influences from the outside.

The yoik has always had a special place in Sami consciousness because of its traditional role as identity marker and as the shaman's music in the old religion. Yoik has also served as a way to remember acquaintances and loved ones, and, in more recent years, it has experienced a renaissance as a source of inspiration for modern musicians both in world music and experimental jazz or techno-yoik. The concept "juoigat" (to yoik) is found over the entire Sami area, but the yoik itself has different names in the different Sami dialects or languages.

Even if the yoik is mainly a music form where melody is primary, there has been and still are areas where the text has great significance. The text was important in the epic yoik tradition, but also in the South Sami *vuelie* and the East Sami *levd* tradition, the text is an essential part of the total expression. In the eastern variety of Northern Sami yoik as well, the text has an independent, content-bearing role. With regard to poetry in yoik it is a fact that its subtlety is on the decline today. Yoik poetry has inspired today's generation of Sami poets, and in earlier periods it was our foremost poets' form. Perhaps it is not entirely fair to express it this way, because here, as in so many other connections to our modern Sami way of life, we are experiencing a change of traditions. It would surely be more correct to say that there has arisen a "division of labor" between the poets and the yoikers. On the one hand the new Sami poetry has taken over the creative text portion of the yoik tradition, and has allowed itself to be inspired by yoik poetry's subtle word use and intended double communicative content. In this way, one expresses oneself in a specific and secretive way to the already informed "insider"; in content this differs from the way the "outsider" interprets the message, even though linguistically it is identical. On the other hand, the music side has kept its original character with certain "traditionalists," but changed with other "innovators." The innovators have wanted to be creative in both form and content, not only because of influences from the outside, but also as a new creation from their own point of departure.

Another important dimension of the Sami yoiks is their exclusive and, to some extent, excluding form of communication. Nils-Aslak Valkeapää once expressed it this way: "In a yoik text the intention can sometimes be to tell a story only to the one who knows. For others its content is obscure."[4] The double communication builds on a long tradition in Sami cultural history, going all the way back to the colonization of Sámiland when the yoik was developed into an oppositional medium (Gaski 1993: 120-22). Its object and purpose is that the Sami should understand more than the non-Sami. This does not represent a devaluation of others, but plays on a form of communication where Sami speakers can derive more meaning from what is said or written than those who do not understand the code fully. The idea with this means of communicating is that those "in the know" are presumed to understand the most, while those on the outside are brought far enough into comprehension that they are no longer completely ignorant, yet not entirely "in the know. "

This is interesting methodically and theoretically, and not sufficiently researched, least of all in the case of indigenous peoples' forms of communication, but also with regard to the presentation and interpretation of hidden messages. Often this type of language usage develops in situations where persons or people groups are forced to communicate through coded messages because of repression and fear of reprisals. However in the Sami case, it seems to have had a connection with a latent linguistic creativity that blossomed and developed for historical reasons as well. The artistic usage of language developed as a means to oppose colonization, acculturation and assimilation. In order to find out more about this, one must know the language well, and look at the expressions in both their social and cultural contexts. As stated, this constitutes a technical, methodological challenge that one hopes post-colonialism and indigenous, methodologically-based interpretative scholarship will take hold of and develop. However, this must happen in co-operation with the indigenous peoples themselves, with their own knowledge and models of interpretation and understanding being respected and appreciated as a resource in the methodological work.[5] As far as the Sami are concerned, traditional poetry's subtle use

---

4   Personal communication while collaborating with him on a manuscript that actually was never published, an antecedent to the later collection of art work and poetry, Trekways of the Wind, DAT 1994 (Sámi original Ruoktu Váimmus, DAT 1985).

5   See more about this topic and the different challenges for an "insider"-interpretation in my essay "The Secretive Text," Gaski 2000, especially pages 195-204, where I briefly discuss Arnold Krupat's term ethnocriticism (Krupat 1992). Ethnocriticism is a variant of post-colonial theory and praxis, interested in the meeting place of different texts and cultures, that is open to allowing indigenous peoples' own voices to be heard. In a more recent book, *Red Matters: Native American Studies* (2002), Krupat elaborates on the terminology. He carries it further from ethnocriticism to cosmopolitan comparativism as opposed to a nationalist or indigenist approach to the criticism of Native American literature today. Still this cosmopolitan comparativism is eclectic and cross-cultural in the sense that it takes into account the nationalist and the indigenist views as well, but does not allow only one way of understanding to be the ultimate and decisive interpretation. It is interesting, however, to register how few references there are in the international post-colonial literary study field to people like

of the connotative potential of the language is quite clearly such a challenge, best able to be analyzed by indigenous principles of interpretation.

Modernization and Alienation?

Traditionally, the audience was located within the same frame of reference as the yoiker. The listeners therefore never represented a threat. What is interesting today is what happens to this delineation–inside and outside–when the yoiker and the yoik free themselves from that function in which language and situation, presentation and reception, were indissolubly tied together. For example will the possibilities of understanding yoik poetry's content be reduced or actually lost when the yoik is no longer used only in culturally (closed) internal contexts, but also becomes more public, for instance on CDs, on radio and TV, in electronic media, in concerts, and even as dance music? Will this lead to an alienation from the tradition within which yoik has previously functioned? That would mean a shift in perspective, but would it also imply a change in perspective? Can the original characteristics of the yoik exist or be maintained when the new usage transcends the traditional frame of communication.

In the traditional understanding of yoik ownership it is the person yoiked, the object of the yoik, who owns the yoik. The one who created the yoik and who performs it, in other words, owns nothing other than momentary permission to perform it. But what can be said about a person at a venue with several hundred listeners in the hall? How revealing can one be, for example, about a person's private life? What is the limit to the portrait, the character sketch, or the libelous song? Several older yoikers guard themselves against yoiking close acquaintances in contexts other than among friends. One thus has examples of a number of yoiks being slightly revised and perhaps moderated for use in public settings. Therefore, it is important to remember this point when one is going to discuss and evaluate yoik from the selection found on LP and CD recordings, as well as to listen to what is presented in connection with the Sami Grand Prix during the traditional Easter festival in Guovdageaidnu in Norway.

The Sami yoik is in the process of being professionalized in the form of artistry and acting. We can begin to sense a segmentation and specialization within yoik art in the same way as in the society in general, with experts in all the areas where cultural practices can be turned into work that brings in a steady income[6]. Yoik is becoming a public concern.

Arnold Krupat and others dealing primarily with indigenous peoples' literatures. It should be obvious that the experiences of indigenous peoples are very relevant for post-colonial critique, but again it seems that the stateless indigenous minorities are usually left out, and the focus is mainly on the previous colonial states. I cannot but see this as a parallel to the lack of interest on the international stage in general in addressing seriously the issues of indigenous peoples.

6   This is also a point made by Nils-Aslak Valkeapää in an essay of 1984 ("Ett sätt att lugna renar" *Café Existens* 24: 43-47), referred to in Gaski 2000: 194)

When Mattis Hætta and Sverre Kjellsberg won the Norwegian Grand Prix final in 1980 with the song/yoik "Sámiid eadnan" and were heading for Europe to represent Norway in the final of the Eurovision Song Contest, the well known Norwegian orchestra leader Kjell Karlsen came out and accused the yoik portion of the song of having been plagiarized from a melody that he had arranged early in the 1970s.[7] It is quite clear that the same yoik is the basis for both versions, but what, in any case, is plagiarized from what? Is the version that was first recorded more original than the one that has been yoiked among people for a long time? And, on the other hand, is it right to use an already extant yoik in a musical competition where the demand for originality is central? Is it at all possible to bring originality and copyright into questions having to do with traditional folk art?

Another side of the issue is that suddenly several Sami owners of the yoik that Mattis Hætta performed came forward. From many Sami villages it was maintained that this yoik was really another person's yoik, different from what "Sámiid eadnan" was being presented. Nor is *this* at all unusual with regard to yoik. Fine melodies have been borrowed and dedicated to new persons and occasions, and it is not at all strange that some yoiks are reminiscent of others, just as are certain persons. Actually, the notion of plagiarism is relatively recent in art. The problems of originality entered in earnest with Romanticism. Until then, one could become famous as a great artist by being good at making versions of themes that were familiar earlier. That is also what one does with yoiking. Authors, and other creators of art, are influenced both consciously and unconsciously by each other; they point to the texts of others and of earlier times, they cite and weave in themes from other works without it necessarily being plagiarism. This obviously happens in Sami art, and consequently in yoik tradition too. Perhaps it is just a healthy sign that several owners of a beautiful Sami yoik appeared, as that showed more than anything else that the yoik is alive and has meaning for people.

The genre shift that can follow the modern use of yoik, for example, that "Sámiid eadnan" won a competition and became famous far beyond Sami circles can, in a sense, be a transformation of and a transfer from traditional Sami folk art to modern popular art. If that is the case, then it will have consequences for the creation, reception and evaluation of yoiking in a social as well as an aesthetic connection. The most important thing with respect to the traditional use of yoik is that this genre shift will certainly influence the possibility of mediating the content of a yoik across the close/distant boundary quite generally, and also in an ethnic sense. The text of the yoik will be just as unfamiliar for a Sami from a different area as it is for a non-Sami when the closeness of the relationship between the yoiker and the listener is gone. A Sami-speaking Sami

---

7   The recording in question was Karlsen's "*Lapplandsminner*," the B side of the single "Ante," a yoik used in a TV series with the same name.

will most likely still have cultural advantages for understanding the meaning between the lines.

Sami popular culture and uncomprehending goodwill

The Eurovision Song Contest and Sami Grand Prix represent popular music, and the entries in the European music festival that have had an indigenous character are part of this tradition. However, it is interesting to note that almost no research has been done in this sphere at all. As most often happens in majority cultures, film and popular music have been placed in the category of "pop" culture, but, in the Sami case, even the most serious critics classify the film *Pathfinder* and the music of, for instance, the well-known Sami artist Mari Boine as Sami high culture. It is a valid question to what extent one should even think that there is a Sami high art, or that the distinction between high and popular culture is relevant in the Sami case.

Still, there exists a dividing line between Sami pop culture and more advanced (musical) compositions, but the question is whether the confused and confusing distinction reflects the views critics from the outside have of Sami art and culture. To what degree should one base oneself on professional and methodological analyses, or should one perhaps not distinguish equally sharply on the scale of a minority's forms of cultural expression compared to the larger societies? Does this, in any case, lead to an intentional positive discrimination or should one not be as strict with the dividing lines for Sami culture as for the majority's art? Or is the reason rather the lack of knowledge about Sami culture among those who review Sami art? Is it in the final analysis about affirmative views (positive discrimination), where the non-Sami critics contribute to leveling out the high-grade art by mixing it, for example in the case of yoik, with musical expressions that belong after all to the entertainment industry?

These are important approaches to the problems that one needs to be aware of when evaluating Sami popular culture and Sami art. It is not a positive act towards Sami culture when outside critics with misdirected goodwill blot out real, surviving Sami ways of evaluation, just because these are not given space in the national media. Moreover the Sami language discussion is never thematized because it is not translated or disseminated due to lack of funds for publishing relevant professional and analytical texts in that area. Could it be that the internal Sami criticism is suppressed, or not heard, because it may not be as positive as criticism from without? So, in practice one can end up shutting a minority out, and the majority's intended goodwill can actually become a neo-colonial[8] neglect of and attack against the minority's own knowledge in the field. Therefore, it is important to develop suitable Sami training within these fields,

---

8 As commented on in footnote 6 the coverage of indigenous peoples' literature is quite insufficient even in the majority of *post*-colonial discourse as well.

so that Sami assessments and critiques for these also find expression. This is not because they are necessarily so much "more correct" than the outsiders' understanding, but because they represent their own culture's self-understanding. To the extent that the minority's own understanding never has the opportunity to be publicly presented we will lose an important dimension in interpretive potential. This, indeed, is a matter of granting the indigenous peoples the same right as the majority to apply our own principles of interpretative scholarship as normative for our texts, art work and music.

The emphasis of recent decades on the importance of building up ethno-knowledge and providing room for indigenous peoples' own methods within academia, is simply expressing the idea that indigenous peoples' self-representation would be different from the picture others have created of them. Without "the indigenous voice" being represented, the multitude of voices will be defective, and the world will be deprived of the chance of creating a richer picture of interpretive possibilities and ways to understand existence. Still, one might contend that the very act of expressing Sami canons and values in any other language will be a kind of submission to neo-colonial terms. This seems to be like a vicious circle, but the other option–to use only Sami in speech and writing, without ever translating it–will lead to cultural isolation, and deny the Sami a fair chance of reaching out with our art. Therefore, bi- and multilingualism is very common among the Sami, and for most of us, the use of Sami as the primary language is important, both as a way of countering the assimilationist powers and of gaining the full benefit from the rich potential of our mother tongue.

Cultural fusion

One aspect of this picture is the international dimension that the Sami cultural activity is part of and enters into. The fact that we can see the same cultural developmental features and phenomena among Sami youth as in the rest of the world is confirmation that the Sami no longer live in isolation and without contact with what is happening elsewhere. We Sami are influenced by and, hopefully, we ourselves will manage to influence others. Traditions change, and there is a question mark over what is authentic. The yoik too has surely changed over time; in any case, it is quite likely that there existed more yoik forms at an earlier period compared to those that are dominant today.[9] How does one define tradition, and who determines what is traditional? Ideas are exchanged, adopted and adapted. Conflict can arise between purists and innovators, where

---

9   The Northern Sámi *luohti* yoik is the best known type of yoik today, and the common denominator for yoik in general, especially in the terminology of the Sámi Radio station and in mass media in general. There exist several other types of yoik as well, such as the already mentioned Eastern Sámi *levd* and the Southern Sámi *vuelie*, but I am also quite confident that there must have existed specific genres of the Shamanistic-religious yoiks, and the more epic-poetic historical yoiks that depicted, retold and renewed Sámi history and myths.

the former want to maintain the traditional while the latter see progress and development in breaking with tradition, perhaps even by contributing to the breaking down of tradition. The purists, however, experience loss of traditions where others see exciting new creations, because everything is in the process of change. Thus, it always has been. Modern mythologies are part of shaping us in the same way as our local values are part of setting the terms of how our way of living will have an effect on the society around us.

In order to be able to adapt the tradition or possibly to oppose it, there should be within a culture some respected and authoritative body that holds the recognized responsibility for deciding what is authentic in that culture. This will always be a controversial question, but within indigenous cultures there has existed a respect for *the elders* and for traditions, and it is by no means certain that it would be an advantage to break it down. It is a debate about values within the cultures that these cultures are perhaps dependent on in order to survive. The Sami yoik is a distinctive language, with clear parameters for creation, performance and learning. Like language in general, it is limited in how much one can distort it before it is no longer authentic. In principle it is no better to mix for instance Northern Sami and Maori together, even though both are indigenous languages, than it is to Norwegianize Sami. The question here is whether this is also the case for musical and artistic language, even if the means of expression here are somewhat different.

A certain modernizing of traditions has always been popular, something the example of Nils-Aslak Valkeapää's revitalization of the Sami yoik clearly shows. His "symphonic" yoiks, however, will still be defined as yoik, while much of that which is performed today contains a leveling out of the yoik's strict demands for mastery of the entire spectrum of stresses. Other artists have chosen to present the traditional as illustrative additions to creative melodizing of material that has its origin in the tradition. This is the case with several Sami artists, and the same tendency could also be registered among other indigenous peoples in recent decades, where names such as Yothu Yindi[10] in Australia and Kashtin[11] in Canada have stood out as very well known exponents of ethnically based modern popular music.

The group that performed the Swedish entry in the Eurovision Song Contest 2000 at Globen in Stockholm, in a way represented Sami, Inuit and Native Americans, as well as being a national contribution from Sweden in the Contest. Viewed this way, the group with the Swedish singer Roger Pontare stands for something new in regard to representation that perhaps takes hold of and comments on the tendencies in the present day and age. The national aspect,

---

10 I am thinking of their breakthrough CD, *Tribal Voice*, Hollywood Records, HR-61288-2, 1992.

11 CDs like *Innu,* TriStar Music, WK 57832, 1991, and *akua tuta*, TriStar Music, WK 67203, 1994

namely that those who are performing on stage are supposed to be understood as representatives of the country they are singing for, is toned down in favor of the multinational element where the message in the song is, nevertheless, both old-fashioned and, in some people's eyes, strongly nationalistic. Thus the song is an example of the time it stems from, that is, a conglomeration of contrasts, but with a message meant both to praise beautiful Sámiland and to be a tribute to the long cultural struggle of indigenous peoples for their own rights and self-respect.

Another relevant question in this era of globalization, however, is what is implied when musical elements from different indigenous peoples are fused together into world music. What happens then to the traditional forms of expression? When two different traditions are fused together can one any longer call the new product traditional music? What happens for example when yoik is mixed together with Native American chanting, or when traditional yoik is performed as throat singing inspired by the Tuvan people of Siberia?

In comparison with the rest of society, our Sami cultural expressions are changed and renewed through internal development as well as through influence from the outside. It is not at all a question of preserving a museum culture, rather of developing and renewing a living culture so that one still shows respect for the traditions, but also allows the new forms of expression to experiment freely with their way forward without the constraints of tradition. There is no general constraint that all new Sami art should stick to tradition, because art claims itself to be an autonomous and free institution, but to the degree that the traditions are used one hopes that this still happens in a worthy fashion.

Among the Sami public it is most often interpreted as positive that people want to learn to yoik. This reduces the danger that yoik will die out. Yet it is a double-edged sword because the demands of traditional yoik masters are strict before they accept new yoikers as competent practitioners of the traditional art form. Yoik, in fact, has its own aesthetics and clear demands for mastering definite modes of expression. This is affirmed not least by scores of concepts for different ways of stressing special sequences of the yoik melody, something an experienced yoiker must know (Nielsen 1979: 196)[12]. So when a person who has not grown up with yoik creates his own yoik form that, to an experienced yoiker's ear, does not correspond with the traditional demands, yet that person nevertheless has great success in world music with something he and the media still call yoik, important questions arise: What are the consequences for yoik, and, perhaps just as important, what about the signal this sends out to young people who want to learn to yoik? Does the fact that yoik has gradually become popular contribute to watering down its authenticity? Should a Sami be happy that yoik is becoming popular among non-Sami people, and not worry so much

---

12 Entry 331 a, and corresponding explanations for the specific terms in the dictionary.

that it is simultaneously being vulgarized from the point of view of the tradition, or do the traditionalists have a responsibility to fight for the "genuine" yoik? If they do so fight, how is genuineness to be defined, and by whom?

Regressive nostalgia or utopian idea of equity?

My position, however, is that as with all other music, yoik too can of course be learned. One does not have to be a Sami to know how to yoik, even if non-Sami up to now have very rarely performed yoik in public at concerts and on CDs. There is, however, nothing to prevent it from happening in the near future, even if yoik until now has been mainly a feature of Sami culture, almost a Sami greeting reserved for Sami performers. Thus, one also hears the story of how Nils-Aslak Valkeapää used yoik to prove that he and the Sami delegation really were an indigenous people during the first meeting of the World Council of Indigenous Peoples in Port Alberni, Canada in 1975. Several of the indigenous representatives from other places in the world were, in fact, skeptical about the Sami because of their white skin color;[13] but when Valkeapää performed a yoik for the assembly the skepticism was blown away and the Sami were accepted on a par with the others. Since that time the Sami have continued to be active participants in the international indigenous movement.

Indigenous cultures meet this sort of challenge all the time–not least when a traditional art form becomes popular among larger population groups. The question is always raised whether the new and modernized version is only a commercialized appropriation of traditional material. There is also a cultural-political aspect to this having to do with the historical dimension of preserving an authentic tradition or letting it all be watered down into a blend of common indigeneity. For example, what should one call the music of a group that consists of a Sami yoiker, a Norwegian who plays an Australian aborigine instrument, the didgeridoo, and a fiddler from Norway who mixes in elements of Norwegian folk music? Are the yoik, and the yoiker, strong enough to let the yoik dominate over the instruments, or will the yoik have to surrender to another concept of music? Or, for that matter, how should one discuss the performance when Roger Pontare, dressed in a prairie Indian outfit at the Eurovision Song Contest, accompanied by a Norwegian-Sami fellow performer in Sami garb on the stage, sings a rock song with sound from the 1980s?

I do not ask these questions in order to be nostalgic or reactionary, or to oppose musical experimentation and new creation, but, on the contrary, to point out that a consciousness is demanded on the part of the musicians, reviewers and researchers about what is being done. There should also be a respect for the tradition such that one clearly distinguishes between it and new creation.

---

13 This also provides some of the background for my choice of the title for my essay in *American Indian Culture and Research Journal*, "The Sámi People: The 'White Indians' of Scandinavia."

Experimentation with traditional music is new creation too, regardless of how big a hit it is with the public. Popularity is no guarantee of authenticity or faithfulness to tradition. Let it be clear, however, that there is no ban on developing new music. In fact a lot of very exciting new music is created in the spirit of hybridism, but one must be aware of what one is doing We must all show respect for tradition by allowing it to be traditional, and should call the truly new by a new name. Why in the world must almost all Sami music be associated with yoik when only a fraction of it actually has anything to do with traditional yoik? However, it must be clearly understood that there are Sami yoikers who know what they are doing, who experiment because they want to and who are knowledgeable both about the yoik's essence and about contemporary musical genres. They collaborate with musicians who appreciate the value of tradition, but who at the same time have the desire to create something new which stands on its own and points to the future. These people still form a minority of today's Sami related music.

A distant alarm bell is ringing that raises a worrying question: when at some time in the future yoik can be heard only as an element in a common indigenous sound, is yoik then dead as yoik? And was it really progress when hybrid forms were so praised that over time they grew together to become a conglomeration of politically correct cosmopolitan (indigenous) expressions? Or is the yoik actually so strong that it will prevail over all kinds of pressure from outside in the same way that it survived attacks from missionaries and assimilationists?

"A note in the embrace of eternity" was once the name of a play at the Sami theater Beaivváš in Guovdageaidnu, Norway. The title was only meant to be poetic for a music and dance presentation, but looking back now, it can perhaps be interpreted as a prescient and prophetic title about what can happen to yoik: Will there be only a note, an opening note, left of the traditional music of the Sami? Will yoik be transformed into a type of world music with no more than indigenous Sami roots? The genuine traditional yoik will probably continue for a while yet, but my guess is that we will experience a lot of fusion and experimentation, in which different indigenous components in the music and in other types of art will be blended into new forms and moulds, and over time drift into the common property of the global as the indigenous peoples' contribution to the global culture of hybridism. At the same time, there will be an acknowledgement and alienation, an acceptance and a redefinition, a gain and a loss–the way development in most areas of human activity will one day be.

References

Gaski, Harald. 1993. "The Sami People: The 'White Indians' of Scandinavia. *American Indian Culture and Research Journal* 17 (1): 115-128. UCLA. Los Angeles.

Gaski, Harald. 2000. "The Secretive Text." In: Pentikäinen, Juha et al. *Sami Folkloristics*. Nordic Network of Folklore: 191-214. Turku.

Gaski, Harald. 2004. "When the Thieves Became Masters in the Land of the Shamans." In: *Nordlit*. No. 15, Summer 2004: 35-45. University of Tromsø. Also available on web-site: http://uit. no/getfile.php?SiteId=22&PageId=977&FileId=184

Krupat, Arnold. 1992. *Ethnocriticism. Ethnography, History, Literature*. University of California Press. Berkeley.

Krupat, Arnold. 1996. *The Turn to the Native*. University of Nebraska Press. Lincoln.

Krupat, Arnold. 2002. *Red Matters: Native American Studies*. University of Pennsylvania Press. Philadelphia.

Nielsen, Konrad. 1979. *Lappisk (Sámisk) ordbok / Lapp Dictionary*. 2nd impression. Oslo.

Turi, Johan. 1910/1997. Songs of the Sami. In: Gaski, Harald (ed.)1996/7. *In the Shadow of the Midnight Sun: Contemporary Sami Prose and Poetry*. Davvi Girji. Karasjok. Originally published in Sami and Danish edition in 1910, *Muittalus Sámid birra*. Græbes bogtrykkeri, København. Also available in English translation by E. Gee Nash, *Turi's Book of Lappland*, London: Jonathan Cape, 1931.

Valkeapää, Nils-Aslak. 1984. "Ett sätt att lugna renar" *Café Existens* No. 24: 43-47. Göteborg, Sweden.

CDs:

Valkeapää, Nils-Aslak 1992. *Sápmi lottážan*, Reproduction. AAD. DATCD-13/1

Valkeapää, Nils-Aslak 1988 *Beaivi áhčážan*, DAT CD-4

Valkeapää, Nils-Aslak 1990 *Eanan, eallima eadni*, DAT CD-5

Valkeapää, Nils-Aslak 1994 *Goase dušše*, DATCD-15

Yothu Yindi. 1992. *Tribal Voice*, Hollywood Records, HR-61288-2

Kashtin. 1991. *Innu*, TriStar Music, WK 57832

Kashtin. 1994. *akua tuta*, TriStar Music, WK 67203

CHAPTER 19

Nationalism, Indigenism, Cosmopolitanism: Three Critical Perspectives on Native American Literatures[1]

ARNOLD KRUPAT

Criticism of Native American literatures in the US today procedes from one or another of the critical positions I call nationalist, indigenist, and cosmopolitan. The nationalist and indigenist positions in some regards overlap, and both nationalists and indigenists frequently tend to see themselves as in opposition to the cosmopolitans. In what follows, I hope to show that all three positions are inevitably interlinked; each can achieve its full coherence and effectiveness only in relation to the others. All three positions may be enlisted for the project of an anticolonial criticism–I will speak about post-colonialism and Native American literature a bit later–as all three may also operate to reproduce colonial dominance in the cultural realm under other names. Nationalists, indigenists, and cosmopolitans also have differences regarding which critical methods are most appropriate to Native literatures, and differences as well as to the most appropriate pedagogical and anthological locations for Native literatures, that is, in which academic departments or institutes Native literatures might most appropriately be taught, and in which sorts of anthologies they might most appropriately belong. There is, as yet, no consensus on these matters in the US today.

Before going further, I should point out that in the US, the terms I have given for *critical* positions also serve as terms for what might be called *identity* positions for Native people. Thus, regardless of a critic's *perspective* on Native American literatures, her *critical* identification, there is also the question: How might she identify as an Indian *person*? Blood quantum as it is called, is an important concern for almost all the tribes. That is, can you trace your descent to two Indian parents? Two Indian grandparents? Two Indian great-grandparents? For some tribal nations–and tribe and nation are synonymous in the US, as they

---

1   This chapter uses material more fully developed in the first chapter of my book, *Red Matters*. It contains, however, a number of reflections on possible relations between the Native American materials I know fairly well and Sami materials in regard to which I am only a beginner, as these have been introduced especially for this occasion. This chapter was a paper I offered as a talk at an international conference honoring the birthday of Johan Turi, and although I have edited it for publication, I have not altered its oral performative nature.

decidedly are not, for example, in Africa–government enrollment records may serve to imply "Indian blood": if you wish to be a citizen of the Mashantucket Pequot Nation of the state of Connecticut, for example–and citizens of the Mashantucket Pequot Nation are entitled to share in the benefits of the millions and millions of dollars that their Foxwoods Casino generates weekly–you must trace your descent to persons on the government rolls in 1910. In other cases, it may be the rolls for 1887 or 1924. For all that these criteria derive from the history of American colonialism, Indian nationalists nonetheless insist upon documentation of one's membership in a particular tribe or nation.[2]

Differently from Indian nationalists, Indian indigenists, assuming biological descent from Indians regardless of any documentation, identify as Indians on the basis of a claim to what is often termed TEK, Traditional Ecological Knowledge, with the much more substantial claim of an alternative epistemological relation to the world than that of the dominant Euro-American society.[3] It is the way in which they know and relate to the world, and the values derived from that knowledge and that relation, that foremost makes indigenists Indians.

Cosmopolitan Indian persons, once more with some assumption of biological descent regardless of its documentation, base their Indian identity in some important measure on a felt connection to other indigenous persons the world over, as well as to their own people or nations. Cosmopolitan Indian identities, are, to borrow from the Anishinaabe–Chippewa, Ojibwe–writer, Gerald Vizenor, more nearly tribal than national. Here, Vizenor would indeed disrupt the usual synonymy I have mentioned between these two terms, tribe and nation. American Indians–and Vizenor has recently taken to writing "*indians*" in italics and with a lower-case "i"–are Indians not because of blood quanta or enrollment cards, not even necessarily because of alternative knowledges, but, rather, because of a commitment they share with indigenous people everywhere to what Vizenor has called the tribal values of *continuance* and *survivance.*

---

2 I should also note that there is no consensus as to the appropriate way to refer to Native people. Many dislike the misnomer "Indian," although the prolific and prominent young Spokane/Coeur d'Alene writer, Sherman Alexie, insists that Indians is what Native people are and should be called. Alexie mocks those who call themselves Native Americans. One can also refer to indigenous people--although practice in the US does not include, as it does in Canada, terms such as First Nations or First Peoples. The Anishinaabe (Ojibwe) writer, Gerald Vizenor, has referred to Native American Indians, as have others, and, as we will note, Vizenor has lately taken to writing of *indians*.

3 The dominant Euro-American view can be generalized as "modern," with reference to a post-Enlightenment commitment (ostensibly, at least) to rationality and a rationalized (e.g., clock-time and rule-governed) life-world. Indigenous peoples' views might by way of contrast be called pre-modern but such an appellation already labels them backward. Perhaps the best contrast (not an opposition) to the modern is the "traditional." But here, too, there is no consensus in regard to terminologies.

Continuance and survivance, the latter, one of this writer's many neologisms, propose themselves as tribal alternatives to what Vizenor sees as European and Euro-American values of *progress* and *domination*. I watched a video of *The Pathfinder* once more before leaving for Sweden (I also re-read Tom DuBois' fine essay on it), and it certainly seemed to me that Nils Gaup's film could be described in Vizenor's terms: the film is about many things, to be sure, but it is very much about continuance and survivance: there will always be a pathfinder. I think this sort of narrative thematics is implied in Turi's work as well.

The commitment to continuance and survivance that cosmopolitan Indians believe they share with indigenous peoples everywhere includes a commitment to a more or less common history of dispossesion and displacement by invader-settlers from Europe, and as well to the common history they foresee of resurgence and renewal. Regardless of what some nationalists and indigenists may think of them–that their cosmopolitan commitments threaten to undermine national sovereignty; that their concern for the global and the historical threaten to undermine concern for the local and spatial–cosmopolitan Indians also feel a particularly strong solidarity with other Indian peoples in the US. Philip Deloria has recently noted the manner in which the late Louis Owens paints "a complex portrait of a mixed-blood identity that can remain every bit as fiercely loyal to Indian legal and political struggle" (Deloria 2003: 673) as the loyalties of those who identify exclusively as Lakota or Creek nationalists.

In the same way, the poet, Ralph Salisbury, whom some of you may know (he has worked with Harald Gaski and Lars Nordstrom on translating Nils-Aslak Valkeapää's *Trekways of the Wind*), identifies passionately as a Cherokee person, also "fiercely loyal to Indian legal and political struggle," and yet intensely interested in Sami people, and welcoming to anyone who shares his tribal values. In a prefatory note to *Trekways*, Salisbury writes, "I am one of many writers of Native American descent who feel a commitment to brotherhood and sisterhood with native populations around the world....Certainly I feel close to Nils-Aslak Valkeapaa's poetry, and it is clear from his poems about Native Americans that he feels himself a brother to my Native American people." (n.p.)

To go no further with this matter of identity positions, let me say what may already be obvious, that it is likely but not at all necessary that the critical positions of Native scholars will coincide with their identity positions. As for the critical positions of non-Native scholars like myself, these are also likely to be tied to some aspect of our perceived identities which identities may or may not closely parallel those of nationalist, indigenist, or cosmopolitan Indians.[4]

---

4   I have published an account of the intersections and divergences of my own personal/historical and critical identities in "A Nice Jewish Boy Among the Indians."

In the United States, the nationalist finds a basis for her critical position by a translation into the cultural realm of the legal and political meanings of the term sovereignty. As Russell Means and Ward Churchill (1995) have written,

> Within the understandings of International Law, it is the right of *all* sovereign nations and sovereign peoples to enter into treaty relationships with other sovereign nations and peoples. Conversely, *only* sovereign nations and peoples are entitled to enter into such relationships. (3)

Thus Native "nations and peoples" were and are sovereigns inasmuch as, according to Pauline Turner Strong and Barrik van Winkle (1993), in North America,

> between 1607 and 1775 the [British] Crown and the various colonies entered into at least 185 treaties with Indian peoples..., treating them as sovereign political entities, if only to limit their sovereignty. (11)

Once the United States achieved its own independent existence as a "sovereign political entity," for almost one hundred years, from 1776 until 1871 (when Congress ended the treaty-making practice), it continued to enter into nation-to-nation treaties with the tribes. Thus, for example, the Cherokees of Georgia, in opposing the Indian Removal Act of 1830–the Act sought to provide the president with authority to make treaties with the eastern Indians for their removal to lands west of the Mississippi River–noted, in a "Memorial" to Congress, that

> the power of self-government abided in the Cherokee nation at the discovery of America...; that the Indians were found here by the white man, in the enjoyment of plenty and peace, and all the rights of soil and domain, inherited from their ancestors from time immemorial (Krupat 1992: 165-166).

Thus, they continued,

> It remains to be proved, under a view of all these circumstances, and the knowledge we have of history, how our right to self-government was affected and destroyed.(Krupat 1992: 166).

This most cogent argument did not, however, prevent the passage of the Indian Removal Act, which finally had the consequence of sending the eastern Cherokees, in 1838, on what has become known as the infamous "Trail of Tears," their forced emigration to Indian Territory.

The nationalist's critical position, as I have said, is constituted by an attempt to extend the legal and political meanings of sovereignty to the realm of culture, to Native American literary expression. To date, it seems to me that this project has had its most fruitful results with traditional oral narrative. Because questions about sovereignty, as the late Elaine Jahner noted in a recent article, are "questions about the boundaries of communities," it has been possible to demonstrate the ways in which specific communities use the transmission and reception of particular narratives as a way of defining their distinctive, bounded identity.[5]   Examining Lakota–Sioux–"Stone Boy" narratives, Jahner shows how Lakota people assert their "communal identity" (Jahner 1999: 6) by the transmission and reception of these stories. The historical process of selecting certain stories and story-versions rather than others over the years is, in Jahner's words, itself "an exercise in sovereignty," (7) one that can be taken as consistent with the dictionary meaning of the word, i.e., the right to independence and self-governance as a nation or people. To borrow a phrase from the anthropologist, Julie Cruikshank (1998: 155), Native communities "*negotiate with narrative*" to "establish[...] cultural identity," (my emphasis) an identity which in turn supports a particular sense of distinctiveness connected to a particular geoscape, and implies autonomy and a full capacity for self-governance, or, indeed, sovereignty.

This account of the relationship between narrative culture and political integrity may well be familiar to students of Sami literature. Just before the middle of the nineteenth century, Lars Levi Laestadius wrote that Lapp "folk tale resources can be seen to be that much richer amongst a people where the folk tale tradition is the same as the history of the nation." (in Pentakainen 61) Does the ascription of an identity between the "folk tale tradition" and "the history of the nation" arise from an implicit sense that apart from the "folk tale tradition" there just is not much of any "history of the nation?" I think that may be exactly what is meant by the remark of Laestadius' contemporary, M.A. Castren, who wrote that, "Ethnography could be regarded as a part of cultural history; but not all nations possess a history in the higher sense; instead their history consists of ethnography" (Pentikäinen 2000: 62). History "in the higher sense," I imagine, is political history: wars, conquests, perhaps attempts at such "high" things as genocide and ethnocide. In any case, the point to emphasize is that there are important ways in which "the folk tale tradition *is* the same as the history of the nation," as Laestadius put it (my emphasis); and that history *can* most certainly consist of ethnography, in the terms of Castren. In the US, and I should add, in Canada, the courts have of late been somewhat willing to allow oral testimony in the form of stories to be entered into evidence, permitting them a certain equivalence, as it were, with the "high" historical subjects chronicled in writing.

5   I have published an introduction to Jahner's essay in Elliott and Stokes, q.v.

As for critical methods, nationalists are wary of "foreign" perspectives, concerned that borrowings from a variety of marxist, psychoanalytic, or feminist approaches, for example, might obscure the local meanings and functions of traditional oral performances–as well as later written work. Thus, Craig Womack (1999: 76), a Creek nationalist critic, reasonably suggests that any particular corpus of Native oral and written materials "must surely provide models for interpretation and principles of literary esthetics," and that criticism should therefore be text- or performance-specific. And, indeed, Womack's own studies of Creek literature have importantly begun to indicate just what those "models" and "principles" might be. Inasmuch as these nationalist commitments seem to me to be based upon cultural and epistemological premises, I will conflate them with indigenist approaches to Native literature, which I will take up in just a moment.

Nationalists are extremely wary of the inclusion of Indian literatures in anthologies of *American* literature. Such inclusions, usually made in the name of multiculturalism, and/or diversity, can easily become, in Philip Deloria's terms, "paternal and incorporative" (Deloria 2003: 679). Womack has firmly insisted on the difference between "*our* canon," and "*their* canon." "I see them," he writes, "as two separate canons" (Womack 1999: 7). I think this distinction has more rhetorical force than descriptive accuracy, given the five hundred years of contact between "our" canon and "their" canon, the standard–but surely of late somewhat fluid–Euro-American canon. Nationalists would prefer Native American texts to appear in anthologies of Creek literature, Lakota literature, pueblo literature, and the like.[6]

So far as institutional locations for pedagogy are concerned, nationalists are, again, wary of the appearance of Native American literature classes in English or American Studies departments, for just the same reasons they are wary of Indian literatures in American literature anthologies. They would prefer to see these courses taught in Native Studies or American Indian Studies departments at some of the larger universities, and some think it would be best if such courses were "separately" taught only in tribal colleges where instruction would procede in a manner consistent with each institution's understanding of the Lakota or Navajo "way" or worldview, an ostensibly strict adherence to a particular *national* hermeneutics, whatever that might look like.

* * *

---

6   But, to say what must be obvious, the *anthology* has no Creek or Lakota or Mohawk parallel. And, while we may soon hope for bi-lingual anthologies, and, surely in time, for exclusively Native language anthologies with a significantly wide readership, there is no way to conceive of these things *separately*, as standing altogether apart from European influence. Womack is a powerful thinker but the insistence on ours and theirs, even as heuristic devices is, to my mind, counter-productive.

From an indigenist perspective, it is not the nation, but the "earth" that is the source of the values on which a critical perspective must be based. Thus, in Linda Hogan's novel, *Power* (1998: 229), Omishto, the narrator, remembers a time when "The whole earth loved the human people." *Power* concludes with Omishto dancing, while "someone sings the song that says the world will go on living." (235) The "world," here, is obviously not the world of nations and nationalisms; rather, it is the animate and sentient earth. Indigenists look to a particular relation to the earth as underlying a worldview–an epistemology–that can be called traditional or tribal. It is this worldview that determines one's perspective on literature as on all else, often regardless of national allegiances (e.g., whether one is or is not a documented "citizen" of a particular Native nation).

Winona Stevenson, a Canadian Cree woman, has quoted her mother as saying to her, "You are of this land, you are Indigenous, and that's what makes you different from everybody else" (Stevenson 1998: 37) – from "ethnic" persons or other Canadians, that is to say. Ward Churchill explains his indigenism as founded

> upon the traditions–the bodies of knowledge and corresponding codes of values–evolved over many thousands of years by native peoples the world over (Churchill 1993: 403).

The late Louis Owens wrote that today,

> in spite of the fact that Indian authors write from very diverse tribal and cultural backgrounds, there *is* to a remarkable degree a shared consciousness and identifiable worldview reflected in novels by American Indian authors... (20 my emphasis)

And José Barreiro affirms that "the principles that guide Native cultures bear a remarkable resemblance to one another" (Whitt 1994: 225). These "principles," "bodies of knowledge," and "codes of value," this "shared consciousness" and "world-view," as I have noted, are said to derive from the special relationship to the land that indigenous peoples everywhere are presumed to share–again, regardless of their sovereignty or any political relation to the dominant settler states that surround them.

In these regards, we may consider another quotation from Stevenson that is typical of indigenist discourse. She writes that indigenous people are not only attached to the earth or the land generally, but that they

> are spiritually attached to [a particular] place...we never left the bones of our ancestors behind. Every hill, mountain, river, coulee, and forest has ancient stories that tell us how we are related to it and to each other (Stevenson 1998: 42).

The latter part of Stevenson's statement is no doubt accurate. Meanwhile, the first part of her statement can only be true, in point of fact, for longtime residents of northeast Africa. Within historical memory, Stevenson's people may well claim "never" to have "left the bones of [their] ancestors behind." The archeological and genetic record, however, indicates that almost everyone has come from somewhere else (indeed, from northeast Africa). Thus the question–a highly political question–arises of just how long it takes to *become* indigenous. In Hawa'i, for example, some claim indigenousness after seven generations of residence, while others would require a hundred and fifty generations of residence as necessary for indigenousness. In the southwestern United States, the Hopi people claim indigenousness based upon settlement dating back over a hundred generations. But Navajo people, in place for perhaps thirty generations can hardly imagine themselves as anything but indigenous to the landscape they know so well, and to which they are "spiritually attached." These matters, to say the obvious, are complex–particularly when we consider, as Julie Cruikshank (1998: 53) has noted, that land ownership "claims made by adjacent First Nations inevitably overlap, forcing communities into competition with one another." This is to say that the "ancient stories" a mountain, river, or hill may tell one Native narrating community may not be exactly the same stories it tells another.

Indigenist geocentric knowledge explicitly seeks to contest the knowledge of European modernity. Insofar as the latter is the knowledge which undergirds colonialism, the former wishes to found a different social order. In order to do this, however, the indigenist is sure to discover that she needs the nationalist because contemporary political realities in the US and doubtless elsewhere still make it necessary to combat colonialism in terms of the nation. And the indigenist will also find herself in need of the cosmopolitan to translate between the two language/knowledges–let us call them geocentric and Euro-modern–and to translate in such a way as to cause the language of the dominant culture to be changed by its encounter with an Other language, what I have elsewhere called anti-imperial translation. I will take this up further in just a moment.

In regard to critical methods, indigenists are wary of European approaches to Native verbal expression which might reductively accomodate and assimilate Native expression to the various agendas of Western criticism, performing a second erasure of Native agency, in Julie Cruikshank's words, "first by colonial forces, then by poscolonial analyses," that ignore the local meanings and functions of these performances and texts (Cruikshank 1998: 139). There are surely powerful ethical and political reasons urging resistance to any criticism that treats the literary production of indigenous peoples as no more than grist for the mill of Euro-American academic interests. But this resistance need not, indeed, in practical fact it *can*not, take the position of rejecting out of hand any idea that cannot be shown to have a homegrown pedigree.

There have been of late a number of attempts to consider such matters as how and to what degree language use in the English texts of some Native writers might parallel usage in tribal languages–this, of course, for writers who speak or know a tribal language--or how imagery and description in a given text–its references to colors, numbers, plants, animals–might reflect the specifics of one or another traditional culture. Similarly, texts by Native writers have begun to be examined to see whether and how their constructions of the self or person, the family or community, or, indeed, the meaning and function of gift-giving and exchange might derive in significant measure from traditional, indigenous understandings of these matters.

All this is to the good. But we should not lose sight of the fact that even indigenist criticism of indigenous literature must always-already be what I have elsewhere called *ethnocriticism*, a meeting or conjuncture, if you will, of the traditional and modern or postmodern; of the local and the European or global. When we look, for example, at Tom DuBois' (1996) fine essay, "Native Hermeneutics: Traditional Means of Interpreting Lyric Songs in Northern Europe," we should not be surprised to find on its first page reference to Dell Hymes and Dennis Tedlock and Richard Bauman, along with John Miles Foley and Alan Dundes, among many other non-Native critics. My point is not in the least to call DuBois' commitment to outlining a "Native Hermeneutics" into question, quite the opposite. Rather, it is only to say that if you are doing *criticism*, even if you are critically offering a "Native Hermeneutics," you are inevitably engaged in ethnocriticism. One further example: Harald Gaski, in an important study of the *yoik* published in 2000, shrewdly and poignantly writes of positioning himself between certain "established methods of criticism and the rather esoteric exposition of each specific culture" (Gaski 2000: 195) – although for him Sami culture, lived and experienced as well as studied, is not so very esoteric. Gaski studies the yoik as DuBois or I could not, as an insider. But even as he practices a form of indigenist criticism, he acknowledges that his practice is what he wittily calls a "Samified ethnocriticism"–a phrase that is, in fact, a tautology, in that a "Sami critic"–like a Lakota or a Creek critic–by her cultural identification on the one hand, and her engagement in critical practice, on the other, is inevitably an ethnocritic.

Indigenous critics whose work is based upon bodies of knowledge that contest the knowledge sustaining the colonial order may well find cosmopolitan critics and their ethnocritical comparativism useful for translating between these different bodies of knowledge. In the same way, indigenist critics will also find useful an engagement with nationalist critics for the simple reason that presently and for the immediately foreseeable future, culture and politics are contested on the specific terrain of the nation–whose demise, often proclaimed of late, nonetheless seems premature. I will return to this point later.

Indigenists would probably disperse Native literary expression among anthologies and pedagogical locations. Fourth and Fifth world anthologies containing the literatures of indigenous persons around the globe, something like the volume called *The Indigenous Voice*, would appear more suitable than, again, standard anthologies of American literature. While Native Studies programs could surely present the alternative knowledge the indigenist finds in Indian literature, courses throughout the curriculum with titles such as–and I have found these titles in a variety of college and university offerings in the US–"Epistemological Pluralism," Nonanthropocentrism," or, indeed, "Environmental Ethics," might also be acceptable–as would a variety of courses oriented toward what is the developing field of ecocriticism.

* * *

Just as Winona Stevenson's mother encouraged her to "remember that you are of this land," so did his father, Kwame Anthony Appiah writes, urge his children to "'Remember that you are citizens of the world,'" (1992: 91) a cosmopolitan perspective. The "world" invoked by contemporary cosmopolitans has a long history going back to strands of the Classical tradition as these are revived in the Renaissance and substantially developed in Enlightenment thought, although, as I will note in just a moment, there most certainly were and are non-European cosmopolitans.

Anthony Appiah and his father, for example, developed their particular understanding of "the world" not only by reading books about the classical, renaissance, and enlightenment periods of Europe, but also by experiencing the traditions of their own part of the world, Asante territory in Ghana. And here I wish to the existence of parallel cosmopolitanisms, the development elsewhere than in Europe and in other times than the European Enlightenment of concepts like those of worldliness, universality, and internationalism. I am thinking, for example, of such things as Amitav Ghosh's wonderful book, *In An Antique Land* (1994), which tells of commercial relationships, friendships, and cultural exchanges among South Asians and Egyptians, Jews and North Africans, among others involved in the Indian Ocean trade from the twelfth to the early sixteenth century–at which time, the Portuguese arrived, and, as Ghosh writes, "declared a proprietorial right over the Indian Ocean: since none of the peoples who lived around it had thought to claim ownership of it before their arrival" (Ghosh 1994: 288).

I am thinking as well of Barry O'Connell's sense "that indigenous peoples in North America might very likely have developed their own forms of the cosmopolitan." O'Connell refers to the "extensive trading networks…that connected many different [indigenous] cultures not only within geographic regions but across vast distances…Crossing cultural lines had to have happened," he continues, "and even though the number of 'cosmopolitans' may have been small, they surely existed as mediators, traders, translators, etc." (personal communication, 4/4/01) I suspect many of you can provide parallel examples in the north. Surely Turi's work was impelled by the desire to tell the *world* about Sami experience.

Cosmopolitan critical perspectives on Native American literatures study them with an eye to other minority or subaltern literatures elsewhere in the late-colonial or post-colonial world; cosmopolitan criticism is always in some degree comparative. Cosmopolitan comparitivism is, to my mind, only another version of ethnocriticism. In regard to traditional oral performances, for example, the cosmopolitan critic, like the rigorous nationalist, will insist upon the necessity to develop competence in the particular language in which what we have as a text in English was orally performed, and in the cultural practices that shaped that performance. The cosmopolitan critic, thus, would not dispute Craig Womack's observation that Creek literature derives from a "geographically specific Creek landscape and the language and stories that are born out of that landscape" (Womack 1999: 20). But the cosmopolitan critic might also want to understand things about Creek (or Apache or Hopi) literature that could only be answered by *informed comparison* to other texts or traditional performances–those of tribal neighbors, or of tribal peoples in a variety of landscapes. For the earliest written Native American literature, the cosmopolitan critic will certainly try to set the text on its "own ground," while recognizing other relevant texts that are similarly and differently grounded. Here, I will take just a few moments say something about postcolonialism and Native American literature.

The first thing to be said is that if some contemporary Native American literature shares certain traits with the postcolonial literatures of the world, Native American peoples do not share a postcolonial status in the world. Thomas Biolsi and Larry Zimmerman (1997: 4) have suggested that the conditions under which Indian peoples live today are those of the "late imperial," and these conditions are, quite simply, appalling. Indians experience twelve times the US national rate of malnutrition, nine times the rate of alcoholism, and seven times the rate of infant mortality. As of the 1990s, the last years for which I have statistics, the life expectancy of a reservation-based male was just over forty-four years, with reservation-based women enjoying, on average, a life-expectancy just under forty-seven years. Teen-age suicides among Indians are the highest in the country; so, too, is unemployment and poverty. Were we to examine the statistics on diabetes, domestic abuse, fetal alcohol syndrome, and on and on, the picture would only get dimmer.

This is why in the forthcoming *Columbia History of Native American Literature Since 1945*, Michael Elliott and I, in the section on Native American fiction, have pointed out that the date–chosen, of course, to indicate post-World War II literature–is meaningful for Native American literature only if it is taken as marking an early point in the resistance to colonialism around the world and possibly to resistance to late imperialism in the United States. Thus, we have tried to read the novelists of the period 1945 to the present–more familiar ones like N. Scott Momaday, Leslie Marmon Silko, Gerald Vizenor, and the late James Welch, along with some younger writers–in the context of a resistance literature.

But of course, Momaday and the others I have mentioned did not actually publish in the 1940s or 1950s, and I suspect the question of *periodization*, the degree to which the usual temporal categories of the dominant culture do or do not mark important dates for subaltern or minority literatures might be as important here in the north as it is in the States. Anthologies in the US often are divided into periods like 1620-1776 or thereabouts, from the Pilgrim invasion of what is now Massachusetts to the thirteen American colonies' revolt against English domination. Or we go from 1865 to 1914, these literary dates determined by that wonderful history "in the higher sense" that gave us the Civil War (1861-5) and World War I (1914-18). But these simply are not meaningful dates for Native American history *or* literature. I'm not sure to what extent anthologies of Norwegian or Swedish or Finnish literature include Sami literature, but, if they do, I would guess that the dates most important to those national literatures are not the dates most important to Sami literary expression, from Turi's remarkable work forward.

In literary and cultural studies, particularly those which are influenced by cosmopolitanism, postcolonialism has often also meant something like post-nationalism. The anthropologist, Arjun Appadurai (1996), for example, has elaborated the ways in which "media and migration," have created communities which do indeed feel themselves to be integral communities without any particular loyalty to the nation states they have willingly or unwillingly departed. Richard Falk (1996: 57) has stressed the ways in which "regional and global market forces" operate as "a structural and defining attribute of the current phase of international history," so that to "project a visionary cosmopolitanism as an alternative to nationalist patriotism without addressing the subversive challenge of the market-driven globalism [of] transnational corporations and banks...is to risk indulging a contemporary form of fuzzy innocence." Falk and others speculate interestingly on the ways in which non-fuzzy cosmopolitanisms and broad-minded nationalisms might co-exist and support one another.

There is, as I noted much earlier, some danger that these cosmopolitan perspectives, for all their importance, do tend in some degree to erode the status of the nation at exactly the moment when Native American peoples rely on the concept and construct of the nation as a matter of rights and entitlements– when, as I have said earlier, the foremost contestation of colonialism occurs on the terrain of the nation. For Native nations, the timing of cosmopolitan commitments, then, are suspect or at best awkward–as, for example, the timing was awkward when post-structuralism attacked the primacy of the voice at very much the moment when women and minorities everywhere, having long been silenced, claimed the right for their *voices* to be heard. So, too, did poststructuralism deconstruct the notion of a coherent, unitary "self," at exactly the moment when women and minorities everywhere, having been treated as Others and/or objects, began to insist on their human subjectivities, expressing themselves as *selves*. I do not in the least mean to demonize post-structuralism, something it is all-too-easy to do in our current post-theoretical moment. I wish only to call your attention to the fact that current attempts to deny the importance of the state and to demonstrate the constraints on nationalism–constraints that are indeed very real–are occurring at a time when Native American nations depend importantly on their own sustained sense of sovereign nationhood. No responsible cosmopolitan critic can procede without powerful awareness of these facts.

Critics both Native and non-Native who work from the cosmopolitan perspective can, like the nationalists, fully acknowledge the importance of the issue of sovereignty in the political struggle of colonized peoples all over the world and at home, and, like the indigenists, take traditional, place-specific values and principles with the utmost seriousness. The cosmopolitan critic knows that a commitment to sovereignty, the home place, and the oral tradition are "roots" that every Native American writer seems to have carried wherever he or she may have gone–or, indeed, wherever these writers have chosen to remain.

Cosmopolitans wish to see Native American literatures not paternalistically appropriated by but *included* in anthologies of American literature. The degree to which this is possible–inclusion without appropriation–remains to be seen. Cosmopolitans would also site Native literatures in resistance anthologies–or, as I have said, treat them in relation to anti-colonial resistance in any collection or survey of these materials. I have a sense, for example, that an interesting comparative study could be done of the boarding school experiences of Sami and Native American persons, in that both Sami and Native Americans were subjected to efforts at ethnocide, what the historian David Adams (1995) has termed an "education for extinction." For all of that, I do want to note the legitimate concern of nationalists and indigenists that such comparativism might obscure the very particular situation of different colonized peoples around the world. They are wary–with good reason–of any attempt at the universalizing of resistance.

Cosmopolitans of every sort can agree with indigenists on the importance of reading and teaching Native American texts that powerfully present non-Western worldviews. Cosmopolitans are very much interested in exploring how "seeing with the Native eye"–a Native hermeneutics in some measure–can question Western modes of vision and, however modestly, produce shifts in Western epistemology and ethics. Cosmopolitan comparativism, as I have said, is another name for ethnocriticism, a practice at points of cultural contact that recognizes differences in power as well as culture. Cosmopolitan comparativism as an ethnocriticism seeks to achieve the sorts of anti-imperial translations that would avoid the wholesale submission of the Native voice to that of the Western hegemonic voice. Translations of this sort, so far as they are possible–no fullscale optimism is warranted–would achieve a mediation between languages. To put this as simply as I can, this would mean a translation that does, as all translations do, inevitably lose something of the original, but a translation that would as well–and as most translations across cultures thus far have not done–provide a challenge to the understanding of speakers of the target language and culture.

As for pedagogical location, cosmopolitans would disperse the instruction of Native American literatures widely among departments of English, American Literature, American Studies, Cultural Studies, American Indian Studies, and Native American Studies. Although anthropology's history as the handmaiden of colonialism is wellknown, that history is not binding on the present as it need not be on the future. Cosmopolitans, fully aware of the animus against anthropology still expressed by any number of Native writers today, nonetheless might support the teaching of Native American literatures in departments of anthropology (at least in some departments of anthropology!) in courses like "Representation and Self-Representation," "Ethnography and Literature," or "Postcolonial Literatures."

We culture workers *as* culture workers can only have indirect influence on the material conditions of indigenous peoples. But we are the ones who can and do assert some fairly direct, if limited effect on the representation of indigenous people and the reception of their verbal expression. While it is imperative to avoid any illusions as to our power to change not only minds but socio-political facts, it is also imperative to resist the illusion that we are utterly powerless. We must do what we can, as nationalist, indigenist, and cosmopolitan critical allies.

References

Adams, David. (1995). *Education for Extinction: American Indians and the Boarding School Experience, 1875-1928.* Lawrence: University Press of Kansas.

Appadurai, Arjun. (1996). *Modernity at Large: Cultural Dimensions of Globalization.* Minneapolis: University of Minnesota Press.

Appiah, K. Anthony. (1992). *In My Father's House: Africa in the Philosophy of Culture.* New York: Oxford University Press.

Biolsi, Thomas and Larry J. Zimmerman. Eds. (1997). *Indians and Anthropologists: Vine Deloria, Jr. and the Critique of Anthropology.* Tucson: University of Arizona Press.

Churchill, Ward 1993. "I Am Indigenist." In: *Struggle for the Land: Indigenous Resistance, to Genocide, Ecoside, and Expropriation in Contemporary North America.* Monroe, Me.: Common Courage.

Cruikshank, Julie. (1998). *The Social Life of Stories: Narrative and Knowledge in the Yukon Territory.* Lincoln: University of Nebraska Press.

Deloria, Philip J. (2003). "American Indians, American Studies, and the ASA." *American Quarterly,* (December) 55: 669-680.

DuBois, Thomas A. (1996). "Native Hermeneutics: Traditional Means of Interpreting Lyric Songs in Northern Europe." *Journal of American Folklore.* 109: 235-266.

DuBois, Thomas A. (2000)."Folklore, Boundaries and Audience in *The Pathfinder.*" In Juha Pentikäinen et al. Eds. *Sami Folkloristics.* Turku, Finland: Nordic Network of Folklore.

Elliott, Michael and Claudia Stokes. Eds. (2003). *American Literary Studies: A Methodological Reader.* New York: New York University Press.

Falk, Richard. (1996). "Revisioning Cosmopolitanism." In Joshua Cohen. Ed. *For Love of Country: Debating the Limits of Patriotism.*Boston: Beacon Press.

Gaski, Harald. (2000). "The Secretive Text-Yoik Lyrics as Literature and Tradition." In Juha Pentikäinen et al. Eds. *Sami Folkloristics.* Turku, Finland: Nordic Network of Folklore.

Ghosh, Amitav. (1994). *In An Antique Land: History in the Guise of a Traveler's Tale.* New York: Vintage.

Hogan, Linda. (1998) *Power.* New York: Norton.

Jahner, Elaine. (1999). "Traditional Narrative: Contemporary Uses, Historical Perspectives." *SAIL* (Studies in American Indian Literatures), 11: 1-28.

Krupat, Arnold. (1996). "A Nice Jewish Boy Among the Indians." In *The Turn to the Native: Studies in Criticism and Culture.* Lincoln: University of Nebraska Press.

Krupat, Arnold. (1992). *Ethnocriticism: Ethnography, History, Literature.* Berkeley: University of California Press.

Krupat, Arnold. (2002). *Red Matters: Native American Studies.* Philadelphia: University of Pennsylvania Press.

Krupat, Arnold and Michael Elliott. (2005). "Native American Fiction Since 1945." In Eric Cheyfitz. Ed. *Columbia History of Native American Literature Since 1945.* New York: Columbia University Press.

Means, Russell and Ward Churchill. (1995). *TREATY: A Platform for Nationhood.* Denver: Fourth World Center for the Study of Indigenous Law and Politics.

Owens, Louis. (1992). *Other Destinies: Understanding the American Indian Novel.* Norman: University of Oklahoma Press.

Pentikäinen, Juha. (2000). "Finnish Research on Sami Folklore." In Juha Pentikäinen et al. Eds. *Sami Folkloristics.* Turku, Finland: Nordic Network of Folklore.

Salisbury, Ralph. (n.p.). "Trekways of the Wind." In Nils-Aslak Valkeapää, *Trekways of the Wind.*

Stevenson, Winona. (1998). "'Ethnic' Assimilates 'Indigenous': A Study in Intellectual Neocolonialism." *Wicazo Sa Review.* 13: 33-52.

Strong, Pauline Turner and Barrik van Winkle. (1993). "Tribe and Nation: American Indians and American Nationalism." *Social Analysis.* 33: 9-26.

Whitt, Laurie Ann. (1994). "Indigenous Peoples and the Cultural Politics of Knowledge." In Michael Green. Ed. *Issues in Native American Identity.* New York: Peter Lang.

Womack, Craig. (1999). *Red on Red: Native American Literary Separatism.* Minneapolis: University of Minnesota Press.

ABOUT THE AUTHORS

RUSSEL LAWRENCE BARSH is Director of KWIÁHT (Center for the Historical Ecology of the Salish Sea), a non-profit conservation research laboratory in the San Juan Islands between Washington State USA and British Columbia, Canada. He studied human ecology at Harvard before taking his law degree there in 1974. Since then, he has pursued his parallel interests in ecology, traditional knowledge, and customary systems of land law by working as a lawyer and researcher for Indigenous nations in Atlantic Canada, the northern Prairies, Alaska and the Pacific Northwest. He has also been involved in United Nations policy negotiations on Indigenous issues. He coordinated the UN work of the Four Directions Council, a North American indigenous peoples NGO, from 1982 to 2002; was science advisor to the International Indigenous Commission of the UN Conference on Environment and Development from 1989 to 1992; and served on the advisory committee of First Peoples Worldwide. In addition to field research and practice, he has taught at the University of Washington, University of Lethbridge, and New York University.

DEMETRIO COIJTI CUXIL, is Maya Kaqchikel. He has a PhD in Social Communication from the Catholic University of Louvain, Belgium, and a MA in Development from the Universidad Del Valle de Guatemala. In his academic career he has worked as professor and researcher at several universities in Guatemala and in other countries, and has been a consultant for international organizations. He was vice-minister of education in Guatemala 2000-2004. He is presently a consultant in the programme Democratic Values and Political Leadership in the Organization of American States. He is the author of several books and articles on the rights of indigenous peoples; some of his work has been translated into English and other languages. He has been and is a voluntary consultant for indigenous organizations and institutions in Guatemala.

ULF JOHANSSON DAHRE is PhD. in Social Anthropology at the University of Lund, Sweden. He has conducted field research in Hawai'i, Sweden, and at the United Nations in Geneva. Has published on indigenous issues both in English and Swedish; publications include books on legal anthropology, indigenous movements and human rights.

JONATHAN FRIEDMAN is Directeur d'Etudes at the Ecole des Hautes en Sciences Sociales, Paris and professor of Social Anthropology at the University of Lund, Sweden. He has done research and written on Southeast Asia, Oceania and Europe. He has written on more general issues concerning, structuralist and Marxist theory, models of social and cultural transformation, and, for the past twenty-five years, on the anthropology of global processes, cultural formations and the practices of identity. He is co-editor of several journals, including, Social Analysis, Anthropological Theory, Ethnos, Theory, Culture and Society. He has contributed to international journals and books on issues ranging from globalization, to ethnicity, to the nature of political correctness. His books include Cultural Identity and Global Process (1994, London: Sage), (ed) Consumption and Identity (1994 London: Harwood), System, Structure and Contradiction in the Evolution of 'Asiatic' Social Formations (1998; 2nd edition Walnut Creek: Altamira), Globalization the State and Violence (Altamira in press), with R. Denemark, B. Gills and G. Modelski, World System History: The Science of Long Term Change (2000 Routledge), with S. Randeira, Worlds on the Move (London: Tauris), and with Kajsa Ekholm-Friedman, Essays in Global Anthropology (Altamira, in press).

HARALD GASKI is Associate Professor in Sami literature at the University of Tromsø, Norway. IIc is the author and editor of several books, journals and articles on Sami literature and culture. Gaski has been a visiting scholar at several universities in the US, Australia, and in Greenland. Gaski's research topics include indigenous peoples' literatures with a specific emphasis on Sami literature. He has also specialized on oral tradition–especially the transition of the traditional Sami singing, the yoik poetry, into contemporary lyrics. Gaski has been co-translator of Sami prose and poetry into English. In 2006 Gaski was awarded the The Nordic Sami Language Prize, Gollegiella, established by the Nordic Sami Ministers and the Presidents of the Sami Parliaments in Norway, Sweden and Finland. The same year he also received the Award for Outstanding Dissemination of Research at the University of Tromsø.

LINA GASKI is a doctoral candidate at the Department of Comparative Politics at the University in Bergen, Norway. Her research interests are identity formation and identity politics, ethnic relations and nation building. She is currently preparing a thesis on Sami politics and the discursive construction of Sami national identity.

VICKI GRIEVES, is Worimi from NSW (New South Wales), Australia, with three decades experience as an educator, manager and consultant within Indigenous affairs in universities, governments and Aboriginal organisations. As a NSW Premier's Indigenous History Fellow (2003-2005), she is developing an Indigenous knowledges approach to the development of mixed-race families in the early colonial period (PhD to be submitted in 2007). She has published on the "history wars" debate and reported on the connection between Indigenous wellbeing and cultural heritage for the NSW government. In 2008 she will be located at the University of Sydney as recipient of an ARC grant, exploring the nature of internecine conflict and violence in Aboriginal communities in NSW.

SVEIN JENTOFT is a sociologist and professor at the Centre for Marine Resource Management, Norwegian College of Fishery Science, University of Tromsø, Norway. He specializes in social and institutional aspects of fisheries and coastal governance and how this affects indigenous communities. Dr. Jentoft has thirty years of research and teaching experience within this and other social science areas in Norway and internationally. Among his recent books is: Fish for Life. Interactive Governance for Fisheries (edited with Jan Kooiman, Maarten Bavinck and Roger Pullin), Amsterdam University Press (2005); In Disciplinary Border Lands: On Interdisciplinarity (edited with Torill Nyseth, Anniken Førde and Jørgen-Ole Bærenholdt), Bergen: Fagbokforlaget (2007) (in Norwegian), and; The Rama People – Struggling for Land and Culture (edited with Miguel Gonzalez, Arja Koskinen, and Diala Lopez Lau) Managua, Nicaragua: URACCAN, (2006). He was also co-editor of the book preceding this volume: Indigenous Peoples: Resource Management and Global Rights on Eburon, Delft, The Netherlands, with Henry Minde and Ragnar Nilsen, (2003).

ARNOLD KRUPAT has published widely in a number of critical journals, and his essays have been included in many anthologies. He has edited (with Brian Swann) I Tell you Now: Autobiographical Essays by Native American Writers (1987, rpt. 2005), and a follow-up volume, Here First: Autobiographical Essays by Native American Writers (2000). He has also published, among other books, Ethnocriticism: Ethnography, History, Literature (1992), The Turn to the Native: Studies in Criticism and Culture (1996), and Red Matters: Native American Studies (2002). He was a recipient of a Guggenheim Foundation Fellowship for 2005-6, which allowed him to complete a new book, All that Matters: Native Studies (forthcoming). He has published a novel, Woodsmen, or Thoreau and the Indians (1994), and he is the editor for Native American Literatures for the Norton Anthology of American Literature. He teaches literature as a member of the Global Studies Faculty at Sarah Lawrence College in New York.

RAUNA KUOKKANEN is the Dean of Academic Studies at the Sami University College, Guovdageaidnu/Kautokeino (Norway). She holds a PhD in Education from the University of British Columbia (Vancouver, Canada), an M.A. on Comparative Literature (UBC) and an M.A. on Sami Language and Literature (University of Oulu, Finland). She is the author of Reshaping the University:

Responsibility, Indigenous Epistemes and the Logic of the Gift (UBC Press, 2007) and editor of the anthology on Sami literature Juoga mii geasuha_(2001). Her current research interests include indigenous peoples' higher education and the intersections of autonomy, violence and political economy in the context of indigenous women. She was the founding chair of the Sami Youth Organization in Finland, established in 1991, and served as the Vice-President of the Sami Council in 1997-98.

HENRY MINDE is Professor of History at the University of Tromsø, Norway, where he specializes in Sami and indigenous peoples' cultural, legal and political history. He has received an award from the Government of Canada and has studied the history of First Nations' people at McGill University (1990-91), at Dartmouth College (1999) and University of Hawai'i at Manoa (2007). He was the co-ordinator of an interdisciplinary project called "The Challenge of Indigenousness: Politics of Rights, Resources and Knowledge," founded by the Norwegian Research Council. In English he has co-edited Becoming Visible: Indigenous Politics and Self-government (1995) and Indigenous Peoples: Resource Management and Global Rights (2003). He has published several articles that deal principally with the history of the Sami and Indigenous peoples.

GEORGES MIDRÉ is Cand.sociol. from the University of Oslo and Professor of social policy at the University of Tromsø, Norway since 1986. He was Dean of the Faculty of Social Science, University of Tromsø 1995-1999, and is presently director of the Department of Sociology at the University of Tromsø. From 1999 until present he is academic coordinator of the programme "Maya Competence Building," a cooperation between the Universidad de San Carlos de Guatemala and the University of Tromsø. He has conducted field work in Norway, Russia and Poland, as well as Argentina and Guatemala. He is author of books and articles on social history and welfare policies, including research on poverty. Among his recent publications are Élite ladina, políticas públicas y pobreza indígena (2002, with Sergio Flores), and Opresión, espacio para actuar y conciencia crítica. Líderes indígenas y percepción de la pobreza en Guatemala (2005), both published by the Instituto de Estudios Interétnicos, Universidad de San Carlos de Guatemala.

Dr.Art. JUKKA NYYSSÖNEN works as a university lecturer at the Department of History at the University of Tromsø, Norway. In 2007 he defended his doctoral thesis on Sami identity politics in Finland 1945-1990. In addition to history of minorities, Nyyssönen has published numerous articles in English on the history of Sami reindeer herding and forestry in northernmost Finland from the perspectives of environmental history as well as that of environmental economics. The meeting between the Sami minority and the Finnish society and institutions are among his research interests.

NILS OSKAL is Dr.art. in philosophy, and Professor of Sámi knowledge and understanding at the Sámi University College, Guovdageaidnu/Kautokeino, Norway. He has published on political philosophy and indigenous rights, philosophy of law and indigenous customary rights, philosophical ethics and ethics on Sami reindeer herding. He is now coordinator of an interdisciplinary project called "Democracy and Indigenous Rights" founded by the Norwegian Research Council.

HENRY REYNOLDS is born in Tasmania. He was Professor in history at the James Cook University until he retired in 1998. He then took up an Australian Research Council post at University of Tasmania in his hometown Launceston. His primary work has focused on the frontier conflict between Aborigines peoples and European settlement of Australia. His major works are The Other Side of the Frontier: Aboriginal Resistance to the European Invasion of Australia (1981), The Law of the Land (1987, 1992, 2003) Dispossession; Black Australia and white invaders (1989), Fate of a Free People (1995, 2004). Aboriginal Sovereignty: Reflections on Race, State and Nation (1996), Why Weren't We Told? (2000), An Indelible Stain?: The Question of Genocide in Australia's History (2001).

SIDSEL SAUGESTAD is Professor and Head of the Department of Social Anthropology at the University of Tromsø, Norway. She has done research on ethnic relations in Northern Ireland, on indigenous relations in the Norwegian-Sami context, and since 1992 in Botswana and the southern African region, specifically on the relationship between emerging San (Bushmen) organisations and the states of Botswana, Namibia and South Africa. Her chapter in this volume is based on participation in meetings on the local and national levels, as well as in international fora such as WGIP in Geneva and UNPFII in New York. Saugestad has published a book, The Inconvenient Indigenous: Remote Area Development, Donor Assistance and the First People of the Kalahari (2001), and several articles on the topic.

VIGDIS STORDAHL is Dr. philos from the University of Tromsø, Norway in 1994 and is the Head of Research at the National Centre for Mental Health in Kárášjohka/Karasjok. She has published books and articles on Sami ethnic identity, gender issues, politics of knowledge and transcultural psychiatry.

KAY WARREN served on the senior faculties of Princeton University and Harvard University before coming to Brown University in 2003. She is currently professor in International Studies and Professor of Anthropology at Brown University where she directs the Politics, Culture, and Identity Program at the Watson Institute for International Studies. Her books on indigenous issues include: The Symbolism of Subordination: Indian Identity in a Guatemalan Town (1978); Women of the Andes: Patriarchy and Social Change in Two Peruvian Towns, co-authored with Susan C. Bourque (1981); Indigenous Movements and Their Critics: Pan-Maya Activism in Guatemala (1998); and Indigenous Movements, Self-Representation, and the State, co-edited with Jean Jackson (2002).

JARLE WEIGÅRD is Associate Professor in the Department of Political Science, University of Tromsø, Norway, where he teaches political theory. He is currently a member of a research team working on the project Democracy and Indigenous Rights, funded by the Norwegian Research Council. His publications include co-authored with Erik O. Eriksen (2003).

Also published by Eburon:
Indigenous Peoples: Resource Management and Global Rights.
Editors: Svein Jentoft, Henry Minde & Ragnar Nilsen. 2003.

Indigenous peoples are under heavy pressure from developments beyond their control. Their territories and natural resources are threatened and, hence, also their economies, cultures and customary ways of life. Yet, globally there is also an increasing awareness for the need to secure the rights of indigenous peoples. We also see a growing self-initiated empowerment process among indigenous peoples to meet these challenges. Since the Rio Earth Summit in 1992, a legal process within the auspices of the UN has been underway that may help indigenous peoples to sustain their natural environments, industries, and cultures, This book addresses some of the legal, political and institutional implication of these processes. The international group of authors draw on examples from different parts of the world, and highlight issues that are involved in indigenous peoples' struggle for control of their lives and their future.

This is an important book (...) because it represents the reader with articles that in different ways give important insight in the interplay between etnicity, power and politics.
IVAR BJØRKLUND in **Rangifer**.

I recommend the book not only to graduate and advanced students and profesionals in the social science and area of ethnic studies, but also to those in the natural sciences who would like to understand more about the role of indigenous groups in environmental governance.
FAE L. KORSMO in **Artic**.

The book is a worthy contribution to our general understanding of the problems facing indigenous peoples.
MALGOSIA FITZMAURICE in **International Journal on Minority and Group Rights**.

The book makes a significant contribution to geographic understandings of these issues.
REBECCA LAWRENCE & MICHAEL ADAMS in **Austraian Geographer**.

The book successfully completes the task of showing the familiarity of indigenous approaches to natural resource management.
BAŞAK ÇAH in **PoLAR**

The chapters focusing on global agendas provide helpful summaries of key international forums for Indigenous peoples, and the more specific case studies provide rich, descriptiv accounts.
LIBBY PORTER in **The Geographical Journal**